The Modern Legislative Veto

The legislative veto, which delegates power to the executive but grants the legislature a measure of control over the implementation of the law, raises troubling questions about the separation of governmental powers, a fundamental principle of the American Founders.

In this book, Michael J. Berry uses a multimethod research design, incorporating quantitative and qualitative analyses, to examine the ways that Congress has used the legislative veto over the past eighty years. He finds that, since the U.S. Supreme Court declared the legislative veto unconstitutional in *Immigration and Naturalization Service (INS) v. Chadha* (1983), Congress has strategically modified its use of the veto to give more power to the appropriations committees. Using an original dataset of legislative veto enactments, Berry finds that Congress has actually increased its use of this oversight mechanism since *Chadha*, especially over defense and foreign policy issues. Democratic and Republican presidents alike have fought back by vetoing legislation containing legislative vetoes and by using signing statements with greater frequency to challenge the legislative veto's constitutionality. A complimentary analysis of state-level use of the legislative veto finds variation in oversight powers granted to state legislatures, but similar struggles between the legislature and the executive.

This ongoing battle over the legislative veto points to broader efforts by legislative and executive actors to control policy, efforts that continually negotiate how the democratic republic established by the Constitution actually operates in practice.

Michael J. Berry (Author) is an Associate Professor in the Department of Political Science at the University of Colorado, Denver.

LEGISLATIVE POLITICS & POLICY MAKING

Series Editors
Janet M. Box-Steffensmeier, Vernal Riffe Professor of Political Science,
The Ohio State University
David Canon, Professor of Political Science, University of Wisconsin, Madison

The Floor in Congressional Life
ANDREW J. TAYLOR

The Influence of Campaign Contributions in State Legislatures: The Effects of Institutions and Politics
LYNDA W. POWELL

The Evolution of American Legislatures: Colonies, Territories, and States, 1619–2009
PEVERILL SQUIRE

Getting Primaried: The Changing Politics of Congressional Primary Challenges
ROBERT G. BOATRIGHT

Ambition, Competition, and Electoral Reform: The Politics of Congressional Elections Across Time
JAMIE L. CARSON AND JASON M. ROBERTS

Partisan Gerrymandering and the Construction of American Democracy
ERIK J. ENGSTROM

Party Discipline in the U.S. House of Representatives
KATHRYN PEARSON

Minority Parties in U.S. Legislatures: Conditions of Influence
JENNIFER HAYES CLARK

Leadership Organizations in the House of Representatives: Party Participation and Partisan Politics
SCOTT R. MEINKE

The Modern Legislative Veto: Macropolitical Conflict and the Legacy of Chadha
MICHAEL J. BERRY

THE MODERN LEGISLATIVE VETO

*Macropolitical Conflict and the
Legacy of* Chadha

Michael J. Berry

University of Michigan Press
Ann Arbor

First paperback edition 2017
Copyright © by Michael J. Berry 2016
All rights reserved

This book may not be reproduced, in whole or in part, including illustrations, in any form (beyond that copying permitted by Sections 107 and 108 of the U.S. Copyright Law and except by reviewers for the public press), without written permission from the publisher.

Published in the United States of America by the
University of Michigan Press
Manufactured in the United States of America
⊗ Printed on acid-free paper

2020   2019   2018   2017   5   4   3   2

A CIP catalog record for this book is available from the British Library.

Library of Congress Cataloging-in-Publication Data

Names: Berry, Michael J., author.
Title: The modern legislative veto : macropolitical conflict and the legacy
   of *Chadha* / Michael J. Berry.
Description: Ann Arbor : University of Michigan Press, 2016. | Series: Legislative
   politics and policy making | Includes bibliographical references and index.
Identifiers: LCCN 2015049566| ISBN 9780472119776 (hardback) |
   ISBN 9780472121724 (e-book)
Subjects: LCSH: Legislative veto—United States. | Chadha, Jagdish
   Rai—Trials, litigation, etc. | BISAC: POLITICAL SCIENCE /
   Government / Legislative Branch. | POLITICAL SCIENCE / Government /
   Comparative.
Classification: LCC KF4944 .B47 2016 |DDC 342.73/052—dc23
LC record available at http://lccn.loc.gov/2015049566

ISBN 978-0-472-03693-6 (pbk : alk paper)

To R and H

Acknowledgments

While working on this study over the past decade, I have been fortunate to benefit from the advice and support of many individuals at the University of Colorado, Boulder and the University of Colorado, Denver. My dissertation advisor, E. Scott Adler, was instrumental in getting this project off the ground. He graciously remains an invaluable source of guidance. Kenneth Bickers, Joseph Jupille, Eric Juenke, and John McIver each provided insightful feedback regarding theoretical and empirical aspects of the study. Jana Everett and Tony Robinson also provided helpful guidance and support.

Financial support from the National Science Foundation and the Dirksen Congressional Research Center helped facilitate the data collection and allowed me to travel to Washington, DC, to conduct interviews with lawmakers and congressional staff. My thanks go to many current and former legislators for meeting with me to discuss their perspectives on congressional oversight and the legislative veto.

The College of Liberal Arts & Sciences at the University of Colorado, Denver, also provided financial support, which helped facilitate valuable research assistance from Sara Gouge, Dan Krug, and Shannon Port, who each spent hours assisting with data collection. At the Auraria Library, Eric Baker provided helpful research assistance on many diverse topics, and former U.S. senator Mark Udall's office graciously provided me with access to numerous Congressional Research Service reports..

I owe a debt of gratitude to many individuals at the University of Michigan Press for their assistance in moving this manuscript toward publication. I am appreciative of the helpful critiques of two anonymous reviewers and the support of the *Legislative Politics & Policy Making* series editors, Janet Box-Steffensmeier and David Canon. Melody Herr's editorial advice was tremendously helpful in fashioning this study into a more compelling narrative. I appreciate her patience and willingness to respond to my many inquiries as I developed and revised the manuscript. The manuscript also benefited from the careful scrutiny of production editor, Mary Hashman, and copy editor, John Raymond. All errors remain my own.

Finally, to the many colleagues, friends, and family who have offered me support while writing this book, my most sincere thanks.

Contents

Introduction: Macropolitical Conflict over the Legislative Veto   1

ONE   Origin and Evolution: The Path to *Chadha*   19

TWO   Reassessments and Reformations: The Modern Era   60

THREE   When to Deploy? Strategies of Congressional Oversight   110

FOUR   "Congressional Aggrandizement": The Persistence of Presidential Opposition   138

FIVE   The Conflict's Front Lines: National Security and Foreign Policy   163

SIX   Suspend or Nullify: Veto Oversight in U.S. Statehouses   211

Conclusion: A Tenuous Equilibrium? The Current Landscape and Future Prospects   269

APPENDIXES
  Appendix 1: Laws Containing Legislative Vetoes: 1931–2010   279
  Appendix 2: Legislative Veto Court Cases   309

Notes   311

Bibliography   321

Index   339

Introduction

Macropolitical Conflict over the Legislative Veto

When the 112th Congress took office in January 2011 the protracted conflict over the federal budget loomed large on the horizon. Since the previous Congress failed to enact any of the 12 regular appropriations bills, this task was postponed as a major item of business for incoming lawmakers. Debates over the federal budget were made more contentious following the 2010 midterm elections when the Republican Party gained 60 seats in the House of Representatives and thereby secured majority party status in the chamber. Also in this election cycle, the grassroots Tea Party movement gained popularity and began using its newfound traction to call for, among other things, drastic cuts in federal spending. This set the stage for a bitter partisan fight.

On February 18, 2011, over unanimous Democratic opposition, the Republicans passed a federal budget that included more than $60 billion in spending cuts (112th Congress, House Roll Call No. 147). Three weeks later, the Republican spending package was defeated in the Senate (112th Congress, Senate Roll Call No. 36). The wide chasm between the parties made a potential government shutdown seem increasingly likely. With just hours remaining before the expiration of the seventh continuing resolution passed by Congress as a temporary funding measure, the parties came together and agreed on a 2011 budget compromise imposing $38 billion in spending reductions (125 Stat. 38, Public Law 112–10).

Upon signing the omnibus spending bill into law, President Barack Obama issued a signing statement that expressed his resounding opposition to just three provisions in the 175-page law. As he had on nearly a dozen previous occasions, the president emphasized his "continued strong objection to these provisions" (Obama 2011). The content of two of those three provisions singled out by President Obama has been a persistent source of conflict between the legislative and executive branches for nearly a full century—the legislative veto.

The 2011 omnibus spending bill included 36 separate legislative vetoes—statutes that authorize either or both houses of Congress, or specific committees, to approve, disapprove, or defer certain executive actions.[1] For example, in appropriating more than $3.6 billion to the Food and Drug Administration (FDA) and related agencies, a section in the law identifies 10 program outlays spanning medical research and development as well as food safety and inspection. At the end of the section allocating these funds, a provision states that "funds may be transferred from one specified activity to another with the prior approval of the Committees on Appropriations of both Houses of Congress" (125 Stat. 115, Public Law 112–10). This provision implements a legislative veto, since it conditions an executive action as requiring some legislative action—other than the passage of a law—as a necessary condition in order to be sanctioned. While Congress as a whole passed the appropriations schedule for the FDA in the omnibus spending measure, transfers of funds between FDA program accounts were permitted only with committee consent. By withholding their approval, the spending committees alone held the power to veto or authorize any transfer proposal submitted by FDA officials. Oversight statutes such as this have been referred to as "extra-legislative" functions whereby Congress can affect policy in ways that do not involve the production of new laws (H. Watson 1975).

Members of Congress perform legislative functions when they introduce, amend, deliberate, and vote on legislation. In contrast, "Congress steps outside of the legislative process when it passes and acts according to a statute authorizing later action by resolution or committee vote, thereby retaining jurisdiction over the subject matter of legislation. Such a statute creates a new role for Congress, ambiguously situated between the legislative and executive functions" (H. Watson 1975, 991–92). The legislative veto over FDA spending does precisely this by affording the appropriations committees with a direct veto over proposals to transfer funds. These statutes are a unique means of oversight because they allow individual committees to independently dictate executive action. In this respect, the legislative veto can be conceptualized as an extralegislative function since it involves actions outside the bounds of the traditional lawmaking process.

In addition to the congressional veto imposed over FDA spending and the 35 additional vetoes inserted into the 2011 appropriations bill, Congress has included legislative veto provisions in many major enactments, both recent and historical. Beginning in September 1940, the United States began allocating billions of dollars in foreign aid to the Allied forces through the Lend Lease foreign assistance act (55 Stat. 11, Public Law 77–11). The act provided President Franklin Roosevelt with the primary authority to control the distribution of foreign aid, which ultimately included more than 30 countries. Any Lend Lease assistance, however, was susceptible to congressional veto by concurrent resolution. Seventy years later, the Patient Protection and Affordable Care Act (124 Stat. 532, Public Law 111–148) included three legislative vetoes affecting how Health and Human Services officials and the Independent Medicare Advisory Board implemented aspects of the landmark health care reform. These examples also demonstrate that Congress can use the veto to affect domestic and foreign policy alike.

More recently, the legislative veto had a prominent role in the August 2011 negotiation of the bipartisan agreement to raise the nation's statutory debt limit. This law instituted an immediate $400 billion increase in the debt limit and delegated to the president the authority to raise the limit on subsequent occasions by additional amounts of $500 billion and $1.2 trillion provided that Congress did not block either increase with a joint resolution of disapproval (140 Stat. 240, Public Law 112–25). Since joint resolutions require agreement in both chambers and a presidential signature, President Obama had the ability to veto a joint resolution blocking his debt limit increase request. Under this scenario, Congress could only prevent the increase by overriding the president's veto with a two-thirds majority vote in both chambers. Because it would be highly unlikely that Congress could actually block a proposed increase, this process was deemed "political theater" by the press as a merely symbolic procedural maneuver allowing predominantly Republican lawmakers the opportunity to cast a recorded vote against the increase while making it a virtual impossibility for such votes to actually block it (Kasperowicz 2011; Sonmez 2012).

President Obama requested the $500 billion debt ceiling increase in the fall of 2011, which the House voted to veto (On Passage of H.J.Res 77, September 14, 2011, Vote Number 706). The resolution failed in the Senate by a vote of 45 to 52, meaning that the debt limit would be raised further (On the Motion to Proceed S.J.Res. 25, September 8, 2011, Vote Number 130). As expected, the votes in both chambers were extremely partisan with a combined total of 12 lawmakers crossing party lines. In the

Senate, all but two Republicans voted in favor of the resolution to deny the increase with all Democrats voting opposed with the exception of Senator Ben Nelson.

Shortly before the end of 2011, President Obama sent Congress a second formal request to increase the debt ceiling by an additional $1.2 trillion. When lawmakers reconvened for the second session of the 112th Congress, the House once again agreed to a resolution of disapproval of the president's request largely along party lines (On Passage of H.J.Res 98, January 18, 2012, Vote Number 4). As it had in September, the resolution failed to garner majority support in the Senate with 44 votes in favor of the resolution (On the Motion to Proceed H.J.Res. 98, January 26, 2012, Vote Number 2). Thus, in each instance, while Congress had the authority to veto the increases, there were not enough votes to send the disapproval resolution to President Obama's desk for a certain presidential veto. Despite the fact that Congress was unable to execute a veto of either debt limit increase, the enactment of statutes containing legislative vetoes has become an extremely common check on executive policy making. The increased use of the veto has occurred against a backdrop of an expanding federal bureaucracy wielding greater abilities to affect policy.

The Administrative State as a Venue for Macropolitical Conflict

Interbranch conflict among the legislative, executive, and judicial branches has been characterized by scholars as "macropolitical" (Adler and Lapinski 2006). Conflict of this nature exists when disagreements arise across branches, causing a clash among policy makers from two or even all three branches. Daily newspapers are filled with stories discussing such conflicts, which are a principal hallmark of American politics as the three branches perform their constitutional duties. Confrontations between the two partisan branches are perhaps the most frequent given the interconnectedness of writing and executing the law. Often such conflicts are waged over efforts to control the manner in which bureaucrats implement public policy. In the modern era, the pronounced policy-making importance of the federal bureaucracy has heightened the macropolitical conflict over its terrain.

Over the course of the twentieth century, the growth of the federal bureaucracy has yielded what has been aptly characterized as the "administrative state" (Dodd and Schott 1979; Krause 1999). While a bureaucracy has existed at the federal level since 1789, following the creation of the Departments of War, Foreign Affairs, and Treasury, the size and organizational sophistication of the bureaucracy during the eighteenth and nineteenth centuries bore little resemblance to the present-day bureaucratic behemoth. Following eras of rapid industrialization and urbanization, the initial period of major change occurred during the 1880s, which witnessed civil service reforms implemented by the 1883 Pendleton Act (22 Stat. 403, Public Law 47–16) and related legislation, increases in the number of federal employees, and a commensurate expansion in the functions of the executive.

In response to the Great Depression, President Franklin Roosevelt and a series of Democratic Congresses created myriad organizations with the intention of stimulating economic growth and creating a more complex domestic infrastructure intended to provide the public with employment, security, and economic relief. Many of these newly created bureaucracies involved the federal government in functions it had not previously performed. By 1940, the New Deal agenda had nearly doubled the size of the bureaucracy to encompass more than a million civil service employees (Dodd and Schott 1979).

Throughout the middle part of the century, the growth of the federal bureaucracy continued unabated. The cabinet doubled in size with the creation of eight new cabinet-level departments after World War II—the most recent being the Department of Homeland Security in 2002. In addition to the growth of the cabinet, Congress created more than 180 significant bureaucratic agencies from 1946 to 1997 (Lewis 2003). The result of these actions is the modern administrative state, wherein hundreds of departments, agencies, commissions, offices, and bureaus within the bureaucracy possess broad implementation responsibilities over a vast array of domestic and foreign policies.

As a result of its institutional growth during the past 75 years, the administrative state is at the forefront of today's federal government. Modern bureaucrats are often authorized to independently determine many aspects of public policy. The combined rulemaking and regulatory powers and its enormous size have positioned the bureaucracy as the "nexus of policy making in the post-war period" (Lewis 2003, 1). One meaningful indicator of administrative power is the size of the *Federal Register*. The *Federal Register*, which contains the rules, proposed rules, regulations, and notices from federal agencies, has exponentially increased in size over the last several decades. During the 1960s, it averaged approximately 20,000 pages per year. In 2011, its more than 82,000 pages contained 3,807 rules—an average of 47 rules for every law enacted by Congress (Crews 2014).[2]

Congress has conceded increasing amounts of policy-making power by delegating to the executive and creating an expansive web of executive departments, agencies, commissions, and bureaus. Critics have derided delegation of this magnitude as "legiscide," whereby Congress unconstitutionally transfers legislative powers from elected officials to unelected bureaucrats (Lowi 1969, 1991). Some have argued that the result of this is the creation of a quasi fourth branch of government where "lawmaking power is now lodged in administrative hands without any constitutional assurance that the agencies are responsive to the people's will" (Bruff and Gellhorn 1977, 1373). The rising importance of unelected bureaucrats charged with implementing policy, however, is not a uniquely American phenomenon. One scholar has characterized this trend across the globe as the rise of the unelected characterized by a "striking expansion in the number and role of bodies in society that exercise official authority but are not headed by elected politicians and have been deliberately set apart, or only loosely tied to the more familiar elected institutions of democracy" (Vibert 2007, 4). While this may be troubling in terms of democratic theory and accountability, the delegation of considerable discretionary policy-making authority to the executive has become an inescapable characteristic of modern American governance.

As Congress delegates increasing amounts of policy-making authority to bureaucratic agencies, the relationship between these two entities emerges as fundamental to understanding the implementation of public policy. Large-scale delegation to the bureaucracy necessarily places a premium on the congressional oversight process. In order to ensure that the actions of administrative agencies generally comply with congressional intent, Congress utilizes a variety of institutional oversight mechanisms to keep watch over the bureaucracy. The legislative veto is one such resource.

The Rise of the Legislative Veto

The inclusion of congressional vetoes in many landmark reforms passed by Congress provides evidence of the importance placed on oversight expressed in this manner. Legislative vetoes were included in the Lend Lease Act of 1941 (55 Stat. 31, Public Law 77–11), the Emergency Price Control Act of 1942 (56 Stat. 26, Public Law 77–421), the 1964 Civil Rights Act (78 Stat. 241, Public Law 88–352), the 1973 War Powers Resolution (87 Stat. 555, Public Law 93–148), the Congressional Budget and Impoundment Control Act of 1974 (88 Stat. 297, Public Law 93–344), the 1974 Federal Election Campaign Act (88 Stat. 1263, Public Law 93–443), the 1984 Defense spending bill that included the Boland Amendment prohibiting disbursement of U.S. aid to fund the Nicaraguan Contras (98 Stat. 1935, Public Law 98–473), the Defense Base Closure and Realignment Act of 1990 (104 Stat.1810, Public Law 101–510), the legislation imposing sanctions on Iraq following its invasion of Kuwait in 1990 (104 Stat. 2101, Public Law 101–515), the USA PATRIOT Act of 2001 (115 Stat. 272, Public Law 107–56), the 2002 Homeland Security Act creating the Department of Homeland Security (116 Stat. 2135, Public Law 107–296), the American Recovery and Reinvestment Act of 2009 (123 Stat. 115, Public Law 111–5), the Dodd-Frank Wall Street Reform and Consumer Protection Act of 2010 (124 Stat. 1376, Public Law 111–203), the Patient Protection and Affordable Care Act of 2010 (124 Stat. 119, Public Law 111–148), the 2011 bipartisan agreement to raise the statutory debt limit (140 Stat. 240, Public Law 112–25), and virtually every omnibus spending bill passed over the past 25 years. In addition to congressional vetoes enacted by these historic laws, figure 0.1 provides data regarding the number of laws containing at least one legislative veto, as well as the number of legislative veto statutes enacted by Congress from 1931 to 2010.

As chapter 1 will describe in more detail, the origination of the legislative veto occurred with the passage of a law in 1932 that delegated to the president the authority to reorganize the executive branch, but reserved the ability for either chamber to block individual reorganization initiatives. Following the first implementation of a legislative veto statute, the continued incidence of this unique brand of oversight occurred at a slow and uneven pace. The remainder of the decade witnessed the passage of a mere five additional legislative vetoes. These statutes concerned funding for irrigation projects on Indian reservations (49 Stat. 1803, Public Law 74–742), international trade (54 Stat. 4, Public Law 76–54), immigration law and deportation cases (54 Stat. 672, Public Law 76–670), and two additional vetoes on presidential reorganization authority (47 Stat. 1517, Public Law 72–428; 53 Stat. 561, Public Law 76–19). While the total number of vetoes implemented during the 1940s increased to 20, these numbers pale in comparison to the amount of vetoes passed by more recent Congresses.

Legislative vetoes of the 1930s, 1940s, and 1950s were often limited to a particular set of policy areas such as immigration, energy, defense, government operations, and public lands. It was not until the 1960s that Congress began expanding its use of the veto to a broader range of issues. Against the backdrop of concerns of a runaway presidency, several post-Watergate reforms seeking to curb escalating executive power prominently featured legislative vetoes. The 352 vetoes enacted during the 1970s represented

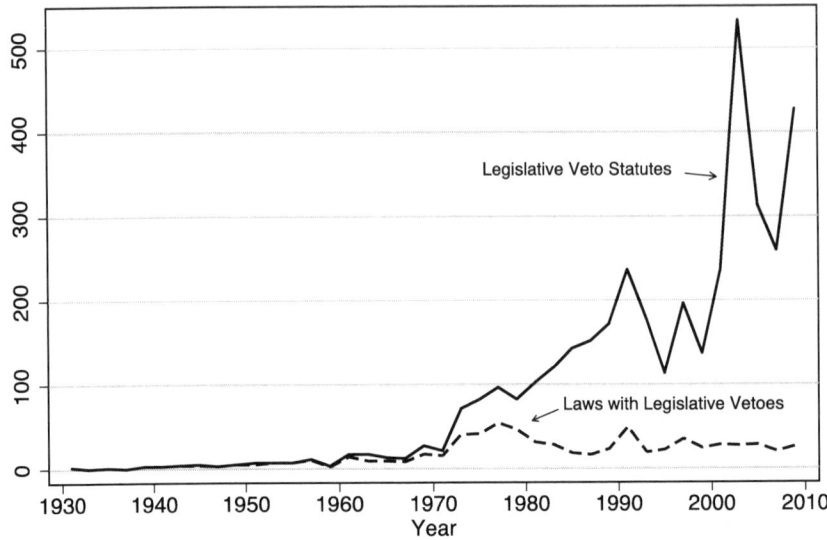

Fig. 0.1. Legislative veto statutes: 1931–2010 (Data compiled by author.)

greater than a 300 percent increase from the previous decade. From the trend data seen in figure 0.1, it is clear that the legislative veto progressed from a sparingly used institutional maneuver tailored to oversee government reorganization initiatives to a widespread component of Congress's statutory oversight framework. The increasingly popular oversight device allowed Congress to intervene in a broad array of actions taken by career bureaucrats and presidents alike.

The 97th Congress was the first to serve in the 1980s and also the first to enact more than 100 legislative veto statutes in total. Just six months after its adjournment, the Supreme Court released its ruling in *Immigration and Naturalization Service (INS) v. Chadha*, 462 U.S. 919 (1983), which declared the legislative veto unconstitutional. Despite the *Chadha* ruling, Congress has continued to use the veto as a vehicle to exert control over the bureaucracy. For their part, presidents have taken many measures seeking to curtail its continued use. However, these efforts have failed to stem the tide of veto oversight—Congress has actually enacted more legislative vetoes since the ruling than it had in all the years prior to it. Congresses serving in the 2000s passed an average of more than 350 legislative statutes per term. And yet, despite its commonality, the legislative veto has received relatively little scholarly attention among political scientists (for exceptions, see Cooper and Hurley 1983; Craig 1983; Fisher 1993, 2005a, 2005b; Gibson 1994; Korn 1996; Levinson 1987; Martin 1997; Wheeler 2008).

Transaction Costs and Congressional Oversight of the Administrative State

In many respects, congressional oversight of executive departments and agencies has always served as one of Congress's chief responsibilities (Oleszek 2010). The emergence of a bourgeoning administrative state and the proliferation of the functions it performs have elevated the importance of oversight in such a way that it now serves as one of Congress's most vital tasks. Indeed, much of the controversy surrounding the use of czars in recent administrations is attributable to the fact that these positions are mostly insulated from legislative oversight (Sollenberger and Rozell 2012). In response to increasing executive authority, Congress, its committees, and individual lawmakers each participate in numerous oversight activities such as direct communication with agency personnel, committee hearings, program reauthorizations, agency reporting requirements, and various program evaluations (Aberbach 1990). While each of these efforts can contribute to an effective oversight design, the foremost component of congressional oversight exists in the content of the laws it writes.

There are a great number of available resources that Congress can use to influence bureaucratic policy making. An obvious first step is to consider the amount of discretion legislators delegate to the executive. This is a strategic calculation that requires consideration of the potential benefits and disadvantages of the act of delegation (Calvert, McCubbins, and Weingast 1989; Epstein and O'Halloran 1999; Gailmard 2002; Huber and Shipan 2002; McCubbins, Noll, and Weingast 1987). In modern American politics, however, congressional decisions regarding delegation center on the amount of delegated power rather than whether Congress should delegate in the first place. Because of the size and complexity of policies and programs administered by the federal government, the primary questions facing Congress are (1) how much policy-making responsibility should be delegated to executive agencies? and (2) what is the most effective way to structure oversight of these delegated powers? Answers to these questions are commonly provided by statute. As many scholars have argued, present-day bureaucrats are simultaneously empowered and constrained by statutes governing policy implementation procedures (Bawn 1995; Gailmard

2009; Huber, Shipan, and Pfahler 2001; MacDonald 2010; McCubbins 1985; McCubbins, Noll, and Weingast 1989). In seeking to more precisely determine the conditions under which Congress delegates and engages in oversight, many path-breaking studies in this area have used a theoretical framework grounded in transaction costs (Cox 2004; Epstein and O'Halloran 1999; Huber and Shipan 2000; Wood and Bohte 2004).

When applied to legislative-bureaucratic relationships, transaction costs principally concern the factors associated with negotiating, enforcing, and monitoring agreements among parties. Epstein and O'Halloran (1999) outline the intuition underlying this theoretical approach in their research on delegation by discussing trade-offs. The principal trade-off for Congress to consider in this context is whether it should write extensively detailed statutes that dictate bureaucratic actions with precision or simply outline general policy objectives and delegate to bureaucrats the autonomy to implement the policy in a manner of their own choosing. Under the former, legislators would necessarily incur costs to gather information necessary to make policy in great detail as well as those involving expended efforts to pass a more complex law through each chamber. Under the latter, bureaucrats may choose not to abide by legislative intent.

Strategic decisions regarding delegation are consequential in shaping policy, which legislators are assumed to prioritize. Due to the costs lawmakers would incur by drafting extensively detailed laws that would hardwire all aspects of a law's implementation, coupled with the desire to benefit from bureaucratic expertise, Congress has many incentives to delegate (Gailmard and Patty 2007). As powers delegated to the executive branch have increased, so too has the need for effective congressional oversight capabilities to help minimize the negative externalities of large-scale delegation.

The very act of delegation surrenders policy-making powers from one branch to another. When given broad implementation powers, agencies may adopt policies that do not accord with prevailing congressional intent. By not delegating, Congress frees itself from this negative consequence of delegation, but is unable to reap any expertise or efficiency benefits. The key problem facing Congress in this regard is how to go about maximizing the benefits of delegation while simultaneously minimizing the costs. One way legislators can protect themselves from undesirable bureaucratic action is to condition delegated powers with certain prohibitions preventing bureaucrats from implementing unauthorized policies (Gailmard 2002; MacDonald 2010). The legislative veto, which has been described as a "unique tool to mold eighteenth-century political institutions to the needs of twentieth-century policymaking" (Gibson 1994, 441), provides one resourceful solution to this dilemma.

Cognizant of the size of the present-day bureaucracy and the tremendous number of policies it is charged with implementing, Congress commonly employs the legislative veto as one of many ways to oversee the execution of the laws it writes. The increase over time in the number of vetoes passed by Congress has not come without controversy. Presidents have almost universally regarded this type of oversight as an excessive encroachment on the executive branch's authority to execute the law.

The President Strikes Back

Although the legislative veto was created with presidential support, every president who has served after its advent has expressed his opposition to the oversight device (Fisher 1993). With varying intensity, presidents have both requested and demanded that Congress cease the practice of including such provisions in legislation. In a special message to Congress, President Jimmy Carter once chastised lawmakers over the veto by arguing that their "proliferation threatens to upset the constitutional balance of responsibilities between the branches of government of the United States" and therefore constitutes a "fundamental departure from the way the government has been administered throughout American history" (1978, 1146). Since Congress refused to acquiesce to these presidential entreaties, the president boldly declared that the administration would not be bound by statutes containing legislative vetoes. Further, because appeals such as this have not produced the desired results, presidents have pursued alternative resources to attenuate legislative veto restrictions on delegated powers. Most notably, presidents have increased their use of the signing statement as a counteractive strategy to this end.

Presidential signing statements are messages added by the president when signing a bill into law. These statements, while not explicitly mentioned in the Constitution, were infrequently issued during the nineteenth century and became increasingly utilized during the latter half of the twentieth century (Kelley 2006). Figure 0.2 provides data on the number of signing statements issued by each president since 1928, and illustrates the increasing number of signing statements issued by modern presidents.[3] While not the first president to use the signing statement in this fashion, President George W. Bush used it to make constitutional objections to hundreds of statutes passed by Congress (Berry 2009; P. Cooper 2005; Kelley and Marshall 2008). For example, in the final signing statement issued by President Bush when signing the 2009 Department of Defense spending bill in October 2008, he declared:

> Provisions of the Act . . . purport to impose requirements that could inhibit the President's ability to carry out his constitutional obligations to take care that the laws be faithfully executed, to protect national security, to conduct diplomatic negotiations, to supervise the executive branch, to appoint officers of the United States, and to execute his authority as Commander in Chief. The executive branch shall continue to construe such provisions in a manner consistent with the constitutional authority and obligations of the President. (Bush 2008, 1346)

This statement explicitly details constitutional objections to sections of the law containing legislative vetoes. By declaring that these provisions will be executed "in a manner consistent with the constitutional authority and obligations of the President," President Bush implicitly suggests that the executive branch may not implement the law precisely as written by Congress.

The bars in figure 0.2 for each president indicate the total number of signing statements issued as well as the number of signing statements containing at least one constitutional objection to a new law. These data demonstrate that presidents have increasingly deployed the signing statement to raise issues pertaining to a law's constitutionality. Across this entire time period about one-fourth of all signing statements contain a constitutionally based protest. More than half of the signing statements issued by three of the past four presidents have made constitutional objections, with over 80 percent of the statements issued by President George W. Bush belonging to this category. According to one estimate, President Bush alone made constitutional objections to over 1,100 sections of enacted law (Kelley and Marshall 2009). In this respect, the signing statement has become a commonly utilized vehicle of presidential power as a weapon against Congress (Berry 2009; Kelley and Marshall 2008).

Every president from Dwight Eisenhower onward has issued signing statements criticizing Congress for including legislative vetoes in legislation (P. Cooper 2002; Dellinger 1995). As the *Chadha* decision occurred during President Ronald Reagan's first term, he was the first president to cite Supreme Court precedent as justification for the presidential opposition to legislative vetoes. In one such signing statement, Reagan declared:

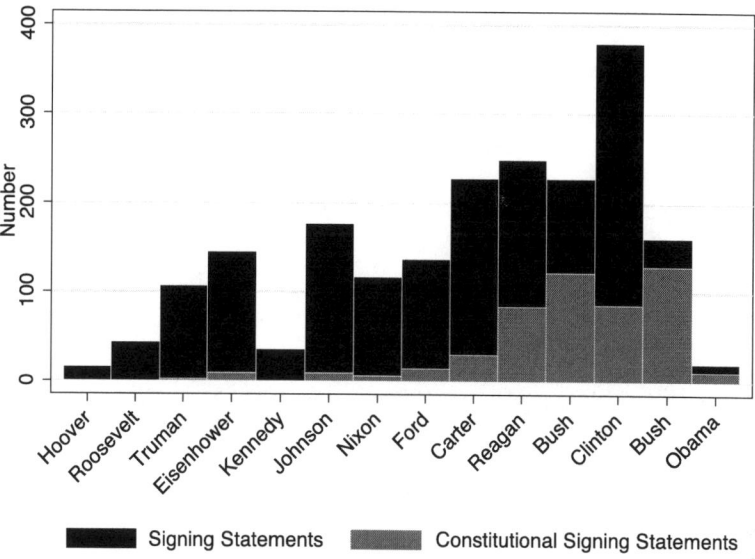

Fig. 0.2. Presidential signing statements: 1931–2012 (Data from the American Presidency Project and compiled by author.)

Many provisions of H.R. 4867 reflect a growing and disturbing trend on the part of the Congress to include unconstitutional committee approval or veto requirements in appropriations bills. . . . In granting authority or making appropriations by law, the Congress may not reserve to its committees approval or veto power over the exercise of that authority or the expenditure of those appropriations. The reservation of such power to congressional committees clearly conflicts with the constitutional principles the Supreme Court enunciated in *INS v. Chadha*, 462 U.S. 919 (1983). The Executive branch will continue to provide committees the notification and full consultation that interbranch comity requires in matters in which the Congress has indicated such a special interest. (Reagan 1988, 1228)

As one would expect, subsequent presidents have likewise used the signing statement to advance this argument. President Bill Clinton issued the following statement when signing a 1994 transportation bill into law:

I also note that section 42104(c) purports to enact a legislative veto with respect to specific regulations issued by the Secretary of Labor. . . . The Supreme Court has ruled definitively that legislative vetoes are unconstitutional. Under the Court's precedents, the legislative veto provision contained in section 42104(c) is severable from H.R. 1758. I therefore instruct the Secretary of Labor to disregard section 42104(c). (Clinton 1994, 1199)

Such is the current state of affairs. When signing bills, presidents have frequently used the signing statement to identify provisions considered unconstitutional, to instruct executive officials how to treat legislative vetoes, and in some instances to state the executive's intent to disregard provisions passed by Congress and enacted into law.

In this research, the signing statement will be examined as a unique device often employed by the president in the macropolitical conflict against Congress. When used in this capacity, both the legislative veto and the presidential signing statement are key institutional resources in the struggle to exert greater control over the bureaucracy.

Overview of the Book

The 30 years that have elapsed since the Supreme Court ruled the legislative veto unconstitutional allow for an extended analysis of these ongoing negotiations between the legislative and executive branches. Rather than sounding its "death knell," as Justice Byron White claimed in his dissenting opinion, lawmakers continue to use the legislative veto with great fervor.

The analysis presented in this book seeks to achieve several goals. First and most important, this research will provide a robust examination of the past and present use of the legislative veto as a statutory oversight device. In their seminal study of congressional delegation, Epstein and O'Halloran state that the "constitutional and political status of the legislative veto remains somewhat murky" (1999, 100). With this in mind, this book aspires to be the definitive study on this topic. Given the continued implementation of legislative vetoes and the varied presidential reactions to their enactment, an informed assessment of this type of oversight is essential to a better understanding of how authority is delegated, overseen, and used to implement public policy. Following in this line of inquiry, this study seeks to answer a series of questions related to how and when Congress elects to delegate power and craft statutes designed to facilitate effective oversight.

Despite its prevalence as an oversight resource, there are a great number of questions concerning the congressional veto that remain, for the most part, unanswered. For example, how did the *Chadha* decision alter the way Congress uses the veto as an oversight device? In what ways do contemporary legislative vetoes resemble or differ from their historical counterparts? How has the executive branch responded to the continued use of the legislative veto? What conditions give rise to the enactment of legislative vetoes? Are they used more frequently under certain circumstances, for specific issue areas, or to restrict certain bureaucratic agencies? Has divided government or ideological polarization affected the implementation of legislative vetoes? What role do committees play in this type of oversight? Answering these questions should therefore enrich our understanding of the process in which modern public policy is implemented, overseen, and reformed.

In order to provide a robust analysis of the legislative veto, I created an original dataset that identifies more than 3,800 veto enactments included in more than 700 laws. These data provide a nearly exhaustive catalog of legislative vetoes from 1931 to 2010. In addition to these data on congressional enactments is a parallel dataset including over 1,400 presidential signing statements. Quantitative analysis of these data will provide greater insight on how Congress uses this particular type of oversight to assert greater control over the execution of the law. The qualitative analysis presented in this book incorporates policy area case studies and interviews with 25 current or former members of Congress and numerous committee staff. These different types of analysis will provide unique perspectives on congressional oversight, bureaucratic policy making, presidential power, and macropolitical conflict.

Following this introductory chapter, chapter 1 provides an introduction to the legislative veto and a general overview of the development and evolution of the oversight device from both legislative and judicial perspectives. On the legislative side, this chapter explores the origin of the legislative veto and chronicles its use over a period of 50 years. Though the veto originated as an institutional compromise, it quickly morphed into a source of considerable interbranch conflict. Given the constitutional questions surrounding its use, this chapter also surveys the beginnings of judicial involvement in the dispute. Court cases challenging the legislative veto began in the late 1970s and culminated in 1983 with the major Supreme Court ruling in *INS v. Chadha*.

To better understand the dynamics associated with its use, this chapter introduces a legislative veto typology. Following the advent of the legislative veto, which allowed either congressional chamber to block presidential reorganization initiatives, lawmakers of both parties have proposed and enacted many different types of veto statutes. Because of the wide variety of legislative vetoes enacted by Congress, it is useful to develop a typology to formally categorize vetoes according to a specific rubric. This typology uses two important criteria: (1) who in Congress is empowered with veto authority, and (2) the procedures that govern how the veto is enacted. Coding legislative vetoes in this manner allows for a more nuanced analysis of its use and the evolution of this oversight device over time.

Chapter 2 begins with a survey of the Supreme Court opinions in *INS v. Chadha* and continues to discuss how the ruling has affected the veto's applications. Cases challenging the veto have become less frequent after the landmark ruling, but there are several worthy of reference that took place after 1983. Judicial review in this area of constitutional and statutory law has almost exclusively benefited the president at the expense of Congress, although the courts have generally been the weakest player in this conflict. That is not to say, however, that the courts have been ineffectual. Congressional vetoes enacted in the post-*Chadha* era differ in several meaningful respects when compared to those before the ruling. Most notably, Congress has largely curtailed its imposition of statutes allowing a single chamber to block executive action in favor of those that bestow veto authority on individual committees.

Chapter 3 introduces the transaction cost theoretical framework used to approach congressional oversight and the legislative veto. Commensurate with the dramatic expansion of the federal bureaucracy is an increase in the powers delegated to bureaucrats to determine many specifics of broader policies passed by Congress. As the scope of delegated powers grew, legislators necessarily developed a variety of ways to oversee policy implementation to ensure that policy outcomes align with congressional intent. With any type of oversight activity there are costs that lawmakers, committees, and chambers must incur. Of central concern for this research are the transaction costs related to policy complexity, conflict, and issue salience.

As legislative vetoes are enacted through the legislative process, the costs of inserting a single legislative veto provision into a bill are typically low. According to interviews with lawmakers and committee staff, the brunt of the costs associated with this type of oversight concern monitoring agency compliance with veto statutes. Ensuring compliance with such statutory requirements passed by Congress can entail substantial amounts of time and attention from individual lawmakers, staff, committees, and Congress as a whole. Because of this, it is expected that lawmakers should generally be more willing to incur costs associated with veto oversight when issue salience, political conflict, or policy complexity are greater. In short, the empirical analysis in this chapter seeks to explain Congress's approach to the legislative veto by considering key transaction costs associated with its use.

Chapter 4 examines presidential reactions to the legislative veto's continued use by focusing on two institutional resources: the presidential veto and the signing statement. Given the steadfast presidential opposition to the veto, the first hypothesis tested in this chapter expects presidents to be more likely to veto legislation containing greater numbers of legislative veto provisions. To date, most of the research on presidential vetoes has examined institutional or contextual factors theorized to affect a president's veto propensity such as divided government, partisan legislative support, legislative productivity, presidential popularity, and various economic and electoral indicators (Lee 1975; Rohde and Simon 1985; Shields and Huang 1995; Woolley 1991). These studies have advanced our understanding of the president's veto power, but few have systematically examined the content of legislation presented to the president as an explanatory factor affecting veto use (although see Cameron 2000; J. Gilmour 2002). By testing whether specific oversight components included in bills sent to the president are more likely to elicit a veto, this analysis does precisely that. A related hypothesis concerning signing statements expects that in the absence of a presidential veto, presidents will be more likely to issue a signing statement making constitutional objections to bills that include legislative vetoes.

Chapter 5 examines the legislative veto from a policy perspective by analyzing the issue areas where it is most commonly used. Of particular focus is the evolution of veto statutes tailored to affect policies related to national security, defense, and foreign policy. Differences in the policy applications of the veto are also analyzed by comparing different configurations of divided government and congressional partisan majorities. By considering measures of agency and cabinet secretary ideology (Bertelli and Grose 2011; Clinton and Lewis 2008), this chapter also tests whether legislators are more apt to impose veto oversight when greater policy disagreements exist across branches. These analyses aim to further our understanding of the conditions that give rise to legislative veto enactments and differences that exist in terms of the veto's oversight role across the policy spectrum.

Chapter 6 examines the use of the legislative veto at the state level. While it originated in Congress, many U.S. states have subsequently adopted similar types of oversight procedures. Beginning with a Kansas enactment in 1939, dozens of states have codified some means of legislative veto authority. The use of the veto by state legislatures exhibits many differences when compared to Congress. Most notable of these is that legislative vetoes imposed by Congress are enacted through individual laws that specify which actions are potentially subject to subsequent override. Though there are some exceptions, most state-level applications of the legislative veto occur through the imposition of statewide rulemaking systems permitting legislators to veto agency rules. The primary distinguishing characteristic of rulemaking processes that permit direct legislative involvement concern whether legislators can nullify rules entirely or impose a suspension period that temporarily blocks a rule's adoption. At present, 12 states permit legislative rule nullification and 16 allow rule suspension.

Though some rule review systems permitting legislative vetoes have since been abolished, a total of 29 states have experimented with at least one type of veto oversight. State constitutions in Connecticut, Iowa, Michigan, Nevada, New Jersey, and South Dakota explicitly protect the legislature's veto oversight power. An additional 18 states permit their legislature to nullify or suspend agency rules with a statutory, rather than constitutional, authorization.

State supreme courts have generally not been receptive to arguments in favor of legislative veto oversight. Of the rulings in 13 states where the veto has come before a high court, only two have affirmed the practice. Even amid such judicial hostility, many states provide joint rules review committees, standing committees, or the legislature as a whole with strong powers to affect agency rulemaking. In sum, this chapter discusses the history and varied applications of the legislative veto at the state level and provides an empirical analysis of veto systems over time. Among the primary findings from this analysis is that legislative veto adoption is generally more likely with a Republican governor in office and single-party control of the state legislature.

The concluding chapter summarizes the evolution of the legislative veto and the major reforms that have occurred following the *Chadha* ruling and discusses the main findings from the empirical analysis. Potential avenues for subsequent research are also identified. A discussion of the current landscape segues into a prognosis of how this unique type of oversight will likely evolve in the future. Finally, the concluding chapter emphasizes the key contributions of this study concerning the legislative veto, congressional oversight, and macropolitical conflict more generally.

ONE

Origin and Evolution: The Path to *Chadha*

The government created by the Framers in Philadelphia's Independence Hall positioned Congress as the most powerful of the three branches. James Madison underscores this point in Federalist No. 51, stating, "In republican government, the legislative authority necessarily predominates" (1788). Partially as a means to constrain legislative power, the Constitution established a bicameral Congress as the country's principal policymaking body. Ratification of the Constitution meant that executive and judicial branches would exist alongside the legislature, which had been the only federal institution under the Articles of Confederation. Although the Constitution establishes a federal republic with three distinct branches of government, Madison draws from the political philosophy of Montesquieu and states that the separation of powers embedded in the Constitution does "not mean that these departments ought to have no *partial agency* in, or no *control* over the acts of each other" (1788, Federalist No. 47; emphasis in original). Through both formal and informal channels, each branch possesses a variety of checks capable of influencing the actions of the others.[1] Because of this, many have described the framework of the U.S. constitutional republic as an "invitation to struggle" (Crabb and Holt 1992; Davidson 1988; Fisher 1997).

Given its constitutional charge to execute the law, the executive branch has often asserted its prerogative to do so unencumbered by legislative interference. Conversely, the legislature has always maintained an interest in ensuring that executive officials faithfully execute the laws it passes.

To this end, Congress has developed many resources to help oversee the bureaucracy. One important type of statutory oversight empowers legislators with a veto over designated executive actions.

Legislative vetoes represent a broad range of congressional actions used to directly influence the execution of the law. To reiterate, legislative vetoes are statutory provisions that authorize the House, Senate, or individual committees to approve, disapprove, or otherwise review specific bureaucratic actions. Congress frequently conditions delegated powers with such provisions as a safeguard to prevent executive officials from enacting policies that deviate from its preferences. By inserting them into legislation, Congress can benefit from delegating while maintaining some modicum of control over delegated powers. Lawmakers advocating on behalf of the veto's legitimacy have maintained that it "has not been a sword which Congress has used to aggrandize itself at the expense of other branches. Rather, the veto has been a means of defense. The veto reserves the ultimate authority necessary if Congress is to fulfill its designated role as the Nation's lawmaker" (DeConcini 1983, 300). Underscoring its importance, scholars have argued that the proliferation of the legislative veto is one of the "most significant institutional developments in twentieth century American politics" (J. Cooper 1985, 364).

Since its inception, the legislative veto has taken many forms. At its extremes, the veto has ranged from a power exercised by a single individual (the House Appropriations Committee chairperson) to those requiring a two-thirds majority vote in both Houses.[2] The development of many different types of vetoes is illustrative of its malleability as an oversight resource. While the constitutionality of this procedure has been questioned both in and out of the court system, Congress has crafted the legislative veto into a versatile oversight tool. The following sections provide a discussion of the legislative veto's origins and development, as well as the introduction of a legislative veto typology that will be utilized throughout the book.

Legislative Veto Antecedents

Informal congressional vetoes date back to the colonial period when General George Washington made the decision to racially integrate the Continental Army in 1775 with the caveat that the Second Continental Congress could overrule the action. Upon notifying delegates of this strategic decision aimed at fortifying the rebels' war effort, Washington declared that "if this is disapproved by the Congress, I will put a Stop to it" (quoted in

Ellis 2007, 35). Following victory in the Revolutionary War and ratification of the Constitution, lawmakers of the first session of Congress enacted multiple statutes seeking to exercise control over executive action without having to adopt new laws as the means to exert influence.

In 1789, Congress created the departments of Foreign Affairs, Treasury, and War as the first cabinet-level institutions responsible for executing policies associated with diplomacy, fiscal policy, and defense, respectively.[3] The enactment creating the Department of the Treasury included one of the first extralegislative efforts to control departmental functions. By law, the secretary of the treasury was required to submit reports to Congress following agreement to a resolution in either chamber making such a request (H. Watson 1975). As its first secretary, Alexander Hamilton complied with these congressional requests and submitted several reports on a variety of matters. In the 1830s, Congress began using House and Senate resolutions to instruct executive officials to provide surveys and reports regarding domestic public works projects (H. Watson 1975). Thus, early in American history, Congress recognized the importance of interfacing with the executive beyond the act of merely passing and amending laws. While extralegislative functions date back to the country's founding, the origins of the legislative veto can be traced to the Treaty of Versailles and federal efforts to combat the Great Depression, which occurred long after this early foray into extralegislative oversight.

Origins of the Legislative Veto

Lawmakers began proposing legislative vetoes at least a decade before the enactment of the first veto statute into law. After the end of World War I, President Woodrow Wilson fiercely lobbied both Congress and the American public to support U.S. entry into the League of Nations. Massachusetts senator Henry Cabot Lodge led the opposition to joining the international organization primarily because of concerns regarding alliance requirements mandating U.S. military action following aggression against any alliance state. During debates on the ratification of the Treaty of Versailles and the merits of the League of Nations, the Senate added a controversial amendment to the treaty that gave Congress the ability to unilaterally withdraw from the international organization (H. Watson 1975). This clause empowered Congress to vacate U.S. involvement with the League of Nations and rendered the president powerless to prevent a withdrawal approved by majorities in the House and Senate. However, since two separate ratification votes in the Senate failed to reach the necessary two-thirds majority, the legislative veto permitting Congress to abrogate U.S. membership in the League of Nations was rendered moot.[4]

Following these unsuccessful votes, the 66th Congress once again attempted to implement a legislative veto, this time dealing with domestic policy. The Budget and Accounting Bill of 1920 passed by Congress proposed, among other things, a new executive office under the authority of the comptroller general. A provision included in the bill authorized Congress to remove the comptroller general from office pursuant to agreement on a concurrent resolution so directing. Perceiving this as an unconstitutional encroachment on his power of executive appointment, President Wilson vetoed the legislation. The same year, Wilson also vetoed a spending bill empowering the Joint Committee on Printing with veto authority over the publication of certain government documents (H. Watson 1975). By virtue of the president's vetoes, neither of these legislative vetoes became law. Slightly more than a decade later, the nation's first legislative veto was enacted when President Herbert Hoover signed legislation affording him with greater powers of executive reorganization with the caveat that Congress could block the exercise of this power.

Overseeing Presidential Reorganization Initiatives

Near the end of the Hoover administration, the president desired the authority to reorganize institutions within the executive branch without having to lobby Congress to enact legislation making these changes. The desire for greater presidential control over executive organization predates the Hoover presidency. The Committee on Executive Departments appointed by President Theodore Roosevelt has been credited with inciting a paradigm shift concerning government reorganization matters whereby the president explicitly claimed executive organization as a prerogative of the chief executive (Karl 1963). Subscribing to this perspective, President Hoover sought independent reorganization authority as a valuable tool allowing for an expedient restructuring of executive branch agencies to facilitate swift actions in response to the increasing economic problems presented by the Depression (Craig 1983).

Writing in his memoirs, Hoover stated "the executive organization of the Federal government appalled me. . . . The real remedy was to get all the executive agencies related to the same major purpose under one hat—one administrator whom the people could put their finger on, who could trim away the overlaps and obtain unity on policies" (1951, 281). Given the escalating magnitude of the economic depression and cognizant of the potential benefits of delegating reorganization powers to the president, the 72nd Congress considered legislation making such a reform. Many in Congress were fearful of granting sweeping and unfettered reorganization power to the president alone.

Congress was understandably reluctant to delegate such extraordinary reorganization authority to the president, despite the potential gains that might result. As is the case with most decisions regarding whether to delegate to executive officials, Congress considered both the advantages and disadvantages of empowering the president in this regard. Its pragmatic solution afforded the president with unprecedented reorganization powers but made all reorganizations susceptible to congressional veto.

Provisions in the Legislative Appropriations Act for the 1933 fiscal year delegated to the president powers to restructure the executive branch (47 Stat. 382, Public Law 72–212). The law required the president to submit any reorganization orders to Congress for a review period not to exceed 60 days. During this review period, either chamber could veto a reorganization proposal with a resolution of disapproval.[5] If neither chamber elected to veto the proposed reorganization, the president's plan would go into effect. In practice, this procedure reverses the lawmaking process outlined by the Constitution. Rather than Congress passing legislation that is submitted to the president to be signed or vetoed, in the instance of executive reorganization the president submits proposals to the two chambers of Congress for their approval or veto.

The initial rationale for the legislative veto was simply a desire from Congress and the president to devise an institutional compromise facilitating expedited government action under dire circumstances. During debate on the proposal, some lawmakers challenged the constitutionality of delegating such powers to the president. Surprisingly, no objections were voiced concerning the constitutionality of the veto provision itself (Franck and Bob 1985). Despite the lack of a substantive discussion concerning the constitutionality of the legislative veto, Attorney General William D. Mitchell recommended that the president veto the legislation (Ginnane 1953). The president did not heed this counsel. After signing the bill into law, President Hoover began drafting reorganization proposals to send to Congress for review. Though he certainly did not know it at the time, all of his proposals were dead on arrival.

The 72nd Congress elected to utilize its newfound veto power with impunity. In fact, every reorganization proposal put forth by President

Hoover failed to pass congressional review. This outcome would have been surprising from the vantage point of election night in 1930, the results of which positioned the Republican Party to take control of both chambers of Congress following the midterm elections. The Republican advantage in the Senate was by a single seat, and the House majority was by a mere two representatives. However, special elections to fill vacated seats following the deaths of 14 representatives-elect gave the Democrats majority party status in the House when the first session of the 72nd Congress commenced.[6] Under a Democratic majority, the House vetoed all 11 of President Hoover's reorganization proposals (Millett and Rogers 1941). To say the least, this surely altered the president's perspective on the utility of the legislative veto. While President Hoover initially approved of this particular legislative veto provision—as it potentially allowed him to expeditiously reorganize segments of the executive branch without having to secure the passage of a new law—subsequent presidents, and indeed Hoover himself, developed an intense opposition to this novel type of oversight.

Admonishing Democratic leaders in Congress following their veto of his proposal to consolidate 58 separate agencies, Hoover lamented, "Either Congress must keep its hands off now or they must give to my successor much larger powers of independent action than given to any President if there is ever to be reorganization. . . . Otherwise it will, as is now being demonstrated in the present law, again be merely make believe" (1951, 284). While modern presidents have regarded the legislative veto as an unconstitutional encroachment on the responsibilities of executive officials to faithfully execute the law, Congress has generally viewed it as a legitimate assertion of its legislative authority to counterbalance increasing executive power.

Legislative Veto Typology

The first veto statute enacted by Congress delegated executive reorganization powers to the president, but stipulated that either chamber could prevent reorganization initiatives from going into effect. Vetoes of this type are classified as "one-House negative" vetoes since a resolution from a single house is sufficient to block a reorganization proposal. To facilitate a more nuanced analysis of this type of statutory oversight, this section introduces a typology of legislative vetoes used throughout the book. Before this typology is introduced, it is first important to distinguish between legislative vetoes and limitation riders.

Although they can be used for similar purposes, legislative vetoes differ from limitation riders in several important respects. In contrast to legislative vetoes, limitation riders inserted into appropriations legislation explicitly prohibit agencies from spending funds in a particular manner. For example, the 2006 Department of Homeland Security Appropriations Act contained the following provision, which prohibited Department of Homeland Security (DHS) expenditures to research or develop methods to identify air travel passengers deemed to pose a safety risk beyond those listed on government watch lists: "None of the funds provided in this or previous appropriations Acts may be utilized to develop or test algorithms assigning risk to passengers whose names are not on Government watch lists" (119 Stat. 2085, Public Law 109–90). Limitation riders such as this and legislative vetoes both serve the oversight needs of Congress, albeit in different ways.

A first important distinction between the two concerns the scope of their applicability. Legislative vetoes are a more versatile oversight mechanism that can be utilized to exert control over virtually any bureaucratic action. Limitation riders, however, are more limited because their prohibitions only concern federal spending. Second, limitation riders impose unconditional restraints on executive officials by prohibiting certain types of expenditures. In contrast, legislative vetoes do not uniformly limit delegated power, but rather condition delegated powers by reserving the right for the legislature to intervene by approving or rejecting an agency action. For example, consider the following legislative veto enacted in the Consolidated Appropriations Resolution of 2003 concerning funds appropriated for the National Park Service:

> Provided further, That none of the funds provided in this or any other Act may be used to pre-design, plan, or construct any new facility . . . for which appropriations have not been specifically provided if the net construction cost of such facility is in excess of $5,000,000, without prior approval of the House and Senate Committees on Appropriations. (117 Stat. 226, Public Law 108–7)

While the limitation rider unconditionally prohibits spending for a certain purpose, the legislative veto prohibits designated expenditures unless prior approval is obtained from the House and Senate Committees on Appropriations. In this respect, a congressional veto over spending measures is less absolute than a limitation rider. Where a limitation rider expressly prohibits funds from being spent on a specific project, a congressional veto allows funds to be spent provided that the spending is approved through the proper channels. With this in mind, one can begin differentiating legislative veto statutes according to the typology presented in figure 1.1.

Several studies have distinguished legislative veto statutes according to a number of different criteria including veto authorization, procedures, and participants; policy areas; and time constraints (Cooper and Hurley 1983; R. Gilmour 1982; Norton 1976). The schematic illustrated in figure 1.1 illustrates a typology used to classify legislative vetoes according to their type. The two criteria used to categorize legislative vetoes are (1) who in Congress is empowered with veto authority, and (2) the procedure that governs a veto's execution.

The categories corresponding to the first criterion are committee, one House, and dual House. In this classification, committee legislative vetoes empower one or more congressional committees with veto authority. One-House vetoes require the adoption of a House or Senate resolution as the mechanism necessary to implement a legislative veto, and dual-House vetoes require concerted action from both the House and the Senate. Historically, dual-House vetoes typically required bicameral agreement on a concurrent resolution, which does not require a presidential signature, as necessary to execute the veto. More recently, however, dual-House vetoes are often tied to joint resolutions, which require the president's signature.

The second criterion utilized to formulate a typology of legislative vetoes deals with the procedure used to execute the veto. While veto powers of any type are generally conceptualized as authorizations to nullify or invalidate some action, legislative vetoes can be one of three types: negative, affirmative, or deliberative (R. Gilmour 1982). In each of these instances, the legislature begins by delegating powers to an agency. Following this authorization, the agency has latitude in terms of how it chooses to implement policies under the enabling legislation. Negative legislative vetoes allow administrative agencies to exercise those powers unless Congress takes the initiative to veto or override them. In contrast, affirmative legislative vetoes require congressional approval of designated executive actions before they occur. Finally, deliberative legislative vetoes require notification to Congress of proposed administrative actions prior to their execution. The plan of action goes into effect after the prescribed waiting period expires unless the legislature takes some proactive measure to prevent its implementation (Bowers 1990). Each of these veto variants provides Congress with a continued influence in the execution of enacted laws.

Some argue that dual-House vetoes by joint resolution are not properly classified as legislative vetoes because they require a presidential sig-

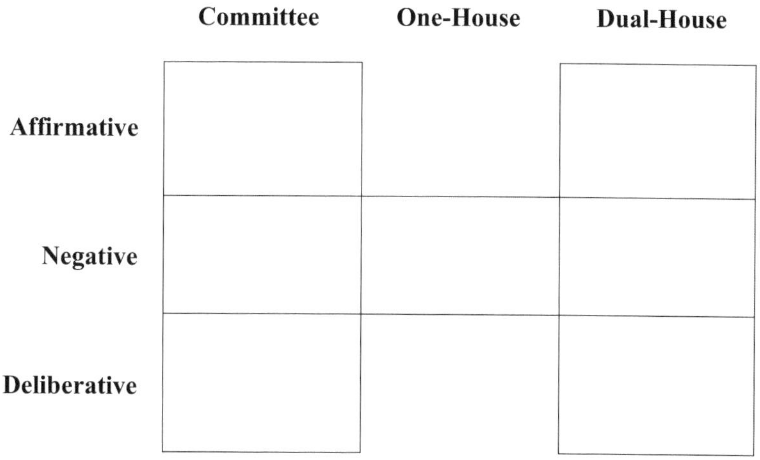

	Committee	One-House	Dual-House
Affirmative			
Negative			
Deliberative			

Fig. 1.1. Legislative veto typology

nature. This study considers such statutes as legislative vetoes for two reasons. First, actions subject to a dual-House affirmative veto requiring a joint resolution of approval are tantamount to one-House negative vetoes since the resolution must receive support in both chambers before progressing to the president's desk. By voting down or refusing to consider a joint resolution of approval, each house essentially holds independent veto power (Fisher 2005a). For actions susceptible to a dual-House negative veto through a joint resolution of disapproval, both houses must act in order to send the veto resolution to the president. As is the case with bills, Congress can override a presidential veto of a joint resolution with a two-thirds majority vote. The practical consequence of this is that Congress may execute this type of dual-House negative veto with majority support provided that the president supports the veto as well. Facing presidential opposition, the veto could only be exercised by a supermajority coalition.

Over time, legislators have adopted many different types of legislative vetoes providing for congressional review, approval, or disapproval of executive actions. Modern Congresses rely heavily on committee deliberative vetoes, also known as "report and wait" provisions. These statutes require administrative officials to formally notify Congress about certain activities prior to their execution, without requiring approval or allowing for a direct veto. Rather, they necessitate a review period—typically 15, 30, or 60 days—before an action takes place. This requirement provides legislators with advance notification of a proposed course of action as well as a stipulated number of days to review the proposal and take action if they desire.

Using the typology presented in figure 1.1, the nation's first legislative veto is properly classified as one-House negative because a resolution from either chamber could block presidential reorganization proposals. When reauthorizing presidential reorganization authority, Democratic majorities in Congress modified this legislative veto from a one-House negative veto to a dual-House negative veto through the Reorganization Acts of 1939 and 1945 (53 Stat. 561, Public Law 76–19; 59 Stat. 613, Public Law 79–263). Consequently, majority opposition in both the House and Senate, as opposed to majority opposition in just a single chamber, became necessary to block presidential reorganization plans. In short, dual-House vetoes such as these require coordinated action from both chambers, while single-House vetoes allow either chamber to execute the veto.

Table 1.1 provides examples of each type of legislative veto from the typology displayed in figure 1.1. The committee affirmative veto example is from a 2007 omnibus spending bill that required any reprogramming of funds by the Forest Service to receive advance approval of the House and Senate Appropriations Committees. Conversely, the committee negative statute passed in 1993 allowed the public works committees in either chamber to veto project-specific spending by the General Services Administration. The committee deliberative example is from the Civil Rights Act of 1964. This statute required 30 days advance notification to committees of jurisdiction before the revocation of federal funds due to failure to comply with the nondiscriminatory requirements contained in the law. Each of these statutes directly involves two or more committees with the execution of the law. Affirmative vetoes require committee approval, negative vetoes allow committees to block an action from occurring, and deliberative vetoes require advance notice to specified committees. These veto mechanisms are similar for dual-House vetoes.

The first veto passed by Congress concerning presidential reorganization proposals serves as the one-House negative veto example. A dual-House negative example is drawn from the War Powers Resolution, which stipulated that Congress may overturn presidential deployments of U.S. forces with the adoption of a concurrent resolution so directing. The dual-House affirmative veto from the International Development and Food Assistance Act of 1975 required agreement on a concurrent resolution to modify the terms of foreign debts owed to the United States, and the dual-

TABLE 1.1. Legislative veto typology examples

One-House Negative—"Whenever the President makes an Executive order under the provisions of this title, such Executive order shall be transmitted during sessions to the Congress while in session and shall not become effective until after the expiration of sixty calendar days after such transmission. . . . Provided further, That if either branch of Congress within such sixty calendar days shall pass a resolution disapproving of such Executive order, or any part thereof, such Executive order shall become null and void to the extent of such disapproval." (47 Stat. 382, Public Law 72-212)

Dual-House Affirmative—"No debt owed to the United States by any foreign country with respect to the payment of any loan made under any program funded under this Act may be settled in an amount less than the first amount of such debt unless the Congress by concurrent resolution approves of such settlement." (89 Stat. 849, Public Law 94-161)

Dual-House Negative—"Notwithstanding subsection (b), at any time that the United States Armed Forces are engaged in hostilities outside the territory of the United States, its possessions and territories without a declaration of war or specific statutory authorization, such forces shall be removed by the President if the Congress so directs by concurrent resolution." (87 Stat. 555, Public Law 93-148)

Dual-House Deliberative—"An obligation of funds for a purpose stated in any of the paragraphs in subsection (a) in excess of the specific amount authorized for such purpose may be made using the authority provided in paragraph (1) only after—(A) the Secretary submits to Congress notification of the intent to do so together with a complete discussion of the justification for doing so; and (B) 15 days have elapsed following the date of the notification." (116 Stat. 2671, Public Law 107-314)

Committee Affirmative—"None of the funds available to the Forest Service may be reprogrammed without the advance approval of the House and Senate Committees on Appropriations in accordance with the reprogramming procedures contained in the explanatory statement accompanying this Act." (121 Stat. 2133, Public Law 110-161)

Committee Negative—"That subject to the exceptions contained in the preceding proviso, in no case shall such funds be made available for any lease, line-item construction, repair, or alterations project referred to in the preceding proviso if prior to February 1, 1994, the lease, line-item construction, repair, or alterations project has been disapproved by the House Committee on Public Works and Transportation or the Senate Committee on Environment and Public Works." (107 Stat. 1243, Public Law 103-123)

Committee Deliberative—"In the case of any action terminating, or refusing to grant or continue, assistance because of failure to comply with a requirement imposed pursuant to this section, the head of the Federal department or agency shall file with the committees of the House and Senate having legislative jurisdiction over the program or activity involved a full written report of the circumstances and the grounds for such action. No such action shall become effective until thirty days have elapsed after the filing of such report." (78 Stat. 241, Public Law 88-352)

House deliberative veto enacted in 2002 simply required 15 days advance notification to congressional leadership before certain funds are spent by the Department of Defense.

Some argue that advance reporting requirements to committees or to Congress as a whole should not be categorized as legislative veto variants since there is no specific statutory procedure for Congress to veto an executive action (Korn 1996). Here it is important to note that there have been cases, where committees have blocked a proposed action through the report and wait process even when no statutory affirmative or negative veto mechanism exists. In some instances, "notification in a statute can become a code word to indicate the need for committee approval" (Fisher 1985, 708). One such example occurred in 2004 when the DHS provided advance notification of a scheduled reprogramming of $900 million in federal air marshal funds.

In this case, the DHS was required by statute to provide 15 days advance notification to the spending committees before making reprogrammings of this magnitude (117 Stat. 584, Public Law 103–272). Shortly after receiving notice of the scheduled reprogramming, both committees informed the DHS that reprogramming was prohibited (U.S. GAO 2004b). Though it is but one example, it demonstrates that deliberative vetoes can result in a direct veto of an executive action. For other instances when a direct veto such as this does not occur, the waiting period provides an opportunity for committees to act should sufficient opposition present itself.

While some adhere to a more narrow definition of legislative vetoes by only classifying provisions that require explicit congressional approval or disapproval of a proposed action as such, a more common approach includes report and wait provisions as legislative vetoes as well. Notably, in their identification of legislative veto statutes, the Congressional Research Service includes all "statutes requiring submission of proposals in advance" because the review period allows for Congress to intervene before the proposed course of action is to take place, should it so choose (Norton 1976, i). Having established a classification typology for legislative veto types, the discussion now shifts to providing greater detail of congressional use of the legislative veto to oversee presidential efforts to restructure the executive branch.

The Evolution of the Legislative Veto

The implementation of the first legislative veto in American history regarding presidential reorganization initiatives represented an innovative means of federal policy making. In its aftermath, Congress was slow to begin incorporating additional vetoes in other legislative acts. Over the eight years following its inception, only five additional legislative vetoes were adopted. This was due in part to opposition to the legislative veto that quickly developed within the executive branch. Attorney General William Mitchell recommended that President Hoover veto legislation on the grounds that the legislative veto provisions contained therein were unconstitutional (H. Watson 1975). One such opinion addressed a legislative proposal passed by Congress included in the Urgent Deficiency Bill (H.R. 13975, 72nd Congress, 2nd session) concerning committee vetoes of federal income tax refund amounts and the Bureau of Internal Revenue. In this opinion, the attorney general addressed a provision that provided an authoritative role for a joint congressional committee to veto or curtail federal tax refunds in excess of $20,000.

> The Constitution of the United States divides the functions of the Government into three departments—the legislative, executive and the judicial—and establishes the principle that they shall be kept separate, and that neither the legislative, executive, nor judicial branch may exercise functions belonging to the others. The proviso in the urgency deficiency bill violates this constitutional principle. It attempts to entrust to members of the legislative branch, acting *ex officio*, executive functions in the execution of the law, and it attempts to give to a committee of the legislative branch power to approve or disapprove executive acts. (Mitchell 1933)

President Hoover heeded the advice of the attorney general in this instance and vetoed the bill citing the "unconstitutionality of the provisions for legislative determination of individual tax refunds" (1933, 969). This did not deter Congress from continuing to insert legislative vetoes into legislation. Two months after President Hoover vetoed the tax reform measure, he signed a spending bill that imposed a second congressional veto over presidential reorganization powers.

Similar to the precedent set by the first, the 1934 Treasury and Post Office Appropriations Act delegated to the president the authority to consolidate and transfer agency responsibilities within the Treasury Department (47 Stat. 1489, Public Law 72–428). In this instance, Congress imposed a veto mechanism that was deliberative as opposed to negative. The version of the bill reported out of committee in the Senate proposed a dual-House negative veto. An unsuccessful amendment offered during

House deliberations sought to instead adopt a one-House negative veto (Ginnane 1953). The bill eventually sent to the president simply imposed a 60-day review period. This implemented a dual-House deliberative veto, as the president was required to provide Congress with advance notification.

Since President Hoover signed the bill into law on his last day in office, his successor had the first opportunity to develop reorganization proposals to submit for congressional review under the new procedure. President Franklin Roosevelt used these delegated reorganization powers frequently with virtually no resistance from Congress, although Roosevelt withdrew one reorganization plan in anticipation of congressional opposition (Harris 1964). The reorganization authority stemming from this legislation expired in 1935. Shortly thereafter, President Roosevelt lobbied Congress to enact a broader reorganization bill affording the president with much greater powers of executive management.

Commissioned by the president, the Brownlow Committee Report on Administrative Management outlined a five-point program aimed at improving the efficiency and effectiveness of the executive branch. Following the report's completion in January of 1937, Congress considered another measure giving the president substantial reorganization powers. Since President Roosevelt failed to consult congressional leaders on this reorganization initiative, its legislative reception was less than enthusiastic (Polenberg 1966). Support for Roosevelt's bill eroded further when Congress began considering the president's Supreme Court packing plan in February. Although the House passed several reorganization measures during this term, agreement could not be reached between the two chambers, meaning that Roosevelt would have to continue his lobbying efforts during the following year.

The administration came closer to successfully passing reorganization reform in 1938. Vocal opposition to the legislation in the Senate proclaimed that the bill would impose "an absolute dictatorship" (quoted in Polenberg 1966, 129). In front of a standing-room-only crowd in the Senate chamber, the Senate passed an amended version of the bill in March by just seven votes. Following passage in the Senate, debate on the measure in the House intensified. One Democratic lawmaker declared that the reorganization battle was the most contentious fight seen on the House floor in 50 years. Another Democrat made the case against further empowering the president by stating that "pretty soon, there will not be any use for Congress," lamenting that if the bill were to pass, lawmakers "might just as well stay at home and endorse Executive directives by mail" (quoted in Polenberg 1966, 166). The House ultimately voted to recommit the bill by a narrow margin of 204 to 196, which temporarily tabled the reform once again.

Republicans picked up 80 seats in the House and seven seats in the Senate following the midterm elections of 1938. The 76th Congress took up a scaled-down version of the failed reorganization reform from the prior term. The Reorganization Act of 1939 (53 Stat. 561, Public Law 76–19) delegated to the president the authority to propose reorganization plans, which were subject to a dual-House negative veto. The law allowed the president to appoint several new administrative assistants, but removed from the bill were broader reforms of the civil service and its accounting procedures, as well as the ability for the president to create new governmental departments (Polenberg 1966).

As was the case in 1932, Congress reserved veto power over presidential reorganization initiatives. House lawmakers proposed a number of amendments seeking to modify the veto mechanism. Representatives considered one-House negative, dual-House affirmative, and dual-House negative vetoes, including some that would have required a supermajority vote. The Senate considered similar measures. House and Senate conferees settled on the concurrent resolution of disapproval as the reorganization plan veto mechanism.

As he had previously, President Roosevelt opposed this proposal, and supported replacing the concurrent resolution with a joint resolution. In practice, this would have made it more difficult for Congress to veto reorganization efforts since joint resolutions require a president's signature. Prior to its passage, both chambers witnessed considerable debate regarding the constitutionality of the single- and dual-House vetoes, as well as the veto more generally. Supporters cited the recent Supreme Court ruling in *Currin v. Wallace*, 360 U.S. 1 (1939) as precedent allowing for an extralegislative influence on government reorganization (Ginnane 1953).

The *Currin* case concerned a set of provisions in the Tobacco Inspection Act of 1935 (53 Stat. 968, Public Law 76-160), where Congress delegated the certification of tobacco standards, sales, and marketing decisions to the secretary of agriculture. In turn, the secretary could not designate particular tobacco markets for inspection and certification unless two-thirds of affected growers voted in favor of a referendum to that effect. Plaintiffs in this case argued that this represented an impermissible delegation of Congress's authority to regulate interstate commerce. The majority opinion written by Chief Justice Charles Evans Hughes found that the act did not represent an unconstitutional delegation of congressional power. The Court recognized that legislation must often be adapted to different circumstances when Congress cannot anticipate future events. In making this argument, the opinion quoted recent precedent, which stated, "The Constitution has never been regarded as denying to the Congress the necessary resources of flexibility and practicality, which will enable it to perform its function in laying down policies and establishing standards, while leaving to selected instrumentalities the making of subordinate rules within prescribed limits and the determination of facts to which the policy as declared by the legislature is to apply" (*Panama Refining Co. v. Ryan*, 293 U.S. 388 (1935)).[7] In sum, placing restrictions on policy decisions made by actors outside of the legislature was acceptable as long as Congress had established a general policy objective.

Supporters of the legislative veto cited the ruling as precedent demonstrating that Congress could constitutionally place postpassage restrictions on executive action. A report from the House Select Committee on Organization also cited *Currin* as legitimizing postpassage conditions or contingencies established by Congress. The committee report argued that "it seems difficult to believe that the effectiveness of action legislative in character may be conditioned upon a vote of farmers but may not be conditioned on a vote of the two legislative bodies of the Congress" (quoted in Ginnane 1953, 579). Following this logic, supporters of the presidential reorganization veto successfully included a provision in the Reorganization Act stating that Congress could block proposed reorganizations deemed "not in the public interest" with a concurrent resolution of disapproval (53 Stat. 36, Public Law 76–19). On April 3, 1939, the president signed the bill into law despite his misgivings on the legislative veto provision. Following the enactment of the Reorganization Act, President Roosevelt's first reorganization initiative, which Congress did not veto, created the Executive Office of the President.

The reauthorization of presidential reorganization power by the Reorganization Act of 1945 maintained the dual-House negative veto enacted in 1939. In 1949, the veto reverted back to the one-House negative variant. On more than one occasion, the Senate prevented the creation of several new executive agencies proposed by President Harry Truman, including one to establish a Department of Welfare (Ginnane 1953). Congress periodically renewed reorganization authority until 1973 when Democrats refused to do so for President Nixon. After a transitory reestablishment during the Carter administration, it expired once again shortly after President Ronald Reagan took office. Presidents Reagan, Bush, and Clinton elected not to request a subsequent reauthorization (Relyea 1996). While the law was in existence, Presidents Truman through Carter submitted a total of 102 reorganization proposals to Congress (Keefe and Ogul 1981). Congress vetoed 19 of them, most of them when President Truman held office. The experience of President Hoover notwithstanding, legislative vetoes in this area have largely functioned as intended. Presidents had more of a free hand to restructure the executive branch and Congress held the authority to veto proposals deemed objectionable on a case-by-case basis—a power it exercised on numerous occasions.

As evidenced by this brief history, the House and Senate have had success using the veto as a constraint on presidential reorganization power. In a complementary fashion but on a smaller scale, congressional committees have also developed novel procedures to oversee and influence the execution of laws falling under their jurisdiction. The first law granting individual committees veto power passed in 1944.

The Advent of Committee Vetoes

The types of legislative vetoes enacted during the 1930s were exclusively single- or dual-House. Committee vetoes emerged in the 1940s as a way to empower committees with greater abilities to control spending for projects under their jurisdiction (H. Watson 1975). Presidents have expressed their opposition to the committee veto dating back to 1920, arguing that the procedure provides committees with an improper role in the execution of the law (Fisher 1993). Congress refrained from testing the president's resolve on the matter until advancing an authorization bill including a committee veto over naval land transactions at about the time President Roosevelt was running for a fourth consecutive term in the White House.

The 1944 Navy Public Works Construction Authorization bill included the first committee veto in U.S. history (58 Stat. 165, Public Law 78–289). This provision required the secretary of the navy to "come into agreement" with the House and Senate Naval Affairs Committees prior to the acquisition or relinquishment of land used for U.S. Navy purposes. This statute for the first time made individual land transactions subject to committee review. In contrast to all previous vetoes, this committee veto did not require an official vote from one or both congressional chambers. Instead, it gave the committees the authority to work directly with the Department of the Navy on these types of transactions. The novelty of this procedure was that rather than having to specifically authorize every land transaction by law, Congress could simply pass a general authorizing statute and allow the Naval Affairs Committees to approve or reject individual projects on a case-by-case basis. These types of vetoes tied to individual committees became increasingly common during the Truman administration and principally pertained to issues involving national security and defense.

Additional committee vetoes overseeing various military functions were enacted with the passage of the Naval Petroleum Reserve Amendment of 1944 (58 Stat. 262, Public Law 78–343), the Strategic Materials Stockpiling Act Amendments of 1946 (60 Stat. 590, Public Law 79–520), and the Long-Range Proving Ground for Guided Missiles Act of 1949 (63 Stat. 98, Public Law 81–60). Presidents Roosevelt and Truman signed these bills into law despite their stated concerns about empowering committees with greater authority to dictate defense policy. When Congress passed the Military and Naval Construction Authorization in 1951, which sought to impose additional committee vetoes, President Truman vetoed the bill, expressing objections about the "gradual trend on the part of the legislative branch to participate to an ever greater extent in the actual execution and administration of the laws. Under our system of government it is contemplated that the Congress will enact the laws and will leave their administration and execution to the executive branch" (1951, 282). President Eisenhower maintained this opposition to the committee veto during his administration.

After vetoing a bill with provisions empowering the Armed Services Committees with veto powers over the development of the surface-to-air Talos missile and the acquisition or construction of facilities for military use, President Eisenhower declared,

> While the Congress may enact legislation governing the making of Government contracts, it may not constitutionally delegate to its Members of Committees the power to make such contracts, either directly or by giving them the authority to approve or disapprove a contract which an executive officer proposes to make. . . . [S]uch provisions violate the fundamental constitutional principle of separation of powers prescribed in Articles I and II of the Constitution, which place the legislative power in the Congress and the executive power in the Executive Branch (1956, 597).

In this instance, Eisenhower took a principled stand by vetoing the military construction bill based on his opposition to the two committee veto provisions contained in the bill, stating, "While I recognize the manifest importance of this measure to national defense, I cannot approve it so long as it contains certain provisions found in sections 301 and 419" (1956, 597).

Later in his administration when presented with the 1956 Department of Defense appropriations bill, which also contained multiple legislative vetoes, Eisenhower signed the bill into law while reasserting his opposition to committee vetoes over executive functions. In a special message to Congress, the president declared:

> The Constitution of the United States divides the functions of the Government into three departments—the legislative, the executive, and the judicial—and establishes the principle that they be kept separate. Neither may exercise functions belonging to the others. Section 638 violates this constitutional principle. I believe it to be my duty to oppose such a violation. The Congress has the power and the right to grant or to deny an appropriation. But once an appropriation is made the appropriation must, under the Constitution, be administered by the executive branch of the Government alone, and the Congress has no right to confer upon its committees the power to veto Executive action or to prevent Executive action from becoming effective. (Eisenhower 1955, 688–89)

As Congress continued the practice of inserting legislative vetoes in legislation, presidential rhetoric grew increasingly combative. As seen by their public statements, presidents of both parties have argued that committee vetoes in particular represented an even further unconstitutional encroachment into the executive sphere. Every president following Roosevelt's death in 1945 has expressed his unequivocal opposition to this brand of legislative oversight (Fisher 1993; H. Watson 1975). From a congressional perspective, these provisions serve as an important means to oversee the execution of the law. Both of these perspectives were on display when Congress passed the Administrative Procedure Act (APA) in 1946.

Administrative Procedure Act

Following the exponential growth in federal agencies and programs created during the New Deal era, many lawmakers in Congress became concerned with the increasing number of rules and regulations issued by bureaucrats. The magnitude of these regulations was, and continues to be, vast. In an effort to impose a more uniform and institutionalized review process regarding increasing executive rulemaking powers, allow for public input, and facilitate greater transparency, Congress passed the Administrative Procedure Act (60 Stat. 237, Public Law 79–404). This landmark enactment is the most "comprehensive, authoritative, and enduring legislation governing administrative practice in the United States today" (Warren 2004, 143).

The APA codified a broad range of rulemaking procedures that also affected the issuance of regulations, licenses, sanctions, orders, and public records. Understanding that rules and regulations issued by executive agencies carried the same legal weight as statutes enacted by Congress, the APA required agencies to provide opportunities for interested parties to submit information and arguments to particular agencies prior to the issuance of regulations. Additionally, certain agencies were required to hold public hearings to consider testimony from experts and public groups interested in participating in the rulemaking process. The final component of the APA provided adversely affected individuals with a legal means to challenge agency actions. Statutes in this section stipulated which agency actions were subject to judicial review, the interim relief available to individuals filing suit, and the scope of agency decisions and actions that were reviewable by the courts.

The APA imposed numerous changes to the rulemaking system, but stopped short of subjecting rules to a formal congressional veto as part of the process. Subsequent efforts to institutionalize the veto, further reform the federal rulemaking process, and overhaul the national regulatory system began in earnest during the late 1970s. Before this renewed interest in rulemaking reform, Congress gradually increased the number of enacted veto statutes and began the practice of including multiple veto provisions in individual bills.

Escalation and Expansion

The first legislative veto delegated to the president the ability to restructure the executive branch without following the traditional process of having a lawmaker sponsor a bill by request and securing congressional passage. The practical consequence of this institutional compromise was that the president no longer needed majority support in both chambers to enact reorganization initiatives, but majorities in either chamber could obstruct them. Following this initial accommodation between the president and Congress, subsequent legislative veto statutes began to vary in terms of the structure of the veto procedures. Both before and after the Supreme Court's 1983 ruling in *INS v. Chadha* against the one-House negative veto,

Congress has utilized the legislative veto to suit an extraordinary variety of oversight purposes.

From figure 0.1, one can see the gradual increase in the number of enacted legislative veto statutes and the number of laws containing legislative vetoes from 1931 to 1983. During the first several decades of its existence, a small number of vetoes were implemented annually, and bills containing them tended to include a single veto provision. The nearly identical two trend lines up until about 1964 demonstrate this phenomenon. This trend changed in the late 1960s and 1970s as laws began to contain multiple sections with veto provisions rather than just one.

The 87th Congress, which served from 1961 to 1963, passed 14 laws with legislative vetoes. The 1963 independent agencies appropriations bill contained three legislative vetoes, making it the only one of these laws containing more than a single veto statute (76 Stat. 716, Public Law 87–741). Over the 10 years following its adjournment, more than 40 percent of all laws containing them included multiple legislative vetoes. The watershed enactment that altered the landscape of veto oversight was an energy conservation initiative passed in 1975.

The Energy Policy and Conservation Act (EPCA) of 1975 (89 Stat. 871, Public Law 94–163) imposed 17 separate veto statutes affecting energy policies made by the president or the administrator of the Federal Energy Administration (FEA).[8] Of these vetoes, 16 were one-House negative that allowed either chamber to block designated "energy actions" with a House or Senate resolution (89 Stat. 965, Public Law 94–163). The law provided Congress with a 15-day window to exercise its veto power. After this period ended, proposals would go into effect. The remaining veto was a dual-House affirmative that required both chambers to agree to a concurrent resolution to sanction any energy rationing contingency plan submitted by the president. These vetoes provided Congress with opportunities to affect an extensive variety of national energy policies including domestic oil production incentives, levels, and storage; oil pricing regulations; emergency oil rationing plans; regulations regarding the trans-Alaskan pipeline; crude oil and refined petroleum product imports; energy conservation plans; the Strategic Petroleum Reserve; and many other regulations promulgated by the FEA administrator. With just one exception, the greatest number of legislative vetoes Congress had included in a bill prior to this enactment was six.[9] In exceeding by far the number of veto provisions Congress had previously included in an individual bill, this law set the important precedent whereby legislators inserted over a dozen to oversee major energy reforms.

The FEA proposed 11 energy actions that were subject to congressional veto in the two years after the passage of the EPCA (Chubb 1983). Resolutions of disapproval for several of the actions were sponsored in the House and Senate. Committees from both chambers held hearings soliciting expert testimony regarding eight of the 11 proposals. Three of these FEA actions "provoked sufficient concern and opposition to prompt Congress to consider a veto seriously" (Chubb 1983, 154). These actions principally concerned the competitive benefits enjoyed by oil refiners and companies with access to lower priced crude oil, and the removal of price controls affecting home heating oil, diesel fuel, and other refined energy sources. With the exception of those that testified in committee hearings on behalf of large petroleum producers, a sizable majority of those that testified was opposed to the three most controversial actions (Chubb 1983). Ultimately, neither chamber elected to veto any of the FEA energy actions.

At least two studies examining these controversial FEA energy actions have argued that the brevity of the 15-day review period imposed by the EPCA and the complex nature of the energy proposals may have been more responsible for the lack of a congressional veto than the support each of the measures enjoyed (Bruff and Gellhorn 1977; Chubb 1983). The Senate Interior Committee favorably reported disapproval resolutions for two of the energy actions, while hearings concerning a third action were ongoing as the 15-day review deadline approached. The disapproval resolution for the third case was discharged out of committee and voted down on the final day of the review period (Bruff and Gellhorn 1977). On the same day, the two actions recommended for a veto in the Senate also failed to garner majority support in the chamber. The disapproval resolution counterparts in the House were similarly defeated by roll call vote.

Despite congressional requests for additional time and information to consider the proposals, opposition from expert and industry witnesses, as well as committee opposition, each of the energy actions went into effect upon the expiration of the review period. In sum, although the EPCA enacted statutes that reserved the possibility for a congressional veto over a broad range of energy policies, these FEA energy action cases "illustrate the difficulty of exercising the legislative veto power when the period for review is short" (Bruff and Gellhorn 1977, 1396). Partially due to this experience, more contemporary veto statutes often impose lengthier review periods.

In the end, despite the fact that Congress did not exercise its veto prerogative over any of the FEA's 11 energy action proposals, the EPCA did set an important precedent regarding veto oversight. The principal legacy of this energy reform is the imposition of multiple veto statutes rather than the actual exercise of these veto powers to affect energy policies. Without the EPCA as a precursor, it is unlikely we would witness the passage of legislation containing nearly 150 legislative vetoes as occurred in 2004 (118 Stat. 2809, Public Law 108–447).

While Congress can include scores of veto provisions into individual laws, a coalition in favor of a "generic" veto sought to institutionalize the ability for lawmakers to veto agency actions without having to predetermine which actions would be subject to potential override. This substantial reform movement gained supporters from both parties during the 1980s, but was ultimately unsuccessful in achieving its primary goal.

The "Generic" Veto Movement

In 1981, a series of hearings before the Subcommittee on Rules of the House examined in detail both the theoretical and procedural consequences of the legislative veto's increased use. One witness who appeared before the subcommittee was a University of Chicago Law School professor, consultant for the American Bar Association's Coordinating Group on Regulatory Reform, and future Supreme Court justice, Antonin Scalia. Scalia spoke before the committee as someone who had developed an opposition to the legislative veto while "laboring in the vineyard of regulatory reform."[10] Scalia conceded the "psychological appeal" of the legislative veto but argued that it provided an inefficient means of agency oversight. The primary basis for this inefficiency, Scalia argued, was the amount of legislative staff necessary to oversee the process of monitoring and ensuring compliance with veto requirements. In practice, this created a system to review and control a burgeoning bureaucracy with another layer of bureaucracy. In addition to the testimony from Scalia, the subcommittee also heard from eight members of Congress, including Representative Elliott Levitas, the leader of the movement seeking to permanently empower Congress with greater legislative veto authority over agency rules and regulations.

Residents of Georgia's 4th Congressional District elected Levitas to represent them in the midterm elections of 1974. He would serve five consecutive terms in office before unsuccessfully running for a sixth term a decade later. Prior to serving in Congress, Levitas was a Rhodes Scholar and had received law degrees from Emory Law School in Atlanta and Oxford University in Great Britain.[11] During his decade in Congress, Levitas is most known for his advocacy for the legislative veto as a check on an unelected bureaucracy. In an interview with the author, Levitas claimed that his administrative law background piqued his interest in the legislative veto. In discussing how he became the flag-bearer for this type of oversight, he stated, "I think that I had probably come to the conclusion even before [serving in Congress] that there needed to be some control over the rulemaking and regulatory process. I felt from experience in dealing with legal matters and from reading history that administrative rulemaking had such sweeping power and seemed so uncontrollable that there needed to be, in my opinion, some mechanism that would provide effective and efficient oversight of the process."[12]

In addition to providing expert testimony in favor of Congress's continued use of the legislative veto and lobbying fellow representatives to support this type of oversight, Levitas also sponsored legislation seeking to establish a far-reaching generic veto. Its proposed reform would allow Congress to exercise broad veto powers without having to include such provisions in individual bills. The movement to establish a generic congressional veto occurred as the number of veto statutes tailored to oversee specific grants of delegated power increased. Rather than continuing this piecemeal application of the legislative veto, Levitas dedicated considerable time and energy trying to institutionalize it as a resource Congress could use at any time.

The first attempt by Levitas to pass legislation providing Congress with a generic veto occurred in 1975 with the introduction of the Administrative Rulemaking Control Act (H.R. 3658, 94th Congress). The proposal stipulated that any agency rule would take effect only (1) if published in the *Federal Register*, (2) after the expiration of 30 days of continuous session of Congress after its publication date, and (3) if neither House of Congress agreed to a resolution disfavoring the rule. This bill was referred to the House Committee on the Judiciary, but was not reported out for consideration by the full chamber.

Despite being unsuccessful in this first attempt to empower Congress with a comprehensive veto over agency rulemaking, Levitas actively continued his efforts, believing that the legislative veto was "the single most effective method of providing this type of regulatory, rulemaking review." A subsequent initiative sponsored by Levitas generated considerably more support with more than half of representatives in the House signed on as cosponsors of the Administrative Rulemaking Reform Act (H.R. 1776, 97th Congress). The number of cosponsors on this legislation is particularly impressive when considering that his first bill did not have a single one.

As its title suggests, the Administrative Rulemaking Reform Act sought to significantly reform the existing federal rulemaking system in two distinct respects. First, it required all federal agencies to provide at least 45 days for public comment on any proposed rule. Public comments could be either written or oral, which, in the case of the latter, mandated opportunities for public comment at scheduled agency hearings. Second, the bill mandated that agencies submit copies of all proposed rules to both chambers of Congress. Upon receipt, lawmakers could veto rules, thereby preventing them from going into effect. Specifically, the legislation enabled Congress to veto any proposed rule with a concurrent resolution of disapproval within 90 days of continuous session. Alternatively, agreement to a resolution of disapproval by one chamber within 60 days that was not followed by any action from the other chamber would also prevent a rule's adoption. Levitas's bill also included a similar review and veto procedure for existing rules. In sum, while the initiative provided for greater public involvement in the bureaucratic rulemaking process, its centerpiece was the empowerment of Congress to veto proposed or existing rules.

At the time of its introduction, Levitas secured 251 cosponsors supporting this major rulemaking overhaul. The bill was referred to both the House Judiciary Committee and the House Committee on Rules, which held multiple hearings on the proposal. The Rules Committee also took the step of requesting comment from the attorney general and officials at the Office of Management and Budget. Despite these actions, once again the bill failed to make it beyond the committee stage. Seeking to force the bill out of committee for debate on the House floor, Levitas filed an unsuccessful discharge petition during the summer of 1982.[13] Levitas recalled that support for the proposal was "broadly bipartisan," but opposition from key committee chairs, House Speaker Tip O'Neill, and President Reagan proved too much to overcome. In an interview with the *Washington Post*, Speaker O'Neill stated that he felt Congress's reliance on the legislative veto had become excessive and plainly stated that he had "always been an anti-veto man" (Lardner 1983). Congressman Levitas reflected on the lack of success in these legislative initiatives:

> In looking back on it, I suppose that I was trying to do too much too soon. What the generic legislative veto approach entailed was such a major shift in direction from what had existed previously that perhaps if it had done incrementally it would not have confronted the type of resistance that it did. I think the concept was valid and from a purely objective point of view it made sense to have a com-

prehensive system embodied in a legislative veto mechanism, but as a practical matter what that meant is that you were stepping on more toes at one time that caused a broad group of people who opposed the idea to get involved. I think it made logical sense to have a comprehensive mechanism in place that would be applicable across the board.[14]

Though these attempts to establish a generic legislative veto spearheaded by Levitas were ultimately unsuccessful, the early 1980s witnessed a flurry of additional regulatory reform efforts seeking to legitimize and expand Congress's use of the legislative veto.

A more modest reform proposal introduced in 1981 by California representative George Danielson sought to establish a limited congressional veto over major rules, which were defined as those having more than a $100 million annual impact on the economy.[15] Following submission to the committees of jurisdiction, rules meeting this criterion were subject to a 30-day review period (England 1981). If a majority of lawmakers on the committee opposed the rule, the committee could report a resolution of disapproval. Such an action would delay the rule from going into effect for an additional 60 days. In order to permanently block the rule from going into effect, both chambers of Congress would have to agree to a joint resolution of disapproval. Unlike Levitas's measures, this scheme involved the president who would have to sign such a resolution in order to execute the veto. The Judiciary Committee reported this scaled-back version to the floor, but it failed to gain passage in the full House. Despite this setback, the coalition in favor of a bipartisan rulemaking reform initiative appeared to be growing. Similar proposals in the Senate enjoyed considerable support.

Sponsored by Nevada senator Paul Laxalt with four-fifths of all senators signed on as cosponsors, the Regulatory Reform Act (RRA) proposed to amend the APA by adding legislative veto capability as an additional layer to the rulemaking process (S. 1080, 97th Congress). With a handful of exemptions, the RRA required the submission of proposed rules to Congress along with a detailed analysis of the proposal including its costs, cost effectiveness, benefits, and alternatives. For major rules, as determined by the agency or the president, a 60-day review period must expire before the enactment of the rule. During the review period, the House and Senate committees with primary jurisdiction could report a resolution disapproving the rule for consideration by the full chamber. If such a resolution were agreed to, the other chamber would have a period of 30 additional days to do the same in order to execute the veto. In short, this reform would have institutionalized a dual-House negative veto over major agency rules.

The extraordinary number of cosponsors who signed onto the RRA demonstrated that the reform had broad bipartisan support in the Senate. The bill made it to the floor following a number of hearings by the Senate Judiciary Committee and the Committee on Governmental Affairs. After the passage of three amendments to the bill, the RRA passed by a unanimous vote of 94 to 0 (97th Congress, Senate Vote No. 62). Despite the fact that the House was considering many of its own regulatory reform proposals, Speaker O'Neill elected not to take action on the RRA, leaving the bill to die at the session's adjournment. This inaction preserved the status quo whereby Congress continued to pass bills including legislative veto provisions tied to specific grants of power.

With the failure of the generic veto movement, legislators pursued alternative avenues to extend their oversight reach by expanding the types of policies made susceptible to veto oversight in an ad hoc manner. The increasing number of enactments containing legislative veto provisions provided greater opportunities for judicial challenges. Courts began hearing cases concerning the veto in the late 1970s, several years before the Supreme Court would make its landmark ruling.

The Judicial Path to *Chadha*

The inception of the legislative veto created a novel procedure for executive reorganization that deviated from the traditional process of reorganizing by statute. Because congressional vetoes empower legislators with the authority to direct or constrain executive action without passing a law, they raise a multitude of constitutional questions. Given the dynamics of this oversight mechanism, which is not explicitly sanctioned by the Constitution, it is surprising that no federal court directly addressed the veto's legitimacy for over 40 years after its creation. The passage of nearly 300 legislative vetoes over this span was not sufficient to invite Supreme Court intervention. The nation's highest court remained silent on the matter until 1976.

Although many factors likely affected this stretch of judicial inaction, there are two main explanations for why the Court elected not to intercede until the latter half of the twentieth century. First, the legislative veto emerged as a product of interbranch bargaining that imposed a unique means of oversight in accordance with duly enacted law. This initial political accommodation between the branches precluded any immediate need for the federal courts to get involved since the two branches agreed on its use. A second set of factors concern the legal issues related to standing and the application of the political question doctrine.

The 1932 Legislative Appropriations Act imposed a congressional veto over executive reorganization. In order to challenge the constitutionality of this statute in federal court an individual must possess standing to file such a case. This normally requires a plaintiff to demonstrate that they have suffered an injury, attribute causation regarding how the injury occurred, and argue that the injury is somehow redressable by action of the court (see *Lujan v. Defenders of Wildlife*, 504 U.S. 555 (1992)). In the case of presidential reorganization initiatives, it would likely require a federal employee directly affected by a reorganization proposal vetoed by Congress to satisfy the standing requirement. Heffron (1994) argues that agencies subjected to some type of legislative veto would be the most likely candidates to have standing to file suit. However, because Congress "controls appropriations and authorizing statutes, most agencies will normally be hesitant to invoke a constitutional confrontation" (374).

Then there is the matter of the political question doctrine, which holds that certain political questions are nonjusticiable. This doctrine has a number of applications, including the 1979 case *Goldwater v. Carter*, 444 U.S. 996 (1979), which concerns the president's authority to abrogate or withdraw from treaties. Finding the case to pose a fundamentally political question, the Court's ruling declared, "The Judicial Branch should not decide issues affecting the allocation of power between the President and Congress until the political branches reach a constitutional impasse. Otherwise, we would encourage small groups or even individual Members of Congress to seek judicial resolution of issues before the normal political process has the opportunity to resolve the conflict" (444 U.S. 996 (1979)). With this in mind, one could argue that the legislative veto poses a similar political question that would preclude a judicial adjudication. The combined effects of legal standing and the political nature of the legislative veto as an interbranch compromise combined in such a fashion that the federal courts remained on the sidelines for decades. Once the courts became involved in the controversy, a litany of rulings sought to clarify the veto's constitutional status.

Judicial intervention in the macropolitical conflict over the legislative veto spanned approximately a decade from 1976 to 1986. Federal court rulings issued during this period generally ruled against the legislative veto, resulting in a number of victories for the executive branch. In turn, these precedents provided the president with a legal basis from which to continue to oppose these measures, which Congress continues to pass. After this decade-long flurry of judicial involvement, the courts have once again receded to the sidelines.

Long periods of judicial inaction spanning from 1932 to 1975 and 1987 to the present, combined with a lack of enforcement power, have rendered the judiciary the least influential of the three branches in the controversy surrounding the legislative veto. This should not be interpreted as evidence that the courts have failed to spur changes to this type of oversight. Among the most important consequences brought about by the courts is Congress's near complete abandonment of the one-House veto after the *Chadha* ruling. This reformation is discussed in detail in the next chapter.

At their core, cases pertaining to the legislative veto have required judges to consider the constitutionality of this oversight device in a system of shared powers. Constitutional law scholars addressing this question have concluded that there exists "no clear *a priori* answer to the question of the constitutionality of the veto or its consistency with the statutory scheme of administration" (Bruff and Gellhorn 1977, 1378). Before discussing key rulings that set the stage for Supreme Court intervention in 1983, the following section briefly outlines the primary arguments on each side of the debate surrounding the constitutionality of the veto.

The Legislative Veto's Constitutionality

Over the past 100 years, the legislative veto has elicited considerable controversy. Its constitutional status remains somewhat undetermined, despite the fact that when given an opportunity courts have most often ruled against it. Because the veto can be attached to virtually any grant of power, its constitutionality is truly a matter of degree and contextually dependent (Habig 1981). One type may appear to be more or less constitutional than another when considering the nature of the law that each is applied to and the veto procedures they impose. Considering the veto in more general terms, supporters often argue that this oversight mechanism allows a government designed by an eighteenth-century Constitution to adapt to the demands of twenty-first-century governance. Opponents, initially within the Justice Department, argue that regardless of any potential benefits, the legislative veto is an unconstitutional procedural shortcut that violates multiple constitutional principles. As the debate over the legislative veto has evolved, politicians, judges, and scholars have proffered a variety of constitutional and normative arguments for and against its use.

Arguments Supporting the Legislative Veto's Constitutionality

Supporters of the veto contend that it provides Congress with an invaluable means to oversee the bureaucracy, and that it is justifiable on both political and constitutional grounds.

> 1. *The necessary and proper clause empowers Congress to utilize the legislative veto as a means to influence policies made by executive officials.*

The necessary and proper clause contained in Article I, Section 8 gives Congress the authority to make all laws necessary and proper to carry into execution the legislative powers granted to Congress by the Constitution. Proponents of the legislative veto argue that the considerable expansion of policy-making powers delegated to executive officials has necessitated that Congress develop and utilize novel oversight methods in order to ensure that policies correspond with legislative intent. From this perspective, the legislative veto is conceptualized as a necessary oversight device that maintains Congress's rightful position as the primary federal policy-making body. This clause has been used as the basis for expanding congressional power throughout American history and can similarly be used to justify the legislative veto.

> 2. *The legislative veto satisfies bicameral passage and presidential presentment required by Article I, Section 7.*

While the execution of many types of legislative vetoes does not require bicameral action and presidential presentment, statutes containing legislative veto provisions are passed in accordance with this process. By virtue of this, supporters argue that it is inconsequential that the veto procedures themselves do not require bicameral action and presidential approval because the law containing the veto has satisfactorily followed this procedure.

> 3. *The legislative veto is a parliamentary procedure that can be classified as a rule governing congressional proceedings.*

Article I, Section 5 states that "Each House may determine the Rules of its Proceedings," which allows each congressional chamber to establish its own procedural rules. While this section is most appropriately interpreted as applying to each chamber's parliamentary procedures, it theoretically could also be extended to additional rules such as those governing appropriations. Committee legislative vetoes affecting bureaucratic spending, for example, often require advance approval from the Appropriations Committees. While not specifically rules governing parliamentary procedures, legislative vetoes such as these could be conceptualized as procedural rules developed by Congress consistent with its constitutional authority to do so.

4. *Because the Constitution did not intend to construct a strict separation of all government functions, the legislative veto is an acceptable means of congressional oversight.*

Although Articles I, II, and III of the Constitution establish three distinct branches of the federal government, proponents of the legislative veto argue that the Framers did not intend to construct a rigid separation of powers structure since the Constitution allows for considerable power sharing across branches. For example, the president as an executive actor has a prominent role in the legislative process by virtue of the presidential veto and the authority to recommend measures to Congress. Beyond these constitutional powers, this argument asserts that other executive officials act in a legislative capacity by adopting rules and regulations. In effect, this practice allows executive officials to dictate policy through the rulemaking process much in the way that Congress does through the legislative process. By considering the rulemaking process as one that allows executive officials to "legislate," supporters argue that lawmakers should likewise be permitted to act in an executive capacity or otherwise place restrictions on executive actions deemed legislative in nature. Expressed in a slightly different fashion, the veto can be properly categorized as one of many power-sharing mechanisms allowing for congressional oversight of executive administration.

Arguments Opposed to the Legislative Veto's Constitutionality

Opponents of the legislative veto typically approach the issue using a strict constructionist perspective that adheres to the legislative procedures sanctioned by the Constitution. Among the notable organizations that have taken a formal position against the legislative veto are the American Bar Association and the Administrative Conference of the United States. The failure of many types of legislative vetoes to satisfy the constitutional requirements of bicameral passage and presidential presentment are the most commonly cited arguments against the legitimacy of the legislative veto and provided the primary basis of the majority ruling in the *INS v. Chadha* case, 462 U.S. 919 (1983), which declared the one-House veto unconstitutional.

1. *The legislative veto violates the Constitution's separation of powers.*

Article II, Section 1 of the Constitution empowers the president as the nation's chief executive by stating, "The executive Power shall be vested in a President of the United States of America." Opponents of the legislative veto argue that the process of subjecting decisions and actions of executive officials to any type of subsequent veto from lawmakers in Congress violates the separation of powers structure created by the Constitution. This argument holds that the only way legislators are constitutionally able to directly affect executive action is by passing statutes in accordance with the procedures outlined in Article I.

2. *The legislative veto violates legislative bicameralism as required by Article I, Section 1.*

The first sentence of the Constitution following the Preamble states that "All legislative Powers herein granted shall be vested in a Congress of the United States, which shall consist of a Senate and House of Representatives." Some have interpreted this section as a constitutional mandate that all congressional activities be bicameral in function. The Supreme Court has stated that there are but "four provisions in the Constitution, explicit and unambiguous, by which one House may act alone with the unreviewable force of law, not subject to the President's veto" (*INS v. Chadha*, 462 U.S. 955 (1983)). These single-chamber actions are voting on articles of impeachment in the House and impeachment trials in the Senate, and the Senate's confirmation of presidential appointees and ratification of treaties. Beyond these four actions, one can argue that Congress must act in a bicameral fashion in order to exercise any legislative power. While dual-House vetoes requiring coordinated action from both the House and Senate satisfy this requirement, one-House vetoes are clearly not bicameral in function. Committee vetoes may also violate a strict adherence to bicameralism since individual committee decisions would not constitute a coordinated action from the full chambers.

3. *The legislative veto fails to satisfy presidential presentment required by Article I, Section 7.*

The legislative process outlined by the Constitution requires that "Every Order, Resolution, or Vote to which the Concurrence of the Senate and House of Representatives may be necessary (except on a question of Adjournment) shall be presented to the President of the United States; and before the Same shall take Effect, shall be approved by him, or being disapproved by him, shall be repassed by two thirds of the Senate and House of Representatives." With the sole exception of adjournment, these guidelines require legislation to be passed by each chamber and presented to the president for approval or veto. All legislative vetoes, exempting those using a joint resolution as the veto mechanism, are not presented to the president for consideration. Thus, opponents argue that they circumvent the president's constitutionally prescribed role in the legislative process.

Beginning Cautiously

The Supreme Court has dealt with complicated questions surrounding the nation's separation of powers system long before the creation of the legislative veto. In *Kilbourn v. Thompson*, 103 U.S. 168 (1880), it considered whether the House of Representatives could force an individual to provide testimony before its committees or order the imprisonment of those that failed to do so. The Court overturned the House's ordered imprisonment of Hallett Kilbourn on the basis that it had neither the expressed or implied constitutional power of this type. Arguing that this authority belonged to the judiciary alone, the ruling emphasized the Constitution's unambiguous separation of powers into three distinct branches. "It is essential to the successful working of the system that the lines which separate those departments shall be clearly defined and closely followed, and that neither of them shall be permitted to encroach upon the powers exclusively confided to the others" (*Kilbourn v. Thompson*, 103 U.S. 168 (1880)). Many of the legal challenges to the legislative veto claim that the oversight device constitutes an unconstitutional encroachment upon the power of the executive branch in the manner that the Court warned against in its *Kilbourn* ruling (also see *Springer v. Philippine Islands*, 277 U.S. 189 (1928)).

Litigation aimed at overturning statutes containing legislative vetoes coincided with the increased utilization of the veto during the 1970s. In particular, Congress confronted a series of legal challenges as a result of including congressional veto provisions in several campaign finance reform initiatives. For the most part, rulings from these early cases failed to take advantage of opportunities to make assertive rulings on the constitutionality of the legislative veto. In this sense, courts began considering legislative veto oversight cautiously, careful to only make game-changing pronouncements when compelled to do so.

Campaign Finance and Federal Employee Salary Litigation

In the longest majority opinion in the history of the Supreme Court, the *Buckley v. Valeo*, 424 U.S. 1 (1976) ruling addressed a series of issues associated with the campaign finance framework created by the Federal Election Campaign Act (FECA) of 1971 (86 Stat. 3, Public Law 92–225) and the FECA Amendments of 1974 (88 Stat. 1263, Public Law 93–443). In 1974, Congress created the Federal Election Commission (FEC) as a six-member commission charged with enforcing, overseeing, and regulating federal elections. In addition to addressing the constitutionality of placing financial limits on campaign contributions, the per curiam opinion issued by the court in the *Buckley* case also addressed the appointment process for FEC commissioners.

The FECA Amendments structured the FEC such that the president pro tempore of the Senate, the Speaker of the House, and the president each nominated two of its commissioners. Each of these nominations was then subject to a majority vote in both chambers of Congress (88 Stat. 1264, Public Law 93–443). Article II, Section 2 of the Constitution empowers the president alone with executive appointment powers and charges the Senate with all confirmation responsibilities. Citing these requirements the *Buckley* ruling declared that the FEC could only exercise its powers with commissioners appointed in this manner. In so doing, the Court struck down the innovative nomination and confirmation process for FEC commissioners in its entirety. Also addressed in the *Buckley* ruling was a provision empowering Congress with a veto over rules issued by the FEC.

The FECA Amendments of 1974 empowered the FEC to prescribe federal election rules and regulations. Before going into effect, the law required the submission of any proposed rules or regulations to Congress for a review period of 30 days where a majority vote in either chamber would prevent their adoption (88 Stat. 1287, Public Law 93-443). This provided either chamber of Congress with the ability to veto any policy change promulgated by the FEC.[16] Although President Gerald Ford was opposed to this provision, he signed the bill arguing that in its totality the legislation provided needed reforms to federal campaign finance law.

In a signing statement issued when signing the legislation into law, President Ford emphasized his opposition to the congressional veto by declaring, "A more fundamental concern is that these amendments jeopardize the independence of the Federal Election Commission by permitting either House of Congress to veto regulations which the Commission, as an executive agency, issues. This provision not only circumvents the original intent of campaign reform but, in my opinion, violates the Constitution. I have therefore directed the Attorney General to challenge the constitutionality of this provision at the earliest possible opportunity" (1976, 1530). Through litigation challenging different aspects of campaign finance law, the Court had the opportunity to address the constitutionality of this legislative veto as requested by President Ford. However, it elected not to take this step because of the holding regarding the impermissible appointment procedures for FEC commissioners. Since the appointment procedures were struck down, the FEC did not retain the power to issue rules, which, consequently, Congress could not veto.

In a separate opinion written by Justice Byron White, he speculated about the future viability of the veto, stating that "nothing in the Constitution would prohibit Congress from empowering the Commission to issue rules and regulations without later participation by, or consent of, the President or Congress with respect to any particular rule or regulation or initially to adjudicate questions of fact in accordance with a proper interpretation of the statute" (424 U.S. 284 (1976)), White concurring in part and dissenting in part). From this perspective, because the president signed the bill providing Congress with veto power over designated FEC functions, the review process was legitimate. In sum, although the Court did not directly address the constitutionality of the legislative veto in this instance, at least one justice indicated that the Court night find oversight statutes of this type permissible.

On two occasions during the following year, judges also neglected to take a position on the constitutionality of the veto (*Clark v. Valeo*, 182 U.S. App. D.C. 21 (1977); *McCorkle v. United States*, 559 F.2d 1258 (1977)). The primary issue in *McCorkle v. United States* concerned the constitutionality of the legislative veto contained in the Federal Salary Act (81 Stat. 644, Public Law 90-206) that allowed either chamber of Congress to veto presidential recommendations to alter federal salary schedules. In the lawsuit, federal employee William C. McCorkle Jr. challenged the Senate's veto of salary increases proposed by President Richard Nixon in 1974. Following the Supreme Court's lead, Fourth Circuit judge John D. Butzner Jr. also refused to explicitly adjudicate the legislative veto's constitutionality.

The *McCorkle* opinion, which affirmed the district court decision, stated that the Federal Salary Act would not have delegated to the president the considerable power of determining federal pay schedules absent a congressional veto to prevent salary changes disapproved by Congress. Accordingly, the one-House veto provision contained in the legislation was ruled "inseparable from those parts of the statute that empower the President to make potentially binding recommendations" (559 F.2d 1262, 4th Cir. (1978)). This holding meant that if the court ruled the legislative veto unconstitutional, the entire law would be struck down. Under this scenario, McCorkle would not be entitled to the salary increase proposed by the president and vetoed by the Senate since the entire law would be inoperable and the president would forfeit the authority to propose salary increases. Declaring that an "important question of public law should not be resolved by a declaratory judgment if that judgment would be futile" (559 F.2d 1262, 4th Cir. (1978)), this ruling paralleled those in both *Buckley* and *Clark*. Although the legislative veto was a prominent feature in both the FECA Amendments as well as the Federal Salary Act, judges refrained from making definitive judgments on the veto. This pattern changed with the ruling in *Atkins v. United States*, 556 F.2d 1028, Ct.Cl. (1977), which took an expansive view of the necessary and proper clause to justify affording Congress independent veto powers.

Rulings with Teeth

Similar to the *McCorkle* case, appellants in *Atkins v. United States* presented a legal challenge to the one-House veto contained in the Salary Act of 1967 (81 Stat. 644, Public Law 90-206). In this instance, 140 federal judges sought to recover lost income following the Senate's veto of a salary increase by asking the court to declare the Salary Act's legislative veto unconstitutional. In addressing this key question, the per curiam opinion issued by the U.S. Court of Claims emphasized that it would not consider the validity of the one-House veto as an "abstract proposition, in all instances," rather it would narrowly address the singular one-House veto contained in the Salary Act (556 F.2d 1058, Ct.Cl. (1977)). In so doing, the 4–3 decision upheld this particular legislative veto as constitutional.

The *Atkins* ruling addressed two fundamental arguments against the legislative veto. The first was whether the one-House veto violated the Constitution's bicameralism, and second, whether it exceedingly encroached on the executive powers vested in the president. Before making these determinations, the court held that establishing pay scales for both judges was an exclusive prerogative of the legislature. Following this declaration, the ruling took an expansive view of the necessary and proper clause as argued in *McCulloch v. Maryland*, 17 U.S. (4 Wheat.) 316 (1819) as the basis for providing Congress with the authority to "delegate the initial power to make proposals to the President, and, then, to select for itself the appropriate method for checking and monitoring the President's action" (556 F.2d 1061, Ct.Cl. (1977)). Citing other congressional functions that do not require bicameral action, the court considered the veto, allowing a single chamber to prevent federal salary modifications constitutionally permissible.

The ruling continued to argue that Congress was not making new law by executing a veto in this instance, but preserving the legal status quo. Justifying their decision to uphold the one-House veto on this basis the court claimed that "at the most, the Act accords the President's recommendations only the potentiality of becoming law—if neither House objects within 30 days of their announcement—and does not give them the force and effect of law *ab initio*" (556 F.2d 1063, Ct.Cl. (1977)). In sum, Congress had the authority to delegate federal salary schedule modification power to the president and the necessary and proper clause allows it to determine the appropriate procedures used to oversee the exercise of this power.

The three dissenting judges in the *Atkins* ruling took a decidedly different position. Judge Byron G. Skelton wrote a scathing dissenting opinion, arguing that the legislative veto violated Article I, Section 1, which vests the legislative power of the federal government in a bicameral Congress; Article I, Section 7, which empowers the president with veto power over congressional proceedings passed by both chambers; and Article II, Section 1, which vests the executive power of the federal government with the president as chief executive. In noting the wealth of constitutional law expertise held by the appellants Skelton found it *"very significant and most persuasive"* that this substantial assembly of federal judges including former Supreme Court justice Arthur Goldberg considered the one-House veto unconstitutional (556 F.2d 1028, Ct.Cl. (1977), 174; emphasis in original).

From a theoretical perspective, Judge Skelton discussed the implications of alternative conceptualizations of the character of the one-House veto. He argued that it was clearly not judicial in character, meaning that it would necessarily be a legislative- or executive-type function. If the one-House veto were legislative in character, Skelton argued that it would violate the bicameralism requirement in Article I. Conversely, if the one-House veto were executive in character, it would violate Article II by allowing legislative officials to exercise executive powers. Given this logic, regardless of whether one considers the one-House veto as legislative or executive in character, it would not pass constitutional muster. Despite these dissenting arguments, the court collectively upheld the statute. To date, the *Atkins* ruling remains the most permissive stance taken by a federal court regarding legislative veto oversight. Following this victory for Congress, the judicial winds quickly shifted during the early 1980s.

Beginning the Judicial Assault on the Veto

A federal district court in Montana made the first notable ruling against the legislative veto by striking down a provision in the Federal Land Policy Act (90 Stat. 2753, Public Law 94-579) that empowered congressional committees to compel the secretary of the interior to revoke public land leases (*Pacific Legal Foundation v. Watt*, 539 F. Supp. 1194 (1982)). In this instance, the court upheld the statute allowing the secretary to abrogate leases, but struck down the statute allowing committees to compel the secretary to do the same. The ruling reached this conclusion by determining that direct committee mandates over the actions of an executive official violated the Constitution's separation of powers.

In another case decided in 1982, a legislative veto over natural gas pricing reached the same fate. In *Consumer Energy Council of America v. Federal Energy Regulatory Commission*, 673 F.2d 425 (D.C. Cir. 1982), a three-judge panel of the federal Court of Appeals for the District of Columbia Circuit unanimously struck down a legislative veto over natural gas pricing included in the Natural Gas Policy Act (92 Stat. 3370, Public Law 95–621). The challenged statute stipulated that natural gas pricing rules proposed by the Federal Energy Regulatory Commission (FERC) would go into effect unless either chamber of Congress agreed to a resolution of disapproval within 30 days. The basis for the suit occurred when the House vetoed a FERC pricing rule affecting both residential and industrial users. Amici briefs submitted by lawmakers in Congress contended that courts should not make a ruling on the legislative veto because the issue was an inherently political one—properly resolved by the legislative and executive branches without judicial intervention. Refusing to heed this advice, the court cited precedent from *Baker v. Carr*, 369 U.S. 186 (1962), which addressed the conditions under which courts should appropriately adjudicate cases presenting questions of a political nature, and noted that more than 50 years of contentious disputes between the elected branches had failed to resolve the status of the veto.

The opinion written by Judge Malcolm Wilkey rebuked the alternative holding in the *Atkins* case by bluntly stating, "The Necessary and Proper Clause does not override other provisions of the Constitution" (673 F.2d 455 (D.C. Cir. 1982)). The ruling further contended that vetoes of FERC pricing rules were legislative in function and therefore concluded that "the Framers were determined that the legislative power should be difficult to employ. The requirements of presentation to the President and bicameral concurrence ultimately serve the same fundamental purpose: to restrict the operation of legislative power to those policies which meet the approval of three constituencies, or a supermajority of two. If the legislative veto represents an exercise of the legislative power, then, it must be exercised only in compliance with these constitutional requirements" (673 F.2d 464 (D.C. Cir. 1982)). Thus, in order for Congress to directly affect FERC gas pricing, it must follow the legislative procedure mandated by the Constitution. Once Congress delegates rulemaking authority to an agency, the process of determining rules fell under the agency's responsibility to faithfully execute the law.

In the last significant ruling before Supreme Court intervention, the federal Court of Appeals for the District of Columbia Circuit similarly struck down on constitutional grounds a legislative veto provision included in the Federal Trade Commission Improvement Act of 1980 (94 Stat. 393, Public Law 96-252). In *Consumers Union of the United States v. Federal Trade Commission*, 691 F.2d 575 (1982), two consumer-oriented nonprofit organizations challenged a Federal Trade Commission Improvement Act provision providing for rules promulgated by the FTC to go into effect following the expiration of a review period of 90 days unless majorities from either chamber voted to prevent their adoption. This occurred in 1981 when the Senate vetoed a rule pertaining to the disclosure of warranty information associated with used car sales. The per curiam opinion from this case cited the recent precedent established by *Consumer Energy Council of America v. FERC* and ruled that the veto statute violated the separation of powers established by the Constitution as well as the legislative procedures set forth in Article I. The next major court case addressing the constitutionality of the legislative veto would be decided by the Supreme Court the following year.

Summary

This chapter provided a survey of the creation and evolution of the legislative veto and introduced a typology to categorize them according to two distinguishing characteristics. The dramatic expansion of the federal bureaucracy, coupled with the devastating effects of the Depression, created the conditions that produced an interbranch compromise resulting in the first legislative veto. The novel expedited reorganization process was intended to benefit both branches, but the legislative veto quickly became a source of intense conflict following the House's rejection of all of President Hoover's proposals. Presidents and attorneys general maintained a consistent opposition to the congressional veto despite its relatively infrequent use during the 1940s and 1950s. During this formative period there were times when members of Congress debated the constitutionality of various legislative veto proposals, but, more often, legislators simply assumed that the device was constitutional.

The primary points of contention regarding the constitutionality of legislative veto oversight concern whether it must abide by the Constitution's bicameral passage and presidential presentment requirements. Supporters argue that since legislative veto provisions must receive bicameral approval and the president's signature to become law, the veto process itself need not also follow this path. Opponents contend, depending on one's perspective, that the device circumvents the president's role in the legislative process or permits legislators to act in an executive capacity by directing the implementation of the law. In either case, it represents a breach of the Constitution.

From its inception through the 1940s, legislative vetoes were almost exclusively of the single- or dual-House variety. Committee vetoes, which do not require action from one or both full chambers, became increasingly common during the 1950s as laws began mandating committee consultation or approval for designated actions. By this time, the legislative veto progressed beyond its original purpose regarding presidential reorganization initiatives. Unfettered by judges, members of Congress ramped up their production of legislative veto statutes and broadened the scope of their application to a variety of domestic and foreign policies. The proliferation of legislative veto enactments during the 1960s and 1970s, as exemplified by the record-breaking 17 vetoes included in the EPCA, provided increased occasions for interbranch conflict and spurred the entrance of federal courts into the controversy.

Concerted efforts to reform the administrative rulemaking system coincided with early judicial rulings on the veto. Championed by Congressman Levitas, many lawmakers worked to secure a more assertive role for Congress in this area. The most notable postwar reform, which predated Levitas's House career, was the APA passed in 1946. Although considerable support existed in Congress in favor of establishing a generic veto that could be exercised universally, proponents were unable to successfully pass any of the major reforms proposed during the 1970s or early 1980s. Largely as a result of the failure of Congress and the president to reach an agreeable settlement on the matter, the Supreme Court finally intervened in 1983.

TWO

Reassessments and Reformations
The Modern Era

In the decades after its creation the legislative veto expanded from its original purpose concerning executive reorganization to scores of additional policy areas. Interbranch conflict surrounding its legitimacy escalated during the 1970s and 1980s as Democratic majorities in Congress, led by Representative Levitas, steadily increased its use. The upsurge in veto statutes over this period represented a concerted effort on behalf of Congress to find ways to check greater executive power (Craig 1983). By 1980, Congresses were passing more than 100 per term. This trend was met with fierce resistance by presidents of both parties.

Presidential opposition to the legislative veto intensified during the Carter and Reagan administrations. The emboldened position of President Carter was to treat any legislative veto provision as having no legal justification.[1] The president claimed that his administration would give such statutes "serious consideration, but we will not, under our reading of the Constitution, consider it legally binding" (1978, 1149). Both he and President Reagan made numerous statements akin to this opposing the veto and seeking to protect executive prerogatives. The proliferation of legislative veto statutes during this period fanned the flames of the macropolitical conflict over its use. The stage was set for Supreme Court intervention.

Chadha, Congress, and the INS

The Supreme Court addressed the impasse between the branches in 1983 after the Ninth Circuit Court struck down a legislative veto in the Immigration and Nationality Act (66 Stat. 163, Public Law 82–414). This provision allowed either chamber of Congress to overrule deportation suspensions authorized by the attorney general.

Members of Congress have used the legislative veto to affect the enforcement of U.S. immigration law dating back to 1940. Among the first legislative vetoes ever enacted was a dual-House negative veto included in the Alien Registration Act of 1940 (54 Stat. 670, Public Law 76–670). In response to increasing numbers of low-skilled immigrants entering the domestic labor force, anti-immigrant nativist groups pressured Congress to overhaul the nation's immigration laws (McClure 1979). The Alien Registration Act passed as a result. Among other reforms, the act delegated to the attorney general the authority to review all deportation orders. Under some circumstances, the attorney general could rescind a deportation order and permit an individual to stay in the country. Congress reserved for itself the last word on these matters by subjecting deportation suspensions to potential veto. A majority vote in both chambers could reinitiate deportation proceedings.

Amendments made by two 1948 laws modified the review procedure by requiring congressional approval of all deportation suspensions (62 Stat. 647, Public Law 80–774; 62 Stat. 1206, Public Law 80–863). The switch from a dual-House negative to a dual-House affirmative veto occurred as a result of congressional dissatisfaction of the effectiveness of the preexisting veto process. A Senate Judiciary Committee report indicated that Congress did not exercise a single veto over any of the 23,604 immigration case rulings submitted by the INS for review over a span of nearly a decade (McClure 1979). Less than a decade later, the review procedure was changed again.

The Immigration and Nationality Act Amendments (71 Stat. 642, Public Law 85–316), which passed in 1957, replaced the dual-House affirmative veto with a one-House negative one. In addition to altering the eligibility requirements for individuals to formally petition their residency status, the law reserved the right of either chamber of Congress to overrule deportation suspensions issued by INS judges. The statute containing the legislative veto mechanism remained in effect until declared unconstitutional by the Supreme Court in 1983.

The litigant in this monumental case was Jagdish Rai Chadha, an East Indian born and raised in Kenya. Both national and international events during the 1960s set the conditions in place for the controversy surrounding Chadha's immigration status. Though he surely didn't know it at the time, his decision to study business and political science in the United States would ultimately threaten to destabilize the federal government's balance of power. Underscoring this, an article in *Time* magazine dubbed Chadha a "foreigner who upset U.S. history" (1983).

From 1960 to 1965, 27 African countries obtained their independence to become sovereign nations. In the midst of this movement Kenya declared its official independence from Britain on December 12, 1963. The Kenyan government declared that all persons born in Kenya prior to independence would automatically receive citizenship status with the exception of those whose parents had not been born in Kenya. Residents with nonnative parents were permitted to apply for citizenship within two years. Chadha's parents had both immigrated to Kenya, his mother from India and his father from South Africa. This required Chadha and his four siblings to apply for citizenship in the country of their birth.[2] Given the uncertainty regarding how Kenyan independence would alter the established class system, many individuals with Asian ancestry declined to apply for citizenship. Of the approximately 140,000 Kenyan Asians who did not have at least one parent born in Kenya, only 14 percent applied for citizenship and less than 10 percent of those had their applications approved (Craig 1988). Individuals who elected not to apply for Kenyan citizenship were presented with extremely difficult circumstances.

Following independence, many Kenyan Asians decided to emigrate elsewhere. As Kenya had previously been a British colony, inhabitants of Kenya were eligible to hold British passports. This resulted in an influx of thousands of immigrants seeking legal residence in Great Britain. Attempting to limit this massive flow of immigrants, the British government announced new immigration quotas, which would restrict the ability of families like Chadha's to start a new life in Europe. Also facing a sudden influx of African immigrants of Asian descent, India and Pakistan took similar measures to prohibit entry into their respective countries. The combined effects of these policies produced a nearly impossible situation for non-African Kenyans. Noncitizens were required to obtain one of a limited number of work permits to work legally in Kenya. Those who stayed in Kenya and risked working without a government-sanctioned license faced imprisonment or deportation. Given the uniqueness of the situation, it is unclear where the government would deport such apprehended lawbreakers.

Chadha found a temporary solution by successfully applying for a student visa to enroll at Bowling Green State University in Ohio. He arrived in the United States in the fall of 1966 and graduated four years later with a degree in business administration. Chadha continued his studies by earning a master's degree in political science and economics in 1971. As a graduate student, Chadha became engaged to his girlfriend who was a U.S. citizen. With his student visa set to expire on June 30, 1972, he wrote to the British consulate regarding the possibility of finding interim employment in Great Britain. The response was far from helpful.

British officials responded to Chadha's inquiry regarding the probability of obtaining a quota voucher for employment in May 1972 by explaining that the chances of receiving a work permit were extremely low. In the unlikely event that Chadha received one of the coveted work permits, it would take more than a year to process. With less than a month left on his student visa, Chadha faced the dilemma of not having a country where he could legally reside. Before his visa expired, Chadha traveled to California, where his fiancée had moved, hoping to find work. Disappointingly, he was unable to secure a job, being ineligible to legally work in the United States. As a last resort, Chadha sought counsel from U.S. immigration officials in a Los Angeles office.

When INS officials became aware that Chadha was in the country illegally, they immediately photographed, fingerprinted, and briefly detained him. Charged with overstaying his student visa, Chadha was subject to immediate deportation. A hearing before INS immigration judge Chester Sipkin was set for November 1, 1973, with a second hearing scheduled for February 7, 1974.

Chadha and his lawyer, Steve Mittleman, requested a deportation suspension based on the "extreme hardship" that Chadha would endure by being deported. In his defense, Chadha described his abnormal immigration situation and lack of a permanent country of residence. Mittleman cited the two degrees he had received from an American university, his pending marriage to an American citizen, and his assimilation into American society after having lived in the United States for more than seven years. Judge Sipkin initially declined the request for a deportation suspension, claiming an inability to find "on the basis of the evidence submitted that Mr. Chadha would suffer the extreme hardship required by the statute" (Deportation hearings 1974, 38). Following this denial, Mittleman proceeded to enter an alternative request for asylum on Chadha's behalf. The request to apply for asylum was granted by Sipkin and the hearing was adjourned. Strangely, Sipkin proceeded to resume the hearing and declared "on further thought I think I might be inclined to grant this application for suspension of deportation" (Deportation hearings 1974, 39). With no explanation for this reversal contained anywhere in the written record, Sipkin granted Chadha the deportation suspension provided he satisfactorily passed a character investigation. This successful appeal no doubt overjoyed Chadha. He surely did not realize at the time that the U.S. Congress lay in wait.

As dictated by existing immigration law, either chamber of Congress held the authority to overrule individual INS case rulings. The relevant section of the Immigration and Nationality Act stated:

> If the deportation of any alien is suspended under the provisions of this subsection, a complete and detailed statement of the facts and pertinent provisions of the law in the case shall be reported to the Congress with the reasons for such suspension. . . . If during the sessions of the Congress at which a case is reported, or prior to the close of the session of the Congress next following the session at which a case is reported, either the Senate or the House of Representatives passes a resolution stating in substance that it does not favor the suspension of such deportation, the Attorney General shall there upon deport such alien. (66 Stat. 163, Public Law 82–414)

This arrangement allowed the INS and the attorney general to review and control the vast majority of deportation cases, while allowing for a direct congressional influence on such rulings through a legislative veto.

The provisions of the Immigration and Nationality Act required two sessions of Congress to elapse before deportation suspensions became official. The first Congress eligible to affect Chadha's immigration status took office in 1973. The INS submitted a total of 208 immigration cases for congressional review during this term. Congress vetoed just six of these cases, none of which belonged to Chadha (McClure 1979). Because neither chamber took action affecting his legal status during either session of the 93rd Congress, Chadha only had to wait an additional two years before securing legal residency. In the interim, he remained in the United States, but did not have a visa or any other official documents with which he could obtain employment.

Chadha's case took an unfortunate turn during the lame-duck session of the 94th Congress when Representative Joshua Eilberg (D-PA) introduced House Resolution 926 to overturn the deportation suspensions for Chadha and five others. At this point, Eilberg served as the chairperson of the Judiciary Subcommittee on Immigration, Citizenship, and International Law, which served as the primary review body in the chamber for these immigration cases.³ The House committee took action on only a fraction of the hundreds of deportation suspensions it received. Following committee review, Eilberg sponsored three separate resolutions opposing permanent residency grants afforded to 10 individuals including Chadha. Successful votes on each resolution meant that deportation orders would soon follow.

The *Chadha* ruling contains the following justification on behalf of the House Judiciary committee for vetoing these cases: "It was the feeling of the committee, after reviewing 340 cases, that the aliens contained in the resolution [Chadha and five others] did not meet these statutory requirements, particularly as it relates to hardship; and it is the opinion of the committee that their deportation should not be suspended" (*INS v. Chadha*, 462 U.S. 926 (1983)). Chadha took his immigration battle to court, claiming that the legislative veto procedure used to overrule his deportation suspension was unconstitutional. On June 23, 1983, the Supreme Court ruled in his favor.

The *Chadha* Majority Opinion

The Court heard oral arguments on February 22, 1982, and again on Pearl Harbor Day of the same year (for an excellent treatment of the case, see Craig 1988). The landmark separation of powers precedent that the *Chadha* ruling would establish was emphasized by Eugene Gressman, who argued before the court on behalf the House of Representatives. Describing the case as a "historic occasion," Gressman stated, "Never before have the two Houses of Congress been forced to intervene as litigating parties before this Court. They have been forced to intervene to protest another episode in the—what this Court once described as the tug of war between the executive and the legislative branches of government" (462 U.S. 919 (1983)). In his opening remarks on behalf of the INS, Rex E. Lee contended that the defenders of the veto faced an "insoluble dilemma" since the oversight device faced two major constitutional hurdles—adhering to Article I's legislative procedures and complying with the Constitution's separation of powers. In a 7–2 majority opinion, the Court broadly declared the legislative veto unconstitutional.⁴

The *INS v. Chadha* decision arguably invalidated nearly 300 legislative vetoes enacted by Congress over a span of 50 years. The actual breadth of the ruling depends on whether its precedent would apply to one-House vetoes only or other types as well, but one could argue that this single

Supreme Court decision overturned more congressional enactments than had previously been ruled unconstitutional in the history of the United States (Craig 1988). Analysis on the front page of the *New York Times* boldly declared that the decision would result in a "grand realignment" of power among the federal branches of government (Hebers 1983). David Broder of the *Washington Post* wrote that a key component of congressional power had been effectively "wiped out" (Broder and Peterson 1983). Due to the enormity and far-reaching effects of this decision, it was difficult at the time to overemphasize its profound significance on U.S. policy making. Chief Justice Warren Burger, who wrote the majority opinion, later ranked the case as "certainly among one of the fifty most important cases in our history" (quoted in Craig 1988, 232).

The majority opinion in *Chadha* advanced two main arguments against the one-House negative veto. First, the Court held that the oversight mechanism violated the Constitution's core separation of powers structure. This argument considered the distinct powers held by the legislative and executive branches as "integral parts of the constitutional design for the separation of powers" (*INS v. Chadha*, 462 U.S. 946 (1983)). In addition to framing the veto as an ill-begotten encroachment into the functions of the executive, the Court also argued that the veto failed to comply with the legislative procedure required by the Constitution. Writing for the majority, Justice Burger outlined its rationale:

> Clearly, when the Draftsmen sought to confer special powers on one House, independent of the other House, or of the President, they did so in explicit, unambiguous terms. These carefully defined exceptions from presentments and bicameralism underscore the differences between the legislative functions of Congress and other unilateral but important and binding one-house acts provided for in the Constitution. These exceptions are narrow, explicit, and separately justified; none of them authorize the action challenged here. On the contrary, they provide further support for the conclusion that congressional authority is not to be implied and for the conclusion that the veto provided for in 244(c)(2) is not authorized by constitutional design of the powers of the Legislative Branch. (*INS v. Chadha*, 462 U.S. 955 (1983))

Noting that the Constitution clearly did not provide Congress with extralegislative veto powers over executive actions of any type, Justice Burger's opinion ruled the veto statute unconstitutional.

To make these arguments the ruling specifically highlighted Sections 1 and 7 of Article I. Article I, Section 1 vests federal legislative power in a bicameral Congress. Because the one-House veto did not require bicameral action by construction, it was summarily struck down. Additionally, Section 7, which outlines the procedure for passing legislation, requires every bill, order, and resolution passed by Congress to be presented to the president for approval or veto. Because the Court conceived the one-House veto challenged by Chadha as "essentially legislative in purpose and effect," failing to provide the president with an opportunity to approve or reject the veto represented an additional breach of the Constitution. Though it understood the pragmatic justification for the legislative veto as a congressional check on powers delegated to executive officials, the Court failed to reconcile the oversight device with the Constitution. The ruling concluded:

> The veto authorized by § 244(c)(2) doubtless has been in many respects a convenient shortcut; the "sharing" with the Executive by Congress of its authority over aliens in this manner is, on its face, an appealing compromise. In purely practical terms, it is obviously easier for action to be taken by one House without submission to the President; but it is crystal clear from the records of the Convention, contemporaneous writings, and debates that the Framers ranked other values higher than efficiency. The records of the Convention and debates in the states preceding ratification underscore the common desire to define and limit the exercise of the newly created federal powers affecting the states and the people. There is unmistakable expression of a determination that legislation by the national Congress be a step-by-step, deliberate and deliberative process.
>
> The choices we discern as having been made in the Constitutional Convention impose burdens on governmental processes that often seem clumsy, inefficient, even unworkable, but those hard choices were consciously made by men who had lived under a form of government that permitted arbitrary governmental acts to go unchecked. There is no support in the Constitution or decisions of this Court for the proposition that the cumbersomeness and delays often encountered in complying with explicit constitutional standards may be avoided, either by the Congress or by the President. With all the obvious flaws of delay, untidiness, and potential for abuse, we have not yet found a better way to preserve freedom than

by making the exercise of power subject to the carefully crafted restraints spelled out in the Constitution. (462 U.S. 956 (1983))

A primary consequence of this ruling was the effective invalidation more than 80 existing one-House negative veto statutes and possibly hundreds more veto statutes of other varieties. Accordingly, many anticipated the *Chadha* ruling to have profound consequences regarding executive independence and the ability of the legislative branch to engage in meaningful oversight. Among the veto's most ardent supporters, Congressman Levitas chastised the ruling by predicting that it would result in a "train wreck government" (129 Congressional Record. H4796, June 29, 1983). Concerned about the extent of the reverberations the ruling would likely create, Justice Lewis Powell's concurring opinion began by stating that the "breadth of this holding gives one pause" and continued to argue that the Court should have decided the case on much narrower grounds.

The *Chadha* Concurring Opinion

Justice Powell wrote the single concurring opinion in the *Chadha* case that agreed with the Court's judgment in favor of Chadha, but disputed the declaration that legislative vetoes violated the Constitution's presentment clause. Justice Powell argued that the House's veto of deportation suspensions exceeded its constitutional authority by exercising a judicial power. Because the legal rights of Chadha and others were directly affected by the House's veto, the concurring opinion argued that the action was "clearly adjudicatory" (*INS v. Chadha*, 462 U.S. 964 (1983), Powell concurrence). Accordingly, Powell favored the determination of the Court as it pertained to Chadha's legal status, but disagreed with its more general holding that one-House legislative vetoes were by construction unconstitutional. Despite disagreement with this aspect of the ruling, Justice Powell elected to vote with the other six justices in the majority.

Opposition to the majority's position was sufficient enough for two of the Court's nine justices to author dissenting opinions. Each dissent provides alternative arguments to those presented in the majority and concurring opinions. On almost every account, dissenting Justice William Rehnquist agreed with the majority, but chose to issue a dissenting opinion, arguing that the Court should have taken a more dramatic action by striking down the entire immigration law instead of only invalidating the section of the law containing the veto. Because this single point is the basis for the dissent by the future chief justice, Justice Byron White's dissent provided the most vociferous defense of the legislative veto.

The *Chadha* Dissenting Opinions

The brief dissenting opinion written by Justice Rehnquist strictly concerned the severability of the legislative veto included in the Immigration and Nationality Act. The majority opinion found the one-House veto severable from the remainder of the law by virtue of the severability clause contained in the act. This text of this brief clause stated, "If any particular provision of this Act, or the application thereof to any person or circumstance, is held invalid, the remainder of the Act and the application of such provision to other persons or circumstances shall not be affected thereby" (71 Stat. 642, Public Law 85–316). Despite the existence of this severability clause, Rehnquist countered by claiming that "the history elucidated by the Court shows that Congress was unwilling to give the Executive Branch permission to suspend deportation on its own." He continued by arguing that

> Congress consistently rejected requests from the Executive for complete discretion in this area. Congress always insisted on retaining ultimate control, whether by concurrent resolution, as in the 1948 Act, or by one-House veto, as in the present Act. Congress has never indicated that it would be willing to permit suspensions of deportation unless it could retain some sort of veto. . . . Congress' continued insistence on retaining control of the suspension process indicates that it has never been disposed to give the Executive Branch a free hand. (*INS v. Chadha*, 462 U.S. 1015 (1983), Rehnquist dissent).

Based on this line of argument, he concluded that the Court should have disregarded the law's severability clause and struck down the Immigration and Nationality Act in its entirety.

The lengthier dissenting opinion written by Justice White provides a meticulous argument in favor of the legislative veto's constitutionality, cognizant of the demands of modern-day governance. While the majority opinion in *Chadha* was firmly positioned in a strict constructionist interpretation of the Constitution, Justice White's dissent took a less constructionist approach regarding the congressional veto's permissibility. The main premise of Justice White's dissent centered on the vast range of policies and programs administered by the federal government that present unique problems for legislators. Chief among these problems was the question of how Congress could continue to delegate on such a large scale while ensuring that policy outcomes conformed to legislative intent. Eloquently presenting the complexity associated with delegated powers and the legislative veto, Justice White wrote:

> The prominence of the legislative veto mechanism in our contemporary political system and its importance to Congress can hardly be overstated. It has become a central means by which Congress secures the accountability of executive and independent agencies. Without the legislative veto, Congress is faced with a Hobson's choice: either to refrain from delegating the necessary authority, leaving itself with a hopeless task of writing laws with the requisite specificity to cover endless special circumstances across the entire policy landscape, or, in the alternative, to abdicate its lawmaking function to the Executive Branch and independent agencies. To choose the former leaves major national problems unresolved; to opt for the latter risks unaccountable policymaking by those not elected to fill that role. (*INS v. Chadha*, 462 U.S. 919 (1983), White dissent)

The dissent continued by noting that Congress had a long history of delegating what were essentially lawmaking functions to executive agencies and departments. Since executive rules and regulations have the force of law, Justice White questioned why these actions need not satisfy bicameral passage and presidential presentment as well:

> If Congress may delegate lawmaking power to independent and Executive agencies, it is most difficult to understand Art. I as prohibiting Congress from also reserving a check on legislative power for itself. Absent the veto, the agencies receiving delegations of legislative or quasi-legislative power may issue regulations having the force of law without bicameral approval and without the President's signature. It is thus not apparent why the reservation of a veto over the exercise of that legislative power must be subject to a more exacting test. In both cases, it is enough that the initial statutory authorizations comply with the Art. I requirements. Nor are

there strict limits on the agents that may receive such delegations of legislative authority so that it might be said that the Legislature can delegate authority to others, but not to itself. . . .

Under the Court's analysis, the Executive Branch and the independent agencies may make rules with the effect of law while Congress, in whom the Framers confided the legislative power, Art. I, § 1, may not exercise a veto which precludes such rules from having operative force. If the effective functioning of a complex modern government requires the delegation of vast authority which, by virtue of its breadth, is legislative or "quasi-legislative" in character, I cannot accept that Art. I—which is, after all, the source of the nondelegation doctrine—should forbid Congress to qualify that grant with a legislative veto. (*INS v. Chadha*, 462 U.S. 986, 989 (1983), White dissent)

This rationale demonstrates a double standard whereby executive agents are left largely unfettered when acting in a legislative capacity while lawmakers are unable to reserve for themselves a postpassage influence on the execution of the law. The increasing quasi-legislative authorities delegated to bureaucrats made the legislative veto all the more necessary to ensure that the elected representatives maintain an influential voice in crafting policy. Indeed, Justice White argued that the history of the veto demonstrates that Congress has not used the oversight device to "aggrandize itself at the expense of the other branches—the concerns of Madison and Hamilton. Rather, the veto has been a means of defense, a reservation of ultimate authority necessary if Congress is to fulfill its designated role under Art. I as the Nation's lawmaker." In essence, legislative veto oversight represents a necessary political indulgence designed to counterbalance increasing executive power.

Justice White's dissent also emphasized the role that the legislative veto served in resolving significant conflicts between Congress and the president. Congressional vetoes helped to "balance broad delegations" of presidential power in the realm of national security and foreign affairs as well as energy, public land management, and trade and tariff agreements, among many others. Emphasizing the importance of Congress maintaining control over the bureaucracy, Justice White stated that the congressional veto "is an important, if not indispensable, political invention that allows the President and Congress to resolve major constitutional and policy differences, assures the accountability of independent regulatory agencies, and preserves Congress' control over lawmaking" (*INS v. Chadha*, 462 U.S. 972 (1983), White dissent). Though he conceded that the veto does raise serious separation of powers concerns, he found it "incomprehensible that Congress, whose Members are bound by oath to uphold the Constitution, would have placed these mechanisms in nearly 200 separate laws over a period of 50 years" if the veto were as blatantly unconstitutional as the majority ruling suggests (*INS v. Chadha*, 462 U.S. 977 (1983), White dissent).

On numerous occasions, Justice White questioned the certainty of the veto's unconstitutionality advanced by the Court's majority. In so doing, he countered the majority's determination that legislative functions must satisfy bicameral approval and presidential presentment by claiming that the "power to exercise a legislative veto is not the power to write new law without bicameral approval or Presidential consideration. The veto must be authorized by statute, and may only negative what an Executive department or independent agency has proposed. On its face, the legislative veto no more allows one House of Congress to make law than does the Presidential veto confer such power upon the President" (*INS v. Chadha*, 462 U.S. 980 (1983), White dissent). Thus, because bills containing legislative veto provisions are necessarily enacted through the legislative process, it should not be a serious concern that the review process does not follow this same path. Justice White further claimed that there was no evidence that delegates to the Constitutional Convention intended the legislative requirements in Article I to apply to congressional actions pursuant to individual laws.

The dissent concluded by characterizing the majority opinion as "regrettable" based primarily on the contention that the veto served as a "necessary check on the unavoidably expanding power of the agencies, both Executive and independent, as they engage in exercising authority delegated by Congress" (*INS v. Chadha*, 462 U.S. 1002 (1983), White dissent). Justice White's arguments on the policy-making benefits and strategic importance of the legislative veto were not lost on the Court's majority, but a strict interpretation of the Constitution did not allow it to sanction the veto, however convenient it may be.

One additional aspect of Justice White's dissent is the allegation of unnecessary judicial activism lodged against the majority. In approaching their job as Supreme Court justices, White argued that "Courts should always be wary of striking statutes as unconstitutional; to strike an entire class of statutes based on consideration of a somewhat atypical and more readily indictable exemplar of the class is irresponsible" (*INS v. Chadha*, 462 U.S. 1002 (1983), White dissent). The majority could have struck down the statute on a more narrow ground in *Chadha*, perhaps ruling that the legislative veto over individual immigration cases represented an impermissible exercise of judicial power by the legislature. The majority ruling took a decidedly more assertive approach.

With a 7–2 ruling in its favor, the executive branch clearly appeared the victor in this landmark conflict. Contrary to what one might expect given the scope and magnitude of the *Chadha* majority opinion, Congress has actually enacted more legislative vetoes since the ruling than it had in all the years prior to it. Several congressional vetoes implemented after 1983 have provided the basis for further litigation; however, none of the subsequent cases have significantly altered the precedent set by *Chadha*. Less than a month after handing down the ruling, the Supreme Court applied the precedent without comment to eight cases (Tribe 1985). Two of these were D.C. circuit court rulings—*Consumer Energy Council of America v. FERC*, 673 F. 2d 425 (1982) and *Consumers Union v. FTC*, 691 F. 2d 575 (1982)—that struck down statutes containing one-House and dual-House vetoes, respectively. Three years later, the Court heard arguments in a case that also concerned broad questions about the balance of power between the legislative and executive branches.

Chadha Redux

In *Bowsher v. Synar*, 478 U.S. 714 (1986), the Supreme Court addressed a series of separation of powers questions related to the Balanced Budget and Emergency Deficit Control Act of 1985 (also known as the Gramm-Rudman-Hollings Act) (99 Stat. 1038, Public Law 99–177). This law aimed to curb federal spending with the intent to reduce budget deficits. To this end, mandatory across-the-board budgetary cuts were scheduled in the event that the federal deficit exceeded designated thresholds. The comptroller general, following recommendations from the Office of Management and Budget (OMB) and the CBO, made decisions regarding the specific programs subjected to budget reductions. The president would then review the report and issue an order imposing the spending cuts. One of the key elements challenged following the passage of the Gramm-Rudman-Hollings Act was the role of the comptroller general acting as the director of the General Accounting Office (GAO), which is an independent, investigatory appendage of Congress.[5] Because the office is housed in the legislative branch, the individual holding the office of comptroller general was removable by congressional fiat.

The ruling in this case mirrored the one handed down in *Chadha*. This should not be surprising since Justice Burger authored the majority opinion in both instances. Burger's opinion in *Bowsher* struck down the statutes empowering the comptroller general to make determinations on spending cuts. Such budgetary decisions were deemed to be executive in function, which led the Court to the conclusion that the authority constituted an unconstitutional separation of powers violation. Specifically, the opinion argued, "To permit an officer controlled by Congress to execute the laws would be, in essence, to permit a congressional veto. Congress could simply remove, or threaten to remove, an office for executing the laws in any fashion found to be unsatisfactory to Congress. This kind of congressional control over the execution of the laws, *Chadha* makes clear, is constitutionally impermissible" (*Bowsher v. Synar*, 478 U.S. 726 (1986)).

Once again, the Supreme Court made an unequivocal separation of powers ruling that left little room for involvement by the legislature in dictating the terms of a law's execution post passage. The Court reaffirmed its declaration that the policy-making spheres of each branch were to remain distinct, and cautioned against the "dangers of congressional usurpation of Executive Branch functions" (*Bowsher v. Synar*, 478 U.S. 727 (1986)). In clear language, the Court again declared that congressional participation in the execution of the law ends with the passage of legislation authorizing executive action. In order to directly affect the implementation of a law after its passage, enacting further legislation increasingly appeared to be Congress's only refuge.

As he had in the *Chadha* case decided three years prior, Justice White wrote a scathing dissent challenging "the wisdom of the Court's willingness to interpose its distressingly formalistic view of separation of powers as a bar to the attainment of governmental objectives through the means chosen by the Congress and the President in the legislative process established by the Constitution" (*Bowsher v. Synar*, 478 U.S. 759 (1986), White dissent). Though the case facts here differed in several respects to those in *Chadha*, Justice White admonished his colleagues for their ill-begotten rigid adherence to keeping governmental powers separate and distinct. Once again, he strongly objected to the idea that the Constitution's separation of powers structure left no room for innovation and power sharing when engaging in art of governing.

The Severability of Legislative Veto Statutes

While the *Bowsher* ruling had a comparatively narrow focus on the newly crafted budget reform law, the enormous volume of federal law affected by

Chadha is truly remarkable. Never before in the nation's history had a single Supreme Court ruling reverberated across hundreds of statutes. When considering all types of legislative vetoes, Congresses from 1931 to 1982 enacted 600 veto statutes in 340 different laws. Fifty-five of these laws contained a combined total of 82 one-House negative vetoes. Typically, when the Supreme Court declares a legislative act or component thereof unconstitutional, it is incumbent on Congress to revise the struck-down law. When judicial rulings are relatively narrow in their focus, as tends to be the norm, they typically place a manageable burden on Congress to revisit a particular law.[6] In the instance of *Chadha*, the constitutional objections against the legislative veto might have compelled Congress to revise an enormous volume of laws containing legislative veto provisions. While Congress did revise some existing legislative veto statutes to conform to the Court's ruling, the vast majority of the veto statutes enacted before 1983 remain unaltered (Fisher 2005a).[7]

Given the failure of Congress to revise an abundance of statutes in the aftermath of the *Chadha* ruling, one might have expected a flurry of subsequent legal challenges to laws containing these unaltered veto statutes. Somewhat surprisingly, only a few cases have challenged legislative vetoes over the subsequent two decades. The issue of standing once again provides a partial explanation for this inactivity. For lawsuits that were filed, a key factor in determining the application of the *Chadha* precedent concerned the question of severability.

As discussed in Justice Rehnquist's dissenting opinion, the issue of severability concerns whether a court may invalidate a section of a legislative act without significantly disturbing the remaining statutes. During oral arguments in *Chadha*, Michael Davidson, counsel for the Senate, declared that the "Court must ask two questions. One is, what is left? Is that fully operative as law?" (462 U.S. 919 (1983)). The traditional approach to determining the severability of challenged provisions centers around "two issues: (1) the functional independence of valid and invalid statutory provisions, and (2) the intent of the enacting legislature" ("Severability of Legislative Veto Provisions" 1984). Following the Supreme Court ruling in *Champlin Refining Co. v. Corporation Commission*, 286 U.S. 210 (1932), its general approach was to consider individual statutes severable from legislative enactments unless it was clear that Congress would not have passed the legislation without including the provision in question.

Above the protests of Justice Rehnquist, the Supreme Court's majority elected not to address the severability issue in the *Chadha* case on account of the severability clause included in the Immigration and Nationality Act. Applying this precedent to laws with veto provisions lacking such a severability clause, judges would first need to determine whether the removal of the veto statute rendered the remainder of the law operable. Because such determinations must be made on a case-by-case basis, courts have considered subsequent challenges to existing legislative veto statutes in an ad hoc manner rather than applying a singular guiding precedent. In making these determinations, courts have tended to find veto statutes severable from the remainder of the law.[8]

The second severability issue regarding the intent of the enacting legislature is considerably more complex. A fundamental question concerns whether the enacting Congress would have delegated certain powers to the executive without a legislative veto safeguard. If a litany of rulings held legislative vetoes inseverable from their enacting legislation, a tidal wave of voided laws would have the effect of hollowing the nation's existing regulatory structure, resulting in an "unparalleled disaster" ("Severability of Legislative Veto Provisions" 1984, 1193).

In discussing the severability issue, constitutional law scholar Lawrence Tribe points out the irony associated with courts adjudicating the question of severability, noting that by severing legislative veto statutes from their enacting legislation, courts are in effect creating new laws in a manner that does not conform to Article I procedures that are the centerpiece of the *Chadha* ruling. Tribe considers it "especially odd for these concerns to be overlooked in *Chadha*—the very decision that held the legislative veto device void precisely because of its failure to meet the bicamerality and presentment requirements" (1985, 80). Of course, the exercise of judicial review is quite distinct from the legislative process, but some have found it disconcerting that, in making determinations regarding severability, courts engage in the practice of amending law much in the way that a member of Congress or individual committees would. Following *Chadha*, several federal courts including the Supreme Court have addressed the severability of legislative veto provisions in several important cases. Many of these initial challenges concerned powers of the Equal Employment Opportunity Commission (EEOC) with an additional case involved the General Services Administration (GSA) and public access to presidential documents and other materials.

Applying the *Chadha* Precedent—the EEOC

With few exceptions, lower court judges have decided most of the post-*Chadha* rulings on legislative veto severability. A collection of cases pertaining to the enforcement powers of the EEOC demonstrated the complexities associated with the application of the *Chadha* precedent.

About one year prior to the *Chadha* ruling, the EEOC filed suit against All State Insurance pursuant to the Equal Pay Act of 1963 (77 Stat. 56, Public Law 88–38), claiming that the company was paying female supervisors a lower wage than their male counterparts. The law originally empowered the secretary of labor with enforcement authority. A 1978 reorganization initiative issued by President Carter transferred this enforcement power to the EEOC. The basis for the president's authority to take such an action came from the Reorganization Act of 1977 (91 Stat. 29, Public Law 95–17), which conditionally delegated executive reorganization power to the president provided that neither chamber exercised a veto. The House voted on a disapproval resolution for this particular reorganization plan, but it did not receive majority support, while the Senate took no action. Absent agreement to a veto resolution in either chamber, the president's reorganization went into effect.

All State's legal counsel argued that despite the fact that Congress did not execute a veto of this reorganization plan, the one-House negative veto contained in the Reorganization Act was unconstitutional and also inseverable from the remaining enactment. If the court ruled the entire act unconstitutional, the EEOC would lack the authority to file suit under the Equal Pay Act. A federal district court found this argument convincing and therefore issued a summary judgment to this effect on September 9, 1983 (*EEOC v. Allstate Insurance Company*, 570 F. Supp. 1236 (1983)). Issued just months after *Chadha*, this ruling established the first precedent regarding the severability of legislative vetoes embedded in enacted law.

In June 1984, the Supreme Court refused to hear an appeal of this lower court holding.[9] Chief Justice Warren Burger and Justice Sandra Day O'Connor each dissented to this decision. The chief justice declared that he found the dismissal "disturbing particularly in light of the importance of the underlying substantive issues," which he deemed "appropriate for resolution by this Court" (*EEOC v. Allstate Insurance Company*, 467 US 1236 (1984), Burger dissent). He continued by highlighting the "substantial questions whether *Chadha* should be applied retroactively, given that the Reorganization Plan was not vetoed by either House and were implemented before *Chadha* was decided, and whether Congress has in any event ratified the transfer of enforcement authority to the EEOC through appropriations and other statutes validly passed" (*EEOC v. Allstate Insurance Company*, 467 US 1232 (1984), Burger dissent). By refusing to hear the appeal, the Supreme Court failed to provide direction on the proper application of the *Chadha* precedent.

Paradoxically, against the backdrop of the Court's refusal to hear an appeal, an appellate court ruling in a similar case also involving the EEOC reached the opposite conclusion. In February 1984, the Fifth Circuit Court of Appeals overturned a lower court ruling by holding the one-House negative veto severable from the Reorganization Act of 1977 (724 F.2d 1188). This case also concerned the authority of the EEOC to enforce gender discrimination prohibitions under the Equal Pay Act. The suit alleged gender wage discrimination among cashiers employed by Hernando Bank. Despite the fact that the law contained no severability clause, the court cited the act's legislative history and ruled the one-House veto severable from the Reorganization Act. This determination affirmed the EEOC's authority to enforce the Equal Pay Act, overturned the summary judgment made by the district court, and remanded the suit for further proceedings.

During the same year, the Second Circuit Court of Appeals further muddied the waters on the severability issue by also addressing the EEOC's power to enforce the Equal Pay Act. In this instance, the court ruled the veto statute inseverable from the Reorganization Act, therefore striking down the entire law and vacating the EEOC's enforcement authority over wage discrimination. Arguing that the veto provision was an "integral and necessary" part of the reorganization act, this stood in stark contrast to the ruling made by the Fifth Circuit on the same issue (*EEOC v. CBS, Inc.*, 743 F.2d 969, 2d Cir. (1984)).

The cumulative result of these cases rendered the EEOC's wage discrimination enforcement powers perhaps less clear than they had been previously. Often when circuit court rulings differ in such a magnitude, the Supreme Court will grant certiorari to an appeal in order to resolve emerging discrepancies. For these cases, however, the Supreme Court's only action came in its refusal to hear the EEOC's appeal in the All State Insurance case. Absent further clarification from the nation's highest court, the EEOC was most likely free to continue its enforcement of the Equal Pay Act in all areas outside of the jurisdiction of the Second Circuit, which includes Connecticut, New York, and Vermont, where the court ruled against the Reorganization Act. Moving forward, federal courts in a number of subsequent cases continued to make severability determinations for a variety of existing legislative veto statutes, but none would experience the oddities of the EEOC cases where multiple suits challenging the same law reached contradictory resolutions.

Applying the *Chadha* Precedent— the GSA, Energy, and Presidential Records

In December of 1983, the United States District Court for the District of Columbia considered the severability of the one-House negative veto included in the Presidential Recordings and Materials Preservation Act (88 Stat. 1697, Public Law 93–526). Passed in 1974, the act delegated to the GSA administrator the authority to establish regulations allowing for public access to presidential recordings and other materials unless vetoed by the House or Senate. In 1975, Congress began exercising its veto power over promulgated regulations. Legislators vetoed the first three sets of regulations submitted to Congress by GSA administrator Jack Eckerd, because of controversies surrounding the ability of the GSA to restrict public access to certain types of presidential materials. It was not until June 1977 that Congress finally allowed GSA regulations to go into effect.

Richard V. Allen, who served on President Nixon's National Security Council, along with 28 other plaintiffs who held public office in the Nixon administration, filed suit against the GSA administrator, Gerald P. Carmen, and Robert M. Warner, the archivist of the United States, seeking to prevent the public release of the "White House Special Files." Since the Presidential Recordings and Materials Preservation Act contained a one-House negative veto akin to the one struck down by the Supreme Court in *Chadha*, the plaintiffs asked the district court to strike down the GSA regulations established pursuant to the act, thereby preventing the release of the files. The verdict reached by the court declared the legislative veto severable from the preservation act, thereby leaving the remainder of the law in effect (*Allen v. Carmen*, 578 F. Supp. 951 (1983)).

While the ruling validated the act's remaining statutes, because Congress exercised its veto on multiple occasions before assenting to the GSA regulations enacted in 1977, the court also struck down the existing regulations, thereby temporarily preventing the release of the nearly 1.5 million pages of material contained in the White House Special Files. By ruling the veto severable from the act, the authority delegated to the GSA administrator to establish regulations regarding the release of presidential materials remained in effect. The court's invalidation of the existing rules meant that the GSA needed to propose a new set of regulations governing the release procedures of presidential documents before making public any further presidential documents. As the law allowed for a legislative veto within 90 days of the administrator's submission of the regulations to Congress, the new regulations could go into effect after the expiration of this waiting period "absent intervening corrective legislation." The main legacy of this ruling is its early precedent supporting the severability of legislative veto provisions from their enabling statutes that began to fill the void on the severability question left by the *Chadha* ruling. A 1984 case regarding petroleum price controls imposed by the Emergency Petroleum Allocation Act (EPAA) (87 Stat. 627, Public Law 93–159) likewise determined legislative vetoes severable.

In *Gulf Oil Corp. v. Dyke*, 734 F.2d 797 (1984) a group of oil companies filed suit against Gulf Oil alleging that they had been overcharged for gasoline over a period of three years. The EPAA contained a one-House negative veto allowing either chamber to overrule petroleum price controls established by the president within five days of their submission to Congress. Although the law did not contain a severability clause, the temporary emergency court of appeals held the veto statute severable from the remaining law. Considering the EPAA's text, legislative history, and other factors, the court determined that the expulsion of the veto left the remainder of the act "fully operative" and maintained the advance notification requirement, therefore providing an opportunity for congressional review. The Supreme Court refused to hear an appeal of this ruling as other courts continued to grapple with the fallout from *Chadha*. An additional case considered the status of the legislative veto contained in the National Emergencies Act (NEA) (90 Stat. 1255, Public Law 94-412), which passed in 1976.

Seeking to clarify presidential powers in times of emergency, the NEA allowed the president to curtail foreign trade following the declaration of the existence of a state of emergency, which could subsequently be terminated by joint action of both houses of Congress. Pursuant to the authority granted under the NEA, President Reagan ordered an emergency embargo against the government of Nicaragua on May 1, 1985. Although the *Chadha* ruling did not directly address dual-House vetoes, a Massachusetts company filed suit against the government claiming that the Court's ruling voided the NEA in its entirety. The appellate court ruling in *Beacon Products v. Reagan*, 633 F. Supp. 1191 (1986 U.S. Dist.), sided with the president and ruled the legislative veto severable from the NEA. Thus, the court upheld the delegation of emergency powers from Congress to the president, while overruling the congressional constraint tied to the delegated authority. This result added to the number of rulings where legislative veto statutes were surgically removed from their enacting legislation, leaving the remaining statutes undisturbed. While lower courts predominantly addressed these severability cases, the Supreme Court finally weighed in on the issue four years after the *Chadha* ruling.

Applying the *Chadha* Precedent—
the Supreme Court and the Airline Industry

Since *Chadha*, the Supreme Court has considered two cases involving different aspects of legislative veto oversight concerning the U.S. airline industry. The first of these cases came in 1987 when 14 commercial airlines challenged a legislative veto included in the Airline Deregulation Act of 1978 (92 Stat. 1705, Public Law 95–504). The act authorized the secretary of labor to issue regulations concerning an employment protection plan that would go into effect unless either chamber of Congress agreed to a resolution of disapproval within 60 days of its receipt. The petitioners in *Alaska Airlines, Inc. v. Brock*, 480 U.S. 678 (1987), argued that by virtue of the *Chadha* ruling against the one-House negative veto, the Court should strike down the employment protection plan on the grounds that it was not severable from the overturned veto provision. In this case, the key question before the Court was simply, would Congress have passed the employment protection plan without including the provision with a legislative veto?

In approaching this question, the unanimous opinion written by Justice Harry Blackmun cited past rulings dealing with the issue of severability, stating that courts should refrain from invalidating more of a statute than is necessary in order to preserve as much of the law passed by elected officials as possible.[10] Applying this principle to the airline case, Blackmun stated that the legislative veto "necessarily alters the balance of powers between the Legislative and Executive Branches of the Federal Government" (480 U.S. 684 (1987)). However, in considering the guidelines and procedural protocol associated with the employment protection plan, the Court ultimately determined that Congress would have most likely passed the program without the veto oversight option.

To support this conclusion, the Court cited the legislative history of the bill that outlined congressional intent on the matter, congressional debate that occurred prior to final passage, and other proposed legislation regarding airline carriers and their employees that did not include veto provisions. With this evidence, the Court found the veto severable from the Airline Deregulation Act, citing an "almost total absence of any contrary refrain" (*Alaska Airlines, Inc. v. Brock*, 480 U.S. 697 (1987)). This ruling contributed to the growing number of cases providing precedent for the severability of veto statutes.

A similar case came before the Supreme Court four years later in *Metropolitan Washington Airports Authority v. Citizens for the Abatement of Aircraft Noise*, 501 U.S. 252 (1991). This case concerned a 1986 law that transferred the operation of two Washington DC airports to the Metropolitan Washington Airports Authority (MWAA) (100 Stat. 3341, Public Law 99–591). The law authorized the creation of a congressional review board that was composed of nine members of Congress who held the power to veto decisions made by the MWAA board of directors. As it had in *Chadha*, the Court struck down this congressional veto power despite the fact that the

MWAA board was not an executive institution and that legislators serving on the review board were charged with doing so in their "individual capacities" as users of the airports. Almost like clockwork, Justice White authored a dissenting opinion, joined by Justice Thurgood Marshall and Chief Justice Rehnquist, admonishing the Court's majority for striking down "yet another innovative and otherwise lawful governmental experiment in the name of separation of powers" (*Metropolitan Washington Airports Authority v. Citizens for the Abatement of Aircraft Noise*, 501 U.S. 277 (1991)). As courts continued to consider how to best apply the *Chadha* precedent, officials in the legislative and executive branches began addressing the political consequences of the ruling.

Post-*Chadha* Reformations

The majority opinion in the *Chadha* case detailed the Supreme Court's perspective regarding the constitutionality of the legislative veto. Despite what some had predicted, the ruling did not constitute the legislative veto's obituary. Lawmakers serving in the congressional term before the ruling enacted 102 veto statutes. The following Congress passed 120. After *Chadha*, the number of enacted veto statutes continued to increase each term to totals of 143, 152, and 172. As a result, each Congress holding office in the 1980s increased the number of enacted vetoes from the prior term by an average of 15 percent. Several government reports provide additional insight into the continued use of the veto in the ruling's short-term aftermath.

A 1985 GAO report provided a survey of DOD appropriations reprogramming proposals requiring congressional approval both before and after *Chadha*. This report identified more than 300 DOD reprogramming requests made to the congressional spending and defense committees involving more than $7 billion from the six fiscal years spanning 1980 to 1985 (U.S. GAO 1985). In the three fiscal years prior to *Chadha*, the DOD submitted an average of 40 such requests per year to Congress. Over the three years that followed, the average number of reprogrammings subject to congressional veto increased to nearly 70 (U.S. GAO 1985). Thus, despite the Court's imposition, Congress continued to enact and exert veto control over a broad range of DOD functions.

The GAO similarly identified more than seven hundred Congressional Presentation Documents submitted to Congress in the 1987 fiscal year alone by the United States Agency for International Development that provided advance notification or requested committee approval. Forty-seven of these requests were denied (U.S. GAO 1989). From these two reports alone, it is clear that legislative veto oversight continued to exist as the post-*Chadha* era began. On first glance, these occurrences may suggest that legislators have largely ignored the Court's admonishment. However, since the ruling Congress has, with few exceptions, completely abandoned its use of legislative vetoes authorizing just one chamber to block executive actions. The vast majority of vetoes enacted in recent decades empower individual committees in both chambers with a broad range of veto authorities.

A Legislative Veto Constitutional Amendment

Seeking to fully legitimize the continued use of the veto in the post-*Chadha* period, Arizona senator Dennis DeConcini put forth a proposal to amend the Constitution to provide Congress with legislative veto power in all instances. Several lawmakers in Congress responded to the momentous ruling by calling for a legislative veto constitutional amendment. Senator DeConcini implored his fellow senators to action by declaring, "We, the Members of Congress, must act to retain our power to make the laws in this Nation" (1983, 296). To this end, DeConcini introduced a resolution proposing a legislative veto amendment to the Constitution:

> Resolved by the Senate and the House of Representatives of the United States of America in Congress assembled, (two-thirds of each House concurring therein), That the following article is proposed as an amendment to the Constitution of the United States, which shall be valid to all intents and purposes as a part of the Constitution when ratified by the legislatures of three-fourths of the several States within seven years after the date of its submission by the Congress:
> "ARTICLE—
> Section 1. Executive action under legislative delegated authority may be subject to the approval of one or both Houses of Congress, without presentment to the President, if the legislation that authorizes the executive action so provides."[11]

Asking "Who shall be responsible for the laws of the land?," DeConcini argued that amendment's ratification would "restore congressional power over the lawmaking functions of Government by enabling Congress to oversee the manner in which the executive branch uses any legislative power which Congress had delegated to it" (1983, 296). The Senate Judiciary Committee's Subcommittee on the Constitution held a hearing on the proposed amendment in March 1984, but it never reached the Senate floor.[12] Thus, this movement to incorporate a legislative veto amendment into the Constitution was short lived and unsuccessful.[13]

Given the varied types of vetoes included in laws passed by Congress, and the *Chadha* ruling's sole focus on the one-House negative veto, the necessity of a constitutional amendment to legitimize different varieties of legislative veto oversight is questionable. As a means to provide some clarity for Congress moving forward, Congressman Levitas wrote to President Reagan to propose a "conference on power-sharing" that would serve to clearly delineate the administrative powers available to each branch of the federal government. This proposal elicited a tepid response from the administration. An internal memo from the White House counsel's office written by future Supreme Court Chief Justice John Roberts mocked Levitas's request by commenting, "There already has, of course, been a 'Conference on Power Sharing.' It took place in Philadelphia's Constitution Hall in 1787, and someone should tell Levitas about it and the 'report' it issued" (quoted in Toobin 2007, 280). Reactions such as these from lawmakers in Congress and officials in the executive branch are hardly surprising given the stark battle lines drawn over the course of several decades.

Post-*Chadha* Bargaining

Among the most important post-*Chadha* test cases regarding continued viability of veto oversight involved a confrontation between the White House and Congress concerning foreign appropriations. The *Chadha* ruling threatened to destabilize the proliferation of legislative vetoes that had occurred in the years leading up to the landmark case. The congressional veto had served for decades as an oversight mechanism that allowed Congress to delegate on any scale while maintaining the power to influence the execution of the law. Given the majority opinion in *Chadha*, Congress might have completely abandoned its use. However, as a *New York Times* analysis put it, "Old habits die hard, particularly comfortable habits" (Tolchin 1989). Understood as a "classic quid pro quo," the legislative veto persists due in large part to Congress's desire to influence delegated powers and the executive's desire for powers to be delegated.

After the *Chadha* ruling, optimists in the executive branch hoped that the legislative veto would cease to exist. This was not to be the case. While presidents, beginning with President Reagan, could elect to veto any bill containing legislative vetoes, it is unlikely that Congress would send the president a bill devoid of such statutes without also revoking powers delegated to the executive. In most instances, the executive would likely prefer the provision of delegated powers with the possibility of a legislative veto than the alternative absence of legislative veto oversight accompanied with the revocation of delegated authority altogether. Indeed, this is exactly how the legislative veto originated. It was fundamentally "an effort to balance the interests of both branches: the desire of administrators for greater discretionary authority and the need of Congress to maintain control short of passing another public law" (Fisher 1985, 706).

About one year after the *Chadha* ruling, President Reagan expressed his displeasure regarding the continued inclusion of committee affirmative vetoes in legislation. In a signing statement attached to an appropriations bill, the president declared, "the provisions in this bill purporting to empower the Appropriations Committees to approve certain expenditures of funds absent participation by both Houses of Congress and the President are unconstitutional," and would therefore be "implemented in a manner consistent with the *Chadha* decision" (1984, 1057). This declaration resulted in the House Appropriations Committee threatening to revoke the ability of NASA officials to request congressional permission to exceed statutory spending limits (Fisher 1985). In response, NASA administrator James M. Beggs asked Congress to maintain the agency's ability to exceed spending limits with committee approval. Though President Reagan threatened to disregard statutes requiring committee approval, the National Aeronautics and Space Administration (NASA) administrator was petitioning Congress to keep such arrangements in place. A more consequential interbranch standoff over the veto's continued viability during President Reagan's second term unfolded in similar fashion.

The Foreign Operations, Export Financing, and Related Programs Appropriations Act of 1988 contained 18 legislative vetoes, 17 of which required State Department officials to secure advance committee approval. One of these committee affirmative vetoes required that funds available for foreign assistance could not be expended through an appropriation account that was not explicitly sanctioned by statute "without the prior written approval of the Committees on Appropriations" (102 Stat. 2268, Public Law 100–461). As expected, the continued practice of including such veto provisions in legislation after *Chadha* led to significant objections from many executive officials.

In 1988, the director of the OMB, James C. Miller III, vocally protested a legislative veto over the transfer of State Department funds included in the Foreign Operations Appropriations Act. Because the removal of the veto provision would open the possibility that the department could allocate funds in a manner opposed by Congress, the House Appropriations Committee threatened in response to eliminate the legislative veto provision and simultaneously prohibit State Department transfer of foreign assistance funds under any circumstance (Fisher 1993). By making good on this threat, however, Congress would incur greater costs by having to write more detailed statutes governing department spending scenarios. Given these positions and likely consequences, both sides had an incentive to compromise. A comparison of the differences in key statutes of the 1988 and 1990 Foreign Operations spending bills illustrates the principal outcome of their mutual agreement.

While the 1988 bill explicitly required advance approval from the Appropriations Committees, the language used in the 1990 bill did not replicate this provision. In its place was the following requirement on funds transfers:

> None of the funds made available by this Act may be obligated under an appropriation account to which they were not appropriated, unless the President, prior to the exercise of any authority contained in the Foreign Assistance Act of 1961 to transfer funds, *consults with and provides a written policy justification* to the Committees on Appropriations of the House of Representatives and the Senate: Provided further, That the exercise of such authority shall be *subject to the regular notification procedures* of the Committees on Appropriations. (103 Stat. 1219, Public Law 101–167; emphasis added)

The primary significance was the exclusion of an explicit legislative veto in the 1990 appropriations bill in exchange for a written justification and advance notification requirement. Constitutional law expert Louis Fisher described the outcome of this comprise by stating, "While not articulated in the public law, those procedures require the administration to notify the Committees of each transfer. If no objection is raised during a fifteen-day review period, the administration may excise the authority. If the Committees object, the administration could proceed only at great peril. By ignoring committee objections, the executive branch would most likely lose transfer authority the next year" (1993, 290). This arrangement provided the committees with advance notification of specified expenditures,

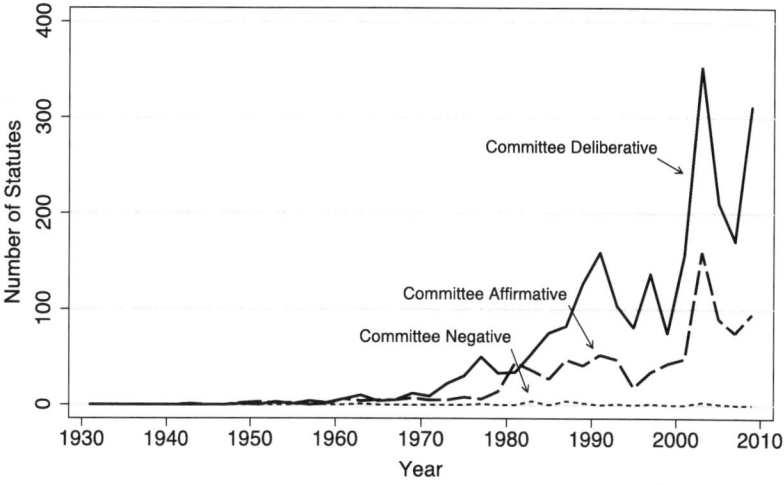

Fig. 2.1. Committee affirmative, negative, and deliberative veto statutes by Congress: 1931–2010

therefore giving them an opportunity to intervene or express an objection. Importantly, this agreement initiated an increased usage of committee deliberative vetoes. In contrast to the one- and dual-House vetoes that commonly existed prior to *Chadha*, the compromise reached over discretionary foreign aid spending implemented a report and wait requirement to bridge the impasse between the two branches. Such agreements existed before *Chadha*, but today these types of committee deliberative vetoes are among Congress's most commonly used statutory oversight resources. Figure 2.1 illustrates the dramatic increase in committee affirmative and deliberative vetoes that has occurred over the past several decades. Thus, while the *Chadha* ruling served as an important catalyst that altered Congress's application of veto oversight, it clearly did not completely eradicate the veto, as some had predicted would happen.

The Veto's Evolution—Oversight and Omnibus Bills

Table 2.1 provides data regarding legislative veto enactments from 1931 to 2010. While considerable variation exists with respect to the number of legislative vetoes enacted by term in recent years, there is surprisingly little variation in the number of laws containing them. From 1993 to 2010, an average of 25 laws contained at least one legislative veto, with a range between 19 and 35. Thus, the increase in the number of veto statutes in recent years is not a result of Congress including vetoes in greater numbers of laws, but rather through an increase in the number of veto provisions included in laws that contain vetoes. In particular, there has been a noticeable increase in the number of veto provisions in appropriations bills passed by Congress. The increased utilization of omnibus appropriations bills in recent years serves as an additional basis for the rise in legislative veto enactments.

In his study of omnibus lawmaking from 1949 to 1994, Krutz (2001) defines omnibus packages in terms of the scope and size of the legislation. The study identifies omnibus enactments as those that address several major policy areas (e.g., transportation, agriculture, defense, and foreign trade) and are significantly longer than an average major law. Recent Congresses have passed several omnibus appropriations packages containing significant numbers of legislative veto provisions. In general, omnibus bills are considered high priority legislation that must pass in order to maintain funding for certain programs or to prevent programs from expiring. Because of the compulsory nature of omnibus legislation, Congress is able

TABLE 2.1. Legislative veto (LV) statutes: 1931–2010

Congress	Laws with Enacted LVs (%)	LVs Statutes	Congress	Laws with Enacted LVs (%)	LVs Statutes
72 (1931–1932)	2 (4.5)	2	92 (1971–1972)	15 (2.5)	21
73 (1933–1934)	0 (0.0)	0	93 (1973–1974)	40 (6.2)	71
74 (1935–1936)	1 (0.1)	1	94 (1975–1976)	41 (7.0)	82
75 (1937–1938)	0 (0.0)	0	95 (1977–1978)	54 (8.5)	96
76 (1939–1940)	3 (0.4)	3	96 (1979–1980)	46 (7.5)	82
77 (1941–1942)	3 (0.4)	3	97 (1981–1982)	31 (6.6)	102
78 (1943–1944)	4 (0.7)	4	98 (1983–1984)	28 (4.5)	120
79 (1945–1946)	4 (0.5)	5	99 (1985–1986)	18 (2.7)	143
80 (1947–1948)	3 (0.3)	3	100 (1987–1988)	16 (2.2)	152
81 (1949–1950)	5 (0.5)	5	101 (1989–1990)	23 (3.5)	172
82 (1951–1952)	5 (0.9)	7	102 (1991–1992)	49 (8.3)	236
83 (1953–1954)	7 (0.9)	7	103 (1993–1994)	19 (4.1)	178
84 (1955–1956)	7 (0.7)	7	104 (1995–1996)	22 (6.6)	113
85 (1957–1958)	10 (1.1)	11	105 (1997–1998)	35 (8.9)	196
86 (1959–1960)	2 (0.3)	3	106 (1999–2000)	24 (4.1)	137
87 (1961–1962)	14 (1.6)	17	107 (2001–2002)	28 (7.4)	235
88 (1963–1964)	9 (1.4)	17	108 (2003–2004)	27 (5.4)	533
89 (1965–1966)	9 (1.1)	13	109 (2005–2006)	28 (5.8)	314
90 (1967–1968)	8 (1.3)	12	110 (2007–2008)	20 (4.3)	259
91 (1969–1970)	17 (2.4)	27	111 (2009–2010)	26 (6.8)	427

to strategically insert legislative veto provisions that might otherwise be objectionable enough to elicit a presidential veto. Krutz emphasizes this general point when he claims that "[c]ongressional leaders used the packages to push through measures the president opposed" (2001, 130). By using omnibus legislation as the vehicle to enact legislative vetoes, Congress has the ability to pass certain provisions that might not receive a president's signature in other settings. An excellent case in point occurred during the 108th Congress when lawmakers passed the three omnibus bills containing a combined total of nearly 400 legislative vetoes.

The first order of business for the newly elected 108th Congress was to quickly complete 10 of the 2003 appropriations bills left unfinished at the adjournment of the previous Congress due in large part to considerable disagreements over domestic and foreign spending priorities. Appropriations for military construction and the DOD were the only major spending bills able to reach consensus during the 107th Congress. As a result, a majority of the appropriations bills were uncompleted and required immediate attention. Largely for the sake of expediency, party leaders combined all of these appropriations into an omnibus package and enacted it into law on February 20, 2003 (117 Stat. 11, Public Law 108–7). The bill spanned more than 3,000 pages and contained 122 legislative vetoes. Divisions over spending priorities during the next fiscal year produced similar results.

The 108th Congress successfully passed six appropriations bills as separate enactments, while the remaining six were combined into an omnibus spending package. On par with the previous year's omnibus spending bill, Congress included 112 legislative vetoes in the 2004 Consolidated Appropriations Act (118 Stat. 3, Public Law 108–199).

Finally, after passing just four of the required appropriations bills prior to the 2004 elections, the 108th Congress passed yet another omnibus spending package for fiscal year 2005 during a lame-duck session (118 Stat. 2809, Public Law 108–447). Not to be outdone by the previous two omnibus bills, the 2005 Consolidated Appropriations Act was packed with 145 legislative vetoes. Thus, the principal reason for the noticeable spike seen in figure 0.1 in the number of legislative vetoes enacted during the 108th Congress was the fact that this term uncharacteristically passed three major omnibus spending packages governing government spending over three consecutive fiscal years. While this term is somewhat of an anomaly due to the circumstances surrounding the appropriations process, recent Congresses have overseen the enactment of hundreds of legislative vetoes every term. A 2008 omnibus bill included nearly 150 legislative vetoes (121 Stat. 1844, Public Law 110–161), while omnibus spending bills passed in

2009 and 2010 contained a combined 268 (123 Stat. 524, Public Law 111–8; 123 Stat. 3034, Public Law 111–117).

Resurgence of the Legislative Veto

By virtue of the thousands of veto statutes enacted since 1983, it is abundantly clear that the *Chadha* ruling failed to eliminate the legislative veto. It did, however, result in the near extinction of the one-House negative veto. To assess the effects of the *Chadha* ruling, table 2.2 provides summary data comparing the pre- and post-*Chadha* periods.

The first column in table 2.2 indicates the number of veto statutes enacted from 1931 to 1984 according to their type. The 99th Congress, which took office in 1985, is used as the first term belonging to the post-*Chadha* period since it is the first full term that served after the ruling. During the pre-*Chadha* period, Congress enacted a total of 721 legislative vetoes. Committee deliberative vetoes were the most common type, constituting nearly 40 percent of all vetoes. In total, 443 statutes were enacted that gave individual committees veto power. In combination, committee vetoes comprised about 62 percent of all veto enactments. The 89 one-House negative vetoes represented 12 percent of the total, and the remaining 26 percent of veto enactments were of the dual-House variety. This distribution of congressional veto statutes where no single veto type constitutes a majority of veto enactments illustrates its versatility. Comparing these data with congressional terms in the post-*Chadha* period indicates that although the Court's ruling did not discontinue the use of the veto, it significantly altered the types of vetoes Congress chooses to enact.

TABLE 2.2. Legislative veto statutes by type: Pre- and post-*Chadha*

Type	Number of Enacted Veto Statutes		
	1931–1984 (%)	1985–2010 (%)	Total
Committee Deliberative	280 (38.8)	2,042 (66.0)	2,322
Committee Affirmative	156 (21.6)	776 (25.1)	932
Committee Negative	7 (1.0)	12 (0.4)	19
Dual-House Affirmative	63 (8.8)	46 (1.5)	109
Dual-House Negative	76 (10.6)	26 (0.8)	102
Dual-House Deliberative	50 (6.9)	188 (6.1)	238
One-House Negative	89 (12.3)	3 (0.1)	92
Total	721 (100.0)	3,093 (100.0)	3,814

Note: Data compiled by author.

The second column in table 2.2 includes the 13 congressional terms from 1985 to 2010. Examining trends in legislative veto use over time shows that one- and dual-House vetoes were utilized much more frequently prior to the ruling. While still used in some instances, these types of vetoes have been drastically reduced in number. After the *Chadha* decision, the cumulative percentage of one- and dual-House legislative veto enactments is less than 10 percent, as compared to comprising nearly 40 percent of all pre-*Chadha* vetoes. Dual-House affirmative vetoes shift from 9 percent of pre-*Chadha* vetoes to less than 2 percent afterwards. Dual-House negative vetoes drop from 10 percent to less than 1 percent, and one-House negative vetoes decrease from 12.4 percent of all pre-*Chadha* vetoes to a nearly nonexistent 0.1 percent of the vetoes enacted in its aftermath.

The one exception to the dramatic decline in one- and dual-House vetoes following *Chadha* is the continued use of the dual-House deliberative veto. From 1931 to 1984, dual-House deliberative vetoes comprised 6.9 percent of all enacted vetoes. While legislators have drastically scaled back their implementation of dual-House affirmative, dual-House negative, and one-House negative vetoes, the use of the dual-House deliberative veto has held relatively steady at about 6 percent of the total. To reiterate, these report and wait provisions provide Congress with a window of opportunity to prevent or modify the proposed bureaucratic action.[14] For example, the following provision was included in an appropriations bill for the Department of Energy during a congressional term immediately following *Chadha*:

> Provided further, That any contract, agreement or provision thereof entered into by the Secretary pursuant to this authority shall not be executed prior to the expiration of 30 calendar days (not including any day in which either House of Congress is not in session because of adjournment of more than three calendar days to a day certain) from the receipt by the Speaker of the House of Representatives and the President of the Senate of a full and comprehensive report on such project, including the facts and circumstances relied upon in support of the proposed project. (99 Stat. 1254, Public Law 99–190)

Statutes such as these are the only type of non-committee veto utilized with regularity in recent decades. Figure 2.2 shows patterns for the three types of dual-House veto enactments over time, each of which saw an increase during the 1970s. The frequency of dual-House affirmative and dual-House negative dissipates after the *Chadha* ruling, while Congress continues to enact dual-House deliberative vetoes, albeit to varying degrees.

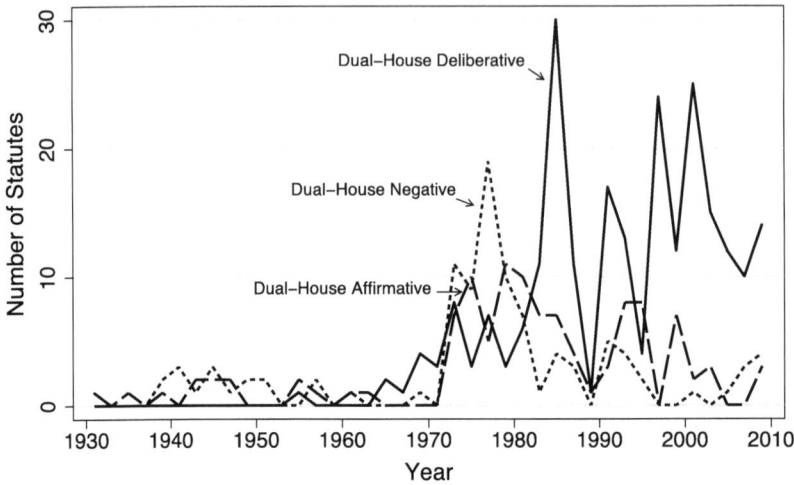

Fig. 2.2. Dual-House affirmative, negative, and deliberative veto statutes by Congress: 1931–2010

In addition to the enactment of 188 dual-House deliberative vetoes, Congress has also passed 46 dual-House affirmative and 26 dual-House negative vetoes since 1985. The veto process for each most often requires a joint resolution of approval or disapproval to execute the veto. In relative terms, then, the number of dual-House vetoes has declined, although dual-House deliberative vetoes continue to be enacted at a rate of about 15 per Congress. In stark contrast, legislators have passed a mere three one-House negative vetoes in the post-*Chadha* period.

The Demise of the One-House Negative Veto

The *Chadha* ruling declared the one-House negative veto unconstitutional. From its inception until 1984, Congress enacted 89 statutes empowering a single chamber with the authority to block executive actions. Figure 2.3 depicts the rise in one-House negative vetoes that occurred during the 1970s. After the passage of the first one-House negative veto in 1932, two decades passed before a second was enacted. During the mid-1970s, the number of one-House vetoes increased appreciably, reaching a peak of 22 passed by the 94th Congress. This trend began to reverse during the early 1980s. The term in office when the Supreme Court issued its legislative veto ruling passed seven such statutes. Since then, with just three exceptions, Congress has abandoned this type of veto.

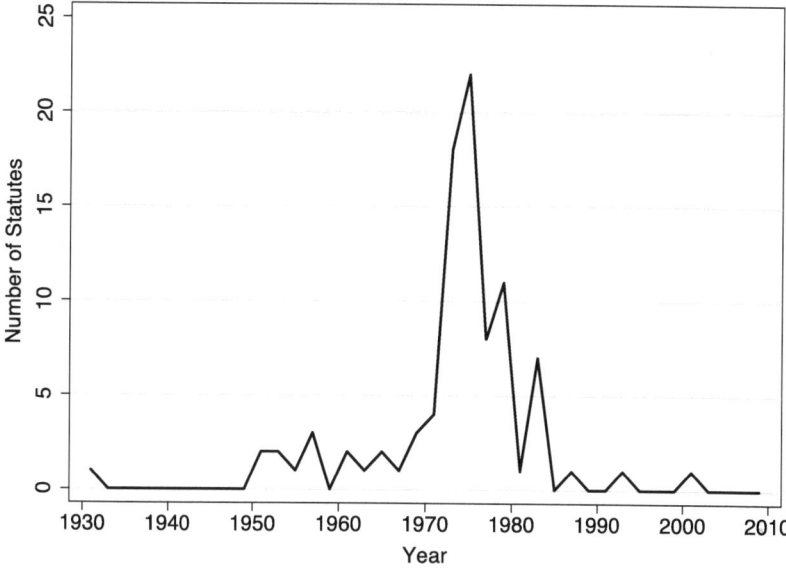

Fig. 2.3. One-House negative legislative veto statutes by Congress: 1931–2010

In May 1994, President Clinton signed into law legislation making major reforms to U.S. transportation policy (108 Stat. 1034, Public Law 103–272). The bill contained three legislative vetoes. A committee affirmative veto required advance approval over automobile and highway safety facility construction projects in excess of $100,000, and a dual-House negative veto allowed Congress to veto proposed Amtrak route additions or discontinuances. The third legislative veto empowered either chamber of Congress to block regulations issued by the secretary of labor regarding employee protection programs. The statute stated, "A proposed regulation under this subchapter shall be submitted to Congress and becomes effective only if, during the period of 60 legislative days after the regulation is submitted to Congress, either House does not pass a resolution disapproving the regulation" (108 Stat. 1159, Public Law 103–272). The resemblance of this to the immigration statute struck down by the Court in *Chadha* was not lost on the president or his advisers.

A signing statement attached to the bill by President Clinton stated, "The Supreme Court has ruled definitively that legislative vetoes are unconstitutional" (1994, 1199). It continued by stating that the administration considered the section containing the one-House negative veto severable from the rest of the law. Citing the *Chadha* ruling as his justification, Clinton boldly instructed the secretary of labor to disregard the one-House negative veto statute. By not attempting to block any regulations pursuant to this statute, Congress did not put the secretary in the precarious position of having to decide whether to do the bidding of the president or comply with the law.

The only other one-House negative vetoes enacted during the post-*Chadha* period were included in the Omnibus Trade and Competitiveness Act of 1988 (102 Stat. 1107, Public Law 100–418) and the Bipartisan Trade Promotion Authority Act of 2002 (TPA Act) (116 Stat. 933, Public Law 107–210). Each of these laws extended presidential diplomatic powers to enter into international trade agreements, a power originally delegated to the president for a five-year period by the Trade Act of 1974 (88 Stat. 1978, Public Law 93–618). The 1974 act required presidential consultation with Congress and permitted an expedited up-or-down vote on presidential agreements. This process was later deemed "fast-track authority" (Sek 2003, 3).

In addition to providing the president with fast-track negotiation authority, the Trade Act is also notable because it imposed eight dual-House and two one-House vetoes governing various aspects of international trade. At the time of its passage, this legislation enacted more veto statutes than any previous law. Five of the dual-House vetoes required congressional approval of trade agreements negotiated by the president. Two one-House negative vetoes allowed either chamber to veto agreements with nations determined to be engaging in unfair trading practices. With this enactment as the baseline, Congress continued the practice of including veto provisions in subsequent reauthorizations of presidential fast-track authority.

The 96th Congress extended fast-track authority for an additional eight years in 1979 (93 Stat. 144, Public Law 96–39). Shortly after its second expiration, the Omnibus Trade and Competitiveness Act of 1988 (102 Stat. 1107, Public Law 100–418) reinstated fast-track powers for a three-year period. New to this reauthorization was a provision allowing the president to request an extension of fast-track authority for two additional years. If requested, the extension would go into effect unless either chamber of Congress voted against it. Many initially considered approval of the extension as a mere formality, but President George H. W. Bush's declaration of his intention to begin work on a North American free trade agreement "triggered a congressional backlash against Fast Track" (Tucker and Wallach 2009, 121). Before the extension went into effect in 1991, committees in both the House and Senate reported resolutions of disapproval, neither of which received majority support. The House resolution was defeated by a vote of 192–231 and the Senate resolution failed by a vote of 36–59 (Destler 2005). Due to these unsuccessful votes, presidential fast-track authority was extended until 1993.

Following the Republican seizure of Congress after the 1994 midterm elections, President Clinton called for the reinstatement of fast-track authority. The remaining three congressional terms of Clinton's presidency each grappled with fast-track renewal proposals, but none were ultimately sent to the president for his signature (Sek 2003). After the presidential election of 2000, President Bush also lobbied for fast-track authority as a way to strengthen the president's ability to enter into bilateral trade accords with an expedited congressional approval process. In July 2002, fast-track authority, which was renamed Trade Promotion Authority (TPA), passed the House by a mere three votes (107th Congress, House Roll no. 370). With approval in the Senate the president received the TPA he had sought for a three-year period ending on June 1, 2005.

As was the case with the 1988 TPA authorization, presidential TPA could be extended for an additional two years to June 1, 2007, following the submission of a written report to Congress outlining the justification for the president's extension request. Once submitted, either chamber of Congress could veto the two-year TPA extension (116 Stat. 1006, Public Law 107–210). Despite President Bush's increased use of the signing statement to make constitutional objections to provisions included in newly enacted laws (Berry 2009; P. Cooper 2005), the TPA Act did not receive a signing statement opposing the extension process. A Statement of Administration Policy released on May 8, 2002, also failed to single out the bill's extension mechanism as objectionable. Instead, the statement claimed that TPA was "more important than ever" and stated the president's opposition to any amendments that would alter the bill reported in the Senate (Bush 2002). According to the U.S. trade representative, President Bush (2005) used TPA during these three years to negotiate significant trade agreements with Chile, Singapore, Australia, Morocco, and Bahrain, as well as the Dominican Republic–Central America–United States Free Trade Agreement, which included Costa Rica, El Salvador, Guatemala, Honduras, Nicaragua, and the Dominican Republic.

On its face, the ability for either the House or the Senate to veto a proposed extension of TPA may appear to violate the *Chadha* precedent. There is, however, an important difference between the veto statute struck down by the Supreme Court and the vetoes enacted as part of the two trade acts. The one-House negative veto challenged by Chadha authorized either chamber of Congress to block rulings made by INS judges acting in their capacity to execute U.S. immigration law. The court held that the Constitution did not permit this type of postpassage ability to dictate a law's execution. In contrast, the one-House negative veto included in Trade Act did not grant Congress the power to veto executive actions made pursuant to U.S. trade law, but instead to block the extension of presidential TPA.[15] A federal court was not given the opportunity to consider these nuances since neither the House nor the Senate elected to veto the two-year TPA extension submitted by President Bush on March 30, 2005. This was not for lack of effort.

The week following the president's TPA extension request, North Dakota senator Byron Dorgan introduced a disapproval resolution to block the extension. The resolution was referred to the Finance Committee, but failed to be reported to the floor. In late June, shortly before the TPA extension would go into effect, Senator Dorgan and eight other Senators sent a letter to Finance Committee chair Charles Grassley requesting that the disapproval resolution be reported for a vote on the Senate floor (Sek 2005). Senator Grassley did not acquiesce to this request and consequently the two-year TPA extension went into effect on July 1.[16]

In sum, while the *Chadha* ruling did strike a blow to the legislative veto, at issue before the Court was one specific type of veto, which Congress has mostly abandoned. The near elimination of the one-House veto coincides with a significant increase in the enactment of committee-based vetoes. Such statutes providing veto power to specific committees constitute over 90 percent of the post-*Chadha* total. These are among the single most significant changes spurred by the *Chadha* ruling.

The committee review process itself exhibits some variation based on the action being reviewed and the committee charged with review authority. Since 1993, nearly 95 percent of committee vetoes bestowed veto power with just six committees—Appropriations (House and Senate), Armed Services (House and Senate), International Relations (House), and Foreign Relations (Senate).[17] The vast majority of these committee vetoes are connected to the Appropriations Committees. Thus, another primary consequence of the post-*Chadha* shift to a greater reliance on committee vetoes is an increased oversight role for the House and Senate Appropriations Committees.

The Oversight Ascension of the Appropriations Committees

The increased use of the committee veto during the last two decades has disproportionately enhanced the oversight reach of the Appropriations

Committees of both Houses. Of all committee vetoes passed from 1993 to 2010, approximately 85 percent have empowered the Appropriations Committees with veto authority. Table 2.3 provides examples of these types of vetoes enacted during the 109th Congress.

The Appropriations Committees hold varying degrees of veto authority over the actions of each of the 15 departments of the federal government. While these committee veto examples all passed during the 109th Congress, they are emblematic of the broad use of the veto to oversee a tremendous range of cabinet functions. Laws that include them often state that specified actions may not be executed without the "prior approval of the Committees on Appropriations of both Houses of Congress," or mandate advance notification by requiring that the "Committees on Appropriations of both Houses of Congress are notified 15 days in advance." Although the language used in such statutes tends to be similar, there is substantial variation with respect to how executive agencies abide by legislative veto requirements in securing committee approval or providing advance notification. Interviews in Washington, DC with Appropriations Committee staff described the procedural protocol associated with the vetoes involving the Appropriations Committees.

Despite the enactment of nearly 2,000 legislative vetoes involving the Appropriations Committees since 1993, the committees have not established a standardized procedure governing their interactions with the executive. Many departments and agencies including the Department of Defense and U.S. Agency for International Development have forms specifically dedicated to complying with congressional veto requirements, while others rely on less standardized means of communication (U.S. GAO 1986). The former staff director for the House Appropriations Committee and White House legislative affairs director from 2011 to 2013, indicated that there exists some variation in terms of how the committee veto process works across individual subcommittees and executive agencies.[18] This is to be expected given the variety of personalities and institutions involved.

Further interviews with House and Senate Appropriations Committee staff generalized that when adhering to veto requirements, most often the executive agency or department will submit a letter to the "big four," the committee chairmen and ranking minority members of both Appropriations Committees. This letter is typically brief and states that the agency is filing a report pursuant to a designated statute. Typically, no votes are officially taken or recorded when executive agencies are required to obtain the approval of the committee. In most instances, the chair of the commit-

TABLE 2.3. Appropriations Committee legislative vetoes: 109th Congress

Department	Public Law	Legislative Veto
Defense	109–114	Requires advance notification to Appropriations Committees for any military exercise in excess of $100,000
State	109–108	Requires advance notice to Appropriations Committees regarding the export of U.S. satellites to China
Homeland Security	109–90	Requires Appropriations Committee approval for Homeland Security immigration enforcement, customs enforcement, and REAL ID identification development
Interior	109–80	Requires Appropriations Committee approval for National Wildlife Refuge System land purchases and partnership projects with the National Parks Service
Education	109–149	Requires advance notification to Appropriations Committees for Energy Secretary to reallocate discretionary department funds
Energy	109–103	Requires Appropriations Committee approval for agency reorganizations in the Department of Energy
Agriculture	109–97	Requires Appropriations Committee approval for certain Food and Drug Administration research and development programs
Housing and Urban Development	109–115	Requires advance notice to Appropriations Committees for reprogramming of Housing and Urban Development technical assistance, training, or management improvement funds
Labor	109–149	Requires advance notification to Appropriations Committees for reprogramming of discretionary funds by the Secretary of Labor
Justice	109–108	Requires Appropriations Committee approval for certain Weed and Seed program expenditures
Commerce	109–108	Requires advance notice to Appropriations Committees regarding reorganizations of the Equal Employment Opportunity Commission
Health and Human Services	109–149	Requires advance notification to Appropriations Committees for reprogramming of Health and Human Services discretionary funds by the Health and Human Services secretary
Transportation	109–115	Requires Appropriations Committee approval for any reprogramming of funds greater than 5 percent of departmental program's budget
Treasury	109–115	Requires Appropriations Committee approval for expenditures regarding Internal Revenue Service information and technology systems modernization
Veterans' Affairs	109–114	Requires Appropriations Committee approval for capital asset acquisition of information technology systems expenditures

tee or subcommittee grants approval for the specific action, although some subcommittees require that the ranking minority member confer their approval as well.

The procedure for obtaining committee approval in accordance with legislative veto requirements is somewhat different in the Senate. Since parties tend to be of more importance in the House due to its adherence to majority rule, it is generally difficult for minority lawmakers on the House Appropriations Committee to have significant influence in the process. A former House Appropriations Committee member's impression of the process was that subcommittee chairs were often the first to review executive proposals after their receipt by committee staff. Committee leadership most often conferred approval without formal deliberations among the full committee or subcommittee. Representatives aware of and opposed to a pending request could approach the committee leadership to express their views. Depending on the situation, this could lead to more discussion of the request among the committee's membership.

Because the Senate frequently operates according to unanimous consent and deference is often provided to individual Senators with strong preferences on an issue of importance, there are occasions when the Senate Appropriations Committee will take more time in responding to letters requesting approval. Even senators that do not serve on the Appropriations Committee can attempt to lobby the committee if they are aware of an agency action of interest to them that requires committee action. Staff members in a former Colorado senator's office stated that they would not hesitate to contact Appropriations Committee leadership if a matter of interest requiring committee review arose. Thus, while Appropriations Committee veto statutes require the same consultation or advance notice to each committee, there can be considerable differences in the procedures associated with how the House and Senate committees ensure compliance.

Committee-based vetoes dominate the contemporary landscape, but Congress has demonstrated a renewed interest in allowing the House and Senate chambers to dictate agency action. At the time, passage of the Congressional Review Act (CRA) in 1996 was considered a significant achievement in providing the collective Congress with the means to prevent bureaucrats from imposing rules it opposed (Herz 1997). As the next section discusses, congressional exertions of influence through the CRA have been extremely rare.

The Congressional Review Act Illusion

After assuming congressional majorities following the 1994 midterm elections, Republicans spearheaded the CRA as part of the Contract with America Advancement Act of 1996, which passed with bipartisan support (110 Stat. 847, Public Law 104–121). This reform required agencies to submit to Congress any proposed regulation along with a concise summary and a proposed effective date. All rule proposals were then subject to a minimum review period of 60 days.[19] During the review period, proposed rules could be barred from going into effect with a joint resolution of disapproval requiring a majority vote in both chambers and a presidential signature. In the absence of this, proposed regulations would become effective on the date proposed by the promulgating agency. A Congressional Research Service report on the legislation sums up the review procedure by stating, "Under most circumstances, congressional disapproval under the CRA is difficult because the President is likely to veto any disapproval of a rule issued by his own administration, and in that case the disapproval can become law only if both houses can override the veto. This obstacle may be mitigated in cases in which the disapproval resolution is presented, not to the President under whom the rule was issued, but to his successor, perhaps especially one of a different political party" (Beth 2009, 1). A testament to the high procedural threshold necessary to execute a veto is the fact that only a single regulation has been blocked under the CRA (Rosenberg 2008).

In the 12 years since the CRA's passage, Congress received 48,271 proposed regulations to review (Rosenberg 2008). Of these tens of thousands of proposals, a total of 47 resolutions of disapproval have been introduced in the House or Senate, meaning that less than one-tenth of 1 percent of the rules subject to congressional veto have warranted opposition sufficient for a member of Congress to sponsor a disapproval resolution. The vast majority of these resolutions were not reported out of the committee with jurisdiction over the agency. The full Senate has voted on three such resolutions—one each during the 107th, 108th, and 109th Congresses—all of which were agreed to.[20] Of the 29 disapproval resolutions introduced in the House, only one progressed to a vote on the floor, which, by a narrow margin, resulted in the only regulation struck down since the CRA's enactment (Rosenberg 2008).

An ergonomics program standard (65 Fed. Reg. 68261) proposed by the Department of Labor's Occupational Health and Safety Administration (OSHA) holds the ignominious distinction as the single regulation vetoed by Congress pursuant to the CRA. This regulation would have imposed a number of requirements on an extremely broad array of industries regarding ergonomics programs associated with work-related musculoskeletal disorders. OSHA began work on a set of ergonomics regulations in 1992, which was partially obstructed by limitation riders prohibiting OSHA from promulgating such rules in 1995, 1996, and 1998 (Rosenberg 2008). Shortly after the 2000 presidential election, OSHA issued its ergonomics regulation, which was voted down in the Senate 54–46 (Record Vote Number 15, 107th Congress) and 223–206 in the House (Roll no. 33, 107th Congress). President Bush signed the resolution consisting of a single sentence, stating that "Congress disapproves the rule submitted by the Department of Labor relating to ergonomics (published at 65 Fed. Reg. 68261 (2000)), and such rule shall have no force or effect" (115 Stat. 7, Public Law 107–5).

Because the CRA's veto procedures have resulted in a solitary vetoed rule out of a pool of tens of thousands, some have concluded that it has been spectacularly ineffective in providing a vehicle for Congress to affect agency rulemaking. In some cases, however, congressional influence has resulted in modifications or revocations of rules even in the absence of an actual veto. One such example occurred in 1997 when former representative and current Mississippi senator Roger Wicker introduced a resolution seeing to overturn an OSHA rule pertaining to exposure to a paint-stripping chemical. Although the resolution never received a vote, Wicker garnered enough support for the resolution to successfully insert a similar provision into an appropriations bill for the following fiscal year (Rosenberg 2008). A concerted effort to block a particular rule could also elicit agency reaction to redress concerns in order to forestall an oppositional coalition.

In recent years Republicans have sought to use the CRA to block Environmental Protection Agency (EPA) rules regarding greenhouse gas emissions. A disapproval resolution sponsored by Alaska senator Lisa Murkowski was narrowly defeated in 2010 after just six Democratic senators joined with 41 Republicans voting to block the issuance of such emissions standards (On Motion to proceed S.J. Res 26, June 6, 2010, Vote Number 184). In January 2014, Senate Minority Leader Mitch McConnell and 40 other Republicans announced their intent to force another vote on the controversial EPA carbon emission standards (Barron-Lopez 2014). The fact that this strategy is unlikely to be successful with a Democrat in the White House has not prevented legislators from attempting it in order to exert pressure on the agency. As the 114th Congress took office, *The Hill* speculated that the CRA could be the Republican majority's "secret weapon" to combat regulations issued by the Obama administration (Devaney 2015). Because the president holds veto power over CRA joint resolutions, veto override votes from all incumbent Republican legislators in addition to 13 Democrats in the Senate and 45 in the House would be required to successfully block a regulation over President Obama's objection.

Though there is some anecdotal evidence to the contrary, a single vetoed regulation in nearly two decades suggests that the CRA has not lived up to its primary intention—to provide lawmakers with an achievable means to block agency rules. To address this perceived inadequacy, several reform proposals have been proffered during recent terms seeking to modify the review process. Among the most notable of these initiatives was the Regulations from the Executive in Need of Scrutiny (REINS) Act sponsored by two Kentucky congressmen in 2011.

Regulations from the Executive in Need of Scrutiny (REINS) Act

With nearly 150 cosponsors in the House and 27 cosponsors in the Senate, the REINS Act was introduced during the early days of the 112th Congress. The stated justification for the proposal was "to increase accountability for and transparency in the federal regulatory process. . . . By requiring a vote in Congress, the REINS Act will result in more carefully drafted and detailed legislation, an improved regulatory process, and a legislative branch that is truly accountable to the American people for the laws imposed upon them" (H.R. 10, 112th Congress). Legislators serving during this term also considered additional proposals to reform the rulemaking process in the form of the Regulatory Accountability Act (H.R. 3010, 112th Congress) and the Regulatory Flexibility Act (H.R. 527, 112th Congress), each of which passed the Republican-controlled House. The REINS Act served as the most ambitious of these proposals.

Arguing that "Congress has excessively delegated its constitutional charge while failing to conduct appropriate oversight and retain accountability for the content of the laws it passes," the REINS Act sought to modify the existing CRA by requiring congressional approval of all major rules proposed by federal agencies.[21] While the CRA presently empowers Congress with a dual-House negative veto to block regulations, the REINS Act would impose a dual-House affirmative veto requiring congressional approval in order for a regulation to go into effect. Of course, this would drastically change the review process. Currently, inaction from Congress results in the enactment of major rules following the expiration of the review period. If the REINS Act passed, inaction from Congress would result in the preservation of the status quo and prevent a rule's adoption.

Committee hearings on the REINS Act were held during the first half of 2011 by the House Judiciary Committee and the Senate Homeland Security and Governmental Affairs Committee. Both supporters and opponents of the bill provided testimony at these hearings regarding the legislation and its constitutionality. Sally Katzen, former administrator of the Office of Information and Regulatory Affairs at the OMB, testified that the joint resolution required to approve agency rules may not satisfy the bicameralism and presidential presentment requirements emphasized by the Supreme Court's *Chadha* precedent. Katzen used a hypothetical example to make this point. Were the Senate to approve a regulation as required by the REINS Act, and the resolution fail to receive majority support in the House, she argues that an action from one chamber would therefore prevent the rule from going into effect (Testimony before the Subcommittee on Courts, Commercial and Administrative Law of the House Committee on the Judiciary, January 21, 2011). From this perspective, allowing a single chamber to affect the execution of the law may violate the spirit of the *Chadha* ruling.

Among those testifying in support of the legislation was law professor Jonathan Adler, who stated that the REINS Act "offers a promising mechanism for disciplining federal regulatory agencies and enhancing Congressional accountability for federal regulations" (Testimony before the Subcommittee on Courts, Commercial and Administrative Law of the House Committee on the Judiciary, January 21, 2011, 6). Adler argued in favor of the joint resolution's constitutionality as the mechanism for approving regulations. In addition to committee testimony, *Washington Post* political commentator George Will has extolled the merits of the proposal, stating that it would "redress constitutional imbalance and buttress the rule of law by compelling Congress to take responsibility for the substance that executive rulemaking pours into the sometimes almost empty vessels that Congress calls 'laws'" (2012). In the midst of divided partisan control of the House and the Senate in the 112th Congress, the prospects of the REINS Act's passage were bleak.

On December 7, 2011, despite a veto threat from President Obama, the REINS Act passed the House on a largely party line vote (112th Congress, House Roll Call No. 901). Four Democrats joined all voting House Republicans to support the passage of the bill by a margin of 241–184. The bill stalled in the Senate after referral to the Committee on Homeland Security and Governmental Affairs.

During the following Congress, Representative Todd Young took over as the leader of this legislative reform. Under his leadership, the House has approved the bill on two additional occasions (113th Congress, House Roll Call No. 445; 114th Congress, House Roll Call No. 482). In an interview with the author, Congressman Young stated that the general goal of the bill is to regain congressional authority in the rulemaking arena in hopes that executive officials will "engage more with Congress as they are writing the regulations based off of the laws we pass."[22] Though this was also the fundamental intent of the CRA, he made the case that the CRA simply did not go far enough. The primary objective in strengthening the ability of Congress to act on major rules is to restore "the constitutional framework our Founders intended when they invested all lawmaking authority in Congress." Young continued by lamenting the fact that agencies can essentially legislate at will by adopting binding rules and regulations. As a means to redress this capability, the act "would restore a measure of accountability to the regulatory process by ensuring that elected members of Congress can't punt on these issues. Congress should have final authority to approve of these major rules because they often do boil down to legislation-by-regulation. Congress has a constitutional responsibility for the laws facing Americans, so votes on major rules should be considered a high priority."

Regarding the additional workload that the passage of the REINS Act would impose on Congress, Congressman Young claimed that major rules account for a very small percentage of agency rules. Citing data from 1997 to 2010, an average of 68 rules per year would require congressional approval, requiring an estimated number of annual votes ranging from 50 to 100. Supporters of the bill contend that placing consideration of major rules onto the congressional schedule is well worth the additional costs that such a reform would necessarily impose. Making this precise point, Congressman Young concluded that "Congress has a constitutional responsibility for the laws facing Americans, so votes on major rules should be considered a high priority." While Congress continues to consider reforms to the CRA, legislators maintain the option to include provisions in individual bills that allow for oversight by resolution. The imposition of one- and dual-House veto statutes in scores of laws is such that modern Congresses consider about 25 resolutions of disapproval or approval each term affecting an array of both domestic and foreign policies.

Vetoes by Resolution

The enactment of many one- and dual-House veto statutes during the latter half of the twentieth century provided Congress with more opportunities to overrule executive actions through House, Senate, concurrent, or joint resolutions. As referenced in chapter 1, Congress has used different varieties of resolutions to direct executive action since its inception. Legislation creating the Department of Commerce and Labor passed in 1903 included provisions that required the secretary to provide reports to Congress should either chamber request them by resolution. During the same era, house resolutions were used to direct the secretary of war to furnish reports on seaways (Fisher 1993).

In his analysis spanning 1972 to 1981, Norton (1981b) finds nearly 750 introduced resolutions seeking to veto an executive action, 85 of which were successful. A more recent study including data from 1932 to 1994 identifies over 125 successful veto resolutions (Gibson 1994). Most of these concerned presidential spending deferral requests pursuant to the Budget and Impoundment Control Act of 1974 (88 Stat. 297, Public Law 93–344), which curtailed the president's ability to withhold funds appropriated by Congress. Under the law, presidents were mandated to notify Congress of any proposal to temporarily delay spending within the current fiscal year. Once notified, deferrals were automatically approved unless vetoed by a House or Senate resolution of disapproval.

Given the large number of sponsored resolutions seeking to veto an executive action, it should not be surprising that a large majority do not receive subsequent legislative action. According to one estimate, while less than 20 percent of such resolutions progressed beyond the introduction stage, those that managed to do so were often successful (Norton 1981a). This suggests that committees and party leaders are strategic when considering whether to invest resources on these types of oversight efforts (also see Balla 2000).

Table 2.5 reports data indicating the number of introduced and adopted resolutions of approval and disapproval from 1989 to the present. Using the THOMAS database, I performed a keyword search for terms commonly used in such resolutions to identify the number sponsored by term. These search terms are listed in table 2.4. Congress considers scores of resolutions that do not seek to affect powers delegated to the executive. For example, there were 37 resolutions of approval introduced in the 111th House alone concerning the use of the Capitol grounds for various events including the Greater Washington Soap Box Derby. Also common are resolutions concerning actions taken by the Washington, DC City Council, compacts or other agreements among states, or those that merely express House or Senate support or opposition to individuals, policies, or events. Each of these resolution types is omitted from the data presented in the table. The remaining 294 resolutions were proposed pursuant to an authorizing statute empowering one or both chambers to veto designated executive actions.

Over a span of 12 congressional terms, House and Senate resolutions of disapproval constitute 75 percent of the total. However, of the 23 successful resolutions, 20 were resolutions of approval. This represents a marked departure from Norton's analysis of approval resolutions in the 1970s. As was the case in the data summary provided by Norton (1981a), most resolutions were referred to a committee and received no further action. A plurality (40 percent) of approval resolutions were not reported out of committee, while three out of every four resolutions of disapproval did not progress beyond the committee stage. Discounting the enacted resolutions, 17 disapproval resolutions were defeated by roll-call vote and 10

TABLE 2.4. Congressional resolution search terms

Congressional approval
Congressional disapproval
Congress approves
Congress disapproves
Expressing approval
Expressing disapproval
Hereby approves
Hereby disapproves
Resolution approving
Resolution disapproving

TABLE 2.5. Approval and disapproval resolutions pursuant to an authorizing statute: 1989–2012

Congress	Approval (#Successful)	Disapproval (#Successful)	Total (#Successful)
101 (1989–1990)	14 (3)	34 (2)	48 (5)
102 (1991–1992)	14 (4)	13 (0)	27 (4)
103 (1993–1994)	9 (3)	6 (0)	15 (3)
104 (1995–1996)	0 (0)	12 (0)	12 (0)
105 (1997–1998)	3 (2)	18 (0)	21 (2)
106 (1999–2000)	0 (0)	18 (0)	18 (0)
107 (2001–2002)	4 (2)	17 (0)	21 (2)
108 (2003–2004)	4 (1)	9 (0)	13 (1)
109 (2005–2006)	4 (2)	15 (1)	19 (3)
110 (2007–2008)	5 (2)	19 (0)	24 (2)
111 (2009–2010)	10 (1)	24 (0)	34 (1)
112 (2011–2012)	4 (0)	23 (0)	27 (0)
Total	71 (20)	208 (3)	279 (23)

Note: Data compiled by author from THOMAS online database.

were agreed to by one chamber alone. The only approval resolution that was defeated by roll call vote was a 1992 measure extending free trade protections to Romania. Although the resolution was resoundingly defeated in the House by a three-to-one margin (102nd Congress, House Roll Call No. 436), an identical resolution was adopted the following year.

Fifteen of the 20 enacted approval resolutions concerned foreign policy or international trade. Seven of these resolutions provided one-year extensions to the economic sanctions placed on Burma through the Burmese Freedom and Democracy Act of 2003 (117 Stat. 864, Public Law 108–61). The 2003 act imposed sanctions including bans on Burmese trade and imports, a freezing of assets connected to the incumbent Burmese regime, an expansion of a visa ban for Burmese political leaders, and U.S. opposition to loans to Burma from international organizations. These sanctions were subject to a congressional dual-House affirmative veto whereby Congress could perpetuate the sanctions with a joint resolution of approval. Such resolutions have been agreed to annually every year following the initial enactment. The remaining approval resolutions concerning foreign policy mostly concern free trade agreements with individual countries. Between 1990 and 1993, Congress authorized independent presidential requests for extensions of nondiscriminatory treatment for the products of Czechoslovakia, Mongolia, Bulgaria, Albania, Romania, and the Union of Soviet Socialist Republics (USSR). Additional approval resolutions enacted over the past two decades concern energy policy and public lands, as well as memorials proposed and designed by the Interior Department.

As seen by their paltry success rate of 2 percent, resolutions of disapproval are much less successful in making their way through Congress. Congress agreed to two dual-House negative vetoes in 1989, the first of which rejected a presidential proposal for federal employee salary increases. The second prohibited the production of hydrocarbons or other minerals in the Cordell Bank National Marine Sanctuary. In 1995, Congress vetoed substantial narcotic sentencing reforms proposed by the U.S. Sentencing Commission equalizing crack and cocaine sentences for both possession and trafficking. The most recent dual-House negative veto enactment was the 2001 veto of proposed ergonomics rules issued by the Department of Labor through OSHA.

Notably, all of the disapproval and approval resolutions agreed to since 1989 are House or Senate joint resolutions. This is in contrast to the concurrent or single-House resolutions that were commonly utilized to execute legislative vetoes in the past. Although there have been several concurrent resolution vetoes introduced in recent years, none has received positive action in both chambers.

Summary

Controversies surrounding the use of the legislative veto have involved all three branches of the federal government. Following the origination of the veto as an interbranch compromise, its expansion produced a considerable degree of conflict between the president and Congress. Federal courts failed to intervene in this political dispute until the 1970s despite the interim passage of nearly 300 legislative veto statutes over a period of four decades. This judicial inactivity is primarily attributable to the political nature of the conflict, as well as the requirement that an individual wanting to challenge a veto statute must successfully demonstrate standing. In 1976, federal courts began hearing challenges to legislative veto statutes beginning with two cases concerning campaign finance reform. In each of these rulings, courts failed to directly address the veto's constitutionality.

The *Atkins v. United States* ruling in 1977 was the first instance where a federal court took a clear position on the legislative veto, arguing that the necessary and proper clause provided sufficient justification for its use. Subsequent rulings during the 1980s leading up to the landmark decision in *INS v. Chadha* reached the opposite conclusion holding that the device violated the Constitution's separation of powers. Though it was decided more than 30 years ago, the *Chadha* precedent remains the definitive Supreme Court position on the constitutionality of the legislative veto.

The majority and dissenting opinions in *Chadha* approached the controversy from divergent perspectives. The majority opinion made a strict constructionist argument claiming that the one-House veto failed to satisfy the legislative requirements of bicameral passage and presidential presentment. In a strong rebuke the Court plainly declared, "Congress must abide by its delegation of authority until that delegation is legislatively altered or revoked" (*INS v. Chadha*, 462 U.S. 955 (1983)). Justice White's dissent reached the decidedly different conclusion that the legislative veto was not only constitutional but also indispensible, since it allowed Congress to reassert itself against an increasingly powerful executive branch.

Most of the cases regarding some aspect of the legislative veto over the last 30 years have involved questions of the severability of veto statutes. Rather than relying on a single guiding precedent, federal courts have made a variety of rulings addressing the proper extraction of legislative vetoes from their enacting legislation. Many have held that vetoes are, in fact, severable. As was the case before judicial intervention in 1976, the lack of judicial activism on the post-*Chadha* use of the legislative veto largely results from the political nature of the dispute and the difficulty in demonstrating legal standing to challenge a specific veto.

In sum, the history of judicial involvement with respect to the legislative veto involved two long stretches of time where federal courts remained largely on the sidelines of the dispute, interrupted by a period from 1976 to 1986 where judges issued a number of controversial rulings. This decade of substantial judicial intervention filled predominantly by rulings against the veto did not result in its extinction. Judicial victories provided the president with a legal basis to refuse to recognize the constitutionality of congressional vetoes, but their primary consequence was to serve as a catalyst that has altered the types of vetoes employed by Congress.

Contrary to what many expected, Congress has actually accelerated its use of the legislative veto following *Chadha*. Its persistence is primarily a function of continued delegation to the executive and the desire of legislators to retain control over key executive functions. Legislative vetoes serve this purpose well, which is why Congress continues its strong reliance on it as an oversight resource. The *Chadha* ruling did, however, bring about some substantial changes in the types of vetoes Congress chooses to adopt. Thus, despite the failure of the short-lived movement supporting a legislative veto constitutional amendment, the veto's survival is largely attributable to its versatility.

The most fundamental change following the *Chadha* ruling is the shift away from one- and dual-House vetoes in favor of those empowering committees with veto power. While the data presented in table 2.5 show that Congress continues to direct policy by concurrent and joint resolution, committee vetoes have become the dominant form following the invalidation of the one-House veto in 1983. Similar to the one-House veto, committee vetoes fail to satisfy bicameral passage and presidential presentment. With limited guidance from courts, the constitutionality of the committee veto remains up for debate. Despite the outstanding constitutional controversies, committees have received an increased role in the execution of the law by virtue of the increased number of enacted committee-based vetoes post-*Chadha*. The primary result of this is a more prominent oversight role for the Appropriations Committees given the disproportionate number of vetoes connected to these committees. Accordingly, the increased number of executive actions requiring Appropriations Committee clearance places the leadership of these committees in a greater position of power in the institution's hierarchy given their greater opportunities to directly affect policy.

THREE

When to Deploy? Strategies of Congressional Oversight

Articles I, II, and III of the U.S. Constitution vest the legislative, executive, and judicial powers in discrete branches of government. This unambiguous division of responsibilities seemingly creates a political environment where each branch operates within its own sphere of influence and retains exclusive authority with regard to its designated powers. However, despite the de jure constitutional separation of these functions, the actual practice of governing typically involves considerable amounts of interbranch collaboration and interaction. Writing in the *Federalist Papers*, Madison makes clear that no branch of government "ought to possess, directly or indirectly, an overruling influence over the others in the administration of their respective powers" (Federalist No. 48, 1788). The preeminent constitutional scholar Louis Fisher echoes this point in the preface to his book *The Politics of Shared Power*:

> To study one branch of government in isolation from the others is usually a study in make-believe. Very few operations of Congress and the presidency are genuinely independent and autonomous. For the most part, an initiative by one branch sets in motion a series of compensatory actions by the other branch—sometimes of a cooperative nature, sometimes antagonistic. Like tuning forks when struck, the branches trigger complementary vibrations and reverberations. (1998, ix)

Some powers shared among the branches are derived directly from the Constitution. Others have evolved over time.

Consider the president's role in affecting the legislative agenda. The Constitution empowers the president to act in a legislative capacity when vetoing legislation, convening special sessions of Congress, and occasionally recommending "necessary and expedient" measures to Congress. Each of these resources affords the president with a role in the legislative realm. The formalization and elevated importance of the annual State of the Union address, the creation of the Executive Office of the President and OMB, the president's role as party leader, and ability to speak directly to the American people have provided the president with further means to influence the congressional agenda and legislative process.

In a similar vein, Congress possesses a constitutionally prescribed role in executive branch politics by confirming presidential appointees and exercising its power of impeachment. It can further affect executive action by enacting laws and passing the federal budget. Additional capabilities developed over time have also helped expand Congress's reach into the executive policy-making sphere—the legislative veto is one such resource.

The evolution of statutory oversight devices such as the legislative veto has occurred as the powers delegated to executive agencies have increased (Epstein and O'Halloran 1999; Huber and Shipan 2002). Once controversial, large-scale delegation to the executive is now the norm. As a consequence, their authority to precisely implement the general policies enacted by Congress places unelected specialized bureaucracies at the forefront of modern policy making. One can see evidence of this in many ways. Over the past decade, federal agencies have published 21 rules for every law passed by Congress. In the 112th Congress alone, the ratio was 36 to 1 (Crews 2014). Given this trend, congressional oversight is more important than ever.

Deciding to Delegate

In the aftermath of the Constitution's ratification, there was no guiding precedent regarding the proper balance of power between the legislature and the executive since an executive branch did not exist prior to 1789—the First Continental Congress (1774), Second Continental Congress (1775–81) and Congress of the Confederation (1781–89) each bore responsibility for both legislative and executive functions. Despite the fact that most of the enumerated powers spelled out in the Constitution are granted to

Congress, early in U.S. history the supremacy of the legislature quickly became untenable given the combined effects of the president's veto power and Congress's delegation of powers to the executive branch (Kiewiet and McCubbins 1991). Operating with little guiding precedent, lawmakers serving in early Congresses were initially cautious in their approach to delegating responsibilities to both legislative and executive agents.

During its first session, lawmakers rarely conceded powers by delegating, even to internal committees. Congressional leaders created scores of ad hoc committees to study individual bills, but did not grant these committees jurisdiction over broad issue areas. It was not until the late 1810s that the House and Senate created a system of permanent standing committees with relatively stable jurisdictions (Davidson et al. 2012). Rule changes made a decade later codified the process whereby bills would be referred to a standing committee following their introduction (Cooper and Young 1989). This reform empowered committees to both prevent and initiate policy changes for select issue areas. Although Congress collectively surrenders control over individual issues by conceding jurisdiction to committees, the development of the committee system transpired as a greater emphasis was placed on the benefits of specialization (J. Cooper 1970; Gamm and Shepsle 1989). In addition to the internal organization of Congress as a means to reduce the uncertainty between policy proposals and eventual outcomes (Krehbiel 1991), informational gains can also be attained by delegating to specialized bureaucratic agencies. Understanding the benefits that could be wrought by delegating to legislative and executive officials alike, Congress gradually began expanding its capacity for delegation.

Initial efforts to delegate to executive agencies typically involved relatively minor policy decisions. Often Congress would specify general program objectives and allow executive officials to independently fill in the blanks. Delegation of this variety, albeit to the judiciary, was sanctioned by the Supreme Court in *Wayman v. Southard*, 23 U.S. 1 (1825). Chief Justice John Marshall's opinion, which upheld legislation affording federal courts with the ability to determine their own procedural rules, stated, "But Congress may certainly delegate to others powers which the legislature may rightfully exercise itself" (*Wayman v. Southard*, 23 U.S. 43 (1825)). This ruling provided an early legal precedent allowing for Congress to grant greater autonomy to nonlegislative actors.

Epstein and O'Halloran (1999) cite the passage of the Interstate Commerce Act in 1887, which empowered the newly created Interstate Commerce Commission with the responsibility for establishing and regulating railroad rates, as the watershed moment when Congress began to delegate substantial powers that were legislative in nature. This and laws similar to the Commerce Act were subject to legal action challenging delegation on this scale as unconstitutional abdications of legislative responsibility.

In *Field v. Clark*, 143 U.S. 649 (1892), and *J. W. Hampton, Jr. & Co. v. United States*, 276 U.S. 394 (1928), the Supreme Court upheld two laws delegating to the president the ability to alter tariff schedules. In the former case, the Court upheld the Tariff Act of 1890 after identifying a litany of laws dating back to the Washington administration where Congress had granted specific powers to the president. In upholding the law, Justice John Harlan quoted a Pennsylvania court ruling as an exemplary presentation of his core thesis: "The legislature cannot delegate its power to make a law, but it can make a law to delegate a power to determine some fact or state of things upon which the law makes, or intends to make, its own action depend. To deny this would be to stop the wheels of government. There are many things upon which wise and useful legislation must depend which cannot be known to the law-making power, and must therefore be a subject of inquiry and determination outside of the halls of legislation" (*Locke's Appeal Commonwealth ex rel. McClain v. Locke et al.*, 72 Pa. St. 498). The law challenged in the *J.W. Hampton* case also delegated to the president the authority to independently modify tariff rates initially established by Congress. Writing for the majority, Chief Justice William Howard Taft upheld the president's control over tariff levels since Congress had outlined an "intelligible principle" or general policy objective (276 U.S. 409 (1928)).

Following a series of mostly unsuccessful subsequent legal challenges, with the important exception of *A.L.A. Schechter Poultry Corp. v. United States*, 295 U.S. 495 (1935), large-scale delegation of policy-making authority to the executive branch proliferated during the twentieth century.[1] Because of the magnitude of these delegated powers, it is incumbent on Congress to consider how to structure forms of oversight concerning a law's execution in order to avoid, in the words of Chief Justice Charles Evans Hughes, "delegation running riot" (*A.L.A. Schechter Poultry Corp. v. United States*, 295 U.S. 553 (1935)). A key question in this regard is how to secure the benefits of delegation and simultaneously minimize the potential for agency loss.

Trade-offs Associated with Delegation

Given the wide range and complexity of issues addressed by today's federal government, it would be unthinkable for Congress to independently administer every government program. Out of necessity, legislators have transferred considerable implementation powers to the executive branch as the functions of the federal government have grown. Interactions between Congress and the bureaucracy can be characterized as principal-agent relationships in which Congress, acting as the principal, authorizes and oversees actions of an executive agent (Bendor 1988; Gailmard 2009; Miller 2005; Weingast 1984). By delegating, Congress can take advantage of bureaucratic expertise, insulate itself from potentially unpopular programs, and make stable commitments to specific policies. However, as is the case in any instance of delegated responsibility, there exists a potential for an agent to deviate in its actions from the preferences of the principal—a phenomenon known as agency loss. This is a persistent problem associated with delegation. A number of studies examining these relationships have shown that legislators can place constraints on delegated powers such that they can maximize the benefits from delegation while minimizing the costs (Bawn 1995, 1997; MacDonald 2010). Carefully crafting legislation provides one avenue to achieve this goal.

Often the most visible forms of congressional oversight are committee hearings and investigations, which allow Congress to investigate a broad array of agency functions (Aberbach 1990; McCubbins, Noll and Weingast 1989; Oleszek 2013). Through direct involvement via investigative hearings, Congress can identify or anticipate problems, solicit expert testimony, and consider potential solutions as deemed necessary. Henry Waxman, the former chairperson of the House Committee on Oversight and Government Reform, identifies this process as the core of Congress's oversight responsibilities by stating, "Proper oversight complements and strengthens the legislative process by identifying problems that may require new laws and by ensuring that existing laws are being executed as Congress meant them to be" (2010, 145). While committee hearings are arguably the most evident form of congressional oversight, statutory guidelines, restrictions, and requirements are the most common oversight resources utilized by Congress, which enacts thousands of such statutes each term (Berry 2009; Hall 2008; Kiewiet and McCubbins 1991; MacDonald 2010; McCubbins 1985). The legislative veto is among the most common statutory oversight devices since it allows Congress to delegate, but reserve the potential for subsequent intervention if lawmakers disapprove of the way agencies exercise their delegated powers. The following section introduces the theoretical approach based on transaction costs and macropolitical conflict that are used to assess conditions under which veto oversight is more likely to exist.

Oversight by Statute

At its most fundamental level, congressional oversight concerns "whether, to what extent, and in what way Congress attempts to detect and remedy executive branch violation of legislative goals" (McCubbins 1985, 729). Since the potential for such violations becomes more likely as the extent of delegated powers increases, Congress relies on numerous means of oversight. The academic literature on oversight has often been framed in terms of the extent to which Congress engages in ex ante and ex post oversight activities (Aberbach 1990; Huber and Shipan 2000; McCubbins and Schwartz 1984; Ringquist, Worsham, and Eisner 2003; Smith 2010; Weingast 1984; Weingast and Moran 1983). Ex ante forms of oversight most often involve placing initial restrictions on the activities of bureaucrats in such a manner that the resulting policies will ultimately be acceptable to Congress. Ringquist, Worsham, and Eisner (2003) characterize this type of oversight as "efforts to control the bureaucratic decision making without the direct intervention of Congress" (143). In contrast, ex post modes of oversight necessarily involve direct congressional intervention to veto or otherwise affect bureaucratic action. Many oversight actions undertaken by Congress can be placed into one of these two categories. Ex ante forms of oversight are most often imposed by statute, committee report, or through the appropriations process. Committee hearings, such as those held in 2010 that focused on mining safety and the operations of the Mine Safety and Health Administration following a lethal explosion in West Virginia that tragically killed 29 miners, exemplify ex post oversight. There are, however, some oversight activities that fit somewhere in between these two types.

Hall (2004) and Cox (2004), respectively, examine short-term authorizations and reauthorizations as forms of oversight that blend characteristics of both ex ante and ex post mechanisms. The content of these original enactments governing bureaucratic action imposes a form of ex ante oversight structuring the parameters under which executive officials may implement the law. Temporary authorizations necessarily provide legislators with the opportunity to engage in ex post oversight by mandating that a specific agency or program come up for reauthorization at a future point. While most would recognize legislative vetoes as a form of ex post oversight, some of their characteristics resemble those of temporary authorizations.

Unlike ex post oversight expressed through committee hearings, which can be held at the discretion of the committee, the opportunity for legislators to veto an executive action is contingent upon a previously enacted statute. By inserting veto provisions into bills, members of Congress engage in a form of ex ante oversight. Because it can designate virtually any agency action as subject to congressional override, such statutes demonstrate that Congress is attuned to specific programs or policies. By construction, legislative vetoes also institutionalize congressional authority to exercise ex post oversight. Through the insertion of vetoes into legislation, Congress can reap the benefits of delegation while reserving the opportunity to veto actions deemed objectionable.

Ex ante oversight is commonly established during the legislative process when the extent of delegated powers is specified. Should an agency have broad authority to reprogram appropriated funds? Does the agency enjoy independence regarding rulemaking and the issuance of other directives? Conversely, what sorts of constraints or impositions are hardwired into the law? Questions of this sort are critical in determining the amount of autonomy granted to individual agencies. In his comprehensive study on the bureaucracy, Wilson (1989) argues that modern Congresses are less prone to directly dictate agency action and more likely to impose restrictions on agency decision making. McCubbins (1985) characterizes initial decisions regarding the degree of bureaucratic independence as the "institutional setting" that stipulates how much discretion administrators will possess. Using slightly different terminology, Wood and Bohte (2004) empirically examine the politics of "administrative design," which broadly refers to the parameters of delegated bureaucratic power. These and other scholars have investigated the degree of agency autonomy in association with ex ante constraints placed on agency action. Once these structures have been codified, elected officials can continue to constrain or expand bureaucratic independence by establishing additional laws, rules, guidelines, and institutions affecting policy implementation (Bawn 1997; McCubbins, Noll, and Weingast 1989).

Oversight imposed by statute is a vitally important resource for Congress (Bawn 1997; Hall 2008; Huber and Shipan 2002; Oleszek 2013). A wide variety of oversight devices fall under its statutory oversight umbrella. Gailmard (2009), for example, argues that Congress benefits most when delegating statutes contain restrictions on the policy choices available to bureaucrats as opposed to "menu laws" that outline differing circumstances that may develop and the specific course of action that bureaucrats should follow depending on what circumstance has occurred. Menu laws are just one variant of statutory oversight that also includes direct implementation requirements, mandatory reporting, reauthorizations, limitation riders, and legislative vetoes, among others.

Reporting requirements are commonly enacted by law as a method to procure information regarding executive branch activities (Smith and Cotter 1957). Kaiser et al. (2007) estimate that Congress receives more than 4,000 reports on an array of programs and priorities from executive officials every year. Another frequently used type of ex ante statutory oversight can be found in the form of limitation riders, which expressly prohibit appropriated funds from being spent in a specific manner. One estimate identified over 4,000 limitation riders enacted into law over a span of five congressional terms during the 1990s (MacDonald 2010). These statutes impose oversight by restricting the universe of agency spending options. The above are just some examples of the many ways that Congress can impose oversight by statute. Weingast (1984) describes the reliance on multiple oversight resources such as these as "an ingenious system for control of agencies that involves little direct congressional monitoring of decisions but which nonetheless results in policies desired by Congress" (148). Over the past several decades, the legislative veto has burgeoned into an increasingly common fixture of Congress's statutory oversight framework. A common approach to understanding congressional strategy regarding this type of oversight is through an analysis of transaction costs.

Transaction Costs and Congressional Oversight of the Administrative State

A theory of transaction costs originated in economics and its applications have since spread to multiple other disciplines (Coase 1937; North 1991). In a political context, transaction costs principally concern the factors associated with negotiating, enforcing, and monitoring agreements among parties. Weingast and Marshall (1988) were among the first to apply transaction cost theory to the legislative arena in their study of congressional organization and the role of committees. Their study asserts that the committees—with relatively stable jurisdictions and membership—minimize enforcement and commitment transaction costs more optimally than simple gains from exchange through vote trading would. Several subsequent studies on congressional behavior and institutions have used this theoretical approach (Cox 2004; Epstein and O'Halloran 1999; Huber and Shipan 2000; North 1991; Wood and Bohte 2004).

While the term "transaction costs" can have alternative meanings in different contexts, Huber and Shipan (2000) provide five specific criteria for the theory as applied to the study of Congress and the bureaucracy. The first two are well known to those familiar with rational choice theory. These principles state that politicians are boundedly rational actors who seek to maximize utility. Third, public officeholders care about policy and seek to implement the most ideal policy given their preferences. In attempting to enact their preferred policies, politicians are presented with transaction costs of varying types. Most commonly these transaction costs involve information asymmetries, policy uncertainty, and the timing in which policies are enacted. The final aspect of the transaction cost approach states that politicians will consider transaction costs associated with a certain policy and seek to impose institutions that will maximize utility (Huber and Shipan 2000). It is this expectation that facilitates the generation of testable hypotheses regarding the conditions under which legislators will implement certain oversight devices. As a charge to political scientists, they conclude that "the transaction cost framework therefore directs attention toward *institutional arrangements as dependent variables*. From this theoretical perspective, it should be possible to explain variation in institutions as a function of variation in the nature of transaction costs themselves, which are the relevant independent variables" (Huber and Shipan 2000, 29; emphasis in original). Several research programs examining congressional oversight have followed exactly this approach.

Epstein and O'Halloran (1999) employ a transaction cost approach to the question of why Congress delegates to executive actors. The main premise of their argument is that delegation occurs when the benefits outweigh the costs of doing so. Examining more than 250 laws from 1947 to 1992, their analysis demonstrates that delegation is function of legislative organization and procedure, interbranch conflict, and issue complexity. In general, the amount of discretionary power afforded to the executive increases for policies of greater complexity and under the condition of ideologically outlying committees. Divided government and the use of restrictive rules exert the opposite effect. Cox's (2004) study of the congressional reauthorization process examines transaction costs related to uncertainty and conflict to predict when Congress will enact temporary authorizations. His research asks how characteristics of individual laws affect the formulation of procedures and structures that enforce the contract spelled out in the legislation. Among the study's main results is that issue complexity and committee staff each increase the likelihood that policies will be enacted through short-term authorizations. Temporary authorizations are less likely, however, when greater intracommittee ideological conflict exists (Cox 2004). Likewise, Wood and Bohte (2004) employ a transaction cost approach that focuses on costs associated with uncertainty, monitoring, and maintaining administrative agency contracts. Their results identify executive-legislative conflict and internal congressional conflict as factors that generally lead to a more independent bureaucracy, while greater party strength is commonly associated with reduced agency autonomy. Finally, Potoski (1999) employs survey data to examine the manner in which states design agencies charged with promoting clean air policy. He concludes that legislatures are more apt to delegate to agencies when policies grow in complexity, and are less likely to do so when greater uncertainty exists regarding the retention of partisan control of the legislature. These studies using transaction cost theory respectively examine the use of delegation, temporary authorizations, and institutional design as dependent variables in the precise manner recommended by Huber and Shipan (2000).

The present study seeks to contribute to this stream of research by analyzing transaction cost considerations associated with the legislative veto. Following in the tradition of Cox's research, the transaction costs related to uncertainty and conflict will be a central focus of the analysis. In the tradition of Ringquist, Worsham, and Eisner (2003), the salience of individual laws is also considered as a factor expected to affect statutory oversight use.

The Legislative Veto as an Oversight Solution

Examining the latitude afforded to bureaucratic agencies Calvert, McCubbins, and Weingast (1989) use a spatial model illustrating a zone of bureaucratic discretion based on the relative preferences of the executive and the legislature. Provided that administrative agencies operate within this zone of acceptability, they do not risk external intervention. Actions falling outside of the acceptability space are conceptualized as belonging to a realm of "active political control" that will likely incite some form of intervention on the part of the executive, legislature, or both (Calvert, McCubbins, and Weingast 1989, 597). While there are many ways that Congress can exert active political control in such instances, the legislative veto is among the most prominent means of intervention.

Every congressional term since 1980 has enacted at least 100 statutes containing legislative vetoes. The costs associated with inserting a single legislative veto provision into a bill are often quite small. The sponsor could include such a provision in the original bill or a veto could be added at various stages of the legislative process. However, because there are transaction costs related to monitoring compliance with veto requirements, Congress is selective in terms of when and where such provisions are inserted.

In an interview with the author, the former staff director for the House Appropriations Committee, stated that monitoring agency compliance with veto statutes requires substantial amounts of time and attention from individual lawmakers, staff, committees, and Congress as a whole. The specific process for ensuring agency compliance varies across committees. Even within a single committee, such as the House Appropriations Committee, the director said that there is not one standardized procedure that executive officials follow when communicating with the committee. In his experience, compliance with committee veto statutes typically involves, at a minimum, the submission of a letter or form to the committee chairperson and ranking minority member providing advance notification or requesting committee approval. In some instances the full committee will meet to take action on a particular issue, but veto monitoring and compliance more often occurs through informal discussions among individual committee members. Unlike committee hearings, which require time and involvement from the entire committee, the transaction costs incurred by monitoring legislative veto compliance are often less since the entire committee need not be involved.

Hypotheses

Many studies examining the phenomenon of delegation and oversight have highlighted the increasing complexity and breadth of issues addressed by modern Congresses. Committee membership affords lawmakers with the ability to develop technical issue expertise, but there remain persistent information asymmetries between lawmakers and executive specialists (Banks and Weingast 1992; Miller and Moe 1983; Niskanen 1971). Although the legislature can obtain some information regarding policies and their cost effectiveness, there exist unavoidable uncertainties regarding policy outcomes and even potential alternatives (Calvert, McCubbins, and Weingast 1989; McCubbins 1985). With regard to exercising oversight over issues of greater complexity, Cox argues that "Congress will choose governance structures that allow future intervention as uncertainty over legislation increases. Intervention allows Congress to manage measurement and observation problems that stem from delegating authority to experts" (2004, 38). The means of intervention from Cox's study is through the reauthorization process. In a very similar fashion, the imposition of legislative vetoes to oversee delegated powers to agencies with technical expertise also provides for an institutionalized means of intervention. Because there are transaction costs associated with developing expertise in technical matters, Congress should frequently elect to delegate to agencies implementing more complex policies. Placing legislative vetoes in bills of greater complexity reserves the opportunity for legislators to intervene in some capacity as they accrue more information regarding the agency's implementation of the law.

Complex Legislation Hypothesis. *Greater numbers of legislative veto provisions will be included in bills of greater complexity passed by Congress.*

Whether through the act of delegation or other means of securing autonomy, bureaucratic agencies often enjoy some degree of insulation from Congress. Wood and Bohte (2004) portray this independence as a form of property rights afforded to agencies through enabling legislation. These powers establish a barrier between the legislature and the executive that may be difficult for Congress to break thorough should it desire to impose changes in policy. As lawmakers well know, control over the federal budget is among their most powerful resources. Although it may be difficult to directly impose changes in agency policy making given some existing degree of political insulation, control over agency and program outlays provides an alternative avenue of congressional control.

As MacDonald (2010) has shown, one way to exercise oversight through spending is by including limitation riders in appropriations legislation that expressly prohibit funds from being spent on designated activities. Legislative vetoes can also provide Congress with direct influence on how funds are spent. Rather than establishing an absolute prohibition on funds being spent for a certain activity, legislative vetoes allow for Congress to consider individual spending proposals with the option of approving or vetoing them. Influence on spending translates to an influence on policy. For example, contemporary spending bills commonly include sections designating broad categories of expenditures as subject to congressional veto such as this statute enacted through the 2012 appropriations bill for the Departments of Transportation, Housing and Urban Development, and related agencies:

> Except as otherwise provided in this Act, none of the funds provided in this Act . . . shall be available for obligation or expenditure

through a reprogramming of funds that: (1) creates a new program; (2) eliminates a program, project, or activity; (3) increases funds or personnel for any program, project, or activity for which funds have been denied or restricted by the Congress; (4) proposes to use funds directed for a specific activity by either the House or Senate Committees on Appropriations for a different purpose; (5) augments existing programs, projects, or activities in excess of $5,000,000 or 10 percent, whichever is less; (6) reduces existing programs, projects, or activities by $5,000,000 or 10 percent, whichever is less; or (7) creates, reorganizes, or restructures a branch, division, office, bureau, board, commission, agency, administration, or department different from the budget justifications submitted to the Committees on Appropriations or the table accompanying the explanatory statement accompanying this Act, whichever is more detailed, *unless prior approval is received from the House and Senate Committees on Appropriations.* (125 Stat. 707, Public Law 112–55; emphasis added)

This statute prohibits seven distinct types of expenditures unless the Appropriations Committees approve an exemption request. Committee affirmative vetoes such as this provide a valuable means of control for the spending committees. As the first two conditions note, no appropriated funds can be used by department officials to create or eliminate program established by Congress without explicit committee approval. Given the importance of appropriations legislation in prioritizing government initiatives and directing programs and policy, it is expected that legislators should be more willing to incur costs related to monitoring compliance with legislative vetoes imposed in this regard.

Appropriations Legislation Hypothesis. *Greater numbers of legislative veto provisions will be included in appropriations bills passed by Congress.*

Similarly, it is also expected that legislative vetoes should be more commonly used to oversee agencies with larger budgets. In this regard, the saliency of agency activity exists as a key transaction cost consideration. In their study of four regulatory agencies over a span of nearly 50 years, Ringquist, Worsham, and Eisner (2003) find that Congress is more likely to pass legislation directing regulatory action for publicly salient issues of greater complexity. In the latter case, they find that policies of greater complexity are more likely to elicit heightened congressional control given the uncertainty that exists regarding policy outcomes. Largely because of the electoral connection, they also argue that lawmakers will be more apt to intervene in the implementation of policies of greater salience. Using a high and low salience dichotomy, they find empirical support for this expectation as well. The present study will also consider issue salience by using agency budgets as a proxy for policy salience.

Budgetary Hypothesis. *Greater numbers of legislative veto provisions will be included in legislation affecting agencies with larger budgets.*

The Appropriations Committees

One way to reduce oversight transaction costs incurred by Congress as a whole is to charge committees with individualized oversight responsibilities (Denzau and Mackay 1983; Weingast and Marshall 1988). By analyzing the oversight role of committees, many scholars have sought to provide a more nuanced view of the oversight process (Balla 2000; Epstein and O'Halloran 1999; Hammond and Knott 1996; Whitford 2005; Wood 1988). For example, in their study of variation over time in the Federal Trade Commission's emphasis on consumer-oriented credit protection, Weingast and Moran (1983) find that the ideological preferences of the Senate and the ideological composition of certain subcommittees had a significant influence on the focus of the Federal Trade Commission. An investigation of the National Labor Relations Board finds that ideological shifts in the committees with oversight of board functions coincided with alterations in the board's regulatory assertiveness (Moe 1985). Wood and Waterman (1993) assess the frequency and substance of committee hearings as important characteristics theorized to affect four types of EPA activities, while Shipan (2004) tests the regulatory activity of the FDA from 1947 through 1995 as a function of different configurations of the ideology of committees and the chamber floor. In a variety of settings, each of these studies demonstrates that the characteristics of individual committees are consequential in affecting bureaucratic oversight and executive action. Given the shift toward a greater reliance on committee vetoes that has occurred following *Chadha*, it is important to consider the role of committees in shaping statutory oversight.

As seen in figure 3.1, the vast majority of modern legislative vetoes are committee-based. Of all the vetoes enacted by the four Congresses from 2003 to 2010, over 95 percent were committee vetoes. By comparison,

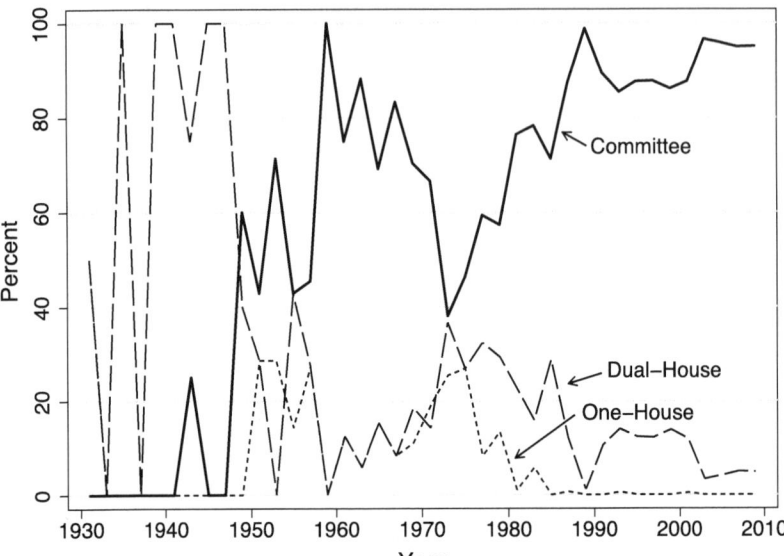

Fig. 3.1. Legislative veto statutes by veto authorization: 1931–2010

committee vetoes comprised slightly more than half of the vetoes enacted by Congresses of the 1970s. Particularly important are the Appropriations Committees in each chamber as 85 percent of the committee vetoes passed during this period have empowered the Appropriations Committees with affirmative, negative, or deliberative veto authority. It is therefore also necessary to consider characteristics of these committees within each chamber.

There are competing expectations concerning how the ideological proximity of the Appropriations Committees and their respective chamber would affect legislative veto use. One could make the case that a greater divergence of preferences between the two should make laws less apt to include veto provisions. Under such a condition, Appropriations Committee vetoes would empower committees that are either more liberal or conservative relative to the chamber's median voter with a greater influence on spending. On the other hand, because the spending committees have a strong hand in the crafting of appropriations bills, we might expect that ideologically outlying committees would strategically seek to add greater numbers of veto provisions. These alternative hypotheses will be tested through an empirical evaluation of patterns in Appropriations Committee veto use over time.

Committee-Floor Ideological Heterogeneity Hypothesis I.
Greater heterogeneity of preferences between the House and Senate Appropriations Committees and their respective chamber floors should result in a greater number of Appropriations Committee legislative veto statutes.

Committee-Floor Ideological Heterogeneity Hypothesis II.
Greater heterogeneity of preferences between the House and Senate Appropriations Committees and their respective chamber floors should result in a fewer number of Appropriations Committee legislative veto statutes.

Executive Influences

As Congress continues to use the legislative veto as a check on delegated powers, it has emerged as a significant source of macropolitical conflict. Modern presidents can, and have at various times, prevented the enactment of legislative vetoes by vetoing legislation. Near the end of 1995, President Clinton vetoed the 1996 National Defense Authorization Act, which contained 15 legislative veto provisions constraining actions of the president and secretaries of defense and energy. President Clinton emphasized his objections to these provisions in the first paragraph of his veto message to Congress by declaring that the bill "would unacceptably restrict my ability to carry out this country's national security objectives and substantially interfere with the implementation of key national defense programs. It would also restrict the President's authority in the conduct of foreign affairs and as Commander in Chief, raising serious constitutional concerns" (1995, 1929). In spite of presidential efforts such as this aimed at scaling back legislative veto oversight, Congress has continued to use different types of vetoes to serve a variety of purposes including the exertion of congressional control over budgetary decisions and the reprogramming of appropriated funds, rulemaking, and other changes in policy.

In terms of its general approach, oversight should generally become more valuable when the preferences of the executive branch deviate substantially from those of the legislature. Congress has used the legislative veto at varying degrees to oversee all 15 cabinet-level departments and many other executive agencies directed by presidential appointees. As the president deviates ideologically from Congress, it follows that administration appointees should do so as well. In addition to the power of appointment, the president has a tremendous number of ways to influence the bureaucracy including performance review, preclearance, and budgetary proposals made by the OMB. Due to the president's ability to direct the leadership and actions of cabinet-level departments and other agencies, Congress is likely to engage in more assertive oversight when the preferences of the president deviate from its own. This expectation is one of the primary hypotheses tested by Epstein and O'Halloran's study on delegation (1999). Their empirical analysis finds support for this theory and demonstrates that congressional delegation to executive agencies decreases during periods of divided government and increases under unified government. Therefore, it is expected that periods of divided government should result in greater amounts of statutory oversight activity expressed through legislative veto statutes.

Divided Government Hypothesis. *Periods of divided government should result in a greater number of legislative veto statutes.*

An additional way to assess interbranch conflict is to test for effects wrought through greater ideological polarization between the president and Congress. A number of studies have demonstrated that the degree of ideological polarization has been on the rise in recent years (McCarty, Poole, and Rosenthal 2006; Sinclair 2006; Theriault 2008). Though divided government and ideological heterogeneity are positively correlated, considering ideological proximities between the president and legislature allows for a secondary assessment of interbranch conflict and statutory oversight. Under the condition of greater ideological heterogeneity between Congress and the president, greater usage of the legislative veto is expected as a means to pull bureaucratic policy outputs toward the preferences of Congress.

Interbranch Ideological Heterogeneity Hypothesis. *Greater degrees of ideological heterogeneity between the president and the House, and the president and the Senate, should result in a greater number of legislative veto statutes.*

Similar to the interbranch ideology hypothesis, committees should also be more likely to utilize the committee veto as they deviate from the president ideologically. Thus, with respect to statutes that empower the Appropriations Committees with veto authority, an additional hypothesis expects greater numbers of committee veto enactments as the ideological preferences of the spending committees and the president diverge from one another.

Interbranch Committee Hypothesis. *Greater ideological heterogeneity between the president and the House and Senate Appropriations Committees should result in a greater number of Appropriations Committee legislative veto statutes.*

To test these hypotheses across an extended time series, it is necessary to collect data on legislative veto enactments. Since identifying congressional vetoes is a complicated enterprise, the following section discusses in detail the data collection processes.

Data Collection

In order to examine how the legislative veto has evolved following *Chadha* and the factors that affect its use, I constructed a comprehensive data set of enacted legislative veto statutes from 1931 to 2010 in a series of three phases. For phase one, a data set of legislative veto provisions was created by aggregating data from Congressional Research Service reports. During the 1970s, the Congressional Research Service produced several detailed reports that identify and often categorize acts containing legislative veto provisions (Norton 1976, 1978). Several additional reports focused on the use and conflict over the congressional veto during the years immediately before and after the *Chadha* ruling (Norton 1981a, 1981b; Cavanagh, Garcia, and Norton 1982).[2] Aggregating data from these sources provided nearly all of the veto statutes enacted before 1975. In total, the data collection process for phase one produced a data set containing 238 legislative veto statutes from 168 separate laws.

For phase two of the data collection, which corresponds to the congressional terms that served between 1975 and 1992, I created an original data set using two data collection processes. First, multiple individuals read the full text of all public laws enacted during this period in attempts to identify as many legislative veto provisions as possible.[3] Extensive training ensured that research assistants became proficient in locating veto provisions both efficiently and accurately. As a secondary means of data collection for this period, I performed an electronic keyword search of the full text of the complete collection of U.S. statutes at large using the process described in the following paragraph.[4] Phase two of the data collection process produced a data set containing 1,185 legislative veto enactments from 306 separate laws.

For phase three, which resulted in a data set containing both proposed and enacted legislative veto provisions, all enrolled bills from the 103rd through the 111th congressional terms were searched for legislative veto provisions using the THOMAS online database.[5] Procedurally, the search was executed by using a two-step process that included the identification of keywords frequently used in veto provisions, followed by a search of the complete text of bills for these words frequently utilized in the statutory language of veto provisions.[6] For example, legislative vetoes often prohibit designated administrative actions without the "advance approval" of the Appropriations Committees. Other legislative vetoes may mandate a "30-day review period," or allow Congress to nullify agency actions pursuant to a "disapproval resolution." While many variants exist, identifying the language frequently used in veto provisions allows for the compilation of a list of keyword search terms. In total, 29 different keywords were used to identify legislative veto statutes. While it is unlikely that this data collection process successfully identified every statute containing a legislative veto across this time frame, searching the full text of legislation for commonly used keywords and phrases provides a systematic process to identify bills containing legislative veto provisions. Table 3.1 lists the search terms used in this process.

The number of enacted vetoes from 1993 to 2010 varies from a low of 113 statutes in the 104th Congress to a high of 533 in the 108th Congress with an average of 265 veto statutes passed per term. Data collection for phase three produced a data set with 2,392 enacted veto statutes from 229 separate laws.

Nonexecutive Legislative Vetoes

Congressional vetoes are also occasionally implemented over the activities of institutions and officials outside of the executive branch. As a first

TABLE 3.1. Legislative veto keyword search terms

15 days	Disapproval resolution
30 days	Expressly approved
60 days	Joint resolution
Advance approval	Notification procedures
After approval	Prior approval
Appropriations Committees	Receive and approve
Approval is obtained in advance	Reporting to Congress
Approval resolution	Reprogramming
Approved by such committees	Requires approval
Approved in advance	Review period
Calendar days	Subject to the approval
Committees on Appropriations	Submit for approval
Concurrent resolution	Such committees approve
Day review	With the approval
Days elapse	Without the approval

example, a provision included in the 2006 Legislative Branch Appropriations Act stipulated that the Architect of the Capitol could not obligate funds for the Capitol Visitor Center unless the Appropriations Committees approved the spending plan (119 Stat. 579, Public Law 109–55). This veto affecting the Architect of the Capitol represents a legislative veto governing the functions of an appendage of Congress. Vetoes over legislative agencies such as this represent a different type of oversight, as separation of powers considerations are not involved. Because the primary focus of this research pertains to congressional oversight of executive bureaucracies, such statutes are omitted from the data.

In a similar fashion, Congress has at times used the veto to oversee functions of the judiciary. In most fiscal years over the past two decades, the funding bill for the federal court system has included a committee deliberative or affirmative veto. In 2010, an omnibus spending bill stipulated that the judiciary could not transfer funds from designated accounts in excess of 5 percent of the account balance without the advance approval of the Appropriations Committees (123 Stat. 3176, Public Law 111–117). For similar reasons, no judicial branch veto statutes are included as cases in the data.

Lastly, Congress has passed legislative veto statutes governing the District of Columbia. Statutes pertaining to matters of DC governance are similarly omitted from the analysis. In 1973, the District of Columbia Home Rule Act (87 Stat. 774, Public Law 93–198) made DC City Council legislation or voter referenda susceptible to congressional veto by concurrent resolution (modified to a joint resolution following *Chadha*). In addition to this generic veto, which has been invoked on just three occasions (Steinhauer 2015), legislative vetoes are often written into the DC Appropriations Act and require interaction among the mayor, city council, and Appropriations Committees (123 Stat. 654, Public Law 111–8). Omitting these three types of veto statutes yields a data set that focuses exclusively on veto constraints on executive departments, agencies, commissions, bureaus, and the president.

Analysis and Results

Chapter 2 provided a descriptive analysis of the evolution of the veto and the fundamental changes in its use since *Chadha*. The analysis presented in the following sections focuses on the factors expected to affect the use of the veto through a quantitative analysis that includes all congressional terms from 1973 to 2010. In order to test the hypotheses regarding transaction cost considerations expected to make legislative vetoes more likely, the first set of models presented in this section uses the individual law as the unit of analysis. The sample includes every law passed by Congress from 1973 to 2010. The list of public laws enacted during this period was obtained from the THOMAS website, which reports public law data extending back to 1973.[7] These 19 congressional terms passed an average of 535 laws per term for a total of 10,167 enactments. The 104th Congress enacted the fewest laws (333) and the 100th Congress enacted the most (713).

In order to examine the effects of ideological heterogeneity on legislative veto enactments, first dimension DW-NOMINATE scores were used to operationalize ideology (Poole 1998). These ideology scores are scaled such that negative values correspond to a more liberal ideological position, whereas positive values correspond to greater conservatism. For each congressional term, the median NOMINATE scores for the House and Senate were used to indicate the ideological ideal point for each chamber. Similar variables were created to indicate the ideological median of the House and Senate Appropriations Committees. In addition to these congressional measures of ideology, common space scores for Presidents Nixon through Obama are used to measure presidential ideology.[8] In order to test the effects of divergent ideological preferences among the president, House, and Senate, independent variables were created to measure the absolute distance between individual dyads of legislative and presidential ideological ideal points. Similar variables measure the absolute ideological distance from the median voter on the House Appropriations Committee and the median voter in the House, between the Senate Appropriations Committee's median voter and the Senate's median voter, as well as between the median voters of the spending committees in each chamber.

A separate variable indicating the presence of divided government is also included as a measure likely to affect legislative veto usage. This variable is coded as a 1 if either chamber is controlled by the party opposite of the incumbent president's party. Other binary independent variables indicate appropriations laws, laws that are designated as major or trivial enactments, and laws enacted by Congresses serving after the *Chadha* ruling. Laws classified as major enactments are those identified by the *Policy Agendas Project* and term-by-term summaries in *CQ Almanac*. These sources designated a total of 397 laws as significant. In order to identify legislation over matters deemed trivial in scope, I used 16 different phrases commonly used in symbolic, commemorative, or otherwise largely inconsequential legislation (see Berry 2009). These types of laws include legislation naming or renaming federal buildings; recognizing or commemorating individuals, groups, or events; making congressional proclamations; expressing the sense of Congress; and private laws for the relief of specific individuals. This systematic coding process categorized 2,438 laws as trivial. Congresses serving after 1985 are coded as belonging to the post-*Chadha* period. Finally, as a proxy for a law's complexity, a variable is included that indicates the total number of pages contained in each law (see Huber and Shipan 2002; Maltzman and Shipan 2008). Table 3.2 contains descriptive statistics for these variables.

Table 3.3 reports estimates from three models examining factors theorized to affect the number of statutes containing legislative vetoes included in a given law. The dependent variable is a simple count variable indicating the number of veto statutes per law. The average number of legislative vetoes included in the 580 laws with at least one such statute is 6.29. A zero-inflated negative binomial regression model, appropriate for this type of dependent variable, is used to analyze factors affecting this type of statutory oversight included in a law.[9] The collective results from these models demonstrate that several law-specific attributes affect whether laws include legislative vetoes. Congress is more apt to include legislative vetoes

TABLE 3.2. Descriptive statistics

Variable	Mean	Standard Deviation	Min	Max
Legislative Veto Provisions	0.36	3.80	0	145
Appropriations Committee Legislative Veto Provisions	0.25	3.58	0	141
President–House Ideology Distance	0.33	0.15	0.17	0.61
President–Senate Ideology Distance	0.37	0.20	0.17	1.21
President–House Appropriations Committee Ideology Distance	0.29	0.21	0.09	0.66
President–Senate Appropriations Committee Ideology Distance	0.30	0.13	0.11	0.55
House Floor–House Appropriations Committee Ideology Distance	0.07	0.03	0.01	0.14
Senate Floor–Senate Appropriations Committee Ideology Distance	0.07	0.14	0.00	0.80
Presidential Public Approval	50.08	11.94	24	86.6
Congressional Public Approval	37.82	12.03	13	84
Law Length	12.27	45.30	1	906
Divided Government	0.70	0.45	0	1
Appropriations Law	0.06	0.23	0	1
Major Law	0.04	0.19	0	1
Trivial Law	0.24	0.43	0	1

in spending measures, major enactments, and more complex legislation, all else equal. These results, which are consistent across each model specification, indicate that legislators are more willing to incur transaction costs regarding monitoring and enforcement for these types of laws. Unexpectedly, legislative veto statutes are not appreciably influenced by divided government or ideological polarization.

The bracketed percentages from this table indicate the predicted change in the rate of veto enactments. For continuous variables, this corresponds to the expected probability change by moving one standard devia-

TABLE 3.3. Zero-inflated negative binomial model estimates of legislative veto statutes: 1973–2010

	Model 1	Model 2	Model 3
Legislative Veto Count			
Divided Government	−0.20	—	−0.20
	(0.14)		(0.14)
President–House Ideology Distance	—	0.82	0.66
		(0.60)	(0.54)
President–Senate Ideology Distance	—	−0.18	−0.02
		(0.23)	(0.26)
Post-*Chadha* Law	−0.22	−0.32	−0.31
	(0.17)	(0.23)	(0.23)
Appropriations Law	2.20*** [7.0%]	2.21*** [3.6%]	2.18*** [10.0%]
	(0.27)	(0.27)	(0.27)
Major Law	0.85*** [50.0%]	0.83*** [48.7%]	0.89*** [50.3%]
	(0.28)	(0.28)	(0.30)
Law Length	0.01*** [0.1%]	0.01*** [0.1%]	0.01*** [0.1%]
	(0.00)	(0.00)	(0.00)
Constant	−1.53***	−1.80***	−1.71***
	(0.29)	(0.38)	(0.35)
Zero Count Inflation			
Trivial Law	28.25***	32.20***	26.11***
	(0.29)	(0.29)	(0.29)
Appropriations Law	−2.70**	−2.61**	−2.76*
	(1.30)	(1.17)	(1.44)
Major Law	−43.10***	−52.18***	−38.91***
	(1.18)	(1.08)	(1.15)
Constant	0.79*	0.79*	0.77*
	(0.46)	(0.45)	(0.47)
Alpha	4.90	4.88	4.93
N	10,167	10,167	10,167
N (Nonzero)	579	579	579
Pseudo Log-likelihood	−2853.94	−2853.98	−2852.66
Wald χ^2	335.39***	236.17***	382.73***

Note: Standard errors clustered by Congress to account for nonindependence within congressional terms are reported in parentheses. Predicted changes in the rate of legislative veto enactments in brackets were calculated using "prchange" in Stata 13. *** $p<.01$, ** $p<.05$, * $p<.10$.

tion above and below the mean while holding the remaining variables at their mean value. For binary variables, this corresponds to the expected change by moving from the absence to the presence of the variable. As seen by these estimates, whether a law is designated as a major enactment exerts the greatest effect on the frequency of veto statutes.

Because of the precipitous rise in Appropriations Committee vetoes that has occurred over time, the models presented in table 3.4 provide an analysis focusing specifically on this specific type of veto. Similar to the modeling approach from table 3.3, a zero-inflated negative binomial model is used where the dependent variable is the number of Appropriations Committee legislative veto statutes per law. With an average of 7.24 per law, 323 laws contain at least one veto of this variety.

As was the case with the prior analysis, several characteristics of individual laws emerge as significant predictors of Appropriations Committee vetoes. When considering all veto types, whether a law is designated as a major policy enactment is most determinative of legislative veto incidence. For Appropriations Committee vetoes, the most important factor is whether a bill concerns spending. Given the jurisdiction over federal spending possessed by these committees, the magnitude of this effect is to be expected. Likewise, major and lengthier enactments are significantly more likely to impose a veto statute as are laws passed after the *Chadha* ruling, although the effects of these factors are of a lesser magnitude than the binary appropriations bill variable, as one would expect.

In the first and second models, there is a dearth of evidence providing support for the ideological and partisan conflict hypotheses. The sign on the divided government variable estimate is actually negative, and only one of the four ideological heterogeneity variables significantly affects the imposition of this type of veto. Such statutes are found to be more likely when the president deviates further from the median voter on the Senate Appropriations Committee. Results from the third model paint a slightly different picture.

Greater ideological heterogeneity between the chamber floors and their respective Appropriations Committee is shown to increases the likelihood of veto statutes connected to these committees. Because the spending committees have a right of origination over appropriations bills, they are conferred with a first-mover advantage wherein legislative veto provisions may be inserted into different segments of a bill. Since lawmakers can amend these measures on the floor, it is also reasonable to expect that the survival of considerable numbers of vetoes should be less likely as the committees deviate from their respective floors. Under such a condition, the parent

TABLE 3.4. Zero-inflated negative binomial model estimates of Appropriations Committee legislative veto statutes: 1973–2010

	Model 1	Model 2	Model 3
Appropriations Committee Legislative Veto Count			
Divided Government	−0.26	—	−0.53**[0.0%]
	(0.20)		(0.19)
President–House App. Comm. Ideology Distance	—	−0.16	−0.42
		(0.56)	(0.58)
President–Senate App. Comm. Ideology Distance	—	1.51* [0.1%]	1.98***[0.1%]
		(0.79)	(0.68)
Floor–House App. Comm. Ideology Distance	—	6.05	8.16***[0.1%]
		(4.43)	(3.70)
Floor–Senate App. Comm. Ideology Distance	—	0.79	1.25***[0.1%]
		(0.50)	(0.48)
Post-*Chadha* Law	1.18*** [0.1%]	1.19*** [0.1%]	1.21***[0.0%]
	(0.31)	(0.24)	(0.21)
Appropriations Law	2.72*** [1.4%]	2.25*** [1.1%]	2.19***[1.2%]
	(0.29)	(0.34)	(0.33)
Major Law	0.37* [0.1%]	0.27	0.40**[0.1%]
	(0.21)	(0.19)	(0.18)
Law Length	0.01*** [0.0%]	0.01*** [0.0%]	0.01***[0.0%]
	(0.00)	(0.00)	(0.00)
Constant	−2.32***	−3.36***	−3.28***
	(0.41)	(0.72)	(0.57)
Zero Count Inflation			
Trivial	23.63***	24.14***	23.55***
	(0.29)	(0.28)	(0.29)
Appropriations	−3.26***	−3.20***	2.19***
	(0.38)	(0.34)	(0.35)
Major	−2.05***	−2.16	−2.09***
	(0.35)	(0.34)	(0.34)
Constant	2.62***	2.72***	2.72***
	(0.28)	(0.30)	(0.28)
Alpha	2.62	2.34	2.33
N	10,167	10,167	10,167
N (Nonzero)	323	323	323
Wald χ^2	173.42	148.24	160.51

Note: Standard errors clustered by Congress to account for non-independence within congressional terms are reported in parentheses. Predicted changes in the rate of Appropriations Committee legislative veto enactments in brackets were calculated using "prchange" in Stata 13. *** $p<.01$, ** $p<.05$, * $p<.10$.

chambers would surrender greater authority to influence a law's execution to ideologically outlying committees. The results from this model suggest that this is not the case. Presidential ideology relative to the Senate Appropriations Committee is again a significant predictor of these types of veto statutes, while the same cannot be said for the House committee.

Perhaps the most surprising result from the third model is the negative effect of divided government. In theory, legislators should be more willing to incur costs related to veto oversight when the president belongs to the opposing party. For Appropriations Committee vetoes, the opposite is actually observed. As analysis presented in the next chapter will demonstrate, presidents are more likely to veto appropriations bills relative to other types of legislation. Because of this, a possible explanation for this divided government effect could be that legislators are strategic in not including excessive numbers of veto provisions in bills due to fear of a presidential veto.

When considered in conjunction, the cumulative results from this empirical analysis demonstrate that lawmakers are much more apt to insert spending committee vetoes into appropriations bills with three additional factors also exhibiting an influence on this specific type of oversight. Notably, these results fail to demonstrate a connection among partisanship, ideology, and legislative veto enactments. These results are perhaps less surprising when considering that the escalation in the number of enacted veto statutes has occurred during periods of both Democratic and Republican control of Congress serving with presidents of both parties. In interviews conducted by the author with more than a dozen current members of Congress, nearly every lawmaker of both parties emphasized the importance of meaningful congressional oversight, believing it to be a critical aspect of their job as legislators.[10] The legislative veto was commonly cited as a useful statutory tool to help procure information and exert control over executive officials.

When asked how she would describe the oversight activities of Congress, a Democratic representative from Connecticut said that oversight actions fall into one of two categories: substantive and partisan. The congresswoman cited the highly publicized Senate Armed Services Committee hearings involving General David Petraeus in September 2007 and April 2008 as examples of highly charged partisan oversight. A Texas Republican expressed his dissatisfaction with partisan-centric oversight such as this, stating that he believed oversight of the bureaucracy to be an "essential part of what Congress does, but when done for theater it is a waste of time." These comments indicate that lawmakers of both parties are cognizant of the fact that some oversight activities undertaken by committees have a distinctly partisan agenda that may provide more in grandstanding than actual oversight. Finding that divided government has no significant effect on legislative veto enactments suggests that the imposition of the veto statutes is an oversight enterprise that is not fueled predominantly by partisanship.

Binder (2001, 2003), Binder and Maltzman (2009), Cox and McCubbins (1991), Fiorina (2003), Howell et al. (2000), Mayhew (1991), and many other scholars have devoted considerable attention to examining the effects of divided government. Challenging the prevailing conventional wisdom, Mayhew found no significant difference in the production of major legislative enactments when comparing divided and unified government. However, Maltzman and Shipan (2008) demonstrate that laws enacted during periods of divided government have a greater likelihood of subsequent revision. Further analysis by Mayhew (1991) demonstrated that congressional investigations of the executive did not appreciably increase during periods of divided government. Examining presidential appointee confirmation rates for judicial and executive appointments, and the use of executive agreements relative to treaties, Fiorina (2003) similarly finds few substantial differences across these regime types. Though a number of studies argue that the consequences of divided government are less severe than one might otherwise expect, analysis by other scholars refute this claim.

Among these studies finding more pronounced effects of divided government, Binder (2001, 2003) identifies greater levels of legislative gridlock, Binder and Maltzman (2009) demonstrate that presidential appointments to circuit court vacancies are less likely to be confirmed, and Howell et al. (2000) find that landmark enactments decrease by a magnitude of about 30 percent. From this sampling of research on divided government, it seems clear that there is no consensus on its consequences. Regarding the use of the legislative veto over the past several decades, this study finds itself more aligned with those finding more attenuated effects of divided government. This finding suggests that members of Congress from both parties generally seek to employ the legislative veto as unique problem-solving device—one that does not revolve principally around partisan agendas (Adler and Wilkerson 2012).

Summary

This chapter has provided a theoretical framework based on transaction costs as the means to assess the legislative veto's oversight role. The considerable growth of the federal bureaucracy throughout American history, particularly during the twentieth century, coincided with greater delegation to the executive branch. Often bureaucrats are empowered to determine many parameters of how policies are put into operation. Decisions to delegate and engage in oversight are wrought with transaction costs that lawmakers incur by monitoring and enforcing bureaucratic contracts. It is expected that increased issue complexity, political conflict, and salience should each make veto oversight more likely.

Research focusing on oversight has surveyed many instruments that Congress can employ to influence the bureaucracy to minimize problems of agency loss. Careful design of enabling statutes serves as an initial step to guide the implementation of the law. When delegating to executive agencies, Congress often imposes legislative veto requirements that allow for a continued legislative influence in a law's execution. Oversight expressed in this manner serves as a particularly appealing arrangement, as it allows Congress to secure many of the benefits of delegation while conditioning bureaucratic functions as susceptible to congressional intervention.

The empirical analysis found that a number of law-specific factors did significantly predict veto incidence. Since 1973, legislative vetoes are more likely to be included in more complex laws, appropriations measures, and major enactments. Under these conditions, legislators are more willing to incur the costs connected to veto oversight. Conversely, interbranch partisan and ideological differences were found to exert little influence on these types of statutes. These results comport with those from existing research demonstrating that other government functions are also somewhat resistant to the party configuration of the national government (Mayhew 1991; Fiorina 2003). An exception to this was found in the analysis of Appropriations Committee legislative vetoes where these particular types of vetoes were found to be more likely when the president and the Senate Appropriations Committee diverge from one another ideologically. Greater numbers of vetoes connected to the spending committees were also seen as these committees exhibit greater ideological heterogeneity relative to their respective chamber floors. This legislative veto variant is by far the most common of the post-*Chadha* era, so it is notable that there are some differences in factors affecting its use when compared to all other types. With this foundation, the following chapter approaches the controversy surrounding Congress's increased use of the legislative veto from the president's perspective.

FOUR

"Congressional Aggrandizement"
The Persistence of Presidential Opposition

The proliferation of legislative veto statutes that occurred during the 1970s provided incumbent presidents with many opportunities to speak out against their legitimacy. These opportunities were often seized. Staking out a new and emboldened position on the veto, President Carter announced in 1978 that the administration would not recognize the legality of any committee, one-House, or dual-House veto, but would instead provide advance notice to Congress only in the interest of interbranch comity (Fisher 1993). Responding to questions about how President Carter would respond to a legislative veto of a foreign arms sale, Attorney General Griffin Bell indicated that the president would not be bound to comply with the congressional dictum, but in the interest of interbranch cooperation may acquiesce provided the president did not strongly favor the transaction (Fisher 1993). The inauguration of President Reagan provided brief optimism for legislative veto supporters in Congress since he had publicly endorsed the oversight device prior to his Electoral College victory (Gazell and Pugh 1987). Moreover, at the Republican National Convention held in Detroit where Governor Reagan was nominated, party leaders inserted a statement supporting the legislative veto into the party platform that cited concerns over the "unremitting delegation of authority to the rule-makers by successive Democratic Congresses and the abuse of that authority have led to our current crisis of overregulation" (Republican Party Platform 1980).

Despite these affirmations from the president-elect and the Republican National Convention, once elected the Reagan administration's position on the legislative veto was virtually no different than its predecessor.

Why the sudden change in position? As the leader of the veto movement, Congressman Levitas recalls a frank conversation he had in the Senate with Republican congressman Trent Lott and incumbent Vice President George H. W. Bush where Bush informed them that the administration would not support measures to impose legislative vetoes over executive branch actions. Informing the two of this abrupt change in position, Bush stated, "You've got to understand that at the time we endorsed the legislative veto we weren't in the government. Now we are."[1] Levitas lamented that "when it wasn't his [Reagan's] administration, he was in favor of that type of check on the executive branch. Once it became his administration, the attitude was different." Expressing his displeasure about this change of position in testimony before a Senate Judiciary subcommittee, Levitas rightly stated that the Republican platform and Governor Reagan's positions in support of the legislative veto were "very clear," but blamed "a bug known as Potomac fever that bites people once they get to Washington and they forget what it was they came here to do to begin with."[2] The change of course by the administration intensified conflicts over the oversight role of the legislative veto as Congress began enacting in excess of 100 veto statutes per term. As this trend escalated, presidents began using retaliatory measures, such as the presidential veto and signing statement, more assertively.

Presidential Vetoes as Efforts to Control Bureaucracy

In addition to serving as an agent of Congress, the bureaucracy answers to the president by virtue of being chief executive. Through appointments, executive orders, signing statements, directives, and budgets, the president has a variety of tools to guide the direction of the policies made by executive officials (P. Cooper 2002; Howell 2003). After the 2010 and 2012 elections, President Obama has touted many of these options to make policy when faced with an intransigent Congress. Among the most powerful of these resources is the presidential veto.

Since statutes containing legislative vetoes are codified through the legislative process, the president is afforded a powerful role in the imposition of this oversight technique. The presidential veto allows presidents to single-handedly prevent the passage of legislation with majority support in both the House and the Senate. As one would expect, use of the veto has varied quite significantly over time. On average, presidents veto 60 bills during their tenure in office (Galemore 2001). President Franklin Roosevelt exercised the power most often by vetoing 635 bills, which corresponds to 25 percent of all presidential vetoes in American history. In contrast, eight American presidents—all prior to the twentieth century—did not veto a single piece of legislation. Table 4.1 presents veto data for each president from Hoover to Obama.

Early studies of presidential vetoes typically examined aggregate data and sought to explain variations in veto usage across administrations, congressional terms, or years (Copeland 1983; Lee 1975; Rohde and Simon 1985; Spitzer 1988). Subsequent studies have used independent variables including divided government, party support in Congress, amount of legislation passed by Congress, presidential popularity, and various economic and electoral indicators, among others (Cameron 2000; J. Gilmour 2002; Horr 1991; Shields and Huang 1995, 1997; R. Watson 1993; Woolley 1991). In large part, these explanatory variables capture institutional and contextual factors theorized to make presidential vetoes more or less likely. Notably few studies have specifically examined the content of legislation passed by Congress as an explanatory variable affecting the propensity of presidents to veto legislation (for exceptions, see Cameron 2000; J. Gilmour 2002).

TABLE 4.1. Presidential vetoes and signing statements: 1929–2014

President	Years	Vetoes	Vetoes Overridden (%)	Signing Statements	Constitutional Signing Statements (%)
Hoover	1929–1933	37	3 (8.1)	16	0 (0.0)
Roosevelt	1933–1945	635	9 (1.4)	44	0 (0.0)
Truman	1945–1953	250	12 (4.8)	107	2 (1.9)
Eisenhower	1953–1961	181	2 (1.1)	145	9 (6.2)
Kennedy	1961–1963	21	0 (0.0)	36	0 (0.0)
Johnson	1963–1969	30	0 (0.0)	177	9 (5.1)
Nixon	1969–1974	43	7 (16.3)	117	6 (5.1)
Ford	1974–1977	66	12 (18.2)	137	14 (10.2)
Carter	1977–1981	31	2 (6.5)	228	30 (13.2)
Reagan	1981–1989	78	9 (11.5)	249	84 (33.7)
Bush	1989–1993	44	1 (2.3)	228	122 (53.5)
Clinton	1993–2001	37	2 (5.4)	380	86 (22.6)
Bush	2001–2009	12	4 (33.3)	161	129 (80.1)
Obama	2009–2014	2	0 (0.0)	33	17 (51.5)
Total		1,467	63 (4.3)	2,058	508 (24.7)

Note: Presidential veto data: http://www.senate.gov/reference/Legislation/Vetoes/vetoCounts.htm#2. Signing statement data: http://www.presidency.ucsb.edu/signingstatements.php

Advancing beyond aggregate analyses of veto use, Cameron's (2000) analysis differentiates among types of legislation presented to the president by classifying bills into landmark, major, ordinary, and minor categories. Progressing further down this path, Gilmour's (2002) study uses several bill-level characteristics expected to affect presidential veto propensity. The primary factors the study considers concern majority and minority party opposition to a given bill as well as the president's position on it. His analysis generally finds that each of these factors, exempting majority party opposition in the Senate, do affect the use of the veto. However, the sample used in the study includes only about 10 percent of bills passed by Congress over a span of nine nonconsecutive terms. By restricting the sample in this manner, the study investigates a little over half of the vetoes issued by presidents during these terms.

A key question posed in this chapter is whether presidents have systematically used the veto as a resource to prevent the imposition of legislative veto requirements. By accounting for the number of veto provisions included in bills sent to the president and using the full universe of bills from 1989 to 2010, the analysis aspires to build on existing research by modeling bill-level characteristics expected to make presidential vetoes more likely.

The Persistence of Presidential Opposition

Presidents have frequently expressed concerns regarding the use of the legislative veto during periods of divided government. This is to be expected since such statutes allow majorities of the opposing party to veto executive branch actions. However, it is important to make clear that presidents have maintained a consistent opposition to the veto during periods of unified government as well. Statements made by recent presidents serving during at least one term of unified government help demonstrate the degree of this opposition.

Upon receiving the news that an appellate court had ruled against the legislative veto as the *Chadha* case progressed to the Supreme Court, President Carter responded positively by stating that the ruling "sustains the position that I and many of my predecessors have taken in signing into law otherwise meritorious bills containing a legislative veto provision under which a resolution of one or both Houses can nullify an executive branch action" (1981, 2836). President Carter's position on the veto is especially notable since Democrats held 292 seats in the House during his first two years in office and 277 seats in the following term. The Democratic advantage in the Senate was also substantial with 61 and 58 seats, respectively. And yet, despite the sizeable partisan advantage in Congress, the president worked assiduously to prevent members of Congress from interfering with the execution of the law.

Presidents Bill Clinton, George W. Bush, and Barack Obama each opposed the use of the legislative veto during periods of unified government as well. President Clinton refused to recognize the legal status of many vetoes passed by the 103rd Congress controlled by Democrats, and President Bush maintained this position during his first six years in office when Republican majorities existed on Capitol Hill. In 2001, when signing appropriations legislation for the Department of Agriculture and the FDA, President Bush declared, "The Administration also objects to a number of provisions in the Committee bill that would require congressional approval before Executive Branch execution. The Administration will interpret these provisions to require only notification of Congress, since any other interpretation would contradict the Supreme Court ruling in *INS v. Chadha*" (Bush 2001a, 1457). President Obama likewise followed suit. On the occasion of signing an omnibus spending bill into law during the first year of his presidency, he declared, "Numerous provisions of the legislation purport to condition the authority of officers to spend or reallocate funds on the approval of congressional committees. These are impermissible forms of legislative aggrandizement in the execution of the laws other than by enactment of statutes. Therefore, although my Administration will notify the relevant committees before taking the specified actions, and will accord the recommendations of such committees all appropriate and serious consideration, spending decisions shall not be treated as dependent on the approval of congressional committees" (Obama 2009, 217). As seen in each of these instances, presidents have consistently opposed legislative veto oversight even when their own party holds congressional majorities.

Based on the expressions of these recent presidents as well as their predecessors, it is clearly not the case that the chief executive's position on the veto has been conditional upon which party controls Congress. For this reason, when Congress includes legislative veto provisions in legislation sent to the president, all else equal, presidents should be more apt to utilize the presidential veto in order to prevent the enactment of such statutory oversight requirements. Greater numbers of legislative veto provisions included in legislation should increase the likelihood that the president will use the veto. This is the first hypothesis tested in this chapter.

Presidential Veto Hypothesis. *Increases in the number of legislative veto provisions included in legislation presented to the president will result in a greater likelihood of a presidential veto.*

The Presidential Signing Statement

Given the president's veto power and the unequivocal opposition to the legislative veto held by presidents since the New Deal, one may question why presidents are not persistently using their veto pen to prevent the enactment of bills containing legislative vetoes. Absent supermajority coalitions in both chambers, presidents could completely eradicate the legislative veto by simply exercising the presidential veto with impunity. In theory, presidents could pursue an obstructionist approach such as this; however, it is not an altogether realistic strategy when considering the types of bills that Congress often uses as vehicles for legislative vetoes.

Cognizant of the president's veto capability, Congress frequently inserts legislative veto provisions in legislation that the president would have some difficulty in consistently vetoing. Unlike Thomas Jefferson's radical assertion in the Declaration of Independence concerning equality at birth among all individuals, all bills are not created equal. In their study investigating bill success, Adler and Wilkerson (2005) distinguish among different types of legislation: compulsory, discretionary, and trivial. Reauthorizations, regular appropriations, and emergency appropriations are considered as compulsory or "must pass" bills. Trivial bills include technical amendments, land conveyances, commemorative, tariff, and private bills. The remaining subset of bills falls under the discretionary category.[3]

Aware that authorizing and spending bills must pass in order to maintain a functioning federal government, legislators have strategically included legislative veto provisions in bills that are compulsory in nature. Most often, Congress inserts vetoes into major appropriations bills. While presidents have the option to veto these bills (as President Clinton did on multiple occasions in 1995 and 1996, which culminated in a federal government shutdown), it is unlikely that they would repeatedly veto spending bills simply because they contain legislative veto provisions.[4] Given this reality, modern presidents have used alternative resources to affect oversight statutes imposed by Congress. The most notable of these resources is the signing statement.

Kelley and Marshall (2008) describe the signing statement as a "multipurpose device" (250). At different times, presidents have used the signing statement (1) as a rhetorical device to garner attention from the press and public, (2) to provide instructions for executive branch officials regarding the president's preferred means of policy implementation, (3) as a means of influencing the courts, and (4) to single out constitutional defects that need correction. To some degree, the issuance of signing statements protesting legislative veto provisions is done with each of these four purposes in mind. In additional to presidential veto data, table 4.1 also presents the number of signing statements issued by presidents from 1929 to the present.

The total number of signing statements issued by presidents has spiked since the Vietnam War. Frequent use of the statement to make constitutional protestations, however, is a more recent phenomenon. Scholars have credited the Reagan administration as a turning point in signing statement usage (P. Cooper 2002; Kelley 2006, 2007a; Kelley and Marshall 2008). According to my analysis of all presidential signing statements issued since the Reagan administration, more than 40 percent of the 1,039 signing statements made at least one constitutional objection to a section of the newly enacted law. Many of these statements challenged multiple statutes as they became part of the U.S. Code. When excluding commemorative and symbolic legislation, presidents have attached a constitutional signing statement to about one of every 12 laws enacted by the federal government. President Bush in particular was unparalleled in his use of the signing statement to challenge multiple sections of law.

It was not uncommon for individual signing statements issued by President Bush to contain objections to more than 30 newly enacted statutes. Nearly half of the 129 constitutional signing statements he issued made at least one direct reference to a legislative veto provision included in the law (Berry 2009). Often President Bush declared that such sections would not be executed as written, stating that the administration would implement law in a manner that conforms with its understanding of the Constitution and the Supreme Court's *Chadha* ruling. Although controversial legislative veto statutes remain part of the U.S. Code, President Bush and other modern presidents of both parties have sought to use signing statements to impose a de facto nullification of dozens of oversight statutes written by Congress. The actual success of these efforts is questionable.

As the number of signing statements issued has gone up, so too have the number of statutes challenged in each individual statement. According to Bradley and Posner (2006), President Carter made constitutional protestations to 39 sections of law enacted during his four-year term. This number increased to 129 and 169 under Presidents Reagan and George H. W. Bush, respectively. President Clinton used the signing statement to identify 144 sections as constitutionally objectionable during the 1990s, while President George W. Bush did the same for more than 1,100 sections of enacted law (Kelley and Marshall 2009). For comparison, a total of 92 statutes were challenged through signing statements from 1789 to 1980 (May 1998). Amazingly, the cumulative number of statutes challenged over a 200-year period was surpassed by President Bush in a single signing statement issued in 2004 that made objections to more than 100 sections of a 658-page bill that he nonetheless signed into law. Nearly half of these sections included legislative vetoes that empowered Congress or individual committees with capabilities to oversee the law's execution. It is extremely common, although not often to this magnitude, for signing statements to profess strident objections to many legislative veto provisions included in bills.

Judging by these trends, it is apparent that the signing statement has been transformed from its more innocuous origins to a controversial unilateral power of the president (Berry 2009; P. Cooper 2005). A second hypothesis expects that in the absence of a presidential veto, presidents will employ the signing statement to single out legislative veto statutes in new laws as contestable on constitutional grounds. In this capacity, presidents can exert countervailing pressures to legislative veto requirements, each seeking to affect the implementation of the law.

Signing Statement Hypothesis. *Increases in the number of legislative veto provisions included in legislation presented to the president will result in a greater likelihood of the issuance of a presidential signing statement.*

Legislative and Presidential Vetoes

Table 4.2 presents the results from four models estimated to test whether bills containing legislative vetoes affect the likelihood that presidents will exercise their veto power. The sample used for these four models consists of all enrolled bills, which are bills passed by both the House and the Senate, from 1989 to 2010. This time frame is selected due to the availability of enrolled bills data on the THOMAS website. There are a total of 6,289 enrolled bills over these 11 congressional terms. The 101st Congress passed the most, with 768, while the 413 bills passed during the 104th Congress are the fewest in the sample. Presidents George H. W. Bush, Clinton, George W. Bush, and Obama issued a combined 95 vetoes over this span, with 19 of those being pocket vetoes. President George H. W. Bush vetoed 44 bills, President Clinton vetoed 37 bills, President George

W. Bush issued 12 vetoes, and President Obama issued 2 vetoes during his first term in office. As the presidential veto hypothesis expects increases in legislative veto provisions to correspond with a greater likelihood of a presidential veto, the dependent variable in each of the models is a dichotomous variable indicating whether the president vetoed the bill.[5]

The primary independent variable of interest—ranging from zero to 145—indicates the total number of legislative veto provisions contained in a bill. The mean number of vetoes included per enrolled bill is 0.36. Additional independent variables included as predictors of presidential vetoes are two partisan polarization variables that measure the degree of the interbranch ideological heterogeneity between the president and each chamber. Again, these variables measure the absolute difference between the median voter in each chamber and the president's ideal point estimate. A dichotomous variable indicating the presence of divided government is also included in three of the models.[6] Binary variables for the Clinton, George W. Bush, and Obama administrations are included to control for the individual characteristics of the four presidents that may affect their veto propensity. Since the sample of congressional terms spans four presidencies, the coefficient estimates on these variables indicate whether each president was more apt to veto legislation, holding all other variables constant, relative to President George H. W. Bush. Two additional dichotomous variables indicate whether a bill is coded as a trivial or appropriations enactment. Lastly, presidential and congressional approval data are included in the fourth model.[7]

The results across each of the four logit model specifications presented in table 4.2 are quite consistent.[8] The principal result to emphasize is that in every model, holding all else constant, greater numbers of legislative veto provisions included in legislation sent to the president significantly increase the likelihood of a presidential veto. This finding is notable for several reasons. First, it demonstrates that presidents are more apt to use their veto power to block legislative enactments containing high numbers of legislative veto provisions. This legislative obstruction allows the president to independently prevent the passage of oversight statutes whereby Congress reserves a direct influence on how a law will be executed. In effect, the president is fighting fire with fire by using the presidential veto to prevent the enactment of legislative vetoes. President Clinton vetoed the bill with the greatest number of legislative vetoes when he prevented the enactment of the 1999 foreign operations appropriations bill, which contained about 50 such provisions (H.R. 2606, 106th Congress). Spending bills constitute nearly all of the cases when presidents vetoed bills containing 20 or more legislative vetoes. However, as models 3 and 4 demonstrate, the number of legislative veto provisions included in bills sent to the president remains a significant predictor of presidential vetoes even when controlling for whether a bill is a spending measure. Second, this analysis is one of very few that accounts for the content of legislation passed by Congress as a factor in determining whether the president will ultimately elect to veto the bill. Further research on presidential veto usage may continue in this line of inquiry by more precisely considering additional bill-specific characteristics theorized to elicit a presidential veto.

Regarding the remaining variables, as expected, presidents are significantly more likely to veto legislation during periods of divided government. The same is true for periods of greater interbranch ideological polarization as seen in the second model. Because the divided govern-

TABLE 4.2. Logit Model Estimates of Presidential Vetoes: 1989–2010

Variable	Model 1	Model 2	Model 3	Model 4
Number of Legislative Veto Provisions	0.05** [0.11%] (0.02)	0.05** [0.10%] (0.02)	0.03** [0.03%] (0.01)	0.03* [0.02%] (0.01)
Divided Government	3.98** [2.21%] (1.87)	—	3.47*** [0.76%] (1.07)	3.40*** [0.68%] (1.02)
House–President Ideology Distance	—	11.22*** [1.13%] (2.81)	—	—
Senate–President Ideology Distance	—	0.74** [0.08%] (0.37)	—	—
W. Bush Administration	−0.97*[−0.46%] (0.59)	−2.45*** [−0.99%] (0.83)	−1.02 (0.72)	−1.62*** [−0.29%] (0.44)
Clinton Administration	−0.28 (0.28)	0.73 (0.51)	−0.53*** [−0.11%] (0.27)	−0.61*** [−0.11%] (0.17)
Obama Administration	2.05 (1.91)	4.75** [27.2%] (2.40)	1.46 (1.09)	1.46 (1.02)
Trivial Enactment	—	—	−3.42*** [−0.92%] (0.36)	−3.42*** [−0.85%] (0.37)
Appropriations Enactment	—	—	1.02*** [0.37%] (0.21)	1.05*** [0.35%] (0.24)
Presidential Approval	—	—	—	−0.05*** [−0.13%] (0.02)
Congressional Approval	—	—	—	0.02* [0.06%] (0.01)
Constant	−7.50*** (1.91)	−12.24*** (3.14)	−6.48*** (1.10)	−3.57*** (0.99)
N	6,289	6,289	6,289	6,289
Pseudo R²	0.0937	0.1103	0.1948	0.2118
Percent Correctly Classified	98.5	98.5	98.5	98.5

Note: Standard errors clustered by Congress are reported in parentheses. *** $p<.01$, ** $p<.05$, * $p<.10$. Predicted probability changes calculated using "prchange" in Stata 13 are reported in brackets.

ment variable is correlated with the interbranch House and Senate polarization variables at 0.77 and 0.63, respectively, subsequent models include only the divided government indicator, which significantly affects veto likelihood in each. The only unexpected result from these models is the effect of the public approval variables. Although one would expect more popular presidents to have greater political capital in bargaining with Congress and therefore utilize the veto more frequently, we actually observe the opposite. The converse is also true when examining the relationship between congressional approval and veto issuance where presidents are more likely to veto bills when faced with a Congress with higher approval levels.

The bracketed percentages in table 4.2 indicate the change in predicted probabilities for each of the variables with a statistically significant coefficient estimate across the four model specifications. For continuous variables, the percentage indicates the change in expected probability of a presidential veto when moving from a one-half standard deviation below the variable's mean to a one-half standard deviation above the mean, holding all other variables constant at their mean values. For binary variables, the percentage corresponds to the expected change in veto likelihood when shifting from the variables absence to its presence. Most variables, including legislative veto provisions, exert a substantively small, yet statistically significant, effect on veto likelihood. In the first two models the insertion of an additional legislative veto provision increases presidential veto likelihood by about 0.1 percent. An alternative model specification that is not reported—replacing the legislative veto count variable with a binary variable indicating whether a bill contains a veto—also positively affects the likelihood that the president will issue a veto. Holding all else constant, the change in predicted veto probability for this dichotomous variable is about 3 percent in most model specifications.

In sum, although presidential vetoes are a relatively rare phenomenon, this analysis demonstrates that greater numbers of legislative veto provisions included in legislation corresponds to a significantly greater probability of a presidential veto. Overall the models do a good job in explaining veto occurrences with each correctly classifying 98.5 percent of bills. One potential critique of this finding is that these models do not account for presidential veto threats, which could influence the content of legislation ultimately sent to the president's desk. For bills that do reach the president, those containing legislative veto provisions are at a greater risk of being vetoed. Similar analyses were conducted in order to test the presidential signing statement hypothesis.

Presidential Signing Statements

Table 4.3 presents a series of models testing the hypothesis regarding presidential signing statements. The sample used for this analysis includes all 10,167 public laws enacted from 1973 to 2010. While the previous analysis used enrolled bills as the unit of analysis, the signing statement models use public laws. This modified approach is necessary since presidents cannot issue a signing statement for an enrolled bill that was vetoed or unsigned. A benefit of this is also a larger sample size due to public law data availability.

The dependent variable for the first two models is a binary variable indicating whether the president issued a signing statement when signing a bill into law. Over this period, an average Congress enacted 535 laws, 78 of which received a signing statement. In total, presidents issued a total of 1,414 signing statements.[9] The dependent variable for the second pair of models is a dichotomous variable indicating whether the president issued a signing statement containing at least one constitutional objection to a section of the law. The number of such signing statements issued per congressional term ranges from a minimum of three issued by Presidents Nixon and Ford during the 93rd Congress to a maximum of 62 issued by President George H. W. Bush during the 102nd Congress. Across the entire sample, presidents issued a total of 469 constitutional signing statements. A logit analysis is used to model factors associated with signing statement use since the values for the dependent variable are 0 or 1.

Models 1 and 3 include 15 independent variables. The only difference in the specification of models 2 and 4 is the omission of the divided government variable in lieu of two variables indicating ideological heterogeneity between the president and each chamber of Congress. In all four models, the main variable of interest is the total number of legislative veto statutes included in each law. In the sample, 579 laws contain at least one legislative veto. The average number of veto provisions included in these laws is slightly greater than six. Recall that the signing statement hypothesis expects a greater likelihood of signing statement issuance when presidents sign bills containing legislative vetoes into law. Greater numbers of veto provisions should increase this probability.

In each model, the coefficient on the legislative veto variable is both significant and positive. This provides consistent empirical support for the signing statement hypothesis. Presidents are also more likely to attach signing statements to more lengthy legislation, major enactments, appropriations bills, and bills with greater numbers of cosponsors. Divided government and presidential approval are the only two variables in the first

TABLE 4.3. Logit model estimates of presidential signing statements: 1973–2010

Variable	All Signing Statements		Constitutional Signing Statements	
	Model 1	Model 2	Model 3	Model 4
Number of Legislative Veto Provisions	0.08** [2.64%] (0.04)	0.08** [2.59%] (0.04)	0.08** [0.45%] (0.04)	0.08** [0.45%] (0.04)
Divided Government	0.08 (0.27)	—	−0.28 (0.42)	—
House–President Ideology Distance	—	1.44 (0.96)	—	3.77*** [0.79%] (1.37)
Senate–President Ideology Distance	—	0.19 (0.25)	—	−0.76** [−0.22%] (0.39)
Major Enactment	0.49** [4.89%] (0.23)	0.48** [4.74%] (0.23)	0.36 (0.32)	0.37 (0.33)
Trivial Enactment	−2.46*** [−13.86%] (0.30)	−2.44*** [−13.69%] (0.30)	−4.32*** [−4.03%] (0.74)	−4.29*** [3.88%] (0.74)
Enactment Length	0.01*** [2.88%] (0.00)	0.01*** [2.92%] (0.00)	0.01*** [0.48%] (0.00)	0.01*** [0.49%] (0.00)
Appropriations Enactment	0.90*** [10.33%] (0.26)	0.90*** [10.31%] (0.26)	1.07*** [2.58%] (0.22)	1.07*** [2.51%] (0.23)
Cosponsors	0.00*** [1.69%] (0.00)	0.00*** [1.71%] (0.00)	0.00** [0.14%] (0.00)	0.00** [0.16%] (0.00)
Presidential Approval	0.01 (0.01)	0.01 (0.01)	0.01 (0.01)	0.00 (0.01)
Presidential Fixed Effects				
Nixon	1.72*** [25.95%] (0.41)	1.52*** [21.59%] (0.25)	0.24 (0.53)	−0.71** [−0.75%] (0.29)
Ford	2.06*** [32.07%] (0.32)	2.03*** [31.37%] (0.17)	1.10* [2.61%] (0.57)	0.57 (0.58)
Carter	2.39*** [38.14%] (0.19)	2.32*** [36.29%] (0.18)	1.29*** [3.21%] (0.27)	1.16*** [2.63%] (0.24)
Reagan	1.73*** [20.94] (0.30)	1.62*** [19.11%] (0.19)	1.98*** [5.43%] (0.40)	1.53*** [3.47%] (0.26)
H.W. Bush	2.39*** [38.09%] (0.31)	2.36*** [37.31%] (0.22)	3.09*** [17.50%] (0.39)	2.63*** [11.76%] (0.25)
Clinton	2.96*** [34.14%] (0.24)	1.86*** [24.98%] (0.27)	1.81*** [5.25%] (0.39)	0.83** [1.57%] (0.35)
W. Bush	1.31*** [15.49%] (0.23)	0.80* [8.16%] (0.43)	2.38*** [8.65%] (0.24)	1.14*** [2.42%] (0.48)
Constant	−4.31*** (0.43)	−4.48*** (0.38)	−5.93*** (0.47)	−5.84*** (0.33)
Pseudo R^2	0.1517	0.1539	0.2252	0.2306
N	10,167	10,167	10,167	10,167
Percent Correctly Classified	86.8	86.9	95.8	95.8

Note: Standard errors clustered by Congress are reported in parentheses. *** $p<.01$, ** $p<.05$, * $p<.10$. Predicted probability changes calculated using "prchange" in Stata 13 are reported in brackets.

model that do not exert a significant effect on signing statement use. These results hold when focusing specifically on signing statements making at least one constitutional objection with the exception of the major enactment variable, which does not achieve statistical significance.

Again, the bracketed percentages reports predicted probability changes for each of the variables shown to significantly affect signing statement use. Appropriations bills are 10 percent more likely to receive a signing statement and major enactments have an increased probability of about half that amount. The substantive effect of the legislative veto variable ranges from 2.6 to 0.5 percent. Replicating these models with a legislative veto dummy variable in lieu of the count measure corresponds to increased probability that a constitutional signing statement will be issued by nearly 10 percent.

Figure 4.1 provides a graphic illustration of the effect legislative veto provisions have on the likelihood of the president issuing a signing statement. Using the CLARIFY software developed by King, Tomz, and Wittenberg (2000), this figure shows the effect of including additional veto provisions in passed legislation on presidential signing statement probability. This figure uses the first model specification from table 4.3. The x-axis ranges from zero to more than 95 veto provisions included in legislation presented to the president. Holding each of the other independent variables at their mean value, the y-axis represents the predicted probability estimates of a signing statement being issued. The solid trend line indicates the predicted probability estimates and the dash lines represent the upper and lower bounds of the 95 percent confidence interval around these estimates.

When Congress passes a bill containing zero legislative veto provisions, there is a probability of about 10 percent that it will receive a signing statement. As the number of veto provisions increases, the predicted probability of a signing statement increases as well. This probability estimate exceeds 50 percent when a bill has eight veto provisions. As seen in the figure, the confidence intervals surrounding several legislative veto provision values are wider in certain sections. For a bill containing 10 veto provisions, the 95 percent confidence interval ranges from a predicted probability of 18 percent to 56 percent. A bill with 30 vetoes has an estimated signing statement probably between 50 percent and 99 percent. As the number of veto provisions increase further, the confidence intervals shrink and converge around a probability of one. This occurred just months into the Obama administration when the president attached a signing statement that made objections to over 50 provisions in an omnibus spending bill that included more than 100 legislative vetoes (123 Stat. 524, Public Law 111–8). The use of the signing statement in this manner by President Obama elicited some controversy.

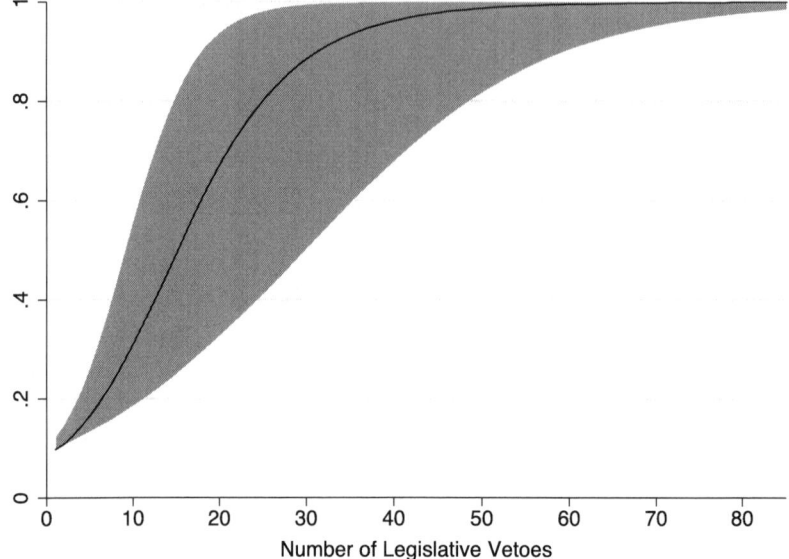

Fig. 4.1. Predicted signing statement probability

President Obama and the Signing Statement

All of the models presented in table 4.3 include presidential fixed effects variables to control for variations in signing statement usage across administrations. President Obama is the omitted president in this panel of dichotomous variables, meaning that these variable estimates capture differences in signing statement issuance relative to Obama. Since each of individual presidency coefficients is positive and significant in the first model, this demonstrates that all presidents from Nixon through George W. Bush were more inclined to use signing statements than President Obama. Likewise, all presidents save Nixon have used the constitutional signing statement more than Obama. An explanation for this can be found in public statements made by Obama when campaigning for the presidency in 2008.

In an interview with the *Boston Globe* during the presidential election primary season, Senator Obama indicated that he would not use the signing statement in the manner that past presidents, specifically President Bush, have employed it. Outlining his perspective on the issue, Obama stated,

> While it is legitimate for a president to issue a signing statement to clarify his understanding of ambiguous provisions of statutes and to

explain his view of how he intends to faithfully execute the law, it is a clear abuse of power to use such statements as a license to evade laws that the President does not like or as an end-run around provisions designed to foster accountability.

I will not use signing statements to nullify or undermine congressional instructions as enacted into law. The problem with this administration is that it has attached signing statements to legislation in an effort to change the meaning of the legislation, to avoid enforcing certain provisions of the legislation that the President does not like, and to raise implausible or dubious constitutional objections to the legislation. The fact that President Bush has issued signing statements to challenge over 1100 laws—more than any president in history—is a clear abuse of this prerogative. No one doubts that it is appropriate to use signing statements to protect a president's constitutional prerogatives; unfortunately, the Bush Administration has gone much further than that. (Savage 2007)

Relative to previous presidents, Obama has used the signing statement with less frequency. By the end of 2014, 17 of the 33 signing statements issued by President Obama made constitutional objections to nearly 140 statutes. When considered in this context, it is clear that Obama has definitely not abandoned this controversial practice, but merely curtailed it.

Whether this scaled-back use of the signing statement constitutes an "abuse of this prerogative" is debatable (Crouch, Rozell, and Sollenberger 2013). White House press secretary Jay Carney explained the seeming disconnect between Obama's words and actions by asserting that the President Obama has made clear his belief that presidents "must retain the right, to have signing statements, to raise constitutional concerns and objections with a law passed by Congress that he signed into law. His [Obama's] concern was with what he saw as an abuse of the signing statement by the previous administration" (White House Press Briefing 2011). President Obama himself explained his rationale for using the signing statement in this manner in 2013 when signing a defense spending bill. President Obama characterized his use of the signing statement in 2013 by stating, "Even though I support the vast majority of the provisions contained in this Act, which is comprised of hundreds of sections spanning more than 680 pages of text, I do not agree with them all. Our Constitution does not afford the President the opportunity to approve or reject statutory sections one by one. I am empowered either to sign the bill, or reject it, as a whole. In this case, though I continue to oppose certain sections of the Act, the need to renew critical defense authorities and funding was too great to ignore" (Obama 2013).

When exercised in this manner the identification of constitutionally questionable provisions is often coupled with explicit or implicit declarations that the executive branch may not implement the law precisely as written. As one of the leading advocates against the signing statement, former Pennsylvania senator Arlen Spector believes "if the president thinks something is unconstitutional, then he ought to veto it" (quoted in Savage 2009). Presidents of both parties have elected to not follow this course of action. Instances where the president makes constitutional objections to sections of newly enacted U.S. law with a simultaneous declaration that the law may not be executed as written have become extremely commonplace over the past several decades. This phenomenon has sparked controversy regarding alleged misuse of the signing statement, as the practice varies substantially from historical applications of the signing statement that were often rhetorical in nature (P. Cooper 2002; Kelley 2006).

Signing Statement Controversies

Presidential directives to disregard sections of U.S. law obviously raise questions regarding their constitutional charge to take care that the laws be faithfully executed. Under some circumstances this could rise to the level of an impeachable offense. President Andrew Johnson's refusal to follow the parameters of the Tenure in Office Act in 1868 was the primary basis for the House's impeachment charges levied against him (Stewart 2009). On the other hand, paramount in the president's oath of office is the affirmation that the president will preserve, protect, and defend the Constitution.

In many contemporary signing statements, presidents have cited Supreme Court precedent to argue that sections of the law are unconstitutional. From their perspective, executing the law precisely as written may violate the oath to defend the Constitution. In this regard, the president's duty to faithfully execute the law may come into direct conflict with the responsibility to uphold the Constitution. Constitutional law scholars have not reached a consensus on this question (Ball 2011; Barron 2000; Johnsen 2000, 2008; May 1998; Strauss 2000).

According to some, the president's responsibility to defend the Constitution does not provide justification for failing to execute the law (Corwin 1940; May 1998). This line of argument has cited the supremacy clause's reference to "[t]his Constitution, and the laws of the United States which shall be made in pursuance thereof . . . shall be the supreme law of the land." Article II, however, makes no similar conditional statement regarding the execution of the laws in pursuance of the Constitution by simply charging the president with the responsibility to "take care that the laws be faithfully executed." Others, including Justice Department counsel provided to President Ronald Reagan, George H. W. Bush, and Bill Clinton, have disagreed with this perspective.

According to one appraisal of the counterargument, "Arguments for routine nonenforcement typically are grounded in a theory of constitutional interpretive authority that emphasizes that the executive is a coordinate, not subordinate, branch of government with coequal authority to interpret the Constitution in exercising executive authority, a power comparable to the authority of Congress and the judiciary in their spheres" (Johnsen 2000, 17). Support for this argument has recently come from Chief Justice John Roberts.

During oral arguments in a case challenging the Defense of Marriage Act in March 2013, Roberts appeared to concur with this understanding when he stated, "I would have thought . . . that the Executive's obligation to execute the law includes the obligation to execute the law consistent with the Constitution. And if he has made a determination that executing the law by enforcing the terms is unconstitutional, I don't see why he doesn't have the courage of his convictions and execute not only the statute, but do it consistent with his view of the Constitution, rather than saying, oh, we'll wait till the Supreme Court tells us we have no choice" (*U.S. v. Windsor*, 570 U.S. ___, Oral arguments). In this statement, Chief Justice Roberts suggests that the president should not enforce laws as they are written, but in such a manner that comports with the president's understanding of the constitution.

Memorandums from the Justice Department provided to presidents of both parties have emphasized that the president holds the authority to refuse to enforce a law believed to be unconstitutional (Dellinger 1993; Flanigan 1992). An analysis of the Ford and Carter administrations shows that this approach predates recent Justice Department positions on the matter since these two presidents were determined to have defied a total of 10 laws containing statutes believed to be unconstitutional (May 1998).[10] As one would expect, the use of the signing statement under this auspice has received significant pushback from members of Congress. One of the most sensational signing statement controversies occurred in 2006 when Congress attempted to impose protections for individuals detained by the U.S. government.

President Bush, the War on Terror, and the McCain Amendment

A signing statement issued by President Bush attached to the DOD appropriations bill for 2006 made constitutional objections to more than 20 statutes in the new law (119 Stat. 2680, Public Law 109–148). Controversy regarding the law's implementation ensued when the president made clear his objection to a portion of the law under Title X (also known as the Detainee Treatment Act or the McCain Amendment). Specifically, the section placed restrictions on the types of detainee interrogation methods U.S. officials were permitted to employ by stipulating that "[n]o individual in the custody or under the physical control of the United States Government, regardless of nationality or physical location, shall be subject to cruel, inhuman, or degrading treatment or punishment" (119 Stat. 2739, Public Law 109–148). Referencing these new detainee standards, the president stated that the "executive branch would construe Title X in Division A of the Act, relating to detainees, in a manner consistent with the constitutional authority of the President to supervise the unitary executive branch and as Commander in Chief and consistent with the constitutional limitations on the judicial power, which will assist in achieving the shared objective of the Congress and the President, evidenced in Title X, of protecting the American people from further terrorist attacks" (Bush 2005, 1919). Though the statement does not explicitly state that the administration will disregard these new detainee treatment standards, the language suggests that the president considers his role as commander in chief and chief executive as providing him with ultimate authority to determine how detainee cases are handled.

The McCain Amendment's definition of "cruel, inhuman, or degrading treatment or punishment" was linked to United Nations Convention Against Torture and Other Forms of Cruel, Inhuman or Degrading Treatment or Punishment. This convention was adopted by the UN in 1984 and ratified by the U.S. Senate a decade later. Torture, as defined by the convention, was specified as "any act by which severe pain or suffering, whether physical or mental, is intentionally inflicted on a person for such purposes as obtaining from him or a third person information or a confession" (United Nations General Assembly 1984).[11] About three years before the passage of the McCain Amendment, an Office of Legal Counsel memo written by Deputy Assistant Attorney General John C. Yoo (2003) forcefully argued that Congress could not interfere in presidential commander-in-chief directives including those concerning detainee interrogation. Perhaps anticipating future congressional intervention on this manner, the memo stated that "[a]ny construction of criminal laws that regulated the President's authority as Commander in Chief to determine the interrogation and treatment of enemy combatants would raise serious constitutional questions.... To avoid this constitutional difficulty, therefore, we will construe potentially applicable criminal laws, reviewed in more detail below, not to apply to the President's detention and interrogation of enemy combatants pursuant to his Commander-in-Chief authority" (2003, 13). Since the McCain Amendment did precisely this, the enforcement of these new detainee protections was in serious question.

A subsequent Office of Legal Counsel memo detailed the use of "enhanced interrogation techniques" used by the Central Intelligence Agency (CIA) during interrogations of dozens of detainees (Bradbury 2005). Among the enhanced interrogation techniques employed by the agency were sleep deprivation, wall standing, dietary manipulation, nudity, water dousing, waterboarding, and other forms of physical abuse. Many of these instances occurred before the passage of the McCain Amendment in December of 2005. Khalid Shaikh Mohammed, for example, was waterboarded 183 times in March 2003 alone (Bradbury 2005). The Office of Legal Counsel claimed that the practice has since been discontinued, although it was not officially prohibited by the CIA until after Michael Hayden became the agency director in May 2006.

On July 20, 2007, President Bush signed an executive order seeking to further clarify the types of interrogation techniques deemed acceptable by the administration. The order identified a broad range of prohibited methods including those deemed cruel or inhumane by the McCain Amendment. Some interpreted this action as evidence that the president had reconsidered his position on the issue. However, as the Congressional Research Service pointed out, "Certain interrogation techniques that have been the subject of controversy and are expressly prohibited from being used by the military under the most recent version of the Army Field Manual—waterboarding, hooding, sleep deprivation, or forced standing for prolonged periods, for example—are not specifically addressed by the order. Whether or not such conduct is deemed by the Executive to be barred under the more general restrictive language of the Order remains unclear" (Garcia 2007, 12–13). Because President Obama declared in April 2009 that the administration would not prosecute CIA officials alleged to have used enhanced interrogation tactics, we may never know whether and to what extent the law was violated. However, in March 2014, Senator Dianne Feinstein, the chairperson of the Senate Intelligence Committee, publicly acknowledged that the committee's review of CIA interrogation and detention methods found that they "were far different and far more harsh than the way the CIA had described them to us" (2014). Although this particular controversy does not concern legislative veto oversight, it is nonetheless an important example where contradictory instructions came from Congress and the president.

Beholden to Two Masters

Although the president may choose to oppose or not legally recognize legislative veto prerogatives enacted by Congress, bureaucratic agencies are faced with a different set of strategic considerations. Fisher (1993) emphasizes this notion by stating that bureaucratic agencies "have to live with their review committees, year after year, and have a much greater incentive to make accommodations and stick by them. Presidents and their legal advisers can indulge in confrontations with Congress on these issues. Agencies cannot risk these types of collisions with the committees that authorize their programs and provide funds" (288). A former member of the House Appropriations Committee made this exact point in an interview with the author. During his time in Congress, he recalls most agencies were careful not to anger committees with control over agency functions and budgets. Recognizing the importance of their relationship with Congress and individual committees, bureaucratic agencies are generally more likely to accommodate legislative veto requirements. Thus, despite presidential instructions giving executive officials permission to ignore these types of oversight provisions, bureaucratic officials have tended to adhere to the legislative veto requirements included in public laws. Of course, there are exceptions. Recent reports by the GAO (2007a, 2007b) shine light on some of these cases.

At the request of multiple committees, the GAO conducted two studies in 2007 of executive action pursuant to statutes recently passed by Congress and subsequently challenged in a presidential signing statement. In total, these reports provided an assessment of nearly 30 individual statutes. Commissioned by the Senate Appropriations and Judiciary Committees, the first report focused specifically on appropriations acts from 2006. As the sample, it drew from 11 signing statements making constitutional objections to 160 individual statutes, about half of which involved sections containing legislative vetoes. Of these 160 statutes, the GAO assessed 19 and found that most were executed pursuant to the law's statutory language or no executive action was necessary since the condition requiring action by the statute did not occur. The report concluded that the execution of six of the statutes under study did not conform to the law's requirements (U.S. GAO 2007a). Three of these statutes contained legislative vetoes.

In one instance, the Department of Agriculture did not request advance approval from the Appropriations Committees for a reprogramming of appropriated funds. The GAO found a similar violation by the Pension Benefit Guaranty Corporation when it failed to solicit congressional approval before making expenditures exceeding its statutory limit. In the third case of legislative veto noncompliance, the Federal Emergency Management Agency (FEMA) failed to submit a housing expenditure plan to the Appropriations Committees for review. The remaining statutes not implemented as written involved the Departments of Defense and Homeland Security. In the Homeland Security case, the Customs and Border Patrol was found to have not relocated checkpoints in Arizona on a weekly basis as the spending measure directed, while the DOD was determined to have violated statutes requiring the submission of an independent budget justification for overseas military contingency operations and the submission of congressionally requested reports within 21 days of the request (U.S. GAO 2007a).

A second GAO study (2007b) from 2007 investigating how nine executive agencies carried out different 10 statutes passed from 2002 to 2006 produced similar results. Once again, a majority of the statutes under scrutiny were determined to have been executed as written. The report identified three instances of statutory noncompliance by the Department of Energy and FEMA. Energy Department officials failed to publicly post information about new protections afforded to whistleblowers as required by law. FEMA was determined to have violated the remaining two statutes regarding a graduate-level education program sponsored by the agency and a contractor registry for those working in disaster areas. None of these violations involved legislative veto requirements.

Overall, these reports found that in most instances the implementation of the law occurred as required despite signing statement claims to the contrary. Likewise, a *National Journal* article that predates these GAO studies also found that most agencies implemented laws as written by Congress (Friel 2006). While the statutes under investigation in these reports constitute an assuredly small sample size from which to draw overarching generalizations, it does suggest that in most cases executive officials comply with the law's statutory requirements even when presidents express clear opposition in a signing statement. Interviews with committee staff provided further corroborating evidence that this indeed is the case.

Interviews with staff on the Appropriations Committees confirmed that most executive officials continue to comply with legislative veto requirements. A few individuals did mention, however, that some of the larger departments, such as the Departments of Defense, Treasury, and State, will occasionally submit reports to the committee when required by law to do so, while emphasizing that they are not legally required to obtain clearance from Congress following *Chadha*. Despite intermittent assertions such as these, most agencies continue to comply with the waiting periods or committee approval procedures. With regard to compliance with veto statutes and other committee requests, executive officials defy Congress at their own peril.

Congressional Retribution

There are many ways Congress can react to unwarranted bureaucratic action. The most influential of these is through the appropriations process (Fisher 1993). In 2006, for example, the Appropriations Committees moved to cut more than 50 percent of the operating budget for the Office of National Drug Control Policy (ONDCP) after the office repeatedly failed to provide information and reports requested by the committee. Included in this budgetary recommendation was a statement by the House Appropriations Committee that expressed their displeasure:

> The Committee is extremely displeased with the performance of ONDCP staff regarding their communication with the Committee and their responsiveness to congressional inquiries. ONDCP's lethargy and the inadequate information provided severely impacts the ability of the Committee to conduct its oversight and make budgetary decisions in a timely manner. This kind of unresponsiveness on the part of ONDCP results in an unnecessary waste of time and energy; numerous follow up communications are required in almost every instance. . . . Therefore the Committee has reduced the salaries and expenses budget to more closely reflect actual performance. (Report 109–293 to accompany HR 5576, 109th Congress, 189)

In addition to the major funding cut, the committee also funded a National Academy of Public Administration study to provide a formal, comprehensive review of the ONDCP and its activities. Also requested was an independent review by the GAO for several specific programs overseen by the ONDCP. On top of this, legislation imposed new mandatory quarterly reports to the committees on staffing levels, hiring plans, and all travel activities. Because of burdensome and punitive actions like these that lawmakers may take, it is inherently risky for agencies to run afoul of Congress and its committees by deviating from statutory obligations.

Summary

In a system of shared powers where policy-making authority is delegated to administrative agents, both Congress and the president possess ways to influence the execution of the law. The president has a strong institutional position by virtue of being chief executive. This chapter provided an analysis of macropolitical conflict surrounding legislative veto oversight by testing hypotheses concerning the presidential veto and signing statement. Each of these devices aims to influence, and often minimize, Congress's statutory oversight reach. As these techniques are used with greater frequency, macropolitical conflict is heightened.

The analyses focusing on occurrences of presidential vetoes and signing statements both provided empirical evidence that legislative vetoes contribute to a greater likelihood of each. When used in this capacity, presidents aim to limit the ability of Congress to independently direct executive action. Presidential vetoes can prevent the enactment of new veto statutes. When in receipt of legislation passed by Congress, presidents and their advisers scrutinize bills from a multitude of perspectives. When controlling for other factors theorized to affect presidential veto propensity, the presence of legislative veto provisions was shown to make presidential vetoes more likely. In spite of this result, presidents continue to sign legislation containing legislative vetoes. Considering that modern presidents unequivocally reject the constitutionality of this oversight device, this may surprise casual observers.

After the Supreme Court ruled against the president's line-item veto power in 1998 (*Clinton v. City of New York*, 524 U.S. 417), the presidential veto reverted back to its original all-or-nothing incarnation. In order to assertively use the presidential veto to prevent the enactment of legislative vetoes, therefore, the president must block bills from becoming law in their entirety. By following such a course of action, the president may, as the old German proverb says, throw out the baby with the bathwater. To help prevent this, the signing statement has emerged as a way for presidents to sign bills into law while also going on record that the administration believes certain sections violate the Constitution's separation of powers.

Though President George W. Bush has received the most notoriety from it, presidents of both parties have used the signing statement to instruct executive officials to disregard legislative veto provisions or to treat them as simply advisory in nature. At its extremes, this can be interpreted as a laudable effort to protect the Constitution and the integrity of the executive branch or as a malevolent attempt to circumvent the rule of law. With thousands of legislative veto statutes in the U.S. Code and hundreds of signing statements issued by presidents since 1932, there are an incredible number of opportunities for interbranch conflict on this issue. Given the differences in how the legislative veto is structured and the delegated powers upon which it is imposed, conflicts over legislative veto vary in their intensity. Government reports suggest that bureaucrats will most often comply with the law when presented with conflicting instructions from Congress and the president. Some exceptions to this have been identified with perhaps more to follow. Thus, while some expected the *Chadha* ruling to serve as the definitive answer to the questions surrounding the legislative veto's legitimacy, macropolitical conflict over the veto continues to evolve.

As Congress continues to propose and enforce legislative vetoes, presidents have escalated their efforts to marginalize their effects. Many of the past and present political debates in Washington fundamentally revolve around efforts to control the bureaucracy, as both the president and Congress seek to wield greater control over public policy. The increasing power delegated to the executive has raised the stakes in this conflict. As the next chapter will demonstrate, the issue areas where the veto is used most frequently—national defense and foreign policy—constitute the front lines of this modern macropolitical conflict.

FIVE

The Conflict's Front Lines

National Security and Foreign Policy

Congress has used the legislative veto to constrain executive actions made by presidents to park rangers. By virtue of a legislative veto over Forest Service spending, Agriculture Secretary Tom Vilsack had to receive approval from the Appropriations Committees in order to allocate $40 million in funds to combat bark beetle infestation in several western states (Udall 2011). In another realm, two Emergency Price Control Acts passed during World War II provided the president with sweeping macroeconomic powers over war-related industries to combat inflation. Any pricing, wage, or other economic changes made pursuant to these laws were susceptible to congressional veto (56 Stat. 26, Public Law 77–421; 56 Stat. 578, Public Law 77–729). Justice White emphasized these broad applications of the legislative veto in his *Chadha* dissent, stating it had been used "in every field of governmental concern: reorganization, budgets, foreign affairs, war powers, and regulation of trade, safety, energy, the environment, and the economy" (*INS v. Chadha*, 462 U.S. 968 (1983), White, dissenting). More than 30 years later, this is still true. In this sense, Supreme Court intervention was less destabilizing than many anticipated. In order to better understand the evolution of this type of oversight, this chapter examines veto enactments according to individual policy areas with a particular emphasis on those areas where the legislative veto is used most frequently—national security and foreign policy.

Use of the legislative veto became commonplace during the latter half of the twentieth century after its inception as a constraint on presidential reorganization power. Its expansion made several trends apparent. The international tumult that led to World War II necessitated greater delegations of power to the president that were frequently conditioned with legislative vetoes (Craig 1983). Greater numbers of military and public works projects also resulted in the passage of greater numbers of veto statutes, most often providing committees with veto authority. The increased utilization of the veto during the 1970s was driven in part by a congressional effort to constrain the rise of the "imperial presidency" and to help offset greater levels of agency rulemaking autonomy (Craig 1983, 27). During this period, "Congress showed a pronounced concern with the degree of its influence compared with the president's over administration and policy. This concern was expressed in many ways, including advocacy of more congressional oversight as one means to redress the balance of influence" (Aberbach 1990, 46). The cumulative effect of these trends was an increased use of the legislative veto across many policy areas, but with a concentration on issues concerning national security and foreign policy. Because of the continued controversy surrounding its use, these issue areas constitute the front lines of this interbranch conflict. A highly publicized prisoner exchange to secure the release of an American prisoner of war approved by President Obama during his second term in office, and the congressional backlash that occurred in its aftermath, is emblematic of the current divide between the branches.

President Obama's Illegal Prisoner of War Exchange

On the day after Christmas in 2013, President Obama signed the National Defense Authorization Act (NDAA), which Congress passed with bipartisan support. Buried in the nearly 500-page law was a section concerning counterterrorism that required the president to provide eight congressional committees with at least 30 days advance notification before any Guantanamo detainee was transferred or released from the detention facility (127 Stat. 851, Public Law 113–66). Statutes such as this requiring advance notification to Congress before a specific executive action occurs, once rare, have proliferated during recent decades. Modern Congresses enact hundreds of them every term.

Congress has passed nearly 3,000 committee vetoes following *Chadha* akin to the one requiring advance notice of detainee transfers included in the NDAA. These requirements, which may necessitate committee approval or mandate advance notification, provide Congress with information and a window of opportunity to take action should a coalition of legislators oppose the proposal. Presidents of both parties have made strong objections to this type of oversight, believing that it violates the Constitution's separation of legislative and executive functions. As detailed in the previous chapter, signing statements issued when bills are signed into law are commonly the vehicle in which these objections are expressed.

The signing statement issued by President Obama upon signing the NDAA asserted that the advance notice requirement regarding detainee transfers might impermissibly interfere with the president's plenary authority over international affairs. Claiming that the requirement may violate constitutional separation of powers, the president declared that the law would be executed "in a manner that avoids the constitutional conflict" (Obama 2013). In essence, if the administration believes a statute to be unconstitutional, the president claims the power to violate the law. All evidence, including statements from administration officials, demonstrates that a prisoner exchange involving five Guantanamo detainees and an American soldier was done in direct violation of the law.

On May 31, 2014, the Department of Defense (DOD) transferred five detainees from the U.S. detention facility on Guantanamo Bay to Qatar in exchange for U.S. Army sergeant Bowe Bergdahl who had been captured in Afghanistan's Paktika Province and held as a prisoner of war since 2009. According to the GAO's (2014) report on the legality of the prisoner exchange, the DOD provided notification to the required committees on the day the exchange took place, presumably after it had been completed. In a five-hour hearing before the House Armed Services Committee, Secretary of Defense Chuck Hagel testified that President Obama authorized the prisoner exchange on May 27 after communication with the emir of Qatar. Citing the "exceptional circumstances" the situation presented, Secretary Hagel claimed that the DOD had to act "quickly, efficiently, and quietly" while acknowledging that the "speed with which we moved in this case has caused great frustration, legitimate questions and concern" (U.S. Congress. House of Representatives. Armed Services Committee, 2014). Committee members of both parties were not reserved about making their frustrations known.

The Armed Services committee chairperson, Howard "Buck" McKeon (R-CA), condemned the administration's actions, calling the initial explanations to Congress from White House officials as "misleading, and at times blatantly false" (House Armed Services Committee Hearing 2014). Without equivocation, McKeon deemed the prisoner exchange a clear violation of the law. His opening statement emphatically concluded,

> There is no compelling reason why the department could not provide a notification to Congress 30 days before the transfer. Especially when it has complied with the notification requirement for all previous GTMO [Guantanamo Bay Naval Base] detainee transfers since enactment of the law. The statute is more than a notification. It requires detailed national security information, including detailed consideration of risk, and risk mitigation that the Congress and American people would expect any administration to consider before a decision is made to transfer GTMO detainees. It was designed and approved by a bipartisan majority in Congress, due to real concerns that dangerous terrorists were being released in a manner that allowed them to return to the battlefield. (House Armed Services Committee Hearing 2014)

The ranking member of the committee, Representative Adam Smith (D-WA), while disagreeing with some of the remarks made by the chairperson, reiterated the concern about the failure of the administration to comply with the advance notification requirement. Smith also dismissed President Obama's signing statement, which called into question the constitutionality of the advance notification requirement, by stating,

> the law is the law. The way you challenge constitutionality is you go to court. And you figure out whether or not the courts say it's constitutional or not. And until the courts rule on that, it is the law. When President Bush was in the White House, he had, gosh, hundreds of signing statements. And there was, I believe, a correct amount of outrage amongst many that those signing statements were put out there as a way to simply avoid the law. It wasn't right for President Bush to do it, it's not right for President Obama to do it, so I would be very curious to understand the argument for why that 30-day requirement wasn't in place and again I'll come back to the fact that there was no reason that 30 days notice couldn't have been given to the leadership of Congress. (House Armed Services Committee Hearing 2014)

Having served two terms representing Nebraska in the U.S. Senate, Secretary Hagel seemed to understand the angst of many on the committee. However, he refused to assure the committee that future detainee transfers would be done in compliance with the law.[1] Throughout the hearing, Hagel remained steadfast in his assertion that the DOD did comply with the law by arguing that the prisoner exchange was more than a detainee transfer, but a "military operation with very high and complicated risks" that invoked the president's "constitutional responsibilities and constitutional authorities to protect American citizens and members of our armed forces" (2014, 4). Secretary Hagel was not the only administration official to publicly defend the legality of the prisoner exchange. National Security Council spokesperson Caitlin Hayden acknowledged that the legal requirement to provide 30 days advance notice to Congress was not followed. Although the law is unambiguous, the National Security Council provided the Orwellian justification that "it is fair to conclude that Congress did not intend that the Administration would be barred from taking the action it did in these circumstances." Failing to adhere to the rule of law in this manner, even for noble purposes, continues to build a dangerous precedent that the president can freely disregard laws passed by our elected representatives.

The GAO report recognized the executive's position that the 30-day advance notification requirement violated the Constitution, while claiming that its report was "not the appropriate forum to decide the constitutionality" of the statute itself (2014, 6). The GAO concluded that the prisoner exchange violated the NDAA advance notice requirement as well as the Antideficiency Act (96 Stat. 923, Public Law 97–258), which prohibits expenditures not authorized by Congress (2014). On September 9, 2014, the House agreed to a resolution condemning the president's actions, while also expressing relief over Bergdahl's safe return. Twenty-two Democrats joined all voting Republicans in condemning the administration's failure to comply with the 30-day notification requirement (113rd Congress, House Roll Call No. 485). In strong language, the resolution deemed further violations of the law "unacceptable" and declared that "these actions have burdened unnecessarily the trust and confidence in the commitment and ability of the Obama administration to constructively engage and work with Congress" (113th Congress, House Resolution 644). Speaking to the media on the subject of the prisoner exchange, President Obama justified his actions by citing the "fragile nature of these negotiations" and ultimately offered "absolutely no apologies" for the prisoner exchange.

President Obama's disregard for U.S. law governing detainees at Guantanamo is illustrative of an increasingly broad conceptualization of presidential commander-in-chief powers. Modern presidents of both parties have used the signing statement and other resources to justify actions taken in the name of national security. It has become increasingly common for presidents to claim the authority to violate duly enacted statutes if they perceive the statutory requirements therein to unconstitutionally infringe on the president's military prerogatives. In this regard, many legislative veto statutes, despite being duly enacted U.S. law, may not provide the types of prohibitions, or induce executive action, desired by Congress.

Policy Prioritization of Veto Oversight

As an initial step toward analyzing the legislative veto from a policy perspective, all 3,814 legislative veto statutes included in the data set were coded according to the *Congressional Bills Project* codebook (Adler and Wilkerson 2011).[2] Based on the original coding system used for the *Policy Agendas Project* (Baumgartner and Jones 1993), the *Congressional Bills Project* codebook divides all government policies into 19 major and 225 minor policy categories.[3] This systematic coding of veto statutes by policy area allows for an examination of usage trends and a careful analysis of those areas where the legislative veto is most frequently employed.

The enactment of nearly 4,000 legislative veto statutes has provided senators and representatives with a greater oversight reach across an enormous variety of both domestic and foreign policies. Table 5.1 provides data regarding the implementation of legislative vetoes by issue area. The first column lists all enacted legislative vetoes by issue area for the congressional terms prior to the *Chadha* ruling (72nd–98th Congresses). The second column provides the post-*Chadha* distribution (99th–111th Congresses). Aggregate data for the entire period are listed in the third column.

As table 5.1 shows, the veto has been used to oversee the execution of laws spanning all 19 major policy areas (see also Cooper and Hurley 1983). There is a substantial skew, however, in the distribution of veto statutes across these issues. In pursuing a selective approach, legislators have most frequently used it to oversee defense-related policies, with more than one quarter of all enacted vetoes affecting the military or national security matters. When combined, vetoes pertaining to defense and foreign policy (international affairs and foreign trade) far exceed those belonging to the remaining categories. Figure 5.1 illustrates the trends in legislative veto use for these two issue areas.

The proportion of defense vetoes has increased slightly following the *Chadha* ruling to 27.4 percent of enacted vetoes as compared to 23.1 percent beforehand. The effort to oversee defense policy in this manner intensified during the 1970s as one of many efforts to rein in expanding executive power. Figure 5.1 illustrates the trajectory over time in the raw number of veto statutes pertaining to defense and foreign policy. Those pertaining to

The Conflict's Front Lines   169

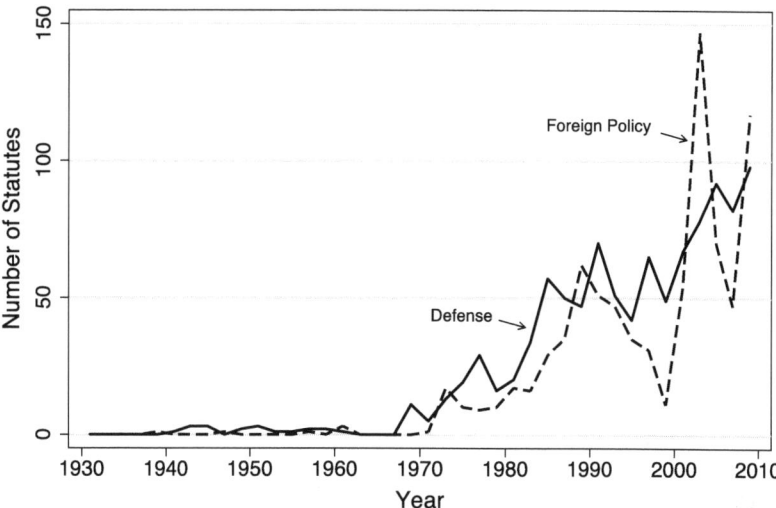

Fig. 5.1. Defense and foreign policy legislative vetoes by term: 1931–2010

TABLE 5.1. Legislative veto statutes by policy area: 1931–2010

Policy Area	1931–1984	1985–2010	Total
Defense	23.1% (166)	27.4% (848)	26.6% (1,014)
International Affairs and Foreign Aid	8.9% (64)	22.6% (699)	20.0% (763)
Government Operations	11.1% (80)	12.9% (400)	12.6% (480)
Law, Crime, and Family Issues	0.8% (6)	10.5% (325)	8.7% (331)
Public Lands and Water Management	11.3% (81)	7.1% (219)	7.9% (300)
Energy	13.3% (96)	2.8% (86)	4.8% (182)
Space, Science, Technology, and Communications	10.1% (73)	2.1% (65)	3.6% (138)
Transportation	5.0% (36)	3.1% (95)	3.4% (131)
Agriculture	1.0% (7)	2.7% (84)	2.4% (91)
Banking, Finance, and Domestic Commerce	1.8% (13)	2.3% (72)	2.2% (85)
Foreign Trade	3.1% (22)	1.2% (37)	1.5% (59)
Community Development and Housing	2.8% (21)	1.0% (31)	1.4% (52)
Labor, Employment, and Immigration	1.4% (10)	0.8% (25)	0.9% (35)
Macroeconomics	0.8% (6)	0.9% (28)	0.9% (34)
Education	2.1% (15)	0.5% (16)	0.8% (31)
Environment	2.1% (15)	0.5% (15)	0.8% (30)
Health	0.4% (3)	0.9% (27)	0.8% (30)
Civil Rights, Minority Issues, and Civil Liberties	0.4% (3)	0.5% (17)	0.5% (20)
Social Welfare	0.6% (4)	0.1% (4)	0.2% (8)
Total	721	3,093	3,814

Note: Percentages may not sum to 100 due to rounding.

defense have reached nearly 100 per term. Given the increases in defense spending during the Cold War and post–Cold War eras, coupled with the tremendous influence wielded by the United States as a global hegemon, it is not at all surprising that lawmakers have relied on the congressional veto as one of many tools to help oversee the enormous range of functions performed by defense officials.

Defense and National Security

The first legislative veto affecting defense policy was a dual-House negative veto of foreign arms sales included in a 1941 enactment promoting the defense of the United States (55 Stat. 11, Public Law 77–11). This statute empowered legislators with the authority to veto sales, transfers, exchanges, or leases of military arms and munitions to foreign countries as negotiated by the president or other defense officials. As noted in chapter 1, the first committee veto passed by Congress in 1943 also concerned defense policy by granting the Naval Affairs Committees the power to block naval land acquisitions and public works projects.[4] Statutes such as this slowly became more common. By 1952, similar requirements had been applied to every branch of the military (66 Stat. 625, Public Law 82–534). It was not until the 1970s that the number of legislative veto statutes pertaining to defense policy began to appreciably increase. Congresses serving during this decade passed an average of about 15 defense-related veto statutes per term. By the 2000s, the number had risen to more than 80. Most often, the requirements imposed by these statutes involved the congressional defense and spending committees.

The specific review mechanisms associated with Armed Services Committee vetoes concerning military land transactions have varied over time. In some cases, committee staff receives DOD proposals and forwards them to lawmakers in the chamber who represent the district or state where the proposed land transaction is to occur. Absent an objection from these lawmakers, proposals are commonly approved. On other occasions, subcommittees have held hearings with DOD officials where lawmakers can raise questions or concerns raised following notifications to the committee (Harris 1964). Legislative veto provisions included in modern defense legislation have affected policies spanning defense contractors and contracts, weapons development, foreign military operations, arms sales, and military aid, among others. Perhaps most notably, Congress has assertively used the veto as a means to oversee policies concerning foreign arms sales and military aid.

Influencing Arms Sales

Following the passage of the first foreign arms sales veto in 1941, Congress has enacted scores of vetoes governing exports and sales of defense articles abroad. The proliferation of statutes allowing for vetoes of arms sales has principally occurred as a result of the increasing size of the foreign arms market and its "importance and impact as a tool of American foreign policy and the belief that then existing and reporting procedures respecting arms sales did not provide the Congress with all the information necessary to exercise effective oversight over foreign military cash sales" (Grimmett 1979, 3). And yet for decades afterwards legislators did not block a single arms sale. By 1974, the value of U.S. arms sales on the foreign market had reached nearly $11 billion (Gibson 1994). Cognizant of the strategic importance of large munitions transfers, Congress reformed the arms sale review process with an important section of the Arms Control Export Act of 1974 (88 Stat. 1795, Public Law 93–559).

The legislative veto's insertion into the Arms Control Export Act occurred with the passage of the Nelson-Bingham amendment, which mandated 20 days advance notification to Congress of any foreign arms sale in excess of $25 million. During the review period, legislators could block individual sales by concurrent resolution. The International Security Assistance and Arms Export Control Act of 1976 lengthened the advance notification period to 30 days and extended congressional veto power to include transfers of defense equipment in excess of $7 million (90 Stat. 729, Public Law 94–329). Institutionalizing a congressional veto over virtually all substantial arms sales empowered Congress to review the merits of each proposed transfer on a case-by-case basis.[5] Though Congress refrained from vetoing any arms sales outright, on multiple occasions it effectively used the threat of a veto to induce concessions from the president (Gibson 1994; Grimmett 1979, 2012).

Congress seriously threatened President Ford with a veto of a proposed sale of Hawk missiles and Vulcan air defense systems to Jordan in 1975. The introduction and subsequent support for veto resolutions to void the sale in both chambers of Congress demonstrated to the president the credibility of the veto threat. To help allay congressional concerns, the terms of the transfer were amended to require the installation of the systems in defensive positions. The following year, Congress successfully leveraged the threat of a veto to reduce the number of missiles sold to Saudi Arabia and Iran. In 1977, Congress similarly influenced the terms of an airborne warning and control systems sale to Iran and aircraft sales to Egypt, Israel, and Saudi Arabia (Grimmett 1979). Early in the Reagan administration, a lengthy battle ensued over a proposed sale of Airborne Warning and Control System aircraft to Saudi Arabia (Goldberg 1990). The House voted 301–111 to disapprove the sale in October 1981 (97th Congress, House Vote No. 243). After the Senate Foreign Relations Committee also voted to disapprove the sale, the full Senate considered the resolution. During congressional debate, the Office of Legal Counsel in the Justice Department began considering how the administration might respond to a veto of the sale. Among its suggestions were treating a veto as a "legal nullity," pursuing emergency exceptions to the congressional review process, or seeking other statutory accommodations (Olson 1981). According to one account of this interbranch standoff, those opposed to the sale who were seeking to invoke the Arms Control Export Act's legislative veto were successful obstructionists "at every legislative step except the last: the final vote in the full Senate" (Goldberg 1990, 71). The vote to disapprove the sale failed in the Senate by just four votes. After the *Chadha* ruling, Congress has continued to utilize veto threats to influence foreign arms sales and military assistance.

In 1985, President Reagan faced a tidal wave of opposition in Congress regarding a proposed $2 billion arms sale of aircraft and aircraft defense systems to Jordan. Failing to consult with members of the Defense and Foreign Relations Committees, the president defined the terms of the sale with DOD officials and submitted the proposal to Congress as required by law. The administration was soundly rebuffed on the measure when the Senate voted 97–1 to reject the sale. While a formal vote was not taken in the House, nearly 300 lawmakers pledged to also stand in opposition. Following this overwhelming expression of congressional disapproval, Secretary of State George Schultz announced that the administration would withdraw the proposed sale (Schweid 1986). During the same congressional term, Congress negotiated the removal of all Stinger missiles, F-15 fighter aircraft, and M-1 tanks from a large arms sale to Saudi Arabia after 356 representatives and 73 senators voted in favor of a veto resolution (Grimmett 2012; Gibson 1994). After vetoing the joint resolution, President Reagan informed Senate Majority Leader Robert Dole that he would acquiesce to the prevailing congressional sentiment by downsizing the proposed sale. Once again, large majorities in Congress made clear their opposition to the existing terms of the sale. Again, these cases help demonstrate that vetoes need not be executed for Congress to exercise meaningful influence on U.S. defense policy through arms sales. Interviews I conducted with several lawmakers serving on the House Armed Services Committee suggest that the imposition of vetoes over arms sales and myriad other defense actions demonstrates that Congress is committed to overseeing DOD actions and may elect to utilize its statutory oversight authority to intervene in some cases.

An Arizona representative likened the oversight effectiveness of veto statutes concerning defense policy to an amendment passed during the aftermath of the exposure of poor treatment of veterans and deteriorating conditions at the Walter Reed Army Medical Hospital in Washington, DC. During debate on legislation addressing Walter Reed, he sponsored a successful amendment concerning a novel system for Veterans' Affairs (VA) officials to record and catalog all complaints at VA hospitals (H.R.1585, 110th Congress). To facilitate oversight, every lawmaker had access to these filed complaints. This provided an avenue for communication and first-hand reporting that did not exist prior to the controversy. Importantly, this represenative described his perception of the main effectiveness of this amendment as a signal to executive officials within the VA that while complaints might not always reach legislators, there was an avenue for oversight, which he argued affected job standards, expectations, and performance. This example parallels legislative veto oversight of arms sales in that Congress does not necessarily have to execute a veto for it to be effective.

The chief military assistant for a former chairperson of the House Armed Services Subcommittee on Oversight and Investigations said that committee deliberative vetoes and statutory reporting requirements can create pressure on executive officials to reassess or clarify policies of importance to committee members. Vetoes such as these often serve as signals to executive officials regarding committee oversight priorities. Thus, the very presence of a veto can illustrate that Congress is watching and capable of exerting influence. Several additional examples embody Congress's continued use of the legislative veto to affect defense policy during the 1980s and 1990s. Among the most prominent cases of congressional-presidential conflict over arms sales occurred during the Iran-Contra controversy.

Iran-Contra

The Iran-Contra controversy principally concerned U.S. aid to Nicaraguan rebels and arms sales to Iran. The Contras were a Nicaraguan opposition group to the socialist Sandinista government, which overthrew the ruling Somoza regime in 1979. Beginning in 1981, President Reagan directed the CIA to provide financial and military aid to the Contras as part of the global effort to combat leftist governments supported by the Soviets. In 1984, Democratic majorities in Congress included a limitation rider, known as the Boland Amendment (sponsored by Massachusetts Democrat Edward Boland), in an appropriations bill that prohibited the CIA or any other government agency from providing direct or indirect financial aid to the Contras (98 Stat. 1935, Public Law 98–473). Due to the controversy that would ensue, the Boland Amendment received considerable notoriety.

In a lesser-known provision included after the Boland Amendment, Congress inserted a dual-House affirmative veto governing U.S. support to the Contras, stating that military and financial assistance could resume following agreement to a joint resolution of approval sanctioning the aid. Combined, these statutes prohibited continued aid to the Contras unless both chambers of Congress acted to approve expenditures to directly or indirectly support military operations in Nicaragua.

As outlined in the Tower Report, members of the National Security Council circumvented the legal prohibition on providing aid to the Contras. The final report issued by Independent Counsel Lawrence E. Walsh summarized the "overarching money crime" in the charges against Lt. Col. Oliver North and three codefendants as conspiring to channel proceeds from U.S. arms sales to Iran into a covert fund, despite the fact that the proceeds belonged to the U.S. government (1993). Unaware of the ongoing back-channel funding to Nicaraguan rebel groups, Congress lifted the ban on aid to the Contras in 1986, providing the president with $100 million to assist the Nicaraguan democratic resistance (100 Stat. 1783–300, Public Law 99–500). The "Baker Accord" negotiated by Secretary of State James A. Baker III and congressional leaders in 1989 allowed the continued funding of the Contras only with the express approval of four designated committees (Fisher 2005b).

While much of the Iran-Contra controversy is illustrative of the inability of Congress to dictate key components of U.S. foreign aid and arms sales negotiated and administered by the Reagan administration, this veto provision passed in 1984 represents, at the least, a concerted effort to constrain the president and oversee foreign aid to the Contras. In addition to the passage of statutes providing for legislative vetoes of arms sales, Congress has also made efforts to extend the veto as a check on the president's power as commander in chief. The most notable instance of this occurred with the passage of the War Powers Resolution in 1973.

The War Powers Resolution

Foreign policy was at the forefront of the congressional agenda during the initial years of the Cold War. The Marshall Plan provided for an unprecedented American investment in rebuilding the European continent devastated by war. Substantial organization reforms to the U.S. defense and national security apparatus occurred with the passage of the National Security Act of 1947 (61 Stat. 496, Public Law 80–235), which created the Department of Defense as a consolidation of the existing armed forces departments including War, Navy, and Air Force. As containment became the centerpiece of U.S. foreign policy strategy, defense spending increased substantially. While defense spending averaged 4.7 percent of the nation's gross domestic product (GDP) from 1947 to 1950, it increased to an average of 10.8 percent of GDP from 1951 to 1960 (Office of Management and Budget 2012). National security concerns during this period resulted in greater delegations from Congress to the president and officials in the DOD. Congress utilized the legislative veto to reserve the right to influence the exercise of many of these delegated powers. Among the most controversial of these efforts occurred when Congress sought to restrict the president's authority to deploy the military following the Vietnam War.

The War Powers Resolution, passed by Congress in 1973, included a potentially powerful legislative veto concerning the deployment of U.S. military forces abroad. Since the repeal of the Gulf of Tonkin Resolution in January 1971 did little to affect President Nixon's war making in Southeast Asia, the War Powers Resolution fundamentally sought to constrain the president's commander-in-chief power. President Nixon vetoed the bill on October 24, 1973. With votes from 284 representatives and 75 senators, this was one of the rare occasions where Congress secured enough votes to override a presidential veto (93rd Congress, House Roll Call No. 563, Senate Roll Call No. 478).

The landmark enactment included two main constraints on presidential war-making power. First, the act imposed a window of 60 or 90 days for the president to unilaterally deploy U.S. armed forces without the explicit approval of Congress.[6] Presidentially directed deployments of this nature were authorized under the sole circumstance of a "national emergency created by attack upon the United States, its territories or possessions, or its armed forces" (87 Stat. 556, Public Law 93-148). Second, a provision in the act empowered Congress to veto any military deployment with a concurrent resolution of disapproval.[7] As a consequence, Congress empowered itself with the authority to legally compel the president to recall military forces from around the globe with the concurrence of majorities in both chambers. In his veto message sent to Congress, President Nixon unequivocally objected to this section by stating that it "would allow the Congress to eliminate certain authorities merely by the passage of a concurrent resolution—an action which does not normally have the force of law, since it denies the President his constitutional role in approving legislation" (1973, 893). How such a monumental interbranch confrontation would play out in reality is far from clear since Congress has never agreed to such a resolution as the means to attempt a military redeployment. Presidential legal advisers have testified that the president would not be compelled to honor such a resolution that so clearly challenges the president's constitutional authority as commander in chief, despite the fact that such measures seek to reinvigorate Congress's power to declare war (Fisher 2007).[8] To date, legislators have yet to assert themselves in this manner, although President Obama's use of the U.S. military in concert with North Atlantic Treaty Organization forces in Libya in 2011 has sparked renewed interest in Congress's ability to counteract presidential deployment decisions.

War Powers Resolution Veto Attempts

Beginning with a resolution introduced by Representative Ron Paul on March 15, 2011, legislators sponsored at least a dozen resolutions expressing their discontent regarding the president's invocation of United Nations Security Council Resolution 1973 as justification for U.S. air strikes on Libyan targets (Hallett 2011). Some even threatened impeachment. On June 3, the House voted on a resolution sponsored by Ohio representative Dennis Kucinich calling for removal of U.S. forces from participation in the Libyan conflict pursuant to the War Powers Resolution (H.Con.Res. 51, 112th Congress). In a vote that divided both parties, with about one-third of Democrats and Republicans voting in favor, the resolution was defeated 148 to 265 (On Agreeing to the Resolution, June 3, 2011, Vote Number 412). In lieu of this measure, the House agreed to a resolution introduced by Speaker John Boehner stating in part, "The President has not sought, and Congress has not provided, authorization for the introduction or continued involvement of the United States Armed Forces in Libya. Congress has the constitutional prerogative to withhold funding for any unauthorized use of the United States Armed Forces, including for unauthorized activities regarding Libya" (H.Res. 292, 112th Congress). This successful resolution mandated the submission of reports to the House by the president, attorney general, and secretaries of state and defense, but stopped short of instructing the president to terminate U.S. involvement.

The insertion of a legislative veto in the War Powers Resolution was symbolic of Congress's willingness to utilize the legislative veto as an operational constraint on presidential power. Unfortunately for those critical of the aggrandizement of presidential war-making power, this effort to exert more congressional influence on military deployments has mostly been a façade. At no point since the passage of the War Powers Act has the Senate voted on a resolution to recall a military deployment. Including the Kucinich resolution calling for the removal of U.S. forces in Libya, the House has voted on seven different resolutions seeking to invoke the veto contained in the War Powers Resolution. These resolutions are listed in table 5.2. In every instance but one, these measures failed to receive majority support. The lone successful resolution concerned U.S. intervention in Somalia (H.Con.Res. 170, 103rd Congress).

By voice vote in November 1993, the House agreed to a resolution calling for full U.S. withdrawal from Somalia by March 31, 1994. The vote occurred about a month after two Black Hawk helicopters were shot down, resulting in 18 American causalities. Despite the unambiguous language in the resolution's title, "Directing the President pursuant to section 5(c) of the War Powers Resolution to remove United States Armed Forces from Somalia by January 31, 1994," Speaker Thomas Foley stated that he believed the resolution to be nonbinding in light of the *Chadha* ruling (Grimmett 2010b). Upon receiving the resolution from the House, the Senate elected to take no further action on the measure, thus leaving Congress's veto power dormant. The 1994 DOD spending bill did, however, bar funds from being spent on military activities in Somalia after March 31 (Public Law 103–139). President Clinton signed the spending bill into law

TABLE 5.2. Legislative veto attempts pursuant to the War Powers Resolution

Year (Congress)	Country	Resolution Number	Outcome	Vote
2011 (112th)	Libya	H.Con.Res. 51	Failed	148–265 (Roll No. 412)
2011 (112th)	Afghanistan	H.Con.Res. 28	Failed	93–321 (Roll No. 193)
2010 (111th)	Pakistan	H.Con.Res. 301	Failed	38–372 (Roll No. 473)
2010 (111th)	Afghanistan	H.Con.Res. 248	Failed	65–356 (Roll No. 98)
1999 (106th)	Yugoslavia	H.Con.Res. 82	Failed	139–290 (Roll No. 101)
1998 (105th)	Bosnia	H.Con.Res. 227	Failed	193–225 (Roll No. 58)
1993 (103rd)	Somalia	H.Con.Res.170	Successful	Voice vote

Note: The House agreed to a nonbinding disapproval resolution of President Bush's Iraq troop surge in 2007 (H.Con.Res. 63, 110th Congress). The resolution succeeded on a party-line vote of 246–182 with just two House Democrats voting against the measure and 17 Republicans voting in favor (Roll No. 99).

after having previously agreed to the March withdrawal date (Grimmett 2010b).

In this particular case, although the House did exercise its authority to veto a military deployment, it is abundantly clear that public reaction to the loss of American lives, rather than any congressional action, dictated the president's decision to extricate U.S. forces from Somalia. In summary, on multiple occasions the House has voted on resolutions invoking the War Powers Resolution's legislative veto over military deployments while a recorded vote on such a resolution has yet to take place in the Senate. Because of this, some have argued that Congress lacks the "collective will to threaten credible use of the legislative veto" (Gibson 1994, 464). Indeed, Congress has yet to invoke the War Powers Resolution's legislative veto over any of the nearly 150 military deployments since the end of the Vietnam War (Grimmett 2010a).

On most accounts, the War Powers Resolution has not functioned as Congress intended. The authority of majorities in Congress to compel the president to withdraw forces deployed abroad remains intact, despite the *Chadha* ruling. All modern presidents have not only challenged the legislative veto contained in the War Powers Resolution, but the entire underlying premise that the Congress can constrain the president's role as commander in chief. Despite this opposition, presidents have often submitted reports to Congress as required by the War Powers Resolution using language that underscores the presidential position that such mandatory reporting requirements are unconstitutional. Legislation passed after the enactment of the War Powers Resolution aimed to further limit presidential war powers.

The National Emergencies Act

The National Emergencies Act (90 Stat. 1255, Public Law 94–412) passed in 1976 as a means to clarify the use of presidential emergency powers delegated to the president by hundreds of existing statutes (Relyea 2005). Signed into law by President Ford, the bill empowered the president with the authority to determine whether a state of emergency existed. Following a declaration to this effect, the president was then authorized to exercise "emergency powers and authorities" following a formal announcement to Congress regarding the specific powers to be invoked (90 Stat. 1257, Public Law 94–412). The law stipulated that absent a presidential renewal of the declaration, states of emergency automatically expired after one year unless terminated at an earlier date by either the president or Congress. Contingent upon agreement to a concurrent resolution, lawmakers could annul a presidential state of emergency at any point following its announcement. Two years after *Chadha*, reform legislation passed modifying the concurrent resolution veto procedure to a joint resolution (99 Stat. 448, Public Law 94–412). This change made it substantially more difficult for Congress to end a state of emergency since the president could veto a joint resolution seeking to terminate it.

Presidents have invoked their emergency powers on more than 50 occasions since the law's passage with only five of them occurring when Congress could end a state of emergency on its own (Relyea 2007). Thirty of these declared emergencies remain in effect (Korte 2014). Most recently, President Obama (2014) sent notice to Congress in September 2014 regarding his sixth extension of presidential emergency powers following the terrorist attacks on the United States originally invoked by President George W. Bush on September 14, 2001. In this brief letter the president stated, "The terrorist threat that led to the declaration on September 14, 2001, of a national emergency continues. For this reason, I have determined that it is necessary to continue in effect after September 14, 2014, the national emergency with respect to the terrorist threat" (2014). The repeated extension of this emergency declaration by Presidents Bush and Obama continued to make a wealth of emergency powers available to the president.[9] In none of these instances has Congress voted to terminate a state of emergency.

Department of Homeland Security and the Dubai Port Controversy

Among the most important post-*Chadha* developments concerning legislative veto oversight of national security policies was the establishment of the Homeland Security Department in 2002. The Homeland Security Act (116 Stat. 2135, Public Law 107–296), which created the department, included five legislative vetoes. These statutes primarily concerned the terms under which functions from existing agencies could be transferred into the newly created DHS. The act provided considerable reorganization powers to the department's secretary, but required 60 days or 90 days advance notification to Congress as well as a justificatory explanation for the proposal (116 Stat. 2243, Public Law 107–296).

From its inception to 2010, Congress has passed more than 150 vetoes affecting the DHS. All of these vetoes are either committee affirmative or deliberative vetoes affecting a broad range of DHS programs and functions including the Secret Service, Customs Service, Transportation Security Administration, Counterterrorism Fund, FEMA, and Office for Domestic Preparedness. As is the case with other issue areas, many of these oversight statutes govern spending. Following Hurricane Katrina, a FEMA spending bill appropriated $552 million for regional, state, or local grants for transportation security and catastrophic event planning and preparedness. The law prohibited FEMA from awarding grants until the Appropriations Committees received and approved detailed disbursement plans (121 Stat. 142, Public Law 110–28).

Given the massive institutional reorganization that occurred with the creation of the DHS, and the increasing numbers of legislative vetoes implemented to oversee other large federal departments, it is unsurprising that Congress frequently employs the veto to constrain DHS actions. Legislators adopted one of the most notable DHS vetoes amid growing controversy concerning the ownership of U.S. ports.

In 2006, Dubai Ports World sought to purchase the Peninsular & Oriental Steam Navigation Company for nearly $7 billion. The sale would have allowed the United Arab Emirates-based company to operate in six major U.S. ports. Both Democratic and Republican opponents of the sale in Congress claimed that transferring such authority to an Arab-based company would pose a substantial national security risk. As the controversy developed, the House Appropriations Committee voted 62–2 in favor of adding an amendment to an omnibus spending bill that would have blocked the sale (Sanger 2006). President Bush supported the sale and threatened to veto legislation that would block it. Perhaps recognizing the growing opposition to the sale and its diplomatic consequences, Dubai Ports World dropped its ownership bid. This action cooled the standoff between the president and Congress, but lawmakers seized upon momentum from the controversy and passed the SAFE Port Act in October of 2006 (120 Stat. 1884, Public Law 109–347).

With an eye toward the possibility of a similar conflict over port operations emerging in the future, the SAFE Port Act required the DHS secretary to submit "policies, initiatives, or actions that will have a major impact on trade and customs revenue functions" to six committees for a 30-day review period prior to their finalization (120 Stat. 1921, Public Law 109–347). The act also required a waiting period of 45 days prior to DHS reorganizations affecting customs revenue and border protection. These review periods allowed legislators and committees to study actions that would have a "major impact on trade and customs" and consider proposing legislation to prevent changes to the status quo. Although the president could veto a bill used for this purpose, these new requirements imposed an opportunity for congressional review that did not previously exist.

Defense Vetoes Post-*Chadha*

Congress began using the legislative veto in 1941 to oversee a tremendous variety of defense policies and programs. Since *Chadha*, vetoes affecting defense policy have followed the broader shift away from one- and dual-House vetoes to the committee variant. About 85 percent of the nearly 850 defense vetoes enacted during this period provided committees with deliberative or affirmative veto power. Only 11 dual-House affirmative or negative vetoes have been passed since 1985 akin to those included in the War Powers Resolution and the National Emergencies Act. In contrast to vetoes by concurrent or single-House resolution commonly included in pre-*Chadha* laws, these 11 statutes calling for support or opposition from both chambers of Congress all require agreement to a joint resolution of approval or disapproval to execute the veto. By law, joint resolutions of disapproval can block nuclear agreements negotiated by the president and impose restrictions on arms sales and military aid to countries determined to be harboring terrorist groups (122 Stat. 4028, Public Law 110–369; 102 Stat. 2627, Public Law 100–526; 109 Stat. 82, Public Law 104–6; 105 Stat. 710, Public Law 102–138). Legislators have also used the veto to address the politically sensitive topic of military base closures.

Legislation from 1990 created the Base Realignment and Closure Commission and devised an expedited process for Congress to consider and potentially reject plans to affect military bases (104 Stat. 1808, Public Law 101–510). On five different occasions since then, the Base Realignment and Closure Commission has proposed closing or otherwise realigning an average of 27 military instillations (Davis 2005).[10] In each instance, majorities in both chambers coupled with presidential support could prohibit the commission's recommendations from going into effect. The only roll-call vote on a disapproval resolution veto taken in the Senate occurred after the 1993 recommendations. In this instance, only 12 senators voted to block the scheduled closures. The House voted on disapproval resolutions in 1989, 1991, and 1995, but in each instance the resolution was overwhelmingly defeated by an average vote of 59–363 (Davis 2005). Thus, in this particular area of defense policy, although the opportunity for a congressional veto exists, lawmakers have come nowhere close to sending a veto resolution to the president's desk.

In contrast to joint resolutions of disapproval required for the above vetoes, joint resolutions of approval were required to approve changes to military personnel assignments to Colombia and Rwanda; military aid expenditures to Columbia, Haiti, or the Soviet Union; or the imposition of wage or price controls pursuant to the Defense Production Act of 1960 (114 Stat. 575, Public Law 106–246; 102 Stat. 2270, Public Law 100–463; 107 Stat. 1474, Public Law 103–139; 100 Stat. 1056, Public Law 100–180; 106 Stat. 4202, Public Law 102–558). Since presidential consent is needed to enact any joint resolution, these vetoes provide Congress with less of a free hand than it had under previous concurrent resolution veto statutes to independently affect the execution of these laws. While many defense vetoes have resulted in interbranch conflict between the president and congressional leadership, committee vetoes imposed on DOD officials exemplify Congress's current approach to employing statutory oversight over defense policy.

Since 2000, Congress has imposed a biennial average of nearly 90 separate veto statutes affecting the DOD and other defense agencies. Many of these statutes require DOD officials to secure advance permission from the Appropriations Committees for any expenditure that "(1) creates or initiates a new program, project, or activity; (2) eliminates a program, project, or activity; (3) increases funds or personnel for any program, project, or activity for which funds have been denied or restricted by this Act . . . (4) proposes to use funds directed for a specific activity for a different purpose . . . (5) augments or reduces existing programs, projects or activities" (123 Stat. 2848, Public Law 111-8). Committee affirmative vetoes such as this are common, but committee deliberative vetoes constitute a large majority of contemporary statutes imposing veto oversight of defense policy. The 111th Congress imposed 65 report and wait requirements on the DOD alone, affecting matters ranging from foreign military aid, arms sales and procurement, weapons system research and development, to private contracting, military installations and training, and a broad array of specific military program spending. This advance notification system allows committees to procure information about designated DOD functions. Armed with a greater understanding of DOD action on these areas of importance, legislators can take subsequent statutory or nonstatutory measures to influence department policy.

Foreign Policy

Interbranch conflicts surrounding foreign policy have existed throughout American history and continue to the present day. The Supreme Court has at times issued rulings affecting this balance of power. In one of the most important cases to date regarding presidential foreign policy authority, Justice George Sutherland's opinion in *United States v. Curtiss-Wright Export Corporation*, 299 U.S. 304 (1936), created the sole-organ doctrine, which designated the president as the sole organ of U.S. foreign policy. Additional rulings in this area have generally added to the increasing power of the foreign policy powers of the president (Adler 1996). The elevated status of the United States as a global superpower over the course of the twentieth century also contributed to the dramatic expansion of presidential foreign policy powers. Particularly during the 1970s, the legislative veto "became a weapon of restraint in the effort to regain control over the executive branch's increasingly cavalier use of authority" (Gibson 1994, 443).

Given its popularity as a means of providing foreign policy oversight, the *Chadha* ruling posed a number of challenges to lawmakers in terms of the veto's continued application (Franck and Bob 1985; Gibson 1992, 1994). Gibson's (1994) studies of Congress's use of the veto to affect foreign policy find that the ruling intensified interbranch conflict for "strategic-salient" issues such as arms sales to the Middle East, as well as "intermestic" issues that meld aspects of both domestic and foreign policy such as most-favored nation status. For diplomatic, crisis, and strategic-nonsalient foreign policy matters, the effect of *Chadha* was less severe. Following a pattern similar to other issue areas, committee-based vetoes have become more common in the post-*Chadha* period and dual-House vetoes are more likely to be tied to joint, rather than concurrent, resolutions as the veto mechanism.

Foreign Trade

International affairs vetoes most often impose policy-making constraints on the president, officials in the State and Defense Departments, and the U.S. Agency for International Development (USAID). Congress's initial foray using the veto in the foreign policy setting concerned international trade. The Neutrality Act of 1939 allowed either the president or Congress to declare the existence of a state of war among specific nation-states (54 Stat. 4, Public Law 76–54). The invocation of this declaration made it unlawful for any American-owned vessel to transport persons, articles, or materials to any country so designated. The declaration also prohibited exports of any type from the United States, including through intermediaries, to the countries engaging in a declared militarized conflict. This reform allowed the president or Congress to independently impose a trade embargo on nations determined to be at war. Since the Neutrality Act's passage, Congress has implemented an additional 34 statutes allowing for vetoes of international trade agreements orchestrated by the president. Typically such vetoes require coordinated action from both chambers, although some statutes have allowed committees to void agreements such as one passed in 1962 allowing the House and Senate Agriculture Committees to block presidential agreements regarding agricultural loan grants and repayments (78 Stat. 1035, Public Law 88–638).

The presence of 10 veto statutes concerning foreign trade agreements included in the Trade Act of 1974 is illustrative of the expanding role of veto oversight that occurred during the 1970s (88 Stat. 1978, Public Law 93–618). Two provisions in the act required a majority vote in both chambers in order for presidentially negotiated trade agreements with nations not receiving nondiscriminatory treatment (also known as "most-favored nation status" or "normal trade relations") to go into effect. This authority was inserted into the bill with the passage of the Jackson-Vanik Amendment (cosponsored by Washington senator Henry Jackson and Ohio representative Charles Vanik), which required nations seeking nondiscriminatory treatment to have a free emigration policy (Pregelj 2005). Congress also made existing trade agreements susceptible to veto by concurrent resolution and included an additional four dual-House negative vetoes of presidential agreements regarding import competition and unfair trade practices. Though Congress has rarely challenged the president regarding most-favored-nation trade status, there have been interbranch confrontations regarding trade relations with Romania, Yugoslavia, Ethiopia, China, and the Soviet Union (Gibson 1994). The president's position on this aspect of international trade was strengthened in 1990 after the veto mechanisms in the Jackson-Vanik were changed from concurrent resolutions to joint resolutions. Amid these changes, Congress began using opposition bills and committee hearings on most-favored-nation status with more frequency (Gibson 1994). The amendment was repealed entirely in 2012 (126 Stat. 1496, Public Law 112–208).

Other bills have imposed similar constraints on presidential powers to alter tariffs (72 Stat. 676, Public Law 85–686; 76 Stat. 899, Public Law 87–794; 91 Stat. 238, Public Law 95–52; 93 Stat. 518, Public Law 96–72). While Congress could veto most proposed alterations with a majority vote in the House and Senate, the Trade Agreements Extension Act of 1958 imposed a rare veto mechanism requiring a two-thirds majority vote in both chambers (72 Stat. 676, Public Law 85–686). Though many concern presidential actions, not all foreign trade vetoes apply to the president.

Foreign trade vetoes have also been imposed on Export-Import Bank loans or financial guarantees in excess of $60 million as well as other loans or aid grants issued by the bank (88 Stat. 2335, Public Law 93–646; 121 Stat. 2290, Public Law 110–161). In addressing trade-related issues, legislators have also used the veto for animal conservation efforts through the State Department. Aspiring to protect dolphins, the International Dolphin Conservation Act of 1992 included two legislative vetoes concerning a ban on yellowfin tuna imports from countries violating the act's dolphin protection standards and the imposition of moratoriums on tuna harvesting practices deemed to threaten dolphins (106 Stat. 3426, Public Law 102–523). Clearly, the applications of veto oversight to matters concerning international trade are broad. In some cases the veto has been used to oversee broad delegations of extraordinary powers to the president to advance U.S. foreign trade, in others its use is directed at more narrow aspects of globalization. Beyond matters concerning foreign commerce and international trade, the legislative veto has also been a common resource used to oversee the distribution of U.S. foreign aid.

Oversight of Foreign Aid

The Lend Lease Act of 1941 contained one of the most notable foreign policy-related legislative vetoes in U.S. history (55 Stat. 11, Public Law 77–11). Understanding that the veto could provide Congress with increased authority to craft foreign policy through foreign aid distribution, the landmark enactment reserved the right for legislators to veto aid administered through the act. During congressional debate on the Lend Lease legislation, Illinois representative Everett Dirksen was able to secure the passage of the veto amendment, the text of which stated:

> After June 30, 1943, or after the passage of a concurrent resolution by the two Houses before June 30, 1943, which declares that the powers conferred by or pursuant to subsection (a) are no longer necessary to promote the defense of the United States, neither the President nor the head of any department or agency shall exercise any of the powers conferred by or pursuant to subsection (a). (55 Stat. 32, Public Law 77–11)

The referenced section was the primary enabling statute that authorized the president to provide considerable amounts of military aid to "any country whose defense the President deems vital to the defense of the United States" (55 Stat. 31, Public Law 77–11). This was the most significant veto passed to that point as it made potentially billions of dollars in foreign aid susceptible to a congressional override, regardless of the preferences of the president.[11]

President Roosevelt strongly opposed this provision, arguing that a congressional veto exercised in this manner would be the functional equivalent to repealing legislation without presidential approval. The president strategically chose not to express this view publicly during the congressional debates on the matter, fearing that revealing his opinion on the controversial provision would result in a loss of support for the bill, which he ultimately wanted to see passed (H. Watson 1975). Although unstated at the time by the president, several lawmakers in Congress agreed with this reasoning.

Utah senator Orrice Murdock argued that if this legislative veto were to pass, Congress could conceivably include similar provisions in every piece of legislation and effectively destroy the president's veto power (Jackson 1953). Despite his opposition to the veto provision, President Roosevelt elected to sign the Lend Lease Act into law because of his overall impression that the initiative was an "outstanding measure which sought to meet a momentous emergency of great magnitude in world affairs" (Roosevelt 1941). Less than a month after signing the bill into law, President Roosevelt took the unusual step of filing a legal memorandum with the attorney general stating his belief that the statute was unconstitutional.

The memorandum filed with the Attorney General's Office began by stating that the president felt "constrained to sign" the legislation because of the unfolding events in Europe, despite his concerns regarding the congressional veto provision contained therein (Roosevelt 1941). The president reasoned that the Lend Lease veto allowed Congress to repeal the legislation with a concurrent resolution. Because the Constitution contained no clause allowing Congress to legislate by resolution, the president argued that any subsequent changes to the enacted legislation must be passed by both congressional chambers and presented to the president. President Roosevelt concluded the legal memorandum with a concise summary of his argument:

> In order that I may be on record as indicating my opinion that the foregoing provision of the so-called Lend-Lease Act is unconstitu-

tional, and in order that my approval of the bill, due to the existing exigencies of the world situation, may not be construed as a tacit acquiescence in any contrary view, I am requesting you to place this memorandum in the official files of the Department of Justice. I am desirous of having this done for the further reason that I should not wish my action in approving the bill which includes this invalid clause, to be used as a precedent for any future legislation comprising provisions of a similar nature. (1941)

Despite the president's position, Congress continued the practice of inserting one- and dual-House vetoes into foreign aid bills.

Legislation providing foreign aid to Turkey and Greece in 1947 allowed Congress to terminate financial and other assistance to these countries through a concurrent resolution of disapproval (61 Stat. 81, Public Law 80–75). The Comprehensive Anti-Apartheid Act of 1986 cut off U.S. foreign aid to South Africa unless its government met certain conditions including the release from prison of all political prisoners including Nelson Mandela (100 Stat. 1103, Public Law 99–440). The law empowered the president to partially or fully recommence aid to South Africa upon his designation that a majority of the conditions had been satisfied and the government was recognized to be making "substantial progress toward dismantling the system of apartheid and establishing a nonracial democracy." Congress, however, could prohibit the resumption of U.S. aid to South Africa with a joint resolution of disapproval. Beyond these vetoes tied to country-specific foreign aid included in the legislation authorizing the assistance, Congress boldly included a generic veto over all U.S. foreign aid in the Foreign Assistance Act of 1961 (75 Stat. 444, Public Law 87–195). This statute provided legislators with a unilateral veto of U.S. foreign aid without having to enact a subsequent appropriations bill.

The legislative veto over all foreign aid is one of the more ambitious vetoes passed by Congress after World War II. Section 617 of the bill stated that any foreign assistance provided by the U.S. government was henceforth subject to a dual-House negative veto by concurrent resolution. This was the first occasion where Congress imposed a generic veto of foreign aid that allowed majority coalitions in both chambers to unilaterally veto any category of foreign assistance for any reason. The passage of this statute made it unnecessary to condition individual foreign aid grants as susceptible to congressional override as had been the case prior to 1961. It was not until 2000 that amendments to the Foreign Assistance Act removed the concurrent resolution veto authority from the U.S. Code and replaced it with a provision requiring the passage of a law to terminate foreign aid (114 Stat. 760, Public Law 106–264).

Despite having the authority to cut aid by concurrent resolution for nearly 40 years, Congress never resorted to using the veto for this purpose.[12] The most likely explanation for this is that it was able to modify foreign aid allotments through annual State Department/foreign operations appropriations bills. Though the veto allowed Congress to quickly cut off foreign aid, at no point did sufficient support arise to block funds appropriated by the current year's spending bill. Because Congress elected to prioritize and curtail foreign assistance levels through the regular appropriations process, the legacy of the generic veto over foreign aid was more symbolism than substance, although it remained available for Congress to threaten its invocation for four decades.

International Diplomacy

While most foreign policy veto statutes concern some aspect of foreign aid, Congress has also used the veto to condition international agreements negotiated by the president such as those concerning nuclear nonproliferation. The most notable of these was the Nuclear Non-Proliferation Act (NNPA) of 1978 (92 Stat. 120, Public Law 95–242), which amended the Atomic Energy Act of 1954. The NNPA delegated the authority to the president to negotiate "binding international undertakings" to control the spread of nuclear materials. International agreements negotiated by the president were conditioned by 12 legislative veto statutes empowering Congress to unilaterally block nonproliferation measures (Clark 1986–87).

Following advance notification to the House Committee on Foreign Affairs and the Senate Committee on Foreign Relations, all agreements were subject to a dual-House veto. Previous administrations followed these procedural requirements by submitting nuclear transfer agreements to the Foreign Affairs Committees for review on a case-by-case basis. Following *Chadha*, the Reagan administration began deviating from this practice by entering into multiple long-term agreements with limited opportunity for congressional review. Arguing that this approach violated the legal framework to enter into such agreements, three members of Congress—California senator Alan Cranston, Michigan representative Howard E. Wolpe, and Maryland representative Michael D. Barnes—in association with six additional plaintiffs outside of Congress filed an unsuccessful suit challenging the president's actions (*Cranston v. Reagan*, 611 F. Supp. 247 (1985)).

Holding that the case presented a nonjusticiable question, the *Cranston* ruling allowed the president to continue to reach agreements with foreign governments concerning nuclear technology as provided for in the NNPA and Atomic Energy Act while largely circumventing the legislative veto procedures contained in the authorizing legislation. Despite this outcome, Congress has continued to enact laws containing legislative vetoes over various nuclear energy agreements (100 Stat. 1101, Public Law 99–440; 122 Stat. 4028, Public Law 110–369). The nuclear accord between the United States and India signed into law by President George W. Bush in 2008 authorized the president to negotiate subsequent nuclear agreements with India or other nations provided that Congress did not veto an agreement with a joint resolution of disapproval (122 Stat. 4028, Public Law 110–369).

Beyond nuclear nonproliferation, Congress has used the veto to constrain other types of foreign agreements. A species conservation law signed by President Carter provided lawmakers with a veto over international fishing accords entered into by the president (91 Stat. 14, Public Law 95–6). During the same term, the International Navigational Rules Act of 1977 specified that a majority vote in both chambers could block the imposition of presidential proclamations amending the Convention on the International Regulations for Preventing Collisions at Sea (91 Stat. 308, Public Law 95–75). More recently, legislation seeking to ensure the integrity of Russian nuclear warhead stockpiles allowed the president to negotiate reductions in debt owed to the United States by the Russian Federation with 15 days prior notification to Congress (116 Stat. 1445, Public Law 107–228). Similarly, the Iran Freedom Support Act of 2006 allowed the president to terminate sanctions on Iran imposed by the act with 15 days advance notice (120 Stat. 1345, Public Law 109–293).

Foreign Policy Vetoes Post-*Chadha*

Beginning with a bill concerning trade with Israel, Congress has passed a total of 12 legislative vetoes affecting trade agreements with foreign nations since *Chadha*. These statutes require the president to submit trade agreements in writing to the finance committees (98 Stat. 3014, Public Law 98–573).[13] As is the case with other issue areas, statutes such as these providing committees with veto power are now the norm. In the post-*Chadha* period, 95 percent of vetoes affecting international affairs are deliberative or affirmative committee vetoes empowering the House and Senate Appropriations Committees, the Senate Foreign Relations Committee, and the House International Relations Committee with veto authority. For example, a 2009 spending bill allocated $50 million for international disaster rehabilitation and reconstruction assistance. USAID administered this type of foreign aid with the proviso that "support may include assistance to develop, strengthen, or preserve democratic institutions and processes, revitalize basic infrastructure, and foster the peaceful resolution of conflict," but required the agency to provide the Appropriations Committees with at least five days advance notification prior to making expenditures on a new program (123 Stat. 845, Public Law 111–8). Although the length of the waiting period can vary, this type is the most common veto mechanism employed by Congress to oversee modern U.S. foreign policy.

Only 17 dual-House affirmative or negative vetoes affecting foreign policy or trade have passed since *Chadha*, all of which require joint resolutions to be executed. Congress enacted 11 of these statutes in the 1980s, the first of which was included in a bill drafted in response to the growing international attention to the 1984–85 Ethiopian famine, which resulted in hundreds of thousands of deaths. This law delegated to the president the authority to determine whether the Ethiopian government was starving its people and engaging in human rights abuses. Congressional concurrence with such a presidential determination would immediately sever all trade with Ethiopia (99 Stat. 265, Public Law 99–83). Four similar trade-restriction measures were included in the Comprehensive Anti-Apartheid Act of 1986 (100 Stat. 1103, Public Law 99–440).

Among the most recent dual-House vetoes affecting foreign policy was one included in a bill concerning U.S. aid to Colombia passed in 2010. This veto statute barred the president from spending funds to support Plan Columbia until a joint resolution of approval sanctioned such a request (114 Stat. 575, Public Law 106–246). During the same year, legislators included a similar provision in a bill addressing commercial communications satellite exports (114 Stat. 849, Public Law 106–280). Because dual-House vetoes such as these are tied to joint resolutions, the president has leverage to influence legislative vetoes affecting the administration's foreign policy by virtue of the presidential veto. Thus, while these statutes provide an avenue for congressional oversight, the joint resolution places the president in a more powerful position and insulates the administration from a direct veto of U.S. diplomatic efforts.

The Legislative Veto, Political Parties, and Policy Subsystems

As data presented in table 5.1 show, it is clear that legislators use a varied approach to this type of oversight. In order to better understand decisions made in Congress regarding the enactment of veto statutes, the remainder of the chapter examines how political parties use the legislative veto during periods of unified and divided government, as well as the effects of partisan majorities in Congress on veto use across different policy subsystems. The analysis section also incorporates ideological estimates of cabinet secretaries developed by Bertelli and Grose (2011) as well as the measures of agency ideology developed by Clinton and Lewis (2008).

The first two columns in table 5.3 provide data regarding the number of enacted veto statutes during periods of unified Democratic and Republican government where the president and both chambers of Congress are controlled by a single party. From 1931 to 2010, 17 congressional terms are characterized by unified Democratic government, almost all of which occurred before 1980. In contrast, from 1931 to 2010, three complete congressional terms had Republican majorities in both chambers with a Republican in the White House. The unified Democratic government terms existed for 34 years, while slightly more than six years have been characterized by unified Republican government control. Because the periods of Republican control occurred more recently, the number of veto statutes passed during the three terms of unified Republican control (854) is nearly identical to the total number passed during the 17 terms of Democratic control (869). This near equivalency exists because periods of unified Democratic government occurred during earlier periods where legislative veto oversight was more limited, in stark contrast to more contemporary Congresses, where its use is widespread. Thus, when comparing partisan differences in veto usage it is most appropriate to examine percentages by policy area due to the considerable increase in veto statutes that has occurred over time.

Unified Government

The first thing to note in comparing veto enactments across unified Democratic and Republican regimes is the general lack of differences that exist with regard to nearly every policy area. For a majority the difference between the parties is less than 1 percentage point. A difference of means test comparing veto enactments by issue area under periods of Democratic and Republican unified government shows no statistically significant difference between the two.

The top five policy areas of veto enactments by percentage during unified Democratic government are defense (23.8 percent); international affairs and foreign aid (20.4 percent); government operations (15.1 percent); public lands and water management (7.3 percent); and law, crime, and family issues (7.3 percent). For periods of unified Republican govern-

TABLE 5.3. Enacted legislative veto statutes by policy area and government type: 1931–2010

Policy Area	Unified Democratic	Unified Republican	Divided Republican President	Divided Democratic President
Defense	23.8% (207)	20.0% (171)	29.2% (480)	34.7% (156)
International Affairs and Foreign Aid	20.4% (177)	23.7% (202)	18.8% (309)	16.7% (75)
Government Operations	15.1% (131)	12.3% (105)	11.6% (191)	11.8% (53)
Law, Crime, and Family Issues	7.3% (63)	14.6% (125)	7.1% (116)	6.0% (27)
Public Lands and Water	7.3% (63)	8.2% (70)	7.8% (128)	8.7% (39)
Energy	6.0% (52)	2.0% (17)	6.1% (100)	2.9% (13)
Space, Science, and Technology	4.8% (42)	1.8% (15)	4.0% (65)	3.6% (16)
Transportation	2.7% (23)	3.0% (26)	4.0% (65)	3.8% (17)
Agriculture	2.8% (24)	4.0% (34)	1.0% (17)	3.6% (16)
Finance and Domestic Commerce	1.3% (11)	2.2% (19)	2.8% (46)	2.0% (9)
Foreign Trade	1.2% (10)	1.8% (15)	1.9% (31)	0.7% (3)
Labor, Employment, and Immigration	1.5% (13)	1.4% (12)	0.4% (7)	0.7% (3)
Community Development	1.3% (11)	1.1% (9)	1.8% (30)	0.5% (2)
Macroeconomics	0.9% (8)	1.1% (9)	0.9% (14)	0.7% (3)
Environment	1.0% (9)	0.7% (6)	0.6% (9)	1.3% (6)
Heath	1.3% (11)	0.9% (8)	0.6% (10)	0.2% (1)
Education	0.6% (5)	0.5% (4)	1.0% (17)	1.1% (5)
Civil Rights and Civil Liberties	0.7% (6)	0.7% (6)	0.3% (5)	0.7% (3)
Social Welfare	0.4% (3)	0.1% (1)	0.1% (2)	0.5% (2)
Total	869	854	1,642	449

Note: Columns may not sum to 100 percent due to rounding. Congressional terms with unified Democratic government were in office during 1933–46, 1949–52, 1961–68, 1977–80, 1993–94, and 2009–10. Congressional terms with unified Republican government were in office during 1953–54, 2001 until Senator Jim Jeffords switched from Republican to independent in May, and 2003–6. Congressional terms where Republicans held a majority in at least one chambers with a Democratic president were in office during 1947–48 and 1995–2000. Congressional terms where Democratic majorities existed in both chambers with a Republican president were in office during 1931–32, 1955–60, 1969–76, 1981–92, and 2007–8.

ment, the top five policy areas of veto enactments are international affairs and foreign aid (23.7 percent); defense (20.0 percent); law, crime and family issues (14.6 percent); government operations (12.3 percent); and public lands and water management (8.2 percent). Across each regime type, the five policy areas with the greatest percentage of enactments are identical. Similar patterns emerge when examining the remaining policy areas.

During periods of unified government for all but five major policy areas, the difference between the two parties is less than 3 percent. Notably, there is only a single policy area where the difference is greater than 5 percent. More than 14 percent of all enacted vetoes during unified Republican government concern law, crime, and family issues, while this percentage for unified Democratic government is about half this amount. The prevalence of law and crime veto statutes enacted during Republican unified government is almost entirely driven by the creation of the DHS in 2002, which was followed by consecutive terms of unified Republican government. Virtually all of the vetoes implemented to constrain functions performed by DHS officials are included in this category by virtue of the *Congressional Bills Project* coding rubric. Absent the creation of this new department, it is doubtful that this percentage would deviate substantially from unified Democratic government. The similarities seen when comparing unified Democratic and Republican government regimes are striking not only due to the nearly identical policy applications of the veto but also because these regimes occurred for the most part during different eras.

Divided Government

The third and fourth columns in table 5.3 provide data regarding the percentage of veto enactments for all policy areas during periods of divided government where at least one chamber of Congress is controlled by the party opposite the president. From 1931 to 2010, there are four congressional terms where Republicans controlled both chambers of Congress with a Democratic president, and 12 congressional terms where Democrats controlled at least one house of Congress with a Republican president. As is the case with veto enactment trends during periods of unified government for both parties, few differences exist with regard to veto usage during periods of divided government. Again, a difference of means test comparing these different configurations of divided government shows no significant differences in vetoes adopted across each of the 19 issue areas.

For nearly every policy area, veto enactment percentages are extremely similar when comparing divided government under Democratic and Republican presidents. There are only two issue areas where the difference in veto enactment percentages is greater than 3 percentage points—defense and government operations. During periods of unified Democratic government vetoes affecting defense policy constitute 23.8 percent of all vetoes. In contrast, defense legislative vetoes increase to 29.2 percent of all veto enactments during periods of divided government with Republican president. This increase of more than 5 percent may indicate a desire by Democratic Congresses to impose greater numbers of veto constraints on defense officials, including the president acting as commander in chief, as a means to exercise greater oversight influence in this policy area. Interviews with Democrats serving on the House Armed Services Committee provided anecdotal evidence supporting this assertion.

Given the increased importance of defense policy and issues related to national defense in the post-9/11 world, two of the interviewed Democrats serving on the Armed Services Committee emphasized the importance of engaging in oversight activities with regard to the DOD, including the incorporation of legislative vetoes into authorizations and appropriations legislation. An Arkansas representative cited several instances when the committee had difficulty obtaining information from the DOD. Whether it is requests for testimony, reports, or other data, he claimed that the committee does not always receive the information it desires. When asked about the increasing number of report and wait mandates imposed on the DOD, the congressman expressed confidence that such requirements at the least alerted the committee to a pending action. In these cases, the committee typically receives the requested information, and the reporting agency is attuned to the fact that the committee is cognizant of certain activities.

Based on this comparison, the use of the legislative veto by Democratic congressional majorities is, for the most part, not affected by the partisanship of the president. The increase in veto enactments as a means to institutionalize oversight over defense policy, and an actual decrease in government operations vetoes, are the only notable change according to presidential partisanship. Republican majorities in Congresses act in largely the same way by not adapting their application of legislative vetoes when a Democratic president holds office.

There are only three policy areas where the percentage of vetoes enacted with Republican congressional majorities differs by more than 3 percent when comparing terms serving with Republican to those with Democratic presidents. Vetoes affecting law, crime, and family issues represent nearly 15 percent of all vetoes enacted during unified Republican government and only 6 percent of enacted vetoes during divided government with Republican control of Congress. Again, this difference is almost entirely a function of increases in the number of recent vetoes enacted as a means to constrain DHS actions.

The second policy area where Republican congressional majorities alter their application of veto provisions based on presidential partisanship is defense. Similar to the increased use of defense-related vetoes by Democrats during periods of divided government, Republican majorities have increased the number of vetoes passed when a Democrat is commander in chief. Defense vetoes constitute 20 percent of all vetoes during periods of unified Republican government. This percentage increases to nearly 35 percent of all vetoes during periods of divided government with a Democratic president. This increase of over 15 percent is by far the greatest difference in terms of veto usage when examining the effect of legislative and executive partisanship. Similar to the increase use of vetoes over defense policy by Democrats with a Republican president, this large discrepancy suggests that Republican majorities are also more apt to utilize the legislative veto to increase their leverage in shaping defense policy during Democratic administrations.

Lastly, the percentage of vetoes enacted by Republican Congresses regarding international affairs and foreign aid actually decreases by about 7 percent during periods of divided government. On its face, this trend seems strange. However, as is the case with the dramatic increase in vetoes affecting the DHS from 2002 to 2008, contemporary appropriations bills for the State Department and foreign operations have contained greater numbers of veto provisions. The increasing numbers of vetoes included in appropriations legislation affecting foreign affairs following the 9/11 terrorist attacks occurred during periods of unified Republican government. The most likely explanation for this development attributes the increased number of foreign affairs vetoes enacted during the most recent congressional terms, which have largely been characterized by unified Republican government, as the basis of this disparity. Discounting the difference in veto use in the law category attributable to the creation of the DHS, defense issues and foreign policy are the only policy areas where a considerable difference exists in the implementation of veto provisions by Republican congressional majorities depending on the partisanship of the president.

In sum, the distribution of veto enactments is remarkably similar when comparing periods of unified and divided government. Very few differences exist when assessing the relative percentages of veto enactments across policy area during periods of unified Republican, unified Democratic, and different configurations of divided government. These relatively constant patterns illustrate the fairly stable oversight role of the legislative veto. Legislators rarely employ the device to oversee policies concerning social welfare, civil rights, health, education, environment, macroeconomics, and community development issue areas, irrespective of the partisanship of Congress or the president. Vetoes affecting other issue areas also exhibit little variation according to partisanship. The lone exception to this stability is defense policy vetoes, which exhibit an appreciable increase during periods of divided government. Progressing beyond a simple examination of the percentages of legislative vetoes passed by policy area under different configurations of divided and unified government, the section that follows provides a more detailed analysis of the effects of partisanship on the likelihood of veto enactments more generally, as well as an analysis of Democratic and Republican policy subsystems.

Partisan Policy Subsystems

The effect of party on the interchange between presidential initiatives and congressional oversight is likely to vary across issue area. Scholars have found that policy subsystems in a partisan environment tend to be tied to a particular party by arguing that the relationship between presidents and interest groups is structured by the relationship of interest groups to the president's party, and the varying opportunities for presidential leadership (Tichenor 2005). For example, Democratic presidents are generally more inclined to focus on policy subsystems of historically liberal issues such as the environment, consumer protection, civil rights, poverty, education, labor, and community development. Conversely, Republican presidents tend to invest more resources on conservative policy subsystems including defense, business, finance, industry, and energy (Tichenor 2005). Wood (1988) finds similar support for the effect of partisanship on bureaucratic policy making by analyzing changes in EPA enforcement following the 1980 elections. Further electoral research on partisanship and issue ownership has identified certain issues that are "owned" by one of the two major parties (Petrocik, Benoit, and Hansen 2003).

Given these partisan allegiances tied to particular policy subsystems, congressional partisanship may likewise have an effect on legislative veto use. Because traditionally liberal policy subsystems will tend to be more important to Democratic lawmakers it is reasonable to expect that they should be more willing to incur transaction costs connected to monitoring compliance with legislative veto oversight of agencies related to these policy areas as a means to ensure policy outcomes are acceptable to Democrats. Republican lawmakers should be willing to do the same for agencies addressing traditionally conservative policy subsystems. Although considering legislative vetoes in the aggregate does not take into account the policy significance of individual vetoes, which can vary widely, increases in the number of enacted veto statutes should generally be indicative of greater efforts to impose statutory oversight.

Partisan Policy Subsystem Hypothesis. *The majority party in Congress should implement more vetoes connected to bureaucratic agencies that are related to the policy subsystems supported by the party in power.*

In order to model the effect of partisanship on legislative veto enactments by policy area over time, I created a panel data set that contains the number of veto enactments by policy area during each Congress from 1931 to 2010 where the congressional term serves as the time component and individual policy areas are the panels.

Research on issue ownership by Petrocik, Benoit, and Hansen (2003) is used to code policy areas into Republican and Democratic subsystem categories. Examining presidential campaign discourse from 1952 to 2000, the study identifies 13 issues areas owned by Democrats, Republicans, or neither party. Based on their evaluation of appeals and rhetoric by presidential candidates, civil liberties, civil rights, social welfare, agriculture, social class, women's rights, and organized labor are all classified as issues owned by Democrats. Civil and social order, defense, and federal taxing and spending are classified as issues owned by Republicans. Foreign relations, the economy, and government functioning are classified as belonging to neither party.

Table 5.4 presents estimates from three random effects regression models where the unit of analysis is the policy area/term spanning a period of 39 congressional terms over a period of nearly 80 years for a total of 741 cases.[14] To test whether party majorities systematically vary their application of the legislative veto across different issues, the dependent variable in each model is the number of enacted veto statutes by policy area. Congress enacted an average of five veto statutes per issue area across all terms included in the sample with a standard deviation of 13.7. Each model includes a variable indicating the number of veto statutes passed by the prior Congress to account for serial correlation in the data (Beck and Katz

1995). It is also important to include a lagged veto variable because spending bills often include legislative veto provisions that recur across fiscal years.

First included in the 1996 DOD appropriations bill was a committee deliberative veto stipulating that the department could not expend funds to facilitate certain arms transfers abroad unless the international affairs committees were notified 15 days in advance (109 Stat. 677, Public Law 104–61). Every subsequent DOD appropriations bill has included this provision. As approximately two-thirds of all enacted legislative vetoes from 1931 to 2010 are included in appropriations legislation, many veto requirements persist over time.

TABLE 5.4. Random effects regression models of legislative vetoes by issue area: 1931–2010

Variable	Model 1	Model 2	Model 3
Lagged Number of Legislative Veto Enactments	0.89***	0.88***	0.89***
	(0.02)	(0.02)	(0.02)
House Majority Party (0=Dem, 1=GOP)	–1.16	–1.48	–0.85
	(1.03)	(1.10)	(1.15)
Senate Majority Party (0=Dem, 1=GOP)	–1.09	–1.27	–1.33
	(0.83)	(0.90)	(0.96)
Divided Government	1.20**	1.17**	1.19**
	(0.58)	(0.58)	(0.58)
Post-*Chadha*	0.94	1.12	0.99
	(0.75)	(0.75)	(0.75)
108th Congress	18.03***	18.00***	18.02***
	(1.86)	(1.85)	(1.86)
Republican Policy Subsystems	—	0.81	—
		(0.87)	
Republican Policy Subsystems* House Majority Party	—	1.69	—
		(2.44)	
Republican Policy Subsystems* Senate Majority Party	—	1.58	—
		(2.17)	
Democratic Policy Subsystems	—	—	–0.86
			(0.72)
Democratic Policy Subsystems* House Majority Party	—	—	–1.23
			(2.01)
Democratic Policy Subsystems* Senate Majority Party	—	—	0.98
			(1.81)
Constant	0.25	0.16	0.49
	(0.41)	(0.43)	(0.45)
N observations	741	741	741
N groups	19	19	19
R^2	0.7280	0.7307	0.7288
Wald χ^2	1964.65	1983.74	1964.65
Prob > χ^2	0.0009	0.0000	0.0000

Note: Standard errors in parentheses. *** $p<.01$, ** $p<.05$, * $p<.10$.

As expected, the coefficient estimate for the lagged dependent variable is significant and positive in each model, which suggests that the number of vetoes enacted by Congress in a given policy area is a good predictor of the number of vetoes that the following Congress will enact. When controlling for the lagged number of veto enactments, several other factors are also found to exert a significant influence on veto oversight. Because lagged dependent variables exert a suppressing effect on the relationship between the remaining variables, these findings are particularly notable (Achen 2000).

Additional independent variables included in this analysis indicate the partisan majority of the House and Senate, the presence of divided government, Congresses serving after the *Chadha* ruling, and a dummy variable for the 108th Congress. The variables measuring partisan control of the House and Senate are included as a means to isolate the effects of partisanship on the likelihood of veto enactments. The measure of divided government is coded as a 1 when the party opposite the president holds a majority in at least one of the two congressional chambers.

As previously discussed, the 108th Congress has the notoriety of passing the most legislative veto statutes in U.S. history. The more than 500 vetoes passed during this term correspond to about 15 percent of all veto statutes. This inordinate amount of veto statutes is partly a function of the failure of the 107th Congress to pass nearly all of the second session spending bills prior to adjournment. This is especially notable due to the fact that Democrats held majority party status for most of the 107th Senate, while Republicans regained control of the chamber following the 2004 elections. Now serving during a period of unified Republican control, the 108th Congress passed a holdover omnibus spending package that contained about 125 legislative vetoes. Because of the failure of the prior Congress, which served during a period of divided government, to pass 10 of the 12 major spending bills for the 2003 fiscal year, the 108th Congress had a rare opportunity to pass three years' worth of budgets. This spending anomaly likely exerts a suppressing effect on the relationship between divided government and veto enactments. One way to account for this spending irregularity would be to simply attribute the 2003 budget passed by the 108th Congress to its predecessor. Such an approach would be inappropriate since the omnibus appropriations bill was fully sponsored, debated, amended, and passed by the 108th Congress. A more suitable alternative is to simply include a dichotomous variable for the 108th term.[15]

Three of the six independent variables from the first model presented in table 5.4 correspond with increases in veto use. The lack of significance on the variables indicating partisan control of the House and Senate suggests that there are no significant differences in terms of partisan control of the Congress and the use of the veto across all issue areas. This result is expected given that the desire for effective oversight is not unique to Democrats or Republicans, but is typically a shared congressional objective where partisanship may, at times, play an important role. Indeed, the expansion of legislative veto oversight spanning eight decades has taken place during periods of both Democratic and Republican control of Congress. The post-*Chadha* variable is also an insignificant predictor of veto usage. Although Congress has enacted several times as many vetoes as it had passed before the ruling, when accounting for the number of veto statutes enacted by the prior Congress, and thereby the general trend of increase in vetoes over time, the Congresses serving after the ruling have not accounted for substantially more legislative veto statutes.

While variables indicating congressional partisanship and the post-*Chadha* period in the first model are not statistically significant, the remaining variables significantly affect legislative veto oversight. Although veto statutes are no more likely to be enacted when comparing party majority status in each chamber, both parties are more apt to impose veto oversight during periods of divided government. Lastly, since the three omnibus spending measures passed by the 108th Congress contained scores of veto provisions, this variable is also positively associated with greater numbers of veto enactments.

There are two primary points to take away from the results of this first model. The first is that the numbers of veto statutes enacted by issue area in a given term are not appreciably affected by which party is currently in the majority in the House or Senate. Second, when controlling for veto statutes passed by the previous Congress, the uniqueness of the 108th Congress, and the *Chadha* ruling, lawmakers are more likely to propose and enact oversight provisions imposing legislative vetoes during periods of divided government. Under unified partisan control, this type of oversight is less common.

The second model in table 5.4 includes a variable indicating the three policy areas that Republican officeholders and candidates often emphasize. This variable is interacted with the House and Senate majority party variables to test for a conditional effect of Republican majority party status on the enactment of vetoes in these three issue areas. Since the majority party variables are coded as a 1 when Republican possess majority party status, the expected sign on the interaction term coefficients is positive, which would signify that Republican majorities generally seek to impose greater oversight through the legislative veto for executive agencies addressing these issues.

As is the case with the first model, the lagged number of congressional vetoes is a strong predictor of the contemporary number of vetoes enacted. The only remaining factors included in the model exerting a significant effect on veto statutes are the divided government and the 108th Congress dummy variables. Although the coefficients on the two interaction terms have the expected sign, neither is statistically significant, indicating that no meaningful difference exists in the passage of veto statutes affecting these three issues of importance to Republicans.

The third model includes a variable indicating policy areas traditionally considered as Democratic policy subsystems. This variable is interacted with the two majority party variables. Given the coding of these party majority variables, the expected direction of the interaction term coefficients is negative. As is the case with the previous model, Democratic majority party status in either chamber does not correspond with greater use of the veto to oversee the execution of laws in these select areas. The lagged number of veto enactments along with the divided government and 108th Congress variables remain the only independent variables that correspond with greater numbers of veto enactments.

Results from this empirical analysis demonstrate that the imposition of statutes containing legislative vetoes does not vary in any systematic fashion depending on which party currently holds the majority in the House and Senate. Given the fact that each party prioritizes various policy areas differently, it is reasonable to expect, for example, greater numbers of vetoes related to defense policy during periods when Republicans are the majority party. This expectation, however, is not borne out by the analysis.

In each of these models, the only significant predictors of veto enactments are the number of vetoes passed during the prior term, whether there is split party control of the federal government, and the dichotomous variable for the 108th Congress that passed a record 533 veto statutes. Although majority party status in both chambers was not found to affect veto oversight, the model results demonstrate that greater levels of veto enactments exist during periods of divided government. These coupled findings indicate that it is not the majority party in Congress that influences veto oversight, but rather congressional majority party status relative to the president's party. When controlling for other factors, the number of veto statutes imposed on the executive branch increases when the party opposite the president controls at least one of the two chambers. This result holds true when examining nearly the full universe of vetoes passed from 1931 to 2010. Earlier analysis comparing the relative use of the veto across issue area showed few differences when comparing unified and divided government. Considering these findings in tandem suggests that while divided government generally does not correspond with changes in the issue areas where veto oversight is used, Congress does often increase the number of veto statutes passed during periods of divided government. To provide an alternative perspective on the veto's policy applications, analysis in the following two sections parses the data according to executive agency or department rather than by issue area alone. Of particular focus is the imposition of veto oversight on cabinet-level departments and independent regulatory commissions.

Targets in the Cabinet—Defense and State

The bias toward veto use in defense and international affairs has disproportionately affected the Departments of Defense and State. So far, this chapter has discussed veto oversight across distinct policy areas. To provide an alternative perspective, figures 5.2 and 5.3 differentiate veto statutes according to the executive department or agency that the veto requirement affects.[16] A committee deliberative veto statute included in the 2004 Intelligence Authorization Act required seven days advance notification from the CIA director and Defense Secretary regarding proposals to construct or improve intelligence community facilities (117 Stat. 2610, Public Law 108–177). This statute is coded as pertaining to defense policy according to table 5.1, and is tabulated as a veto over both the DOD and the CIA in figures 5.2 and 5.3. While there is considerable overlap between these categorization approaches, not all vetoes coded as pertaining to defense policy impose constraints on the DOD. Congress has passed a broad array of vetoes affecting defense-related programs restraining the departments of State, Veterans Affairs, Energy, Interior, and Justice, as well as the president.

Given the distribution of veto enactments across issue area, it is unsurprising that veto oversight has disproportionately affected certain cabinet-level departments. Vetoes are most commonly imposed on the DOD, which has been subjected to one-third of all veto statutes affecting the cabinet. When combined with vetoes pertaining to actions of State Department officials, these two categories constitute about 50 percent of the cabinet total. Beyond Defense and State, a second tier of eight departments have each been subjected to legislative veto requirements on more than 100 occasions. Congress has rarely imposed legislative veto oversight on the

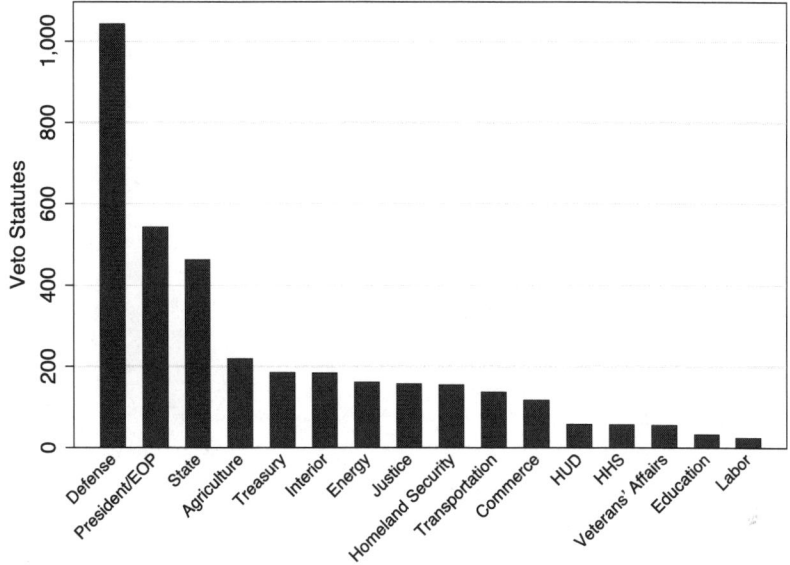

Fig. 5.2. Legislative veto statutes by department: 1931–2010

remaining five departments—Housing and Urban Development, Health and Human Services, Education, Veterans' Affairs, and Labor. Only 25 statutes containing vetoes have applied to actions of officials in the Labor Department. In addition to the cabinet, Congress has passed more than 450 vetoes aimed at constraining or otherwise overruling presidential actions. With a few notable exceptions, veto oversight is less commonly found for executive branch institutions beyond the president and the cabinet.

Focusing specifically on veto enactments affecting cabinet-level departments, table 5.5 provides fixed effects panel regression model results using a data set where the unit of analysis is the department/congressional term.[17] Legislative veto data extend back to 1931, which predates several cabinet departments. The departments of Homeland Security (2002), Veterans' Affairs (1988), Education (1979), Health and Human Services (1979), Energy (1977), Transportation (1966), and Housing and Urban Development (1965) are each added to the sample during the congressional term of their creation, producing a total of 451 cases.[18]

Each model includes a variable indicating the number of veto enactments imposed on each department by the previous Congress. As expected, this variable is a strong predictor of the number of department vetoes enacted each term. A divided government variable spanning the full time period is also used. To account for issue saliency, which is one of the transaction cost factors expected to affect the congressional approach to veto oversight, several models include measures of department spending. These spending data across departments are made available by the OMB and date back to 1962 (Office of Management and Budget 2012). Since the time increment in this panel data set is the congressional term, the spending variable indicates the average amount appropriated to each department for the two fiscal years during each term. Also, because the OMB reports department outlays in current dollars, the Consumer Price Index from the Bureau of Labor Statistics is used to adjust the spending outlay variable for inflation into 2010 dollars. Two additional variables measure the ideological heterogeneity between each chamber of Congress and each cabinet secretary.

In a 2011 study, Bertelli and Grose construct ideological estimates for

TABLE 5.5. Fixed effects regression models of legislative vetoes by department

Variable	Model 1 1931–2010	Model 2 1962–2010	Model 3 1962–2010	Model 4 1991–2004	Model 5 1988–2006
Lagged Legislative Veto Statutes	0.84***	0.72***	0.71***	0.37	0.38*
	(0.03)	(0.04)	(0.04)	(0.24)	(0.23)
Divided Government	0.13	−0.78	1.66*	—	—
	(0.74)	(1.01)	(0.92)		
Average 2-Year Appropriations Outlay (2010 dollars)	—	0.00**	0.00	0.00***	0.00***
		(0.00)	(0.00)	(0.00)	(0.00)
108th Congress	—	—	20.39***	—	—
			(2.16)		
Secretary-House Ideological Heterogeneity	—	—	—	8.03	—
				(17.11)	
Secretary-Senate Ideological Heterogeneity	—	—	—	−7.69	—
				(16.77)	
Department-House Ideological Heterogeneity	—	—	—	—	6.59
					(11.89)
Department-Senate Ideological Heterogeneity	—	—	—	—	−17.98
					(14.10)
Constant	1.62***	2.35**	0.55	−5.63	6.15
	(0.57)	(1.01)	(0.92)	(6.37)	(8.60)
N observations	451	327	327	89	100
N groups	15	15	15	15	15
R^2	0.6300	0.6927	0.7569	0.2090	0.2318
F	369.50	110.64	128.99	2.42	2.88
Prob > F	0.0000	0.0000	0.0000	0.0561	0.0276

Note: Standard errors in parentheses. *** $p<.01$, ** $p<.05$, * $p<.1$.

cabinet secretaries for a period spanning 1991 to 2004. Performing a content analysis on committee testimony made by leaders of all 15 departments, they impute secretary positions on designated roll-call votes for legislation discussed in the committee hearing. These inferred positions facilitate ideological ideal point estimates akin to those previously constructed for lawmakers in Congress and the president (McCarty and Poole 1995; Poole 1998; Poole and Rosenthal 2000). The resulting data provide ideology measures that are directly comparable to lawmakers for a total of 46 cabinet secretaries. Considered in association with legislative ideology estimates, the second model includes variables indicating the absolute distance between the median voter in each chamber and each cabinet secretary.

A subsequent model incorporates an alternative measure of department preferences using an agency ideology measure created by Clinton and Lewis (2008). Using a multirater item response model, Clinton and Lewis transform expert survey responses into ideology scores for 82 agencies from 1988 to 2005. These scores range from -2.07 (Action—a federal volunteer agency dissolved in 1993) to 2.40 (the Department of the Navy). Since this analysis focuses exclusively on the cabinet, only the ideology measures for the 15 departments are included. Among these, the DOD and Commerce Departments are the most conservatively rated, while the Departments of Labor and Housing and Urban Development represent the most liberal. Similar to the variables created with secretary ideology data, two variables are created with the department ideology measure that indicate the absolute distance between the median voters in each chamber and the department. Although each department receives one ideology score for the entire period, changes in membership in the two chambers allow these ideological heterogeneity variables to vary across time.

The dependent variable for the models in table 5.5 is the total number of legislative vetoes enacted during a congressional term by department. This variable has a mean of about seven, and ranges from a minimum of zero to a maximum of 102 veto statutes passed affecting the DOD during the 108th Congress. Model 1 includes the only two variables available across the entire time period. The number of vetoes passed affecting each department emerges as a significant predictor of the number of veto statutes enacted in the following term. Divided government, however, does not correspond with substantially more of these types of oversight statutes. The next model adds the average appropriation amount allocated to each department during each term. Like the lagged dependent variable, greater levels of funding received by departments also correspond with greater levels of legislative veto oversight. This suggests that legislators are more willing to incur the costs associated with veto oversight of departments with larger budgets, all else equal. The presence of divided government again does not exert a significant effect on veto enactments.

The third model adds the dichotomous variable for the 108th Congress. With this specification, the coefficient on the divided government variable is positive and significant. Prior veto enactments remain a significant predictor of the current number of such statutes, while the p-value of the spending variable coefficient is 0.12, which very nearly reaches the conventional 0.1 significance level. Thus, across a period of nearly 50 years, when controlling for the uniqueness of the 108th Congress, lawmakers are more likely to enact greater numbers of legislative vetoes constraining departments of the federal government during periods of divided government.

The fourth model adds the two variables capturing the ideological distance between the cabinet secretaries and the median voter in the House and Senate. The coefficient estimates on each of these variables are not significant, and the coefficient on the Senate's measure is actually negative. There are a number of plausible explanations for this result. First, because the secretary ideology measures are only available from 1991 to 2004, the number of department/years is dramatically reduced from previous models. Second, many of the department/years included in this limited sample represent departments where Congress rarely uses veto statutes to oversee departmental functions. More than half of the department/years in the smaller sample receive less than five legislative veto directives during each two-year period. Splitting the sample to only include the departments incurring greater numbers of veto enactments produces a similar noneffect. A third possible explanation concerns multicollinearity, as the two ideological heterogeneity measures are correlated at 0.9. Specifying the model with an alternative singular measure in lieu of the two ideology distance measures also finds no significant effect on veto enactments. In the end, experimenting with several different measures and model specifications fails to establish a connection between the ideological distance between cabinet secretaries and Congress with the number of enacted legislative vetoes.

The variables indicating ideological heterogeneity between each chamber and individual departments included in the fifth model likewise do not significantly affect the numbers of legislative veto statutes passed during a congressional term. These two measures are also highly correlated with one other, but model specifications using a single congressional-departmental ideology measure similarly failed to establish a link between this factor and veto enactments.

Despite the finding that variations in secretary and departmental ideology do not produce noticeable changes in veto oversight, this analysis does demonstrate that Congress is more likely to rely on statutory oversight through the legislative veto for departments with greater levels of funding when controlling for other factors. This result corroborates the transaction cost theoretical framework expectations, as lawmakers are generally more apt to incur costs related to proposing, passing, and monitoring executive actions thorough legislative vetoes for departments that are allocated greater shares of federal spending.

Most every variable included to capture interbranch political conflict did not engender significant differences in the passage of veto statutes. However, when accounting for the abnormal number of spending bills passed by the 108th Congress, at least one model identifies a connection between divided government and the legislative veto. This too, fits with the transaction cost approach, suggesting that lawmakers are more apt to incur costs related to veto oversight when the president belongs to the opposite party.

In sum, legislative veto oversight requirements are most commonly imposed to exercise control over actions of the president and the cabinet. A coding of all veto statutes enacted by Congress demonstrates that more than 80 percent have affected the president, the Executive Office of the President, or the cabinet, with a disproportionate number of cabinet vetoes addressing the Departments of Defense and State. The remaining share of legislative veto statutes affecting executive actors beyond the cabinet have disproportionately been applied to USAID, GSA, and NASA.

Exempting the president, the Executive Office of the President, and the cabinet, Congress has used the legislative veto with most frequency to affect functions of USAID, as figure 5.3 shows. These statutes usually place conditions on how the agency can disburse foreign aid for certain programs. Over 300 legislative veto statutes imposing requirements on USAID have passed since *Chadha*. Vetoes over NASA functions typically come in the form of committee deliberative vetoes, whereas those most commonly applied to the GSA belong to the committee affirmative category. Nearly all GSA vetoes concern spending on construction or building projects, which require approval from the spending committees. After the hundreds of veto requirements levied on USAID, GSA, and NASA, there is a large drop-off in the number of legislative vetoes affecting the remaining executive institutions. With just a few exceptions involving the Nuclear Energy Regulatory Commission and the FEC, veto oversight is rarely applied to regulatory commissions.

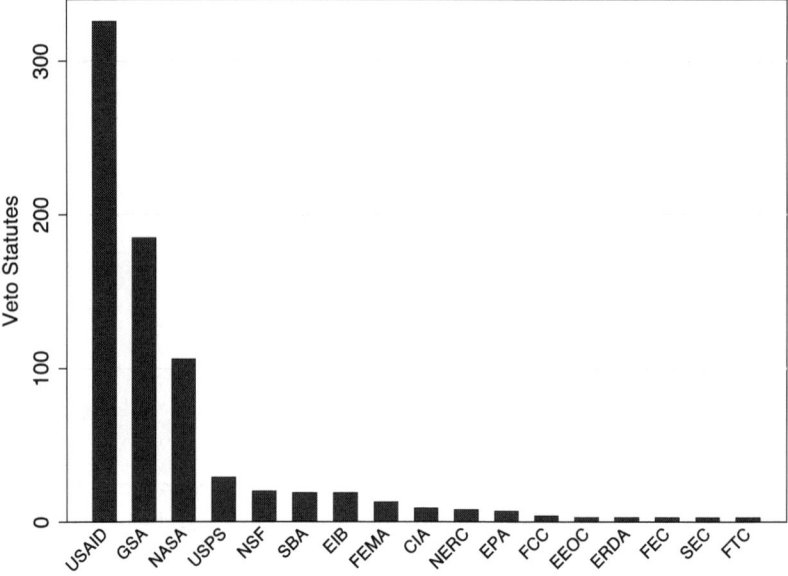

Fig. 5.3. Legislative veto statutes by agency: 1931–2010

Summary

The legislative veto, which began as an instrument to oversee presidential reorganization initiatives, has dramatically expanded to scores of other issue areas addressed by the federal government. Congress has applied this type of oversight to subjects as different as nuclear energy agreements made with foreign states and office redecorating expenses for government workers, NASA research and development and FTC rules on cigarette advertising, large-scale military deployments and forest fire prevention, as well as billions of dollars in foreign aid and post office construction. There are few reaches of the executive branch that have been completely insulated from this type of oversight.

Although lawmakers have used the veto in some capacity to oversee agency actions in each major policy area identified by the *Congressional Bills Project*, there is a tremendous amount of variation in the distribution of statutes containing vetoes across these 19 different issue areas. Over one-quarter of all vetoes enacted in U.S. history have affected defense and national security policies, while those affecting social welfare issues constitute a mere two-tenths of 1 percent.

For most major policy areas included in this analysis there exists little variation in the relative frequency of veto enactments before and after *Chadha*. Defense, for example, serves as the category where the veto is most often used during each of these periods. Veto enactments concerning government operations, public lands and water management, transportation, and others have also displayed consistency over time. Likewise, there are many policy areas where legislative veto oversight remains sparse. While Congress has periodically implemented vetoes in these areas, these statutes tend to be infrequent measures aimed to address a specific matter.

Other issue areas have witnessed considerable changes with regard to veto use over time, particularly when examining the post-*Chadha* era. The creation of the DHS drastically increased the number of vetoes classified as applying to law, crime, and family issues. Vetoes enacted in this issue area were less than 1 percent of all veto enactments during most of the twentieth century, but have increased to nearly 8 percent of vetoes enacted in recent decades. As the number of veto enactments has increased for certain policy areas, it has declined for others. Space, science, and technology vetoes constituted greater than 10 percent of all veto enactments from 1931 to 1983 and have since fallen to about 2 percent. Most vetoes from this category were implemented to oversee NASA functions, and although the number of these statutes has remained relatively constant over time, the huge increase in the total number of enacted veto statutes in recent decades has rendered approximately the same number of NASA vetoes as a smaller percentage of the overall total. Despite changes in veto use over time for policy areas such as this, trends in veto use for most policy areas display considerable stability.

Comparing veto use according to congressional majority party status provides further evidence regarding the steadiness of this type of oversight. Regardless of which party is in control of Congress, legislative vetoes are most often used to oversee policies related to defense, international affairs, and government operations. Although there are a small number of policy areas where veto use varies depending on the majority party in Congress, the manner in which Democratic and Republican majorities employ the legislative veto is remarkably similar.

Models estimated to test the congressional partisan policy subsystem hypothesis failed to provide empirical evidence to support its theoretical expectation. Although support did not materialize for this hypothesis, it is noteworthy to emphasize that this result illustrates that veto use does not vary wildly by policy area over time, but rather follows fairly predictable patterns. Most enacted veto provisions have been concentrated in a small number of policy areas. Regardless of the partisan control of Congress, the presidency, or the partisan subsystem to which these areas belong, Congress has applied the veto most prominently to oversee policies related to national security and international affairs.

The examination of legislative veto oversight as it affects the cabinet showed that greater levels of department funding often correspond with additional legislative veto constraints. Results from this chapter also demonstrate that the legislative veto is not appreciably affected by ideological disagreement between the two chambers of Congress and individual cabinet secretaries or departments in their totality. It is certainly reasonable to expect statutory oversight to increase when the preferences of lawmakers substantially diverge from those of department leadership; however, the empirical analysis spanning more than a decade found no evidence of such an effect. The following chapter transitions to an examination of how individual states have used the legislative veto to oversee the agency rulemaking process.

SIX

Suspend or Nullify

Veto Oversight in U.S. Statehouses

By creating the legislative veto in the early 1930s Congress planted the seed—or, as some have described it, a virus—whereby states would soon begin adopting similar reforms (Dean 1992). Beginning with a Kansas law passed in 1939, a total of 30 states have experimented with some type of legislative veto oversight (Bonfield 1986; Levinson 1987). State constitutions in Arkansas (Article V, § 42) Connecticut (Article XVIII), Iowa (Article III, § 40), Michigan (Article IV, § 37), Nevada (Article III, § 2), New Jersey (Article V, § 4), and South Dakota (Article III, § 30) empower their legislature with independent veto power over agency rules.[1] In states where it is not constitutionally protected, courts have generally not been receptive to this type of direct legislative oversight. Whether by legislative or judicial fiat, some states have since eliminated the legislative veto as part of the rulemaking process. At present, 25 state legislatures possess some type of veto power over agency rules.

One of the virtues of federalism is that states can experiment with different policies and learn from one another. As we would expect, states have permitted legislative veto oversight in many different permutations. This chapter discusses the history and varied applications of the legislative veto at the state level and provides an empirical analysis of veto systems over time. As a first step, it is important to make some general distinctions between legislative veto use in Congress and among the states.

Federal and State Legislative Veto Comparisons

At the federal level, legislative vetoes are enacted by inclusion in individual laws. As covered in chapter 2, constitutional and statutory efforts to institutionalize a generic veto over all federal agency rulemaking have generally failed, with the exception of the Congressional Review Act of 1996. Because of this, veto oversight is typically imposed on a case-by-case basis as a restraint on specific delegated powers. At the state level, legislative vetoes are typically not included in individual laws, but through the imposition of statewide agency rulemaking procedures. Most often this is done by passing or amending state administrative procedure acts (APAs). Legislators are then free to utilize their veto power as they deem necessary under the conditions established by the APA.

A second difference between state and federal veto oversight concerns the veto mechanisms available to legislators. The typology presented in chapter 2 identified seven different types of vetoes according to whether they were affirmative, negative, or deliberative in execution, and whether committees, a single chamber, or both chambers exercised veto power. In contrast, variations on state-level legislative veto capabilities primarily concern whether the legislature or its committees have the authority to completely nullify agency regulations or to temporarily suspend them.

One additional point of comparison concerns affirmative-style vetoes. As described in chapter 2, committee affirmative vetoes constitute the second most common type of veto enacted by Congress. The other variant of affirmative vetoes are dual-House affirmatives, which require bicameral concurrence. Affirmative vetoes akin to these are infrequently employed at the state level, but have existed in Virginia (1944–75), Michigan (1977–2000), Connecticut (1971–present), West Virginia (1982–present), and Nevada (2009–present).[2] These systems generally require that new rules receive approval from a joint legislative committee. These exceptions aside, most veto systems permit legislators to negate or suspend rules rather than approve them. Before more closely examining differences in state legislative veto powers, it is important to first outline key differences in how state constitutions separate governmental powers.

Constitutional Separation of Powers

Questions about the proper balance of power across the branches of state government date back to May 1776 when the Second Continental Congress called on each colony to draft a state constitution. Today, every state government is characterized by a separation of powers system similar to the one that exists at the federal level. State constitutions differ, however, in the way that the three branches are defined and vested with the authority to govern.

Constitutions in 34 states contain a "strict" separation of powers clause that divides the government into distinct branches and expressly prohibits officials working in one branch from usurping roles performed by other branches (Boyd 1997, 327). As Florida's constitution states, "The powers of the state government shall be divided into legislative, executive and judicial branches. No person belonging to one branch shall exercise any powers appertaining to either of the other branches unless expressly provided herein" (Article II, § 3). In contrast, six state constitutions have a more general separation of powers clause stipulating that the government shall be divided into separate branches. For example, North Carolina's constitution states, "The legislative, executive, and supreme judicial powers of the State government shall be forever separate and distinct from each other" (Article I, § 6). The remaining 10 states have a constitutionally implied separation of powers by virtue of the vesting of legislative, executive, and judicial powers in autonomous branches (Boyd 1997). At times, the nuances of these clauses have been critical in judicial rulings.

In 1970, New Hampshire justices upheld a system for issuing state employee raises that required committee approval. Noting the uniqueness of the state's implied constitutional separation of powers, the opinion stated, "Unlike most state constitutions . . . the language of the New Hampshire Constitution recognizes that separation of powers in a workable government cannot be absolute but should be 'as separate from, and independent of, each other, as the nature of a free government will admit, or as is consistent with that chain of connection that binds the whole fabric of the constitution in one indissoluble bond of union and amity'" (*Opinion of the Justices*, 110 N.H. 359, 266 A.2d 823, 1970). Because of this less absolutist construction, the court declared that each branch need not be surrounded by "impenetrable barriers." As this chapter will survey, other state courts have sought to reinforce these barriers with great alacrity.

Rule Review Procedures

As the twentieth century gave rise to the federal administrative state, so too have state governments grown in size and sophistication. Because of this, state legislators have greater incentives to oversee how laws are executed. Forty-eight states have established formal procedures to review administrative rulemaking (National Association of Secretaries of State 2012; Council of State Governments 2012; Tharp 2001). State APAs, which have been enacted in all 50 states, establish most rulemaking institutions and procedures (De Figueiredo and Vanden Bergh 2004; Jensen and McGrath 2011).

At the time Congress enacted the Administrative Procedure Act in 1946, only 10 states had created a comprehensive framework for agency rulemaking and review (De Figueiredo and Vanden Bergh 2004). During this same year, the National Conference of Commissioners on Uniform State Laws—a nonprofit association of appointed state commissioners that draft model state laws—approved its first Model State Administrative Procedure Act (MSAPA).[3]

The original MSAPA and its successors sought to facilitate rulemaking improvements by establishing a clear, fair, and uniform process that allowed for government and public involvement (Bloomenthal 1963). A majority of states have used at least part of the MSAPA when drafting or revising their own APA (Scholtz 1981). At the point when APAs had been enacted in every state, more than two-thirds had established formal rulemaking review processes. Legislative review in 22 states provided for some type of legislative veto of agency rules (Renfrow and Houston 1987). In addition to this type of legislative review, nearly every state has government offices in the mold of the federal government's Government Accountability Office that provide systematic program reviews of state agencies (Boerner 2005).

States employ different methods of agency rulemaking review, which are reported in table 6.1. In 19 states the legislature serves as the singular review body (National Association of Secretaries of State 2012; Council of State Governments 2012). Missouri, for example, stipulates that "[a]ny agency's authority to propose an order of rulemaking is dependent upon the power of the general assembly to disapprove and annul any such proposed rule or portion thereof" (Revised Statutes of Missouri, Chapter 536.028). Similar to many other states, Missouri has created a joint committee—the Joint Committee on Administrative Rules—that bears responsibility for reviewing rules proposed by state agencies.

In contrast to this type of legislative rule review, six states have established an executive rule review system. A revision to California's APA passed in 1979 created the Office of Administrative Law, which is chiefly responsible for examining rule submissions from over 200 state agencies. Its counterpart in North Carolina is the Rules Review Commission, which must approve agency rules in order for them to go into effect. In Hawaii the governor performs this function, while Maine's attorney general bears the responsibility for judging whether rules are commensurate with enabling statutes. Massachusetts and New Mexico require agencies to periodically perform self-reviews. In each of these states, legislators maintain the ability to modify or repeal agency action by law, but they have no formal responsibility in the rule promulgation, review, or approval process.

The remaining 21 states, exempting Mississippi and Rhode Island, impose a multipronged rule review system involving both legislative and executive actors (Bonfield 1993). For example, North Dakota's Administrative Rules Committee, comprised of 13 senators and representatives, can suspend proposed rules. Following suspension, rules are automatically annulled unless both chambers of the legislature vote for reinstatement (State Law 2001, chapter 293, § 28–32–18). In addition to this avenue for review, state law requires gubernatorial approval of emergency rules, and the attorney general has the authority to veto existing rules. This review process allows legislators to operate in a sphere that is distinct from the governor and attorney general. In contrast, Maryland employs a mixed sys-

TABLE 6.1. Agency rule review authority by state

Legislature (19)	Executive (6)	Combination (23)	None (2)
Alabama	California	Arizona	Mississippi
Alaska	Hawaii	Colorado	Rhode Island
Arkansas	Maine	Delaware	
Connecticut	Massachusetts	Idaho	
Florida	New Mexico	Indiana	
Georgia	North Carolina	Iowa	
Illinois		Kansas	
Kentucky		Louisiana	
Missouri		Maryland	
Montana		Michigan	
Nevada		Minnesota	
New Hampshire		Nebraska	
Ohio		New Jersey	
Oregon		New York	
South Carolina		North Dakota	
South Dakota		Oklahoma	
Tennessee		Pennsylvania	
Texas		Utah	
West Virginia		Vermont	
		Virginia	
		Washington	
		Wisconsin	
		Wyoming	

Note: Data from Cancelosi (2012), Council of State Governments (2012), Tharp (2001), and collected by the author.

tem where legislative and gubernatorial review actions are interdependent. A specialized Joint Legislative Committee on Administrative, Executive, and Legislative Review performs the first level of review. Rules opposed by the committee are transmitted to the governor who can either approve the rule or instruct the agency to modify the rule in accordance with the committee's suggestions. Beyond these two examples, there exist many variations in the design of these types of mixed review systems.

Joint Rule Review Committees

In total, 42 states presently empower legislators with formal opportunities to affect agency rulemaking. Many have established some type of joint rule review committee. Among the primary advantages of having such a committee is that its membership can develop expertise in the state's rulemaking procedures and therefore be "in a good position to assure that the rules of the many state agencies are consistent with each other and can be reconciled with the potentially conflicting legislative policies embodied in statutes other than the enabling act of the particular agency issuing the rule" (Bonfield 1986, 484). Primarily on this basis, the National Conference on State Legislatures has expressed support for such committees. Opponents argue that rule review is a task better performed by standing committees with a membership better versed in the policy nuances of a particular issue area (Bowers 1990). Joint rule review committees currently exist in 28 states. The powers granted to these committees vary starkly.

On the weaker end of the spectrum, Florida's Joint Administrative Procedures Committee has the authority to review rules and make objections to those believed to be an "invalid exercise of delegated legislative authority" (Stengle and Rhea 1993, 470). State agencies are not required to act upon the committee's objections, which are listed as a footnote to the rule when published in the Florida Administrative Code. In this case, the committee acts in an advisory role with no direct authority to affect rules. Many review committees, including those in Alabama, Alaska, Iowa, Michigan, New Hampshire, Ohio, South Carolina, South Dakota, Virginia, and Wisconsin, have the authority to independently impose rule suspensions of various lengths. Among the most powerful rule review committees are those in Nevada, Connecticut, and Illinois. In Connecticut and Illinois, the committees hold veto power over rule proposals, but the committee's veto in each case is susceptible to override from the full legislature. Nevada law requires that all rules receive the express approval of the 12-member Legislative Commission. In this case, and in others, the joint review committee holds an absolute veto power.

Table 6.2 provides greater detail regarding state legislative veto powers. As of 2014, 13 states sanction the use of the veto as a means to nullify agency rules, while 16 permit rule suspension. Although we might expect states with only an implied or general separation of powers clause to permit legislative veto oversight, states with a strict separation of powers clause constitute a majority of both types of veto systems. Table 6.3 categorizes states permitting legislative veto oversight according to their constitutional separation of powers stipulations. Of the 10 states with an implied separation of powers, Alaska, North Dakota, Ohio, and Wisconsin permit the use of the legislative veto. Connecticut, New Hampshire, and South Dakota, representing half of the six states with a general separation of powers clause, likewise sanction this type of oversight. In similar proportion, half of the 34 strict separation of powers states allow one or both types of vetoes. Thus, there is not a substantial difference when considering the proportion of states permitting legislative veto use across the strict, general, and implied separation of powers clause categories. About half of the states in each of the three groups sanction the use of the veto.

One difference that does exist across these categories concerns legislative veto constitutional amendments. All of the states that have ratified an amendment to their constitution sanctioning legislative veto oversight have come from the strict or general separation of powers categories. No state in the implied category has inserted legislative veto authority into the constitution. This suggests that modifications to constitutions in states containing strict and general separation of powers clauses may be necessary in order to reconcile legislative veto powers with stipulations on the division of government authority.

The Evolution of State Legislative Veto Systems

The legislative veto experienced a period of decay during the mid-1980s after a consistent expansion during the 1970s. This decline was mainly driven by judicial rulings in several states against this type of oversight. Also influential were the string of unsuccessful legislative veto constitutional amendments—a total of seven during the decade—and policy changes made by state legislatures (Levinson 1987). This trend, especially for suspension systems, reversed during the 1990s, leading some to conclude that the "[r]eports of the death of the legislative veto may have been premature" (Schwartz 2010, 33). Though most courts have ruled against its constitutionality when given the opportunity, courts in many states have yet to intervene. A total of 29 states have permitted some type of legislative veto, but state supreme court rulings have occurred in only 12 states. Because of this relative judicial inaction, determinations regarding the legitimacy of the veto have most often been left to accommodations made by legislators and governors. Figure 6.1 shows the number of states with suspension or nullification rule review systems over time. Through statutory reforms, judicial rulings, and constitutional amendments, the number of states permitting legislative veto oversight remains fluid.

The adoption of legislative veto powers among the states has not followed a standard pattern. Since rulemaking procedures are most often determined by law, state legislatures and governors have, of course, been two influential actors on this matter. In some cases, voters have had an opportunity to weigh in on the legislature's role in the rulemaking process. On 17 different occasions between 1976 and 2014, voters in 13 states have considered legislative veto constitutional amendments. The first of these occurred during the 1976 presidential election year when voters in Florida and Missouri soundly defeated dual-House nullification veto amendments (Strum and Wright 1978). The same result occurred three years later in Texas. In a change of fortune, the first successful vote happened the following year in South Dakota. This continues to be the exception rather than the norm.

Eleven legislative veto amendments were not successful. To date, only six legislative veto amendments have been ratified.[4] These elections have typically not been close with an average vote of 46.6 percent in favor to 53.4 percent against. In three instances, amendments received support from less than one-third of the ballots cast. On the other end of the spectrum is the 1982 measure in Connecticut that passed with 70 percent of voters in favor of ratification. Figure 6.2 reports the results of each legislative veto amendment election.

Although the three most recent legislative veto constitutional amendment votes were successful (New Jersey 1992, Nevada 1996, and Arkansas 2014), there was a long gap of eight election cycles when an amendment of this type did not appear on any statewide ballot. This is attributable to a number of factors including ballot access challenges whereby it may be difficult to gather a sufficient number of signatures to receive ballot certification, and the tendency for states to adopt and reform their administrative procedures through the statutory process rather than inserting them into the state constitution. It is also likely that veto supporters,

TABLE 6.2. State legislative veto powers

State	Type (Year)	Legislative Veto Description
1) Alabama	S (1981)	Joint Committee on Administrative Regulation Review can suspend proposed rules until session's adjournment (AL. Code § 41-22-24).
2) Alaska	S (1978)	When the legislature is not in session, the Administrative Regulation Review Committee by a two-thirds majority vote may suspend proposed or existing rules until 30 days after the legislature reconvenes (AS § 24.20.445).
3) Arkansas	N (2014)	Legislature can adopt legislation requiring committee approval of new rules (Article V, § 42).
4) Connecticut	N (1971)	Proposed rules require approval of the Legislative Regulation Review Committee (CGS § 4-170).
5) Georgia	H (1977, 2008)	A two-thirds majority vote by both standing committees with jurisdiction suspends a proposed rule until the next session. Rules are vetoed by full legislature following agreement to a veto resolution. If the resolution passes by less than a two-thirds majority in either chamber, the governor may veto the resolution (Ga. Code Ann., § 50-13-4).
6) Idaho	N (1969)	Concurrent resolution can nullify proposed or existing rules (Idaho Code Title 67, Ch. 52).
7) Illinois	H (1980)	The Joint Committee on Administrative Rules can veto proposed rules by three-fifths majority vote. Veto can be overruled by joint resolution (5 ILCS 100/5-115).
8) Iowa	H (1976, 1984)	Committee may suspend a proposed rule's adoption for 60 days (I.C.A. § 17A.4). A 1984 constitutional amendment allows for a concurrent resolution to veto existing rules.
9) Louisiana	N (1980)	Concurrent resolution can suspend, amend, or repeal rules (La. R.S. § 49:969).
10) Michigan	S (1947)	The Joint Committee on Rules can suspend the adoption of a proposed rule for up to 30 days. Rules may be amended or rescinded by statute during this period (MR 8, 2012).
11) Minnesota	S (2001)	A majority vote by both standing committees with jurisdiction suspends a proposed rule's adoption until the end of the current legislative session (M.S.A. § 14.126).
12) Missouri	S (1994)	Joint Committee on Administrative Rules may suspend a proposed rule's adoption for a 30-day period (Mo. Rev. Stat. § 536.028).
13) Montana	S (1997)	If a majority of committee members object to a proposed rule, the agency is prohibited from adopting rule before the expiration of 6-month review period (MCA § 2-4-305).
14) Nevada	H (1981)	The Legislative Commission or its Subcommittee to Review Regulations can suspend proposed rules and require revisions (NRS § 233B.0675). A 1996 amendment to the constitution allows the legislature to veto rules by majority vote in both chambers. A 2009 law required commission approval of all rules (NRS § 233B.067).
15) New Hampshire	S (1994)	Joint Legislative Committee on Administrative Rules can suspend proposed rules for 90 calendar days by voting to sponsor a joint resolution to permanently veto. The joint resolution is subject to governor's veto (N.H. Rev. Stat. § 541 A:2).

TABLE 6.2.—Continued

State	Type (Year)	Legislative Veto Description
16) New Jersey	N (1981)	As amended in 1992, the state constitution allows the legislature to veto proposed or existing rules by a majority vote in both legislative chambers (NJSA 52:14B-4.3).
17) North Dakota	N (1995)	The Administrative Rules Committee can veto proposed rules (NDCC, 28-32-18).
18) Ohio	H (1977)	The Joint Committee on Agency Rule Review can suspend proposed rules. A concurrent resolution agreed to by both chambers of the legislature is necessary to veto suspended rules (RC 119.03, 111.15).
19) Oklahoma	N (1987)	A concurrent resolution, which does not require the governor's signature, can veto proposed rules. Existing rules may be vetoed following the passage of a joint resolution, which requires the governor's signature (75 PS § 250).
20) South Carolina	S (1979)	Legislative Council can suspend proposed rules for 120 days. During this period, rules can be approved or vetoed by joint resolution, which requires the governor's signature (SC Code of Laws Title 1, Ch. 23).
21) South Dakota	S (1975)	The Interim Rules Review Committee can suspend a proposed rule's adoption until July 1 of the following year (SDCL § 1-26-18).
22) Tennessee	S (1995)	Government operations committees can suspend a proposed rule's adoption for 60 days (TCA § 4-5-215).
23) Virginia	S (1984)	Standing committees or the Joint Commission on Administrative Rules can file formal objections to proposed rules in order to impose a 21-day suspension period (VA Code Ann. § 2.2-4015).
24) West Virginia	N (1996)	The Legislative Rule-Making Review Committee reviews proposed rules. Legislature must pass legislation authorizing promulgation of rule in order for it to go into effect (W. Va. Code, § 29A-3-12).
25) Wisconsin	S (1973)	Standing committees and the Joint Committee for the Review of Administrative Rules can suspend a proposed rule's adoption for 30 days each. Statutory action required to permanently veto (W.S.A. § 227.24).

Key: N—Nullification system; S—Suspension system; H—Hybrid system.
Note: Data from Council of State Governments (2012) and compiled by author.

Suspend or Nullify 221

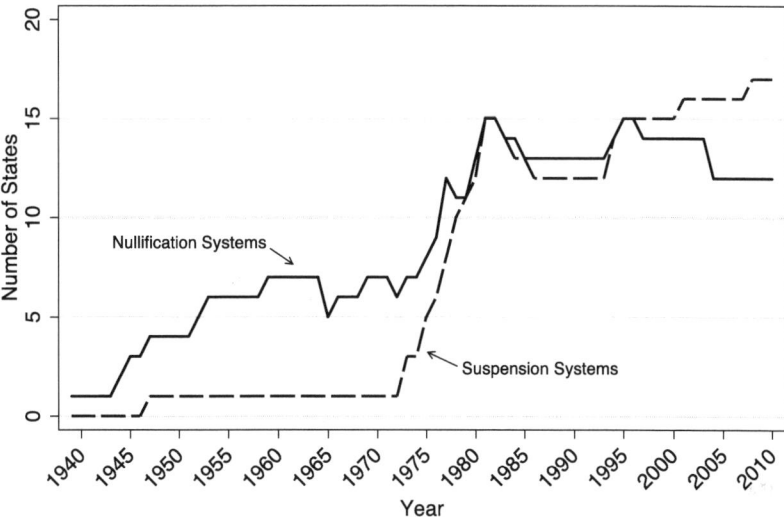

Fig. 6.1. Nullification and suspension veto systems by year

TABLE 6.3. Legislative veto systems by constitutional separation of powers requirements

	Strict (34 States)	General (6 States)	Implied (10 States)
Nullification Systems	Arkansas Idaho Louisiana *New Jersey* Oklahoma West Virginia	*Connecticut*	North Dakota
Suspension Systems	Alabama *Michigan* Minnesota Missouri Montana South Carolina Tennessee Virginia	New Hampshire *South Dakota*	Alaska Wisconsin
Hybrid Systems	Georgia Illinois *Iowa* Nevada		Ohio

Note: States in italics are those where the constitution sanctions legislative veto oversight.

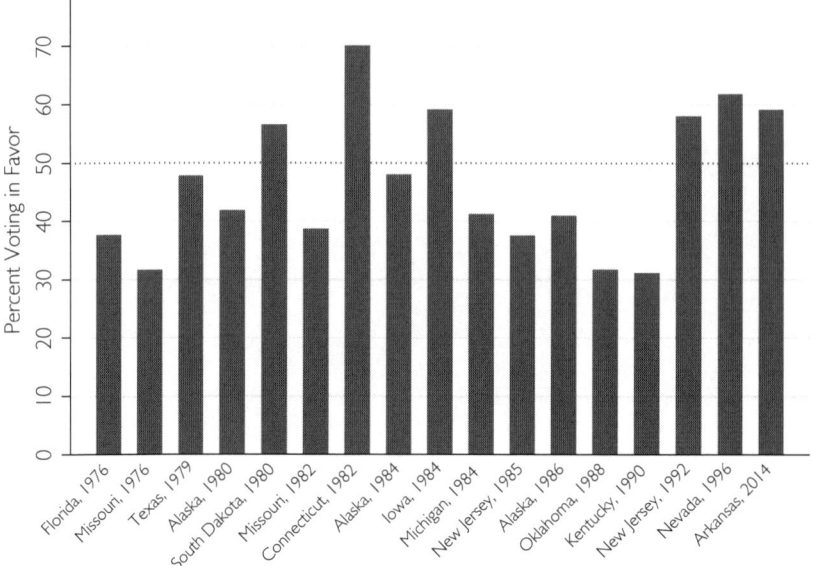

Fig. 6.2. Legislative veto constitutional amendment election results: 1976–2014 (Data from the National Conference of State Legislatures: http://www.ncsl.org/legislatures-elections/elections/ballot-measures-database.aspx.)

aware of the fact that legislative veto amendments have a ratification success rate of less than one-third, have strategically sought to add to the legislature's oversight arsenal by amending APAs rather than the constitution. Through this process, many states have recently expanded their legislature's ability to affect agency rulemaking including Virginia (2002), South Dakota (2003), Michigan (2004), Illinois (2004), Georgia (2008), and Nevada (2009). Lawmakers in Colorado (SB12–027, 2012) and Rhode Island (H. 5183, 2011), among others, have also recently advanced proposals to sanction the legislative veto.

Having introduced several important aspects of state legislative veto use, the sections that follow depict the evolution of the veto within several individual states. The first section covers nullification systems beginning with Kansas. The subsequent section describes selected rule review systems that permit legislative rule suspension. Hybrid systems are discussed last.

Nullification Systems

Nullification-based legislative veto systems came into existence with the passage of a 1939 statute permitting the Kansas legislature to veto certain types of rules (F. Cooper 1965). Since then, 23 states have adopted rulemaking procedures that allow legislators to independently block rules. Most of the 13 nullification systems currently in operation require a majority vote in both chambers to execute the veto. Georgia has the only dual-House nullification system that requires a supermajority vote (Ga. Code Ann., § 50-13-4). Less common are nullification systems that authorize joint rules review committees to unilaterally block rules. These types of committee nullification systems can either allow committees to veto rules deemed objectionable or require committee approval of newly proposed rules. North Dakota and Illinois employ the negative veto system (NDCC, 28-32-18; 5 ILCS 100/5-115), while Connecticut and Nevada (with Arkansas likely to soon join this pair) require affirmative committee action to adopt a rule (CGS § 4-170; NRS § 233B.067). Each of these systems allows committees to block rules. The key difference concerns the effect of committee inaction.

In North Dakota and Illinois, rules are automatically approved unless committees take a proactive measure to block them. In these cases, rules can be adopted as a result of committee inaction. Because rules require committee approval in Connecticut and Nevada, no rules can be adopted as a result of committee inaction. These two approaches parallel the committee affirmative and committee negative veto types according to the typology presented in chapter 1. Most rare are nullification systems that allow a single chamber to veto rules. Virginia was the first state to adopt this type of rule review in 1952 until revising it more than 20 years later. The only other state to permit one-House vetoes was Oklahoma (1975-87).

Beginning with Kansas, the sections that follow describe the development of nullification veto systems in four additional states: Idaho, Oklahoma, West Virginia, and New Jersey. The remaining states that permit legislative rule nullification, with the exception of Louisiana and Arkansas, are discussed in a subsequent section on hybrid veto systems that permit legislators to suspend or nullify rules.

Kansas (Nullification: 1939-1965, 1977-1985)

State use of the legislative veto commenced with a Kansas statute that empowered legislators with the authority to nullify general or statewide regulations by concurrent resolution (F. Cooper 1965).[5] The text of the statute stated that "every such rule and regulation shall remain in force until and unless the legislature, by concurrent resolution duly adopted, shall disapprove or reject the same" (Kansas Laws 1939, chap. 308, § 2). According to the Kansas Legislative Research Department, the legislature only vetoed a single rule, which pertained to income tax deductions for individuals serving in the legislature, during the first seven years it held this veto power (2010). A 1947 law expanded the category of rules subject to veto, but did little to increase the number of rules voided by lawmakers (Kansas Laws 1947, chap. 440 § 11). Legislators refrained from issuing any further vetoes until 1959 when they voided three rules concerning newspaper taxes, the sale of animals for pets at drugstores, and secondary school counselors. The legislature's veto power was significantly altered in 1965 when the concurrent resolution veto mechanism was abandoned in favor of a joint resolution, which required the signature of the governor (Kansas Laws 1965, chap. 506, § 11). No rules were vetoed by joint resolution in the 10 years following the change (Kansas Legislative Research Department 2010).

Beginning in 1974, the legislature embarked on an effort to implement substantial rulemaking and oversight reforms, which resulted in the creation of the Joint Committee on Administrative Rules and Regulations and the reimposition of the concurrent resolution veto in 1977 (Kan. Stat. Ann. § 77–436). These reforms were the cumulative product of interbranch negotiations following the governor's veto of legislation seeking to make new rules susceptible to a single-House veto. In contrast to its original incarnation, the legislature was only permitted to veto newly proposed rules. Any effort to rescind existing rules required the passage of a new law.

In the first year under the new system legislators vetoed four existing rules by law and 17 rule proposals by concurrent resolution. Over the next six years, they vetoed between 10 and 22 rules annually, averaging 17 per year. Lawmakers retained the concurrent resolution veto power until 1984, when the Kansas Supreme Court struck it down as a separation of powers violation. In the years before the court's ruling, legislators utilized the veto with more frequency than they had previously. In total, 128 proposed or existing rules were rescinded. At least 30 of these vetoes were exercised over existing rules with the passage of a statute to nullify the rule, while most were imposed over new rule proposals (Kansas Legislative Research Department 2010).[6] The case brought before the Kansas high court challenged more than 10 vetoes the legislature exercised independently by resolution.

In *State ex rel. Stephen v. House of Representatives*, 236 Kan. 45, 687 P.2d 622 (1984) the court heard arguments in a suit filed through the state's attorney general, Robert T. Stephen, who claimed that the concurrent resolution veto violated the state's constitution. Since Kansas is one of 10 states with a constitutionally implied separation of powers, this was potentially a case where the justices would be disposed to take a more permissive position on the matter. This was not to be. In a divided ruling, the court struck down the legislative veto as unconstitutional.

Chief Justice Alfred G. Schroeder's opinion cited *Chadha* and a number of recent state rulings regarding the constitutionality of legislators exercising veto power. He summarized the court's rationale on the veto by stating:

> We are persuaded by our analysis of the law in this state and a review of the above-discussed decisions that the legislative veto mechanism . . . violates not only the separation of powers doctrine but also the presentment requirement contained in art. 2, § 14 of our state constitution. As made clear by the court in *Chadha*, a resolution is essentially legislative where it affects the legal rights, duties and regulations of persons outside the legislative branch and therefore must comply with the enactment provisions of the constitution. . . . The legislature cannot pass an act that allows it to violate the constitution. (*State ex rel. Stephen v. House of Representatives*, 236 Kan. 64, 687 P.2d 622 (1984))

To comply with the ruling, a 1985 reform modified the statute containing the legislative veto in such a manner that the lawmakers could employ the concurrent resolution as a means of "expressing the concern of the legislature with any permanent or temporary rule and regulation . . . and requesting the revocation of any such rule and regulation or the amendment of any such rule and regulation in the manner specified in such resolution" (Kansas Laws 1985, chap. 307, § 4). This change resulted in the transformation of the concurrent resolution from a mechanism used to directly repeal or amend rules to one that merely informed agencies of the legislature's opposition to a rule and requested some agency action. The authority to advise agencies by concurrent resolution remains part of Kansas law (K.S.A. § 77–426(c)).

More than a dozen years after the nullification veto system was vanquished, the Kansas legislature enacted the Consolidation Act (K.S.A. 1997 Supp. 12–340 et seq.), which outlined the procedure under which county and city governments could form a unified jurisdiction. Following a number of steps to initiate such a consolidation, a plan would go before resident voters for their approval unless legislators adopted a concurrent resolution vetoing the plan. On its face, this would seem to be a direct affront to the *Stephen* ruling. However, this legislative veto applied not to rules made by state agencies, but rather to plans initiated by localized municipalities to form a single government. A case challenging multiple aspects of the consolidation procedure made it to the state's supreme court in 1998. Its reception was once again unfavorable.

The court again rejected the legislature's veto authority by making clear that "the legislature may not reserve the power to take back such delegation by concurrent resolution if it disagrees with the Commission's Plan. If the legislature wishes to take back this delegation, it must do so by passing a statute which removes such delegation and present this statute to the Governor. It cannot do so simply by reserving the power to remove the delegation in the same act which delegates the power to the Commission. This is improper" (*State ex rel. Tomasic v. Unified Government of Wyandotte County/Kansas City*, 264 Kan. 293, 955 P.2d 1136 (1998)). Combined, these rulings dealt a fatal blow to the legislative veto in the state of its origin. The remaining exception to this is the legislative veto power over gubernatorial reorganization proposals whereby the Kansas Constitution designates that executive reorganization orders have "the force of general law" at the start of the next fiscal year unless a majority in either chamber votes to disapprove the proposal within 60 days of its receipt.

Idaho (Nullification: 1969–Present)

In contrast to the Kansas experience, the nullification system adopted by the Idaho legislature is notable since it is the only one of its kind to survive a legal challenge in a state supreme court. In 1969, state legislators amended Idaho's APA, originally passed in 1965, to provide themselves with veto authority over agency rules (Act of Feb. 24, 1969, chap. 48, § 2). The procedure required the submission of proposed rules to both legislative chambers. If the standing committee with jurisdiction determined that a rule violated legislative intent, it could draft a resolution to amend or veto the rule (Heffron 1994). It is unclear from the statutory language whether a single-House resolution could impose such a veto or whether bicameral action was required. A law passed in 1976 revised this section to state that the legislature could veto proposed rules by concurrent resolution (Act of Mar. 19, 1976, chap. 185, § 2). Subsequent modifications to this statute stipulated that lawmakers could use the concurrent resolution to veto existing rules in addition to new rule proposals (Act of Feb. 26, 1985, chap. 13,

§ 2). A 1990 amendment to the APA declared that all agency rules would automatically expire on July 1 of the year following their initial adoption (S.L. 1990, chap. 22, § 2).

A rare judicial victory endorsing a statewide nullification system came in a 1990 ruling by the Idaho Supreme Court regarding sewer systems. The controversy in *Mead v. Arnell* concerned the veto of Idaho Board of Health and Welfare rules regarding subsurface sewage disposal. In order to implement current pollution prevention technology, the board imposed mandatory upgrades of existing disposal systems. Over a four-year span, the board dispensed over 11,000 permits to those working to comply with the new rules. In a state with about one million residents, the number of permits issued by the board was considerable. In 1989, both legislative chambers acted to declare the rules "null and void and of no force and effect." Officials from the board challenged the legislative veto as a separation of powers violation. In the majority opinion, which included citations to Justice White's *Chadha* dissent, the court sided with the legislature.

Addressing the character of rules made by executive agencies, the court argued that although "rules and regulations may be given 'the force and effect of law,' they do not rise to the level of statutory law" (*Mead v. Arnell*, 117 Idaho 660, P.2d 410, 1990 Ida. 34). Primarily on account of this distinction, the ruling held that the state's dual-House rule nullification system did not violate the Idaho Constitution, specifically the executive branch's responsibility to execute the law.

> Here, the legislative action has not invalidated the executive department's "execution of the law." Such would be the case, for instance, if the legislature had passed a concurrent resolution to prevent the Attorney General from taking legal action for some violation of a statute. Enforcing the law of this state is a constitutionally mandated executive department function resting in the office of the Attorney General. In such a case no *delegation* would be involved. Conversely, in this case, the Board's rule making power comes from a legislative delegation. Rulemaking that comes from a legislative delegation of power is neither the legal nor functional equivalent of constitutional power. It is not constitutionally mandated; rather it comes to the executive department through delegation from the legislature. This Court, as noted, has consistently found the executive rule making authority to be rooted in a legislative delegation, not a power constitutionally granted to the executive. (*Mead v. Arnell*, 117 Idaho 660, P.2d 410, 1990 Ida. 34)

Because the legislative veto applied to rulemaking functions delegated to the Board of Health and Welfare from the legislature, it did not constitute a veto over the execution of the law, but rather a veto over the implementation of a delegated power.[7]

This ruling constitutes by far the most liberal interpretation made by a state court regarding legislative veto oversight.[8] The ruling's importance stems from the fact that it "makes clear that some state supreme courts are likely to permit some types of legislative vetoes of particular agency rules by means less than statutory, even in the absence of constitutional provisions expressly authorizing those devices" (Bonfield 1993, 196). Few other states have followed Idaho's lead.

Oklahoma (Nullification: 1975–Present)

Oklahoma's experience with the legislative veto is one of the most unique in the nation. According to those well versed in Oklahoma state politics, public officeholders have frequently waged heated battles over the veto powers held by the legislature as well as the governor. Such interbranch conflicts have "raged virtually since statehood" (Slater 1987, 132). As part of this ongoing debate, the Oklahoma legislature enacted reforms in 1963 that imposed broad changes to the state's regulatory system. The new framework created a timetable for the formal submission of rules to the legislature and allowed rules to be vetoed by joint resolution. This permitted legislators to initiate the process to veto a regulation, but allowed the governor to veto any such resolution calling for a rule's annulment (F. Cooper 1965). Over the following 12 years, legislators introduced a total of just five veto resolutions, only one of which was successful (Slater 1987). In 1975, the legislature amended the rulemaking process to permit a majority vote from one chamber as sufficient to execute a veto rather than requiring consensus among both chambers and the governor (Laws 1975, c. 289, § 1). Altering the veto mechanism to a single-House resolution made Oklahoma the second state, following Virginia, to permit legislative vetoes that did not require bicameral action.

With the adoption of the one-House veto in 1975 "the floodgates opened" and legislators began sponsoring many more veto resolutions than they had previously (Slater 1987, 150). Until the single-House veto power was rescinded in 1987, legislators introduced a total of 72 veto resolutions. During the final few years of its existence, the legislature considered an annual average of over nine veto resolutions. In stark contrast to the single rule struck down when the veto process required bicameral concurrence and the governor's signature, legislators vetoed a total of 43 regulations by house or senate resolution for a veto success rate of 60 percent (Slater 1987). This marked increase in rules vetoed illustrates the importance of the veto mechanism design on the frequency of its execution. This modification to the rule review process did not come without controversy. A decade after its initial adoption, a dispute surrounding horse racing thrust the state's one-House veto procedure into the spotlight.

A rule issued by the Oklahoma Horse Racing Commission permitted the operation of only one major racetrack in the state. Businessman Edward J. DeBartolo Sr., who owned both a professional football team (the San Francisco 49ers) and hockey team (the Pittsburgh Penguins), proposed building a $90 million casino and race track facility in Oklahoma City named Remington Park (Greiner1988). The commission's rule restricting the state to one track meant that approval of the Remington Park proposal would necessarily prohibit any other substantial track developments. In 1986, several representatives sponsored a house resolution calling for the annulment of the one-track rule. Among those seeking to preserve the rule and prevent a majority coalition in the house or senate from vetoing the rule was a state senator from Oklahoma City who made a request to the attorney general's office for an opinion on the constitutionality of the one-House veto procedure.

Following a familiar pattern that had transpired in several other states, the attorney general issued an opinion in February 1986 arguing that a veto exercised by a single chamber did not conform to the state's constitutional requirements of bicameralism and gubernatorial presentment. Citing the *Chadha* precedent as well as five additional state supreme court rulings, the opinion concluded that a veto exercised in this manner should not be binding, but rather would "constitute no more than an expression of opinion of the house which passes it" (OK. Att'y. Gen. Op. 17, 1986). Two actions followed this opinion. First, the commission adopted a revised rule that temporarily banned new construction until betting income at two tracks in the state eclipsed $230 over a two-year period (Greiner 1988). Second, despite the fact that the one-House veto process had not yet been subjected to direct judicial scrutiny, the legislature acted once again to reform the state's rulemaking procedures.

In a first attempt to revise the veto process, those supporting the preservation of the one-track rule backed legislation to eliminate the one-House veto system and require joint resolutions of approval for all regulations. Regarding the one-track rule in particular, the bill sought to retroactively impose the legislative approval requirement. Democratic governor George P. Nigh vetoed the bill, calling it "too overreaching" in its requirement of legislative approval of all agency rules (Slater 1987, 153). No vote was taken to override the governor's veto. Instead, lawmakers passed a substitute measure that revoked the singe-House veto and replaced it with the joint resolution as had previously existed (Laws 1987, c. 207, § 21). Understandably, a number of lawmakers opposed this reform, as it required bicameral action and support from the governor in order to veto a rule. Seeking to reinstate the one-House veto procedure, Republican senator Frank Rhodes led the effort to put the legislative veto on the ballot with the hope that voters would grant the legislature this type of oversight power.

A constitutional amendment permitting single-House veto power over agency rules appeared on the ballot in 1988. Turnout in this election was high since the measure went before voters during the first presidential primary election in state history. The public overwhelmingly rejected the amendment, with nearly 70 percent of ballots cast opposed. This result closed one avenue for reform, so supporters in the legislature pursued the legislative path to alter the state's increasingly controversial oversight system.

Later in 1988, the state's APA was amended again by implementing distinct veto mechanisms for proposed and existing rules (Laws 1988, c. 292, § 19). The new statute stipulated that legislators could veto existing rules by joint resolution, meaning that the governor's approval in association with majority support in both chambers was necessary in order to strike down a duly adopted rule. For proposed rules not yet implemented, the revised procedure stipulated that agreement to a concurrent resolution would permanently bar a rule's adoption. In designating this power, the statute explicitly protected the authority of the legislature to independently veto proposed rules absent any action from the governor by stating that "any such concurrent resolution shall not require the approval of the Governor, and any such rule so disapproved shall be invalid and of no effect regardless of the approval of the Governor of such rule" (75 Okl.St.Ann. § 308, B(2)(a)(3)). With the passage of this act, legislators successfully reimposed a legislative veto point in the rulemaking process.

West Virginia (Nullification: 1976–Present)

West Virginia's initial foray into legislative veto oversight occurred during a period of reform for the state's mining industry. In 1976, the Legislative Rule-Making Review Committee was created as a body responsible for the review of rule proposals (W. Va. Acts 1976, chap. 117). The committee members—six from each chamber—had a six-month period to study regulations and could block the implementation of any rule. The full legislature could reverse this decision by majority vote and allow rules to move forward. In a case concerning regulations made by the Department of Mines, the state's supreme court struck down this procedure five years after its adoption.

In *State ex rel. Barker v. Manchin*, 167 W. Va. 155, 279 S.E.2d 622 (1981), the court held that the committee's veto power violated the separation of governmental powers and circumvented the governor's veto authority. Outlining this rationale, the opinion stated that the "constitutional provision which prohibits any one department of our state government from exercising the powers of the others is not merely a suggestion; it is part of the fundamental law of our State and, as such, it must be strictly construed and closely followed." It concluded that the legislature "cannot invest itself with the power to act as an administrative agency in order to avoid those requirements" (*State ex rel. Barker v. Manchin*, 167 W. Va. 166, 173, 279 S.E.2d 632 (1981)). After this ruling, legislators began work to revise the rulemaking system.

In the reforms that passed after the court's intervention, the joint review committee maintained its authority to review all proposed rules. New to the process was a prohibition on the enactment of any new rule unless the full legislature passed a bill authorizing its adoption (W. Va. Acts 1982, chap. 121). The requirement that all rules had to be approved by statute provided the governor with the opportunity to overrule or sustain the will of the legislature. At the time, this reform made West Virginia's rulemaking system among the most restrictive in the nation due to the fact that agencies were barred from issuing any rules whatsoever without the passage of specific authorizing legislation. By requiring positive action to authorize a rule, the revised system in practice allowed one chamber to block a proposed rule by failing to consider a bill sanctioning the rule. Thus, the state's system essentially was transformed from one where a joint committee wielded veto power to one in which either chamber could veto proposed rules by simple inaction. Because of this, it came as no surprise that the revised system also became the subject of judicial scrutiny.

In 1995, the state's highest court once again invalidated the rulemaking system (*State ex rel. Meadows v. Hechler*, 195 W. Va. 11, 462 S.E.2d 586 (1995)). The controversy in this case involved rules issued by the West Virginia Department of Health and Human Resources regarding the operation and licensure of health-care-providing homes. The department appropriately filed a series of rules in this area with the legislature's rulemaking review committee, which approved them with minor modifications. Bills in both chambers to authorize these rules failed to progress out of committee. This inaction resulted in the suit's claim that it was unconstitutional for legislators to "prohibit the implementation of specifically mandated regulations through purposeful languishment in legislative committees" (*State ex rel. Meadows v. Hechler,* 195 W. Va. 11, 462 S.E.2d 587 (1995)). The ruling in the case found few differences between the existing system and the one it struck down in *Barker* and held that the existing system provided the legislature with an "outright veto power" to block agency regulations. As it had four years prior, the court invalidated the legislative review process as an impermissible "intrusion into the Executive branch's ability to effectuate its mandated responsibilities" (*State ex rel. Meadows v. Hechler,* 195 W. Va. 11, 462 S.E.2d 593 (1995)). Once again, its primary argument concerned the state constitution's separation of powers claiming that it "is not merely a matter of convenience or of governmental mechanism. Its object is basic and vital, namely, to preclude a commingling of these essentially different powers of government in the same hands" (*State ex rel. Meadows v. Hechler,* 195 W. Va. 11, 462 S.E.2d 589 (1995)).

About six months after the *Hechler* ruling, the legislature again modified the statute rejected by the court (W. Va. Acts 1996, chap. 162). In practice, this change was somewhat cosmetic since the new system maintained the requirement that rule proposals receive legislative approval through the passage of an authorizing bill. As was the case before the ruling, agencies must still submit all proposed rules to the rulemaking review committee. According to the secretary of state's office, rules approved by the committee move to the full legislature for review near the beginning of each legislative session. Votes are taken on individual rules and approved rules addressing similar topics are "bundled" into an authorizing bill. Rules do not go into effect until the authorizing bill becomes law. Based on the state's supreme court rulings in *Barker* and *Meadows*, it would seem likely that this system would not pass constitutional muster either, but absent a case challenging the nullification system, the current veto procedure remains intact. At presently constituted, the West Virginia legislature's ability to directly affect rules is among the most powerful in the nation since all rule proposals must receive affirmation from the full legislature in order to go into effect.

New Jersey (Nullification: 1981–Present)

New Jersey's APA was adopted in 1968 (L. 1968 chap. 410, §§ 1–17). About a decade later, legislators made an effort to strengthen their rule review powers. On four occasions, Democratic governor Brendan Bryne vetoed bills passed by the Democratic-controlled legislature seeking to institutionalize legislative veto authority. The fourth such bill passed in a rare unanimous vote in both chambers on November 10, 1980. The vote to override the governor's veto was also unanimous with all 101 legislators voting in favor.

The APA reform measure passed over the governor's objection required virtually all state agencies to submit proposed rules to the standing committees with jurisdiction for review (L.1981, chap. 27, § 12). No later than 45 days after their submission, committees proffered a recommendation on rules to the full legislature. Rules would go into effect after an additional 60-day waiting period unless both chambers agreed to prohibit the imposition of the rule. This revised rulemaking procedure went into effect in March 1981. During this same month, the state's attorney general issued an opinion declaring the review process "inconsistent" with the New Jersey Constitution. Because of this, the attorney general argued that "administrative agencies of state government should be directed that those provisions have no force and effect and state agencies should not conform their rulemaking activities to the provisions of that act on its effective date" (Yaskin 1981, 3). The following year, a ruling by the state supreme court in *General Assembly of New Jersey v. Byrne*, 90 N.J. 376, 448 A.2d 438 (1982) concurred with the attorney general's assessment.

The ruling in *General Assembly of New Jersey v. Byrne* struck down the Legislative Oversight Act (New Jersey Laws 1981, chap. 27), which allowed for the veto of agency rules by concurrent resolution. In line with a growing number of precedents from other states, the court held that the nullification system violated multiple provisions of the constitution by "excessively interfering with the functions of the executive branch" (*General Assembly of New Jersey v. Byrne*, 90 N.J. 378, 448 A.2d 438 (1982)). Despite this outcome, the legislature did not act to repeal its concurrent resolution veto power until 2001 (L.2001, chap. 5, § 11). In a related case that came before the court in the following year, judges upheld a more limited legislative veto, allowing legislators to veto construction and leasing agreements negotiated by the New Jersey Building Authority after they had received approval from the governor (*Enourato v. New Jersey Building Authority*, 90 N.J. 396, 448 A.2d 449 (N.J. 1982)).

In addition to the involvement of each branch of the state government regarding the legitimacy of the legislative veto, two ballot measures proposing to insert legislative veto oversight authority into the constitution allowed New Jersey residents the opportunity to weigh in on this issue.

The first referendum in the off-year 1985 election received scant support with less than 40 percent voters voting in favor of the amendment. Voters reversed course in a second attempt in 1992 that successfully amended the constitution to permit a majority vote in both legislative chambers as sufficient to veto any proposed or existing rule. With 58 percent voting in favor, the ratification of this amendment made New Jersey the fifth state to enshrine legislative veto authority in the state constitution.

Suspension Systems

Suspension systems differ from nullification systems in that the legislature can only delay a rule's adoption to allow for further examination and debate. Regardless of the length of the suspension, once it has expired, subsequent action on behalf of the legislature, governor, agency, or some combination of the three is required to permanently bar the regulation. The procedures for invalidating regulations following their suspension vary from state to state.

Michigan was the first state to adopt a rule review system permitting legislative rule suspension in 1947. For more than a quarter century it was the only such system in existence and it remains the longest-existing suspension system. Other suspension systems have been transitory. Kentucky's rule review system permitting rule suspension lasted a mere two years before the state supreme court struck it down (*Legislative Research Commission ex rel. v. Brown*, 664 S.W.2d 907 (Ky. 1984)). North Carolina eliminated legislative suspension power after only six years (Laws 1983, c. 927, § 2) in favor of an executive rules review commission created in 1985 (Laws 1985 (Reg. Sess., 1986), c. 1028, § 32). Though some states have acted to abrogate these types of legislative review, figure 6.1 shows that the 1970s brought about a tremendous expansion of legislative veto oversight. Eleven new states adopted suspension systems during the decade with four more implemented by 1983.

Michigan (Nullification: 1947–2004; Suspension: 1947–Present)

Beginning in 1943, proposed rules in Michigan required approval from the attorney general before going into effect (Howe 1955–56). Four years later, Michigan became the first state to permit legislative suspension and nullification of rules. This particular reform created numerous occasions for lawmakers to contest rules (Public Acts 1947, No. 35). Regarding nullification, legislators could abrogate rules with a concurrent resolution of disapproval. The law also created a Joint Committee on Legislative Rules, which could suspend rules issued when the legislature was not in session (F. Cooper 1965).

The imposition of these novel veto authorities was the product of considerable interbranch bargaining that spanned several legislative terms. In 1945, Republican governor Harry Kelly vetoed legislation requiring legislative approval before rules could go into effect. Governor Kelly's veto message indicated that he opposed the reform on both political and constitutional grounds (Howe 1955–56, 182). The following legislative term brought compromise on this issue when newly elected Republican governor Kim Sigler signed legislation empowering legislators to veto or suspend rules in lieu of the more tedious process requiring approval of all rules in advance. In 1951, the system was amended further to prohibit the reinstatement of suspended rules unless the legislature so directed by concurrent resolution (Public Acts 1951, No. 9). In a debate that heretofore had involved the legislature and the governor, the state's attorney general elected to enter the fray.

The main conclusion from an opinion written in 1953 by Attorney General Frank G. Millard was that the suspension and nullification systems were unconstitutional encroachments on the functions of the judiciary. By itself, this argument is notable since one of the foremost arguments against the veto is that it usurps executive functions. In the aftermath of the attorney general's opinion, the joint rules committee continued to meet, but did not use its suspension power (F. Cooper 1965). Instead, the committee transitioned to a more advisory role by consulting with agencies about rules that might invite legislative scrutiny. Despite the growing controversy surrounding the constitutionality of these veto powers, courts in the state did not intervene in the dispute. Voter ratification of the state's fourth constitution in 1963 resolved most of the constitutional questions surrounding the matter as it gave legislators the expressed power to create a joint committee for rules review that could suspend rules put forth during a legislative recess (F. Cooper 1965). In a subsequent vote that occurred in the 1984 election cycle, voters rejected a constitutional amendment providing the committee with nullification power.

With the suspension system preserved in the constitution, legislators serving during the late 1970s amended the state's APA to require that new rules receive the approval of the newly created Joint Committee on

Administrative Rules (JCAR) (Public Acts 1977, No. 108). In the absence of committee approval or in the event of committee disapproval, the full legislature had an opportunity to approve the proposed rule by concurrent resolution. If neither of these actions occurred, the agency was barred from adopting the rule. This system was one of few that have existed where legislators must confer their approval of all new rules. Presented with an opportunity, the Michigan Supreme Court struck down the approval system in a suit filed by group of incarcerated persons challenging rules on visitation rights made by the Department of Corrections (*Blank v. Department of Corrections*, 462 Mich. 103, 611 N.W.2d 530 (2000)).

Department of Corrections officials proposed more restrictive inmate visitation rules in 1995. The department submitted the new visitation protocol to JCAR, which held hearings and ultimately did not confer its approval of the rule changes. By law, absent joint committee approval, the only way to impose the rule changes was by obtaining a concurrent resolution from the full assembly sanctioning the policy change. After failing to receive committee approval, the department chose to unilaterally adopt the new rule following its submission to the governor, secretary of state, and the state regulatory office. Since the court refused a request from the governor to issue an opinion regarding the constitutionality of the preclearance requirement, this case provided the first instance where the high court could make such a determination.

The court's main premise in striking down the approval requirement for new rules asserted that the veto mechanism was "inherently legislative" and therefore must follow the constitution's enactment and presentation clause requirements. Justice Marilyn J. Kelly penned the opinion in which she stated, "I conclude that the Legislature cannot circumvent the enactment and presentment requirements simply by labeling or characterizing its action as something other than 'legislation'" (*Blank v. Department of Corrections*, 462 Mich. 103, 611 N.W.2d 538 (2000)). As justification for this holding, Justice Kelly cited similar rulings from other states and devoted an entire section to the *Chadha* precedent and its application in this context.

To comply with the ruling, several sections of the APA were amended (Public Acts 2004, No. 23). The revised system maintained the review functions of JCAR and the approval requirement before rules could go into effect. However, rather than allowing the legislature to approve rules opposed by JCAR, the reformed process stipulated that rules not approved by JCAR must go before the full legislature for its review. At this stage, the general assembly may act to pass a bill or joint resolution vetoing the rule. In both cases, the governor's approval is required. If either measure is unsuccessful, rules may go into effect without JCAR's approval (MCL 24.245a).

Wisconsin (Nullification: 1953–1965; Suspension: 1973–Present)

Wisconsin legislators adopted a new rulemaking system in 1953 that empowered legislators to veto existing rules with a joint resolution of disapproval, which does not require the governor's signature (Laws 1953, chap. 331, § 4). Similar to concurrent developments occurring in the neighboring state of Michigan, an opinion from the Wisconsin attorney general concluded that "the legislature cannot constitutionally abrogate or modify a duly issued rule of an administrative agency by the mere passage of a joint resolution, and therefore the provisions . . . are invalid" (43 O.A.G. 350, Wis. 1954). Shortly after the opinion's release, the legislature created a joint committee with advisory powers to also investigate rule grievances and consult with appropriate agencies (Laws 1955, chap. 221 § 11).

In spite of the attorney general's contrarian argument, the nullification authority held by the legislature lasted for a dozen years and did not receive judicial scrutiny during this period. Absent any judicial provocation, Wisconsin lawmakers repealed their own nullification veto authority in 1965. The following decade they adopted a system allowing standing committees and the Joint Committee for Review of Administrative Rules to suspend a rule's adoption for a period of 30 days (Laws 1973, chap. 336, § 4). During the suspension period, the enactment of a law prohibiting a rule was the only way to block the rule from going into effect. Upon challenge, the supreme court sanctioned the system, which had been struck down by an appellate court, in *Martinez v. Department of Industry, Labor & Human Relations*, 478 N.W.2d 582 (Wis. 1992).

The case stemmed from a conflict between the joint review committee and the Department of Industry, Labor, and Human Relations regarding a proposed a rule allowing employers to pay newly hired workers a subminimum wage for a period of 120 days. The review committee recommended reducing this to just three days and voted to suspend the adoption of the 120-day rule pending review by the full legislature. In considering the constitutionality of the suspension process, the justices found the suspension statute to be "carefully drawn" in order to facilitate "a cooperative venture between the legislature and administrative agencies to make and implement rules that are consistent with their statutory authorization" (*Martinez v. Department of Industry, Labor & Human Relations*, 478 N.W.2d 583 (Wis. 1992)). The ruling further cited the state constitution's implied separation of powers, noting that "the separation of powers doctrine allows the sharing of powers and is not inherently violated in instances when one branch exercises powers normally associated with another branch" (*Martinez v. Department of Industry, Labor & Human Relations*, 478 N.W.2d 585 (Wis. 1992)). In sum, the court upheld the suspension system as a type of interbranch power sharing that was permissible on the grounds that the committee's review did not "unduly burden or substantially interfere" with the functions rightfully exercised by executive officials. This and Idaho's *Mead* ruling constitute the most progressive positions taken by courts regarding the veto's constitutionality.

Alaska (Nullification: 1959–2004; Suspension: 1978–Present)

Alaska's regulatory review structure was developed in the state's infancy. During the first legislative session following statehood in 1959, lawmakers required an annual review of state regulations by a Legislative Council in addition to permitting the annulment of regulations by concurrent resolution, which does not require the governor's signature (SLA 1959, chap. 143, § 3). Twenty years later, Alaska became the first state to have its legislature's veto authority struck down by a state supreme court.[9]

Prior to the court's ruling against the nullification system, Alaskan legislators revised the state's APA to provide for committee suspension of rules as well. A 1975 law created the Administrative Regulation Review Committee (ARRC), which reviewed all proposed regulations and made recommendations to the full legislature (SLA 1975, chap. 27, § 1). Three years later, the ARRC received the statutory authority to suspend proposed rules or regulations when the full legislature was not in session with a two-thirds majority vote of its membership (SLA 1978, chap. 3, § 1). Following such a vote, the deferral period persisted until 30 days after the legislature reconvened. This reform passed after the legislature successfully voted to override Republican governor Jay Hammond's veto. With this addition to the state's APA, Alaska became one of few states to permit its legislature to both suspend and nullify agency rules. This status was short lived.

The ruling in *State of Alaska v. A.L.I.V.E. Voluntary, Inc.*, 606 P.2d 769 (Alaska 1980) was the first instance of a high court striking down a statewide rulemaking framework that permitted legislative vetoes. At odds in the case was a regulation issued by the Department of Revenue concerning limits on the total amount of cash prizes awarded by group fund-raising lotteries and a union-based political action committee, A.L.I.V.E. Voluntary, which had been denied a lottery permit on the basis that it had exceeded the disbursement limit. The group filed suit, hoping to retain the permit.

In a 3–2 ruling, the majority opinion, written by future chief justice of the Alaska Supreme Court Warren Matthews, argued that when vetoing regulations, lawmakers were engaging in a legislative function that did not follow the legislative process required by the state constitution. Responding to the argument that the state's legislative veto system was codified by duly enacted law signed by the governor, the court rejected the notion that "the legislature can free itself, in certain instances, of the constitutional constraints that would otherwise govern its actions. Such an enactment would impermissibly preserve legislative power possessed at one instant in time for future periods when the legislature might otherwise be incapable of acting because of the executive veto. It would also do away with the formal safeguards of article II which are meant to accompany law-making. The requirements of the constitution may not be eliminated in this fashion" (*State of Alaska v. A.L.I.V.E. Voluntary, Inc.*, 606 P.2d 779 (Alaska 1980)).

A dissenting opinion written by the incumbent chief justice, Robert Boochever, noted that the state's constitution made no requirements on the establishment of regulations. Because of this, legislative checks on rulemaking should not be considered prima facie unconstitutional. In fact, because oversight of agency rulemaking properly fell under the legislature's purview to make public policy, the means used by lawmakers to oversee agency actions should be "generously construed." In making this argument, the chief justice stated, "It seems to me that if the legislature, in authorizing regulations, cannot condition that authority with a reasonable provision for oversight because the annulment of a regulation is equated with repeal of a statute, then the regulation itself must be considered invalid as not having been passed with the requirements necessary for enacting a bill into law" (*State of Alaska v. A.L.I.V.E. Voluntary, Inc.*, 606 P.2d 780 (Alaska 1980)). Finally, the chief justice found it salient that many of the 55 delegates to the state's 1955 constitutional convention served in the first legislative session following statehood that sanctioned the legislative veto power. Further, Governor William A. Egan, who served as the chairperson of the constitutional convention, signed the bill implementing the legislative veto into law. The court's majority, however, rebuked both of these perspectives.

Veto supporters seeking to overrule the court successfully placed a legislative veto constitutional amendment on the ballot in 1980. In this election, Alaskan voters considered four amendments to the state constitution, each of which was rejected. The veto amendment appeared on the Alaskan ballot once again in 1984. This time the amendment came closer to ratification than the 1980 amendment had, but ultimately failed with 52 percent voting against it. Hoping that the third time would be the charm, the legislative veto amendment made it onto the ballot once more in 1986. In a likely case of voter fatigue, this amendment fared the worst of the three with nearly 60 percent voting in opposition. The cumulative results of these elections meant that the Alaskan legislature's ARRC may only suspend rules following a successful supermajority vote from its membership.

Virginia (Nullification: 1944–1974, 1981–1984; Suspension: 1981–Present)

The legacy of the legislative veto in Virginia is unique because of the sheer number of different veto procedures the state has employed. In 1944, the general assembly passed the Administrative Agencies Act (1944 Acts, c. 160), which created the Commission on Administrative Agencies. As constructed, the commission's membership consisted of six members from the house of delegates and three from the senate (Howe 1955–56). This made Virginia the first state to create a new institution with the sole purpose of reviewing agency rules. For 14 designated agencies, promulgated rules could not go into effect until they had received formal approval from the commission. This oversight requirement that applied to a subset of state agencies was expanded in 1952 following the enactment of the General Administrative Agencies Act (1952 Acts, c. 703), which also allowed either chamber to veto agency rules by resolution (F. Cooper 1965). Though one-House vetoes were commonly seen at the federal level during this era, this is one of few instances where a single chamber could veto rules independent of any action from the other chamber or the governor.

Virginia maintained this oversight system until 1975, when a report by the Virginia Code Commission proposed repealing the existing system in lieu of a more nuanced one that established separate procedures for rulemaking, administrative hearings and case decisions, and judicial adjudication of contested rules (Philpott et al. 1975). Though the report does not provide specific data, it alludes to the fact that the state's existing legislative veto power was infrequently utilized and further claims that the existing oversight system was insufficient in many respects. The resulting legislation—the Administrative Process Act—repealed the existing veto procedures and simply required a 30-day waiting period before most regulations were operative (1975 Acts, c. 503, 1002).

New requirements adopted in 1981 mandated that agencies submit the text of new rules to the general assembly along with a statement justifying their purpose (1981 Acts, c. 387). Standing committees with jurisdiction over a rule then had 90 days to assess the proposal. During this period, either review committee could defer the effective date by majority vote. Agreement to a joint resolution of disapproval in both chambers would permanently ban the rule. In Virginia, joint resolutions are not sent to the governor, so the adoption of this new system reinstated the legislature's veto authority, although in a different form than had existed previously.

According to the state's Division of Legislative Services, the veto system adopted in 1981 was never challenged in court, but an attorney general opinion from 1982 argued that the system violated the constitutional provisions requiring the separation of governmental powers and the legislative process. In light of this declaration, lawmakers once again substantially overhauled the existing rulemaking system in 1984 (1984 Acts, c. 5). Most notably, this reform eliminated the ability of the assembly to permanently block a rule. In addition to adding procedures for executive review for regulations, the new system allowed standing committees with jurisdiction to file objections to proposed rules with the agency and the state's registrar that would suspend their adoption for 21 days. Rules could progress toward implementation at the expiration of the suspension period unless the agency withdrew the rule or the governor imposed an extension to solicit additional public comment.

The next significant change to the review procedure occurred in 1993, when the legislature permitted standing committees to delay the implementation of a proposed rule until the end of the following legislative session, provided that the governor approved this request (1993 Acts, c. 551, c. 772). During the suspension period, the legislature could block rules by enacting a bill into law. In 2002, the Joint Commission on Administrative Rules was created to facilitate a more effective legislative review of rule proposals (2002 Acts, c. 677). With a membership of 12 lawmakers, the commission made recommendations on individual rules to the governor and general assembly. This level of review primarily concerned whether the agency had the statutory authority to issue a rule and whether it complied with legislative intent. With the governor's concurrence, the commission could prevent the adoption of proposed rules until the end of the next legislative session. The only independent power the commission possessed was the imposition of a 21-day suspension period following a formal objection. Thus, although standing committees and the joint commission could both impose a brief extension of a rule's adoption date, they were each dependent on the consent of the governor to impose a more lengthy suspension period.

In sum, Virginia was among the first states to adopt the legislative veto as a means of direct agency oversight. Through its many incarnations, the state has employed systems requiring committee approval of regulations, allowing committees to suspend regulations, and allowing one or both chambers of the assembly to strike down regulations. The diversity of oversight powers granted to the legislature at various points in time is unmatched by any other state.

Missouri (Suspension: 1994–Present)

The application of legislative veto oversight in most every state that has utilized it has occurred through the imposition of a statewide rulemaking system allowing for some means of direct legislative intervention. Missouri, however, is an exceptional case.

Legislation creating a Joint Committee on Administrative Rules (JCAR) passed in 1975 that charged the committee with primary rule review authority (L. 1975 S.B. 58 § 536.020). If the committee determined that a rule should be rescinded in part or completely nullified, it could report such recommendations to the full legislature for its consideration. Acting in this capacity, JCAR was essentially an advisory body. While Missouri had no statewide veto system at this point, Dean (1992) identifies scores of individual statutes that began to empower JCAR with more consequential veto authorities.

Laws passed during the late 1970s and early 1980s began stipulating that JCAR could suspend rules made pursuant to the enabling statute. The language in such statutes commonly stated, "Any rule or portion of a rule promulgated pursuant to this chapter may be suspended by the joint committee on administrative rules if after hearing thereon the committee finds that such rule or portion of the rule is beyond or contrary to the statutory authority of the agency which promulgated the rule, or is inconsistent with the legislative intent of the authorizing statute" (Dean 1992, 1218). Over a period of about 15 years, at least 80 laws were passed containing a variation of this provision. These grants of power essentially allowed JCAR to nullify rules since the length of the suspension period was indeterminate and there were no instances where the assembly had reinstated a rule suspended by the committee (Dean 1992). In addition to this de facto veto power, the general assembly also passed at least eight statutes requiring agencies to secure advance approval from JCAR before rules could go into effect. Thus, although JCAR was never given a broad grant of authority to veto agency rules, it received substantial powers to reject agency rules through the passage of more than 100 laws providing distinctive veto powers.

As JCAR wielded greater oversight powers, Missouri residents twice voted on constitutional amendments that would grant the full assembly veto power. Less than one-third of Missourians who participated in the election voted in favor of the legislative veto amendment in 1976. A second attempt in 1982 fared slightly better, but was also defeated. Twice, voters had soundly rejected legislative veto initiatives. Assuredly unbeknownst to these same voters was the fact that lawmakers were frequently enacting statutes providing a small subset of the legislature with similar types of veto authority.

Legislation amending the state's APA passed in 1994 and allowed JCAR to suspend proposed rules for 30 days by majority vote (L. 1994 S.B. 558 § 536.018). During the suspension period, the general assembly could act to prevent a rule's adoption. This reform provided JCAR with rule suspension power and provided for nullification following adoption of a resolution in each house. A 1997 Missouri Supreme Court ruling scaled back some of these oversight powers as incommensurate with the state's tripartite structure of government, but the revised system continues to permit JCAR to suspend rules for a period of 30 days (L. 1997 S.B. 850 § 536.024).

At issue in the legislative veto case before the court was a rule proposed by the Department of Natural Resources regarding permits for landfills and waste management facilities. Under existing law, all proposed rules must receive the approval of the JCAR in order to move forward. In this instance, the department failed to submit a rule proposal to the committee and therefore did not secure approval in advance of its promulgation. Following a familiar pattern, the court ruled against this rule review process on the basis that it infringed upon the prerogatives of the executive branch and did not conform to the legislative process imposed by the constitution. Calling for the departments of government to be separate, the ruling further reinforced these delineations by declaring that "neither can lawfully trench upon or interfere with the powers of the other" (*Missouri Coalition for the Environment v. Joint Committee on Administrative Rules*, 948 S.W.2d 133 (Mo. 1997)).

The primary reform adopted following the court's pronouncement concerned the process used to veto rules following disapproval from the review committee. In lieu of a resolution adopted by both chambers, the legislature stipulated that rules could only be barred following agreement to a concurrent resolution. The Missouri Constitution requires the governor's signature on such resolutions, meaning that the governor would need to condone the legislature's effort to prevent the adoption of an agency rule. Provided both chambers of the assembly and the governor concur with the committee's opposition to the rule, it is permanently prevented from going into effect (L. 1997 S.B. 850 § 536.024).

Hybrid Systems

Michigan legislators embarked on an unprecedented reform in 1947 by enacting a law permitting either legislative suspension or nullification of agency rules (Public Acts 1947, No. 35). For decades, it remained the only state in the nation where legislators held both types of power. After a state supreme court ruling against the state's nullification process in 2004, Michigan reverted to a suspension system only. Today, five states carry on the tradition it created.

Ohio became the second state to adopt a hybrid system in 1977, followed by Illinois in 1980, and Nevada in 1981. Iowa joined this club in 1984 with the ratification of a constitutional amendment, and Georgia became the last state to sanction both types of review in 2008. Though each of these review processes is somewhat unique, they all provide legislative actors with the ability to impose rule suspensions or block their implementation altogether. If one considers legislative rule review power on a continuum, on the weaker end of the scale are the eight states where the legislature possesses no formal role in the rulemaking process. Slightly more powerful are those states where legislators have rule review responsibilities, but no authority to independently suspend or block rules. States permitting rule suspension by the legislature would come next, followed by those permitting rule nullification. At the other extreme would be the five state legislatures with both nullification and suspension powers. Considered in this fashion, the Georgia, Illinois, Iowa, Nevada, and Ohio legislatures are among the most powerful in the nation given their extraordinary abilities to exert a direct influence on agency rulemaking.

Ohio (Nullification: 1977–Present; Suspension: 1977–Present)

Ohio legislators substantially reformed the state's rulemaking process in 1977, permitting both legislative suspension and nullification of agency rules (1977, H 257, § 1). Under the new procedures, a majority vote in both chambers would permanently block a rule's adoption provided the vote occurred within 60 days of the rule's initial filing. Vetoes were permitted in the event that the agency had exceeded its rulemaking authority, had not followed legislative intent, or if the proposed rule conflicted with an existing rule. A follow-up reform passed in 1984 also required agencies to provide a summary and fiscal analysis with rule submissions (1984, SB 239, § 1). Failure to include these documents with a rule's submission was added as another basis for legislators to veto rules.

In addition to this nullification veto authority, the 1977 law also created a joint rule review committee with the power to suspend rules. During periods between legislative sessions, the Joint Committee on Agency Rule Review could suspend rules until 60 days after the legislature reconvened with a two-thirds majority vote of committee members. The suspension power of this committee and the veto power held by the legislature continue to exist, despite several efforts to scale them back.

Illinois (Nullification: 1980–Present; Suspension: 1980–Present)

The origin of the legislative veto in Illinois occurred in 1980 with APA amendments permitting the Joint Committee on Administrative Rules to suspend proposed rules (Public Act 81–1514, § 2). With a three-fifths majority vote, the committee could stay the implementation of a proposed rule for 180 days. During the suspension period, a majority vote in both chambers would permanently bar the rule from going into effect. Republican governor James R. Thompson vetoed the bill granting the legislature both suspension and nullification veto powers, but the legislature successfully passed the bill into law over the governor's objection.

Following some minor modifications to the review process, a 2004 reform empowered the review committee to nullify rules instead of merely imposing a suspension and requiring action from the full legislature to prevent their adoption (Public Act 93–1035, § 5). This revision kept the supermajority requirement to object to a rule, but eliminated the 180-day suspension period. Under the new procedure, blocked rules were prohibited from going into effect unless the committee rescinded its objection or the legislature agreed to a joint resolution approving the rule. This change made the Illinois joint rules review committee among the most powerful in the nation. Previously, committee suspension and inaction from the full legislature resulted in a rule's adoption. Under the revised system, committee suspension and inaction from the full legislature sustains the committee's opposition to the rule and prevents its adoption.

Nevada (Nullification: 1981–Present; Suspension: 1981–Present)

Nevada is the most recent state to ratify a constitutional amendment permitting legislative veto oversight. The inception of the veto in the state occurred in 1981 through a law permitting the Legislative Commission to suspend rule proposals and joint action from both chambers to veto them (Laws 1981, c. 264, § 3). In that event, agencies had the option to revise and resubmit the rule or to refuse to make amendments. This had the potential to be an iterative process where compromise between the two sides would hopefully result. For rule proposals where agreement could not be reached, the commission could postpone a rule until the beginning of the following session at which point a concurrent resolution could bar its adoption. This rule review system persisted until a legislative veto constitutional amendment passed in 1996. With 61.8 percent of ballots cast in favor, the successful amendment granted the legislature independent suspension and nullification power. Voter approval of this amendment cemented Nevada's status as one of few states that permit both types of veto mechanisms.

The rule review process was substantially revised in 2009 to require all proposed rules to receive approval from the Legislative Commission (2009, 2287). Before the law's passage, a majority vote in both chambers was required to permanently block an objectionable rule. The new rule-making process requires agencies to submit all rule proposals to the Legislative Commission, which must confer its approval in order for the rule to be filed with the secretary of state and go into effect. The Legislative Commission may reject rule proposals on the basis that the rule duplicates a federal statute or regulation, does not conform to the agency's statutory authority to issue the rule, or does not sufficiently comport with the legislative intent of the authorizing statute (NRS § 233B.067). Agencies may revise and resubmit rules rejected by the commission, but legislative approval is required for all rule proposals. Thus, the 12 lawmakers serving on the committee possess a strong veto power over all new rules.

Unlike most nullification systems, the commission must proactively approve rules rather than take steps to veto them. The only other states with a similar requirement are Connecticut and West Virginia. Like Nevada, rule proposals in Connecticut must receive committee approval. West Virginia requires the passage of an authorizing law in order to sanction a rule proposal. In this respect, these three states are unique in their requirement that the legislature must approve all proposed rules. The nine other nullification states allow legislators to take some action to block a rule's implementation, but do not require advance approval for rules to progress toward implementation.

Iowa (Nullification: 1984–Present; Suspension: 1976–Present)

Before the ratification of a legislative veto constitutional amendment, Iowa's legislature updated the state APA in 1976. Prior to this reform, agencies were required to submit rule proposals to the governor and a joint legislative review committee (I.C.A. § 17A.2). The committee could make objections and, if left unsatisfied, could recommend legislation that would block a rule's adoption. The revised system allowed the Administrative Rules Review Committee to suspend the implementation of proposed rules for 70 days or until the end of the current legislative session (Acts 1976 chap. 1063, § 2).

Originally created in 1974 with advisory powers only, the committee's membership included five lawmakers from each chamber. The party with majority status has the power to appoint three individuals to serve on the committee, and the minority party receives two slots. With this membership criteria, the only possible partisan configurations of the committee would be an even split in the event that each party controlled one chamber, or a division of six to four if a single party held majorities in each. This imposed party composition of the committee is notable since the committee may only suspend the effective date of proposed rules by a two-thirds majority vote.[10]

With seven of the committee members voting in favor, the committee could suspend a rule proposal for 70 days or until the next session (I.C.A. § 17A.4–8). Under either scenario, suspended rules are forwarded to the appropriate standing committees, which have the authority to propose a joint resolution or legislation to permanently veto the rule. Both of these measures would require the governor's signature. If no law or resolution is successful during the suspension period, the rule automatically goes into effect.

A decade after the creation of the review committee with the power of rule suspension, Iowans amended their constitution to allow legislators to veto rules without involvement from the governor. Results from the 1984 election resulted in the ratification of the 38th amendment to Iowa's constitution that read "the general assembly may nullify an adopted administrative rule of a state agency by the passage of a resolution by a majority of all of the members of each house of the general assembly" (Article III, Section 40). By adding this section to the constitution, the state guarded against the possibility of judges striking down the nullification system on constitutional grounds as had occurred in several other states by that point in time.

Georgia (Nullification: 1977–Present; Suspension: 2008–Present)

A reform to Georgia's APA in 1977 permitted standing committees to sponsor resolutions to veto adopted rules (Laws 1977, Act 735, § 3). In order to nullify a rule, both chambers must agree to a resolution of disapproval. If the resolution is supported by at least two-thirds of legislators in both houses, the rule is nullified. Although a few other states require supermajority coalitions to execute a veto, the supermajority requirement imposed by Georgia law is unique because of the governor's potential involvement in the process.

Veto resolutions receiving majority support, but less than a two-thirds majority vote in both chambers, go to the governor's office. If the governor vetoes the resolution, the rule persists and the legislature has no opportunity to overrule the governor's veto. If the governor approves the resolution, the rule is vetoed. This is the only state where the size of the coalition voting in favor of a veto resolution dictates whether the governor has a role in the review process. Since the original passage of this nullification process, lawmakers have made some modifications to the state's APA, but the general nullification procedure requiring supermajority support or support from simple majorities in both chambers in association with the governor's approval remains in effect.

Legislation passed in 2008 allowed standing committees to postpone a rule's adoption until the following term (Laws 2008, Act 389, § 1). Like the nullification process, the imposition of a rule suspension required a two-thirds majority vote from members of the standing committee in each chamber with primary jurisdiction over the rule. Committees maintained the ability to initiate resolutions to nullify agency rules without a supermajority vote. In sum, the Georgia legislature holds the ability to both suspend and nullify agency rules, but in both instances supermajority coalitions are required in order to independently execute either veto type.

Oversight Actions of State Legislatures: Literature and Hypotheses

The cases discussed in the preceding sections help illustrate the varied history of the legislative veto. In some states, lawmakers have a great deal of direct oversight influence, while in others the executive has more rulemaking discretion. Research seeking to explain variations in the oversight activities of state legislatures is diverse, spanning topics including oversight by statute (Hamm and Robertson 1981; Huber, Shipan, and Pfahler 2001), rulemaking review (Clingermayer 1991; Clingermayer and West 1992; Ethridge 1981, 1984a, 1984b; Gerber and Teske 2000; Gerber, Maestas, and Demetrius 2005; Woods 2004), sunset laws (Hamm and Robertson 1981), agency design (Potoski 1999), and the adoption and content of state APAs (Clingermayer 1991; De Figueiredo and Vanden Bergh 2004; Grady and Simon 2002; Jensen and McGrath 2011; Renfrow and Houston 1987; Renfrow, West, and Houston 1986). When scholars have considered legislative veto capabilities, they have served predominantly as an independent rather than dependent variable (for an exception, see Hamm and Robertson 1981).

In one of the most notable studies on the topic, Huber, Shipan, and Pfahler (2001) examine factors affecting the degree to which legislatures engage in statutory oversight. Their analysis of the length of certain Medicaid laws in 48 states demonstrated that the professionalization of the legislature, divided government, and the availability of other nonstatutory oversight resources each corresponded with more lengthy enactments. One of the nonstatutory oversight devices considered is the legislative veto. Here, Huber, Shipan, and Pfahler (2001) show that lawmakers from states where the veto is not permitted are more apt to write more detailed statutes. Applying a new measure of legislative rule review authority to all 50 states, Gerber, Maestas, and Demetrius's (2005) study of agency rulemaking finds that administrators perceived state legislatures with veto power as more influential. Counter to expectations, Woods and Baranowski (2006) actually find the opposite. Using a smaller sample of just 11 states, their analysis of survey data from 400 state officials indicated that legislative veto availability corresponds with lessened perceptions of legislative influence. This unexpected result, they argue, may indicate that legislative veto influence is conditioned by other factors. Examining different types of legislative review power expected to affect environmental compliance costs over a six-year period, Daley, Haiderr-Markel, and Whitford (2007) find that the opportunity for legislative rule review exerts a significant, negative effect on state regulatory compliance costs. An earlier study found that the opportunity for committee rule review had no effect on the strictness of sulfur emission regulations but did correspond with regulations of lower complexity (Ethridge 1981). Judging by this small sample, it is apparent findings on the effects of veto oversight have been somewhat inconsistent, and few studies have sought to examine factors expected to bring about this type of legislative rule review. The remainder of this chapter seeks to make such a contribution.

The emphasis legislators place on vigilant oversight should generally increase as the preferences of executive actors deviate from those of the legislature (Epstein and O'Halloran 1999). Huber, Shipan, and Pfahler's (2001) comparative study on statutory control of the bureaucracy also finds corroborating evidence that divided government affects the oversight actions of legislatures. De Figueiredo and Vanden Bergh (2004) find a partial effect of divided government on state APA adoption, concluding that the likelihood of adoption increases when Democratic legislative majorities face Republican governors but not when Republican majorities exist alongside a Democratic governor. Following in this research tradition, this study will likewise examine the effects of split partisan control of the statehouse and governor's office on the oversight prerogatives of legislators.

It is expected that states will be more likely to enact reforms providing for legislative veto oversight during periods of divided government. By subjecting rules to greater legislative scrutiny and the possibility of a veto, legislators can exercise greater control over policy as a counterweight to the state executive branch. Under divided government, legislators should be more willing to incur the transaction costs associated with efforts to impose legislative veto oversight. However, because changes to state rulemaking procedures are typically imposed by statute, in most instances the governor's signature is required to enact the reform. Because proposals sanctioning the use of the legislative veto raise concerns over separation of powers and, under divided government, would concede a greater ability to affect rules to a legislature controlled by the opposing party, we may actually observe that such reforms are less commonly enacted when state government is divided. In short, it may be more difficult to pass legislation overhauling state administrative procedures when facing opposition from a governor with an alternative partisan allegiance.

Divided Government Hypothesis. *Legislative veto reforms are more likely to be enacted during periods of divided government.*

Grady and Simon (2002) utilize original survey data from government employees in 49 states to assess government control and public input in state rulemaking processes. Examining how government partisanship affects bureaucratic control, they find virtually no difference between unified and divided government. Their results do indicate that shifts to Republican control of the legislature correspond with greater influence over the administrative process. Specifically, they argue that "the shift to Republicanism in the state capitols has been *a*, if not *the*, major cause" in fostering greater political control over agency rulemaking (Grady and Simon 2002, 670; emphasis in original). In order to test whether partisan control of the legislature affects the probability that a state will adopt the legislative veto, unified Republican and Democratic legislatures will be compared to those where each party controls one chamber. Single-party control of the legislature by either party is expected to increase the likelihood that such rulemaking reforms will pass.

Unified Legislature Hypothesis. *Legislative veto reforms are more likely to be enacted during periods of unified legislative control.*

Another partisan factor that may influence efforts to impose legislative veto oversight are prospective assessments of each party's fortunes. If the current majority party expects that its status may be in jeopardy in the next election, we would expect that the party in power would be less apt to incur the costs associated with shepherding reforms permitting greater legislative rulemaking influence. This is, of course, because the opposing party could then use the legislative veto to help achieve its own policy goals during the following term. Thus, if the party in power has some expectation that its majority-party status may be fleeting, we would expect it to be less likely to invest the resources necessary to get some type of legislative veto reform passed.

Future Party Prospects Hypothesis. *Legislative veto reforms are less likely to be enacted when the existing majority party in the legislature is in danger of losing its majority party status.*

Beyond partisanship, several other factors could influence legislative veto reform including the professionalization of the legislature. This concept has been demonstrated to be important in other contexts, although Clingermayer (1991) and Clingermayer and West (1992) find no connection between professionalized legislatures and the presence of legislative rule review authority. Huber, Shipan, and Pfahler (2001) use lawmaker salary as a proxy for professionalization and determine that more professionalized legislatures produce lengthier laws. In assessing state rulemaking restrictiveness in state APAs, Renfrow, West, and Houston (1986) et al. show that restrictive APAs are often found in states with greater legislative professionalism. They further speculate that legislative veto requirements are probably "a function of the ability of state legislators to oversee the implementation of statutes" (375). The present study permits a test of this expectation. Previously, Gerber, Maestas, and Demetrius (2005) did not establish a link between professionalization and the perceived influence of lawmakers in the rulemaking process, and Baranowski (2001) and Woods and Baranowski (2006) found that professionalized legislatures were actually perceived as less influential.

In this analysis, Squire's (2007) measure of legislative professionalism is used to test whether more skilled legislatures are more apt to engage in legislative veto oversight. This hypothesis is attributable to the expectation that lawmakers serving in a more professionalized legislature should have greater capacities to develop expertise in specific issue areas. Further, they may be more likely to have the incentive and wherewithal to obtain information on proposed and existing rules in these areas of specialization made by the state's bureaucracy. Greater legislative resources that exist in a more professionalized legislature should also facilitate the ability to study, oversee, and identify regulations that may warrant additional legislative scrutiny. The imposition of legislative veto authority would provide one avenue for legislators to direct agency action.

Legislative Professionalization Hypothesis. *Legislatures with greater levels of professionalization are more likely to enact legislative veto reforms.*

Another factor that may contribute to the imposition of legislative veto oversight is the size of state legislatures. As problems of collective action generally increase in accordance with the size of a group, states with larger legislative bodies may be more desirous of an expedited rule review process. The largest chambers in the sample that follows are the New Hampshire House of Representatives, which once held a membership of 443 (since reduced to 400), and Minnesota's upper chamber currently consisting of 67 senators. For such large bodies, it may be more difficult to build a coalition in support of legislation altering the status of an agency rule. Because of this, there are likely to be greater benefits to delegating agency rule review to select committees or by providing the legislature with an expedited means to consider a rule's status.

Chamber Size Hypothesis. *States with larger legislative chambers are more likely to enact legislative veto reforms allowing for an expedited process to review agency rules.*

A final consideration concerns the size of state governments more generally. As state agencies grow in terms of the functions they perform and the amount of expenditures allocated to them, it is likely the case that legislators will desire greater amounts of control over agency actions. Following in the example of DeFigueiredo and Vanden Bergh (2004) some models include a variable indicating the change in total state spending from the prior fiscal year.

Data and Methods

To test the hypotheses from the preceding section, I created a data set including all states from 1938 to 2011. This start year is used in order to capture every instance where a state adopted some type of legislative veto oversight beginning with the Kansas law, which was the first to grant veto power to a state legislature. Using the state/year as the unit of analysis, adding Alaska and Hawaii to the data set in their shared statehood year of 1959, and omitting Nebraska due to its unicameral nonpartisan legislature, produces a data set with a total of 3,584 observations.

Information concerning the adoption of legislative veto procedures was collected from a number of sources. Several administrative law texts provided a survey of state legislative veto policies during the first few decades of its existence (Bonfield 1986; F. Cooper 1965; Howe 1955–56), and two studies by Levinson (1982, 1987) provided citations to statutes imposing or reforming state legislative veto procedures through the 1980s. Statutory citation information and enactment dates from these publications provided the necessary information to identify the state/years when legislative veto powers were adopted or amended. Tharp's (2001) summary of rule review powers based on interviews with dozens of public officials provided an exhaustive description of existing legislative and executive rules review procedures. More recently, *The Book of the States* (2012) published by the Council of State Governments lists summary tables concerning the structures, procedures, and powers of legislative review of administrative regulations. Also published in 2012 was a survey of state administrative rule review created by the Administrative Codes and Registers section of the National Association of Secretaries of State. Finally, a comprehensive report by Schwartz (2010) on state rulemaking procedures and oversight also provided detailed information regarding state law and practices. Each of these sources lists details about contemporary state-level administrative rulemaking procedures. With assistance from each of these sources, I identified the sections of state law concerning legislative review of agency rulemaking.

To identify state/years when legislative veto reforms were adopted I used the statutory history of legislative rule review sections from each state's APA. For example, current Nevada law concerning legislative review of proposed rules lists the statute's legislative history as "Added by Laws 1981, p. 510. Amended by Laws 1987, p. 1582; Laws 1997, p. 276; Laws 1999, pp. 902, 2205; Laws 2005, c. 498, § 2, eff. June 17, 2005; Laws 2007, c. 248, § 11, eff. July 1, 2007; Laws 2009, c. 419, § 6, eff. July 1, 2009" (NRS § 233B.067). This provides citations to the original law as well as six subsequent enactments that amended the statute.

Using the Hein Online Session Laws Library, I downloaded the full text of all laws listed in the statutory history of the relevant state laws on legislative rule review. The number of such laws varied from a single amending law in Louisiana to 18 amending laws in Montana. In each law, I identified the section imposing amendments to legislative powers in the rulemaking process. These amendments were then scrutinized to determine whether the change substantially altered the existing review scheme and provided lawmakers with greater capabilities to veto agency rules. Less consequential modifications to the review process, minor adjustments to statutory language, and technical changes were not included as significant amendments in the creation of this variable.

In 1975, an amendment to Iowa's APA imposed a wording change that simply replaced instances of "departmental rules" with "administrative rules" (Acts 1975, chap. 68, § 70). Likewise, a revision to Georgia's APA passed in 1984 required agencies to submit economic impact analyses to lawmakers as part of the review process (Laws 1984, No. 1261, § 1). While each of these laws modified the existing rulemaking process, this analysis is principally interested in accounting for factors contributing to the adoption or substantial expansion of the legislature's authority to veto rules.

For example, South Dakota adopted a rule review process permitting committee suspension in 1975 (SL 1975, chap. 19). Because this enactment constituted the state's first implementation of the suspension variety of legislative veto oversight, this state/year is coded as a suspension veto system adoption. Originally, the law required a three-fourths supermajority vote from the committee in order to impose a suspension. Legislation passed in 2003 made it easier for the rules review committee to suspend rules by eliminating the supermajority requirement in lieu of a simple majority vote (SL 2003, chap. 17, § 3). Since this reform significantly modified existing suspension system procedures, this case is coded as an expansion of suspension veto power.

In most instances, subsequent amendments to rulemaking procedures have allowed for greater participation by the legislature, thereby extending its oversight reach. There are a small number of laws that have made reforms in the opposite direction, such as a Minnesota law passed in 1997 that repealed the ability of the joint rules review committee to suspend new rule proposals (Laws 1997, chap. 98, § 17). In order to take this into account, I coded each amendment according to whether the law expanded or restricted the legislature's veto power. In total, this data collection process identified 20 state/years when a suspension system was first adopted and 14 instances when legislative suspension powers were expanded. Nullification systems were originally adopted on 22 occasions with reforms to expand the legislature's preexisting veto authority passed in 18 state/years.

Data regarding party control of state legislatures were obtained from the Partisan Division of American State Governments data set created by Burnham and the Inter-university Consortium for Political and Social Research, as well as the state politics data set compiled by Lindquist as provided by *State Politics & Policy Quarterly*. Data on the size of legislative chambers and state spending were obtained from separate data sets made available by Klarner.[11] Table 6.4 provides descriptive statistics for these variables.

An initial analysis of legislative veto adoption presented in table 6.5 considers the state government's partisan configuration at the time that suspension or nullification legislative vetoes were originally sanctioned. The party division variable has four possible categories: unified Democratic government, unified Republican government, divided government with a Republican governor, and divided government with a Democratic governor. For the latter two categories, a state is classified as belonging to a period of divided government if the party opposite the governor controls at least one of the state's two legislative chambers. Since the distribution of these four government types is not uniform across the sample, the percentage of state/years corresponding with each type is listed in parentheses.

Of the 19 instances of suspension system adoption that can be placed in one of these four government types, no single category constitutes a majority of these enactments.[12] Eleven suspension systems were adopted during periods of either unified Republican or Democratic government, while eight systems were established under divided government.

TABLE 6.4. Descriptive statistics

Variable	Mean	Standard Deviation	Min	Max
Suspension Veto Adoption	0.01	0.07	0	1
Suspension Veto Adoption/Expansion	0.01	0.09	0	1
Nullification Veto Adoption	0.01	0.08	0	1
Nullification Veto Adoption/Expansion	0.01	0.10	0	1
Democratic Governor	0.56	0.50	0	1
Democratic Majorities both Chambers	0.49	0.50	0	1
Republican Majorities both Chambers	0.32	0.47	0	1
Divided Government	0.44	0.50	0	1
Legislative Majority Party Change	0.11	0.30	0	1
Lower House Size	114.81	61.19	24	443
Upper House Size	38.68	10.78	15	67
Annual Total Expenditure Change	5.09	6.17	−29.55	43.77
Professionalization	0.21	0.12	0.03	0.66
South	0.33	0.47	0	1

TABLE 6.5. Legislative veto adoption and expansion: 1938–2011

Government Type (% of cases)	Suspension (%)	Nullification (%)	Total (%)
Adoption			
Unified Democratic (35.0)	7 (36.8)	7 (33.3)	14 (35.0)
Unified Republican (21.6)	4 (21.1)	6 (28.6)	10 (25.0)
Divided—Republican Governor (22.2)	6 (31.6)	7 (33.3)	13 (32.5)
Divided—Democratic Governor (21.2)	2 (10.5)	1 (4.8)	3 (7.5)
Total	19	21	40
Adoption and Expansion			
Unified Democratic (35.0)	9 (28.1)	12 (30.8)	21 (29.6)
Unified Republican (21.6)	8 (25.0)	9 (23.1)	17 (23.9)
Divided—Republican Governor (22.2)	9 (28.1)	13 (33.3)	22 (31.0)
Divided—Democratic Governor (21.2)	6 (18.8)	5 (12.8)	11 (15.5)
Total	32	39	71

Note: Nebraska's adoptions of nullification (1953) and suspension (1978) systems are not included in the table due to its nonpartisan legislature. Minnesota's expansion of suspension (2001) veto power is also omitted since the governor was neither Democratic nor Republican. Iowa's nullification system was adopted by constitutional amendment in 1984. The partisan division that existed when the amendment was certified to go before voters is used for this case. Columns may not sum to 100 percent due to rounding.

This distribution is contrary to what the divided government hypotheses expects as a majority of suspension systems were enacted during periods of unified party control. Most of the suspension systems adopted during periods of divided government occurred when Democrats controlled at least one chamber of the legislature with an incumbent Republican governor. Only two of these enactments occurred during the alternative configuration of divided government. The distribution of nullification veto system adoption across these four categories is similar with the biggest difference being a greater percentage adopted under unified Republican government.

On 22 occasions states have originally bestowed their legislature with the authority to nullify agency rules. In every instance except one the initial adoption of this type of veto oversight occurred with the passage of a bill into law.[13] As was the case with suspension systems, a plurality of nullification system adoptions occurred during periods of unified Democratic control. In addition to the seven enactments passed during unified Democratic government, six nullifications systems were adopted during unified Republican control. Under divided government, more enactments passed with a Republican governor relative to those with a Democratic governor. Nullification veto adoption under the latter divided government configuration occurred only once—Vermont in 1975. On seven occasions nullification systems were adopted under divided government with a Republican governor. When jointly considered, 60 percent of the instances where states adopted a suspension or nullification system occurred with one-party dominance of the state government.

The second panel in table 6.5 adds the instances where states have adopted reforms expanding the legislature's veto power. While a plurality of suspension systems were adopted under unified Democratic government, only twice have suspension powers been strengthened under this condition. As seen by comparing the first column of the two panels, most instances when suspension powers were expanded occurred with a Republican governor in office. Beyond the four cases when suspension systems were first adopted under unified Republican government, there are an additional four instances where legislative powers to suspend rules were strengthened by a Republican-controlled state government. On three other occasions, rule suspension powers have been expanded under divided government with a Republican governor. Although the adoption of nullification systems is more common under unified government, a majority of the successful efforts to expand rule nullification powers have occurred under divided government. A total of eight were passed under unified government, while 10 expansions have occurred under divided government—six with a Republican governor and four with a Democrat.

Comparing the distribution of legislative veto reforms by government type to their prevalence across this time period shows that the configurations with Republican disproportionately impose this type of oversight. Unified Republican government represents 21 percent of state/years from 1938 to 2011, but 25 percent of legislative veto reforms permitting rule suspension and 23 percent of nullification veto policy enactments. Divided government with a Republican governor exists in 22 percent of these cases, while constituting 28 percent of the suspension system enactments and 33 percent of nullification system reforms. Conversely, those configurations with Democratic governors are disproportionately less likely to adopt either type of rulemaking reform. While 21 of the 71 instances (29.6 percent) when legislative veto powers were adopted or amended occurred under unified Democratic government, this percentage is less than the prevalence of unified Democratic government in the data (35 percent). Least common are legislative veto reforms passed under divided government with a Democratic governor. About one-fifth of all state/years belong to this category, which represents just 15 percent of all suspension and nullification veto enactments. The combined results from this descriptive analysis fails to provide support for the expectation that legislative veto reforms should be more common under divided government, and also suggests that the adoption of legislative veto oversight is more likely when a Republican holds the governor's office.

One caveat to the data presented in this table is the fact that nine of the laws imposing legislative veto reforms were passed over the governor's veto. In total, governors vetoed six bills originally adopting legislative rule suspension, three bills adopting rule nullification, and one bill expanding existing rule nullification power.[14] Without the benefit of additional data on unsuccessful overrides of gubernatorial vetoes of legislative veto reform bills, this distribution suggests that governors are more likely to veto bills first imposing legislative veto powers, that legislatures are more successful at overriding these kinds of gubernatorial vetoes, or, perhaps, both. Of the 11 state/years where suspension systems were adopted during unified government, three were passed over the veto of the Democratic governor (Tennessee 1975, New Jersey 1981, and Kentucky 1982) and one over a Republican's veto (Montana 1997). Suspension systems were adopted over the governor's veto twice during periods of divided government (Alaska 1978 and Illinois 1980). Excluding these cases, seven suspension systems were adopted during unified government and six passed under divided government. This distribution is closer to what the divided government hypothesis expects, but remains short of providing support for its expectation.

Of the three nullification systems that passed over the veto of the governor, one occurred in New Jersey (1981) under unified Democratic government. The remaining two instances, in West Virginia (1976) and Illinois (1980), happened when Democratic majorities in the legislature overrode the veto of the Republican governor. By exempting these cases, 12 nullification systems were originally imposed under unified government, with seven adopted during a period of divided government. This too remains contrary to the expectation of the divided government hypothesis.

When solely considering partisan control of the legislature, most veto systems were originally adopted with Democratic majorities in both chambers. More than two-thirds of the suspension systems (13) and about 55 percent of nullification systems (12) were passed by legislatures controlled by Democrats. That Democratic majorities more commonly impose such reforms is to be expected given the skew toward Democratic legislative control in the data—49 percent of all state/years compared to 32 percent of state/years under Republican legislative control. Of the remaining cases, Republican legislative majorities were responsible for the passage of approximately one-fifth (4) and one-third (8) of suspension and nullification enactments, respectively. Despite the fact that split partisan control of the legislature exists in about 20 percent of the state/years in the sample, only 10 percent (2 each) of both veto types were adopted under this condition. Thus, from a strictly legislative perspective, the imposition of legislative veto oversight is most likely to occur when a single party controls the legislature, with passage by Democratic majorities being the most prevalent condition. To provide a more nuanced analysis, the models presented in the next section consider additional factors expected to affect the likelihood that a state will adopt a rulemaking process permitting legislative vetoes.

Modeling Legislative Veto Adoption and Abolition

Debating different approaches to modeling state policy adoption, scholars have recommended the use of Cox duration models in lieu of the more traditional logit or probit maximum likelihood estimation since they more suitably deal with multiple and competing events both within and across states (Box-Steffensmeier and Zorn 2002; Jones and Branton 2005). A technical advantage of such models is the fact that they do not require a parameterization of the baseline hazard function. Discussing their benefits, Jones and Branton emphasize that they "easily accommodate research questions where multiple events can occur; for example, a state adopting different kinds of legislation. The logit-probit approach is not easily extended to this kind of problem. . . . [T]he Cox model has also been extended to handle the case of repeatable events; for example, a state adopting the same kind of policy multiple times" (2005, 424). Box-Steffensmeier and Zorn (2002) likewise suggest that researchers employ duration models for repeatable event dependent variables. Since the adoption and expansion of legislative veto powers are potentially repeatable events, Cox duration models provide the primary basis to test the hypotheses from the prior section.

The analysis presented in tables 6.6 and 6.7 models the adoption of nullification and suspension legislative vetoes separately given the different types of authority each provides for legislators. The dependent variable

TABLE 6.6. Cox conditional gap-time model estimates of legislative veto suspension systems

Variable	Adoption		Adoption and Expansion	
	(1938–2011)	(1960–2005)	(1938–2011)	(1960–2005)
Democratic Governor	−1.37***	−1.09**	−0.63*	−0.53
	(0.47)	(0.51)	(0.33)	(0.36)
Democratic Majorities	0.46	0.69	0.93	0.94
Both Chambers	(0.84)	(0.90)	(0.77)	(0.80)
Republican Majorities	−0.36	−0.64	0.70	0.25
Both Chambers	(0.67)	(0.74)	(0.68)	(0.68)
Divided Government	−0.77	−0.46	−0.02	0.01
	(0.49)	(0.61)	(0.38)	(0.44)
Majority Party Change in	0.04	0.26	0.40	0.44
Next Legislative Term	(0.87)	(0.88)	(0.50)	(0.48)
Lower House Size	0.00*	0.00*	−0.00	0.00
	(0.00)	(0.00)	(0.00)	(0.00)
Upper House Size	0.00	0.01	−0.00	−0.00
	(0.01)	(0.02)	(0.00)	(0.02)
Expenditure Growth	—	0.05	—	0.08*
		(0.06)		(0.04)
Legislative	—	−1.96	—	−1.05
Professionalization		(2.15)		(1.36)
South	—	−0.08	—	−0.13
		(0.55)		(0.54)
N	3,541	2,229	3,541	2,229
N Veto System Adoption	19	17	32	29
Log Psuedolikelihood	−52.03	−45.94	−74.33	−65.74

Note: Standard errors adjusted for clustering across 49 states are reported in parentheses. *** $p<.01$, ** $p<.05$, * $p<.10$.

used for the first two models presented in table 6.6 indicates each instance when a state first adopted a rulemaking system permitting legislative rule suspension. The first model includes the full sample spanning 1938 to 2011 and captures every instance when a state adopted this type of oversight (exempting Nebraska on account of the partisan variables included as independent variables). The second model spans 1960 to 2005 on account of the data availability of three additional variables. This restricted sample includes all but two suspension system adoptions. The dependent variable used for the third and fourth models adds cases when existing legislative rule suspension powers were strengthened. This variable mirrors the first column in the second panel of table 6.5. The dependent variables used in table 6.7 replicate those of table 6.6 for nullification systems with the first two models including original adoptions of this type of legislative rule review and the third and fourth models adding cases when existing nullification powers were extended.

TABLE 6.7. Cox conditional gap-time model estimates of legislative veto nullification systems

Variable	Adoption		Adoption and Expansion	
	(1938–2011)	(1960–2005)	(1938–2011)	(1960–2005)
Democratic Governor	–1.34**	–1.58***	–0.77**	–0.72
	(0.65)	(0.63)	(0.35)	(0.47)
Democratic Majorities Both Chambers	1.30	—	0.95*	1.35*
	(1.08)		(0.55)	(0.72)
Republican Majorities Both Chambers	1.10	—	1.05	1.07
	(1.50)		(0.69)	(0.83)
Divided Government	–0.31	–0.54	–0.04	–0.10
	(0.66)	(0.50)	(0.36)	(0.42)
Majority Party Change in Next Legislative Term	0.22	–0.22	–0.38	–0.32
	(1.31)	(1.42)	(0.73)	(0.61)
Lower House Size	–0.00	–0.00	–0.00	–0.00
	(0.00)	(0.00)	(0.00)	(0.00)
Upper House Size	–0.01	0.01	–0.01	0.01
	(0.02)	(0.02)	(0.02)	(0.02)
Expenditure Growth	—	–0.06	—	0.03
		(0.06)		(0.03)
Legislative Professionalization	—	–2.65	—	–2.20
		(2.11)		(1.78)
South	—	–0.19	—	–0.92*
		(0.60)		(0.56)
N	3,541	2,229	3,541	2,229
N Veto System Adoption	21	15	39	29
Log Psuedolikelihood	–67.66	–45.30	–99.91	–71.25

Note: Standard errors adjusted for clustering across 49 states are reported in parentheses. *** $p<.01$, ** $p<.05$, * $p<.10$.

The first model in table 6.6 includes seven independent variables. Most of these variables concern some aspect of partisanship. The first variable indicates the party of the governor, and the second two variables are binary variables indicating whether Democrats or Republicans possess majority party status in both chambers of the legislature. The divided government variable is also a binary measure that indicates whether the party opposite the governor controls one or both legislative chambers. In order to take into account future strategic considerations, a lead variable designates cases when the majority party status changes in one or both legislative chambers in the following year. Though such changes may not always be expected, we can assume that party leaders typically have an idea about the fragility of the existing party balance. These future expectations may influence contemporary action. Finally, two separate variables denoting the total membership in each state's upper and lower legislative chamber are also included.

According to the estimates from the first model, few variables emerge as significant predictors that a state will adopt a rulemaking system permitting legislative rule suspension. The singular influential partisan variable is the party of the governor with such reforms being more likely with a Republican in office. Though the coefficient estimate on the divided government variable nearly reaches conventional levels of significance (p-value of 0.12), none of the remaining party variables exhibit a strong relationship with suspension system adoption. Both of the chamber-size variables have a positive coefficient estimate indicating that these reforms are more likely to be adopted by larger legislatures, but the lower house size variable is the only one of the two that reaches statistical significance.

At the cost of a smaller sample size because of data availability, the second model adds variables capturing the annual change in total state spending, legislative professionalization, and a dichotomous variable for southern states. None of the three variables appreciably influence the adoption of legislative rule suspension. Similar to the first model using the full sample, the only statistically significant predictors of suspension system adoption are the party of the governor and the size of the state's lower chamber.

Models three and four include cases where states acted to expand pre-existing legislative rule suspension authority. The results from these two models mostly comport with those that focus exclusively on adoption. Most striking is the lack of statistical significance on the coefficient estimates of most independent variables, although prior studies have also found that few variables explained the presence of legislative rule review (Clingermayer 1991; Clingermayer and West 1992). The most robust result across all four specifications is that legislative rule suspension powers are more apt to increase with a Republican governor in office. In the third model, this factor is the only one shown to significantly influence legislative rule suspension reforms. Model four also has but one variable with a significant coefficient estimate—government spending growth. (The p-value for the governor's party variable in the fourth model is 0.14.) Controlling for annual changes in total state spending shows that legislative rule suspension powers are more apt to grow as expenditures increase. In fact, legislators have enacted suspension system reforms when state spending decreased relative to the prior year when controlling for inflation on just seven occasions.

Table 6.7 provides model estimates of factors expected to affect legislative veto oversight permitting rule nullification. With one exception, the models are identical to the suspension system models in table 6.6.[15] Similar to those results, few variables emerge as significant predictors of nullification veto reforms. Once again, the most consistent finding across all four model specifications is that legislative veto reforms are more likely with a Republican governor in office. Among the 10 variables included in the two nullification system adoption models, the party of the governor is the only factor for which the null hypothesis can be rejected. Models three and four, which add cases when legislative rule nullification powers were expanded, show that such reforms are more likely when Democrats hold majority party status in both chambers. Since the models also include a variable for Republican Party majorities, which also has a positive coefficient estimate, the omitted category is legislatures with split partisan control. Thus, the enactment of nullification veto reforms is more likely under single-party dominance, particularly Democratic Party control. The only other factor with a significant effect is the regional dummy variable for southern states. This type of oversight is less commonly found in this region. Among the 11 states of the former Confederacy, only Virginia, Louisiana, and Georgia have permitted legislative rule nullification.

When jointly considered, these models provide little support for the divided government hypothesis. In seven of the eight model specifications, the estimated effect of divided government on the likelihood of legislative veto adoption or expansion is actually negative, though the effect is not statistically significant in any model. This directional effect is the opposite of what was theorized and may speak to the difficulty of passing reforms permitting greater legislative influence in the rulemaking process when faced with a governor of the opposing party. In most cases, the relationship between single-party control of the legislature and veto adoption was positive as the unified legislature hypothesis posited, although the Democratic Party majorities variable was the only one of these partisan variables with a statistically significant effect. These findings regarding the influence of Republican governors and Democratic legislative majorities on legislative veto adoption align with those of De Figueiredo and Vanden Bergh (2004) who find a similar effect when considering the adoption of APA reforms more broadly.

The effects of the chamber size and future majority party switch were inconsistent across the eight model specifications. The relationship between legislative professionalism and legislative veto oversight was negative in every instance, but not strong enough to reject the null hypothesis in any of the four models. This finding is contrary to the expectation of the professionalization hypothesis. Since Huber, Shipan, and Pfahler (2001) demonstrate that legislative professionalization contributes to a greater use of statutory controls to oversee agency action, it is conceivable that professionalized legislatures are more prone to writing more detailed laws meaning that there is less of a reliance on agencies to issue rules as they execute the law. This may obviate the need for extensive veto powers to influence agency rules. Finally, both types of legislative vetoes are generally less common in southern states. A closer examination of the interplay between these variables, perhaps through case studies, would help further clarify these relationships. What is not apparent from the foregoing analysis focusing strictly on rulemaking procedures, however, is any description of the actual exercise of veto powers. Government data from several states provides at least a partial perspective on the frequency with which legislators vote to suspend or reject rule proposals.

Exercise of Veto Powers: Speak Softly and Carry a Big Stick?

While every state provides at least some legislative resources online, none comprehensively catalogues its legislature's oversight activities. Because of this it remains challenging to obtain detailed information concerning the actual exercise of the veto (Howe 1955–56). Providing testimony at a 1981 hearing before the Senate Judiciary Committee's Subcommittee on Agency Administration, Congressman Elliott Levitas discussed research conducted by his staff on legislative veto use in 10 selected states. Though he did not document veto frequency across each of these states, he concluded that state legislators tended to use their veto powers sparingly.[16] Typical, Levitas argued, was the experience of the Montana legislature, which vetoed just two of the 600 rules it reviewed in 1977. Most active was the Connecticut legislature, which vetoed 23 of the 159 regulations it received in 1974, for a veto rate of nearly 15 percent. This percentage dropped significantly to about 2 percent in the following term when legislators struck down just three of 129 regulations (Levitas 1981). These albeit limited descriptive data help illuminate how state legislators actually wield this type of oversight, yet scholarly examinations of state rulemaking review committees have been few (Gerber and Teske 2000, although see Hahn 2000b). A small collection of studies has provided a window into the oversight actions of these committees (Anderson and Poynor 2012; Ethridge 1984a; Lambert 1982).

A study that scrutinized the actions of Michigan's JCAR, which, at the time, was charged with approving new rule proposals, found that over a six-year period the committee conferred approval on 77 percent of the nearly 1,000 rules it received (Lambert 1982). It vetoed a total of 18 rules—less than 2 percent of all submissions. Agencies withdrew close to 20 percent of the remaining rules that did not receive outright approval or a veto. The sizable number of rules withdrawn was seen as an indication that JCAR exerts a substantial influence on agency action despite the fact that it issued an average of only three vetoes per year. A majority of the rules withdrawn faced committee opposition, which suggests that even in the absence of a direct veto, JCAR had the authority to "force modification" of a substantial number of rules (1982, 116). A subsequent comparative study of Michigan, Wisconsin, and Tennessee examining rule review actions over a four-year span found that 107 rules (29.3 percent) failed to pass committee review in Michigan, while Wisconsin's Joint Committee for Review of Administrative Regulations vetoed 82 rules (32.8 percent) (Ethridge 1984a). Least active was the Tennessee legislature where standing committees from both chambers had to concur in order to block a rule. The 34 rules vetoed by the committees constituted a rule failure rate of 14.7 percent. This variation speaks to the obvious importance of the institutional design of veto procedures in shaping how they are used.

A more contemporary analysis comes from a 2012 article on Iowa's Administrative Rules Review Committee (ARRC). Anderson and Poynor (2012) provide detailed data on the committee's activities from annual reports spanning 1996 to 2010. Under state law, all rule proposals made by Iowa agencies must be submitted to the committee for review. Upon receipt of a rule proposal engendering opposition among its members, the committee can elect to take five different actions: impose a 70-day suspension period, impose a suspension period lasting a full session, object to the rule, request a regulatory analysis, or refer the proposal to the full assembly for further consideration. Over a 15-year period, the review committee evaluated a total of 6,485 rulemaking actions from 116 different state agencies (Anderson and Poynor 2012). Ranging from a high of 26 in 1996 to a low of 9 in 2005, the committee took action on 233 proposals, which corresponds to an average of about 3.5 percent of the proposals it received annually.

According to their data, proposal suspensions and general referrals combine to constitute a large majority of actions taken by the committee. On 98 occasions the committee referred rules to the full legislature. Ninety-one proposals received temporary suspensions, while the committee requested additional regulatory analysis on only 25 proposals. The committee made a formal objection, which is its most powerful resource, to just 19 rules. In most years, the committee dispensed only one rule objection. This veto infrequency corresponds to just 0.3 percent of the thousands of proposals reviewed by the committee over this span.

In Iowa's experience, the ARRC exercises its veto power sparingly. This should not, however, be interpreted as an indictment of its effectiveness. Anderson and Poynor claim, "Many rules that saw no formal action were significantly affected by the AARC's attention. To avoid delay, objection, or possible legislative action, agencies often withdrew or agreed to modify the rule" (2012, 46). Thus, the frequent execution of the veto is clearly not a necessary condition for legislators to influence the rulemaking process. In an interview with the author, the current executive director of Ohio's Joint Committee on Agency Rule Review, agreed with this assessment. He stated that the committee has held veto authority over agency rulemaking for approximately 35 years and had nullified a total of only 14 rules over that period. In his experience, agencies most always worked with committee members to revise rules identified as potentially problematic. Often veto threats will compel an agency to consider revising the rule to somehow address the concerns of the legislature.

Summary

When considered as laboratories for democracy, the tremendous amount of variation in the application of the legislative veto across the states is not unexpected. As of 2014, 25 states permit some type of legislative veto oversight, while it has never existed in 20 others. In some states, legislatures have acted on their own impetus to revise APA procedures and repeal existing legislative rule review powers. The Vermont legislature did precisely this in 1981 when it abolished the veto power it held for six years (1975, No. 211, § 4; 1981, No. 82, § 7). North Carolina did the same thing in 1983 (Laws 1983, c. 927, § 2). Although this has occurred in a few instances, most cases of legislative veto curtailment have come through judicial fiat.

Courts in Alaska, Kansas, Kentucky, Michigan, Missouri, Montana, New Hampshire, New Jersey, and West Virginia have each struck down rulemaking systems permitting legislative vetoes. The general refrain from judges is simply that legislatures may not attach unconstitutional conditions to any delegated powers (Levinson 1987). Given that a majority of states have permitted some variant of legislative veto oversight, and considering the constitutional separation of powers controversy that often surrounds the practice, it is surprising that courts have not been more active in this realm of state politics. Though there are likely many explanations for this, some of which may be state-specific, the primary reasons for judicial nonintervention at the state level mirror those nationally. Individuals must demonstrate standing in order to file a legal challenge. Depending on the circumstances, it might be difficult for a potential litigant to make a convincing standing argument, especially for proposed rules that have not gone into effect. The second factor concerns the political question doctrine, which holds that courts should refrain from intervening in political disputes between the elected branches of government. For this reason, some courts may have an inclination to let these types of interbranch disputes resolve themselves on their own volition.

Among the principal findings from the analysis presented in this chapter is that legislative veto systems of all types are more likely to be adopted when a Republican governor is in office and a single party controls both chambers of the legislature. Conversely, the analysis found no evidence that the presence of divided government contributes to the adoption of legislative veto oversight. In fact, legislative veto adoption more commonly occurs under unified government. Similar to the dynamic that tends to exist at the federal level, controversies surrounding state use of the legislative veto appear to be more about protecting institutional prerogatives rather than furthering a predominantly partisan agenda. Indeed, there are several instances when governors vetoed bills seeking to provide greater veto powers for the legislature when his or her party had majority party status in both legislative chambers.

The frequency in which legislators exercise their veto power varies across state and time. In many cases it is used sparingly. One explanation for this is that credible veto threats are often sufficient to compel an agency to address the legislature's concerns. Rulemaking systems that permit the exercise of a legislative veto, therefore, provide both formal and informal channels for legislators to shape rules. The 25 states that permit legislative vetoes provide legislators with unique means to scrutinize rules and help counterbalance the increased rulemaking powers held by state agencies.

Conclusion

A Tenuous Equilibrium? The Current Landscape and Future Prospects

The 1979 Iranian Revolution prompted the decade's second energy crisis, creating substantial disruptions in the global oil supply. In March 1979, President Carter submitted to Congress a Standby Gasoline Rationing Plan that sought to ration both statewide and individual gas consumption. By virtue of the Energy Policy and Conservation Act (89 Stat. 871, Public Law 94–163) gasoline rationing plans of this type were subject to a dual-House affirmative veto. As mandated by law, President Carter submitted the Standby Gasoline Rationing Plan to Congress. The policy change could go into effect only with Congress's consent.

In a message accompanying its submission, President Carter implored Congress to take positive action on the proposal. The president continued by challenging the constitutionality of the veto provisions contained in the Energy Policy and Conservation Act. Making this objection known once again, the message "strongly recommended" that Congress approve the rationing plan by joint resolution instead of a concurrent resolution in order for it to have "binding legal effect" (1979, 814). Despite being controlled by Democrats, Congress did neither. On May 10, 1979, the House voted against the Standby Gasoline Rationing Plan by a vote of 159 in favor to 246 opposed (96th Congress, House Roll Call No. 128). Republican support for the plan was scant and more than 100 Democrats broke party ranks and opposed the president's proposal. Later that year, Congress vetoed another Carter initiative to modify the strategic petroleum reserve.

Making matters worse for the administration was the fact that these major defeats were caused by legislative vetoes that White House officials considered blatantly unconstitutional.

Following the legislative veto of the Standby Gasoline Rationing Plan and the strategic petroleum reserve proposal, Congress continued to employ its veto power to affect national energy policies. This chain of events is illustrative of Congress's greater use of the veto during the 1970s and exemplifies the considerable degree of power sharing that often exists across the branches of the federal government. Such an institutional design presents a multitude of challenges for both lawmakers in Congress and executive officials, including the president, as they seek to shape policy.

Macropolitical Conflict over the Legislative Veto

The compound republic established by the Constitution separates the functions of government such that those responsible for making laws are institutionally distinct from those responsible for their execution. At the turn of the twentieth century, the federal bureaucracy consisted of just seven cabinet-level departments and comparatively few executive agencies. As the bureaucracy expanded, the magnitude of delegation to the executive increased, albeit with some controversy. Like slow-moving tectonic plates, the executive branch has supplanted in many ways the legislative functions previously held by Congress. The practical consequence of this phenomenon is a greater ability for unelected bureaucrats to determine policy outcomes. Against this backdrop, Congress has created numerous statutory and nonstatutory oversight resources to remain vigilant over the law's execution.

Created during a period of bureaucratic expansion, the legislative veto provides an innovative way for members of Congress to direct executive action. The main appeals of this type of oversight are the veto's malleability and the scope of its applicability. Congress can design veto statutes to provide committees or chambers with affirmative, negative, or deliberative veto authority. These statutes also allow legislators to directly affect an incredibly broad range of actions made by career bureaucrats and presidents alike.

From its modest beginnings in 1932 as a seemingly innocuous restriction on presidential reorganization power, the legislative veto has been transformed into a mainstay of modern statutory oversight. Every decade subsequent to its inception has witnessed an increase in the number of veto enactments. Figure 7.1 illustrates this growth over time.

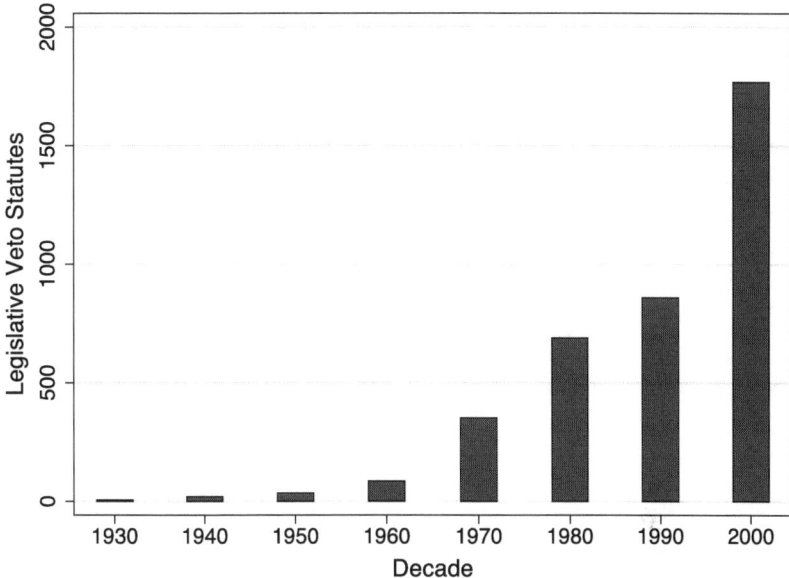

Fig. 7.1. Legislative veto statutes enacted by decade: 1930–2010. (Data compiled by author.)

The 1960s witnessed the imposition of 85 veto statutes. This skyrocketed to a total of 352 over the next decade—the first in which the number of enacted vetoes climbed into the hundreds. The lack of the generic veto movement's success during this period did not deter legislators from continuing to insert veto provisions into individual bills. In fact, the lack of a generic veto compelled legislators to employ the veto in piecemeal fashion, which partially explains its continued increase during this era. The quantity of veto enactments in the 1980s nearly doubled the prior decade's total and climbed even further to 860 during the 1990s. Ten years later, the number of adopted veto statutes more than doubled again. At present, contemporary Congresses enact hundreds of veto statutes every term that are often highly contested by presidents. The dramatic expansion of legislative veto oversight created many opportunities for confrontation between legislative and executive officials.

Much of the legislative veto controversy stems from its use to constrain presidential action. Modern presidents have expressed their steadfast belief that the veto unconstitutionally encroaches on executive power. Congress has passed nearly 500 vetoes that impose different types of oversight restrictions on the president. Among the most notable was the Congressional

Budget and Impoundment Control Act of 1974 (88 Stat. 297, Public Law 93–344), which effectively used the veto to constrain presidential spending authority. More controversially, Congress has also used the veto as a means to restrict presidential actions as commander in chief. The most famous of these types of vetoes was included in the War Powers Resolution.

Upon vetoing the War Powers Resolution, President Nixon argued that presidential decisions made with respect to military strategy and deployments were not susceptible to congressional override. In other settings, presidents have asserted that the exercise of a veto allows members of Congress to extend their reach beyond what the Framers intended by assuming a role as a de facto executive actor. Defense and foreign policy veto statutes in the modern era commonly require notification or consultation with Congress in advance of some action. Legislation passed in January 2014 prohibited the president from making certain arms transactions without providing Congress with 15 days advance notice (128 Stat. 116, Public Law 113–76). Even though such report and wait requirements are not as directly invasive as affirmative or negative vetoes can be, presidents continue to resist this sort of encroachment on executive policymaking. This understanding calls for an extremely limited role for legislators to direct executive action after a law's passage. Because Congress continues to assert its right to do precisely this, there do not appear to be any signs of reconciliation.

Scholarly Contributions

This study follows in a long tradition of research examining congressional oversight and legislative-executive relations. Among the primary scholarly contributions of this research is the compilation of a nearly exhaustive data set of legislative veto statutes in U.S. history. Through these data, it is overwhelmingly evident that the use of the legislative veto has continued in spite of the majority ruling in *INS v. Chadha*. It is therefore inaccurate to assert that this ruling ended the legislative veto or even served to curtail its use. One scholar, writing six years after the ruling, presciently claimed, "*Chadha* may prove to be as effective in limiting vetoes as the Eighteenth Amendment was in limiting the consumption of alcohol" (Mezey 1989, 170). The Supreme Court's bold intervention did, however, serve as the catalyst that shifted the types of vetoes Congress tends to enact. Accordingly, the legislative veto lives on.

Applying a transaction cost theoretical framework used by other scholars of congressional and bureaucratic politics, chapter 3 outlined hypotheses concerning political conflict, issue salience, and policy complexity. Model results including all legislative veto types showed that several bill-specific factors influenced the use of this oversight device, while divided government and ideological polarization did not. Given the nontrivial amount of transaction costs legislators incur by monitoring and enforcing legislative veto requirements, they appear more willing to bear these costs when bills concern spending, propose major policy changes, or address a more complex topic. In sum, the analysis found support for the notion that the transaction costs concerning complexity and issue salience positively affected legislative veto incidence.

When considering factors expected to affect whether bills contain legislative veto provisions, divided government and polarization exhibited little influence. The exception to this was the analysis focusing on Appropriations Committee vetoes, which are the most common type. An examination of these kinds of committee vetoes showed that they are more likely when there is greater ideological polarization between the president and each spending committee. Paradoxically, divided government was found to actually lessen the probability of a bill that could include spending committee veto provisions. It was argued that this might be attributable to a strategic calculation by legislators serving on these committees.

The examination of aggregate veto totals presented in chapter 5 showed that there are generally no substantial differences in how Republican and Democratic congressional majorities exercise this type of oversight. However, when controlling for other factors, we do observe increased veto use during periods of divided government. This apparent disconnect between the effect of divided government at the micro-level (bill) and the macro-level (Congress) certainly merits further investigation. Given the increasing divide between the parties in Congress, the inconsistent effects of divided government and polarization remain notable. They suggest that while many congressional functions are strongly influenced by these factors, the use of legislative veto oversight does not widely fluctuate according to partisan or ideological shifts. Conflicts over the use of the veto, therefore, are driven primarily by separation of powers concerns rather than partisan ones. This is evident at the state level as well. Actors generally appear most interested in protecting the institutional prerogatives of their respective branch of government. This finding corroborates those from earlier studies on legislative veto oversight that claim that "the tug of war between the legislative and executive branches may be a more powerful driver than the partisan political differences" (Anderson and Poynor 2012,

48). Given these battle lines, the veto remains a substantial source of interbranch controversy between the White House and Congress, even when the same party controls both.

In addition to the examination of the legislative veto from Capitol Hill, chapter 4 surveyed the conflict from the president's perspective. Approaching the controversy from alternative viewpoints allows for a more comprehensive assessment of this ongoing macropolitical conflict. In response to the continued imposition of legislative vetoes, presidents have maintained their steadfast opposition to the oversight device that began long in advance of the Supreme Court's intervention. Of particular focus were presidential actions in the form of presidential vetoes and signing statements.

An analysis spanning the past four presidential administrations found that increases in the number of veto provisions included in legislation elicited a greater likelihood of a presidential veto. Cognizant of the president's consistent opposition to this type of oversight, Congress has strategically elected to include the vast majority of veto provisions in legislation considered compulsory in nature. Most commonly, veto provisions are bundled into major appropriations or omnibus spending bills. By including them in compulsory legislation, Congress can often force the president's hand to sign bills containing numerous legislative vetoes. Although the repeated use of the presidential veto remains an option available to the chief executive, it would be difficult for any president to pursue an extended game of brinksmanship on this issue. Because this course of action is one that presidents have chosen not to pursue, they have more frequently resorted to using the signing statement as an alternative counteractive strategy. When used in this capacity, the signing statement aspires to function as a separation of powers defense.

Though the presidential signing statement is not a modern creation, the past several decades have witnessed a dramatic shift in its use. Categorizing signing statements into constitutional and nonconstitutional groupings according to their content illustrates the significant changes that have occurred. An examination of the factors contributing to the likelihood of signing statement issuance demonstrates that there is a greater likelihood of the president issuing a signing statement when bills contain greater numbers of veto provisions. According to one model specification, a bill presented to the president containing at least one legislative veto increases the likelihood of signing statement issuance by nearly 10 percent relative to a "clean" bill. Modern presidents of both parties have frequently used the signing statement as a way to sign legislation while singling out legislative veto provisions as constitutionally suspect. This represents a fundamental change in the use of the signing statement as the functional equivalent of a line-item veto (P. Cooper 2002). Preliminary analysis of the effects of such signing statements indicates that agencies typically, but not always, follow the wishes of Congress. A more focused examination of the consequences stemming from different sets of instructions coming from the president and Congress is a logical next step with respect to research in this area (see Ainsworth et al. 2014; Ostrander and Sievert 2014).

Though their effects may vary, presidents have issued hundreds of signing statements indicating that scores of statutes containing vetoes may not be executed as written. Depending on one's perspective, this can be interpreted as a nefarious erosion of the rule of law whereby presidents unilaterally select which statutes the administration will comply with, or as a noble effort on behalf of the president to preserve constitutionally protected executive powers believed to be under siege from Congress. In either case, the two branches remain at odds.

Judicial Intervention and the Veto's Adaptation

The federal courts have played a punctuated, yet influential, role in the controversy surrounding the legislative veto. Although its constitutionality was, at times, hotly debated in the halls of Congress and the Justice Department, decades elapsed before the oversight device would come before a judicial body. The long stretch of judicial inactivity ended in 1976. During the ensuing 10-year span, most rulings sided with the executive. As interpreted by presidents, these legal precedents provide sufficient justification to ignore statutes containing legislative vetoes or to treat their requirements as advisory rather than compulsory. The Supreme Court's ruling in *Chadha* may not be the final word on the veto's status, but it has been the loudest declaration from the Court to date. Since then the courts have again receded from prominence.

In some sense it is odd that over 80 percent of all veto statutes enacted in U.S. history were passed after the Supreme Court's landmark ruling against it. Applying the seven-category typology as a way to better understand trends in veto use helps clarify exactly how this came to be. In sheer numbers, it is clear that the veto has survived, even flourished, after what some thought to be a fatal blow from the Court. The continued use of this brand of statutory oversight "demonstrates the distance between the court's decision and the operational realities of government" (Fisher 1985, 707). Though *Chadha* failed to eliminate the legislative veto, it did engender several important effects. The first major change involves the type of vetoes Congress prefers to enact. Prior to the 1983 ruling, one- and dual-House vetoes were quite common. Since the statute challenged by *Chadha* contained a one-House negative veto, justices closely scrutinized this particular veto design. Their collective conclusion was far from favorable, primarily on the basis that the veto mechanism was neither bicameral nor presented to the president. In the post-*Chadha* period, the one-House veto is on the brink of extinction.

A corollary to the decline in single- and dual-House vetoes is the rise of committee veto statutes. Modern vetoes disproportionately allocate veto authority to individual committees; namely, Appropriations, Armed Services, International Relations (House), and Foreign Relations (Senate). Over the past decade, 95 percent of all committee veto statutes have been tied to these six committees. While committee vetoes could be tailored to provide veto authority for any of Congress's many committees, there is a substantial skew in those authorized to exercise this type of oversight. Most consequential are the Appropriations Committees, which constitute the vast majority of the committee veto total. When considering all veto types, three out of every four veto statutes in the post-*Chadha* era are connected to the two spending committees. Thus, another consequence of the landmark ruling is the elevated oversight importance of the Appropriations Committees. These committees can obviously shape spending priorities through the annual appropriations process, but can further direct individual expenditures throughout the fiscal year by virtue of the large number of vetoes they possess. The 111th Congress alone passed more than 350 of the statutes affording some type of veto power to the Appropriations Committees.

In addition to the shift away from one- and dual-House vetoes in favor of a greater reliance on committee vetoes, the number of deliberative veto enactments has also increased since *Chadha*. Comparing affirmative, negative, and deliberative legislative veto types, deliberative vetoes have always been most common. Over the past 30 years, deliberative vetoes have increased to such a level that they now represent a large majority—approximately 70 percent—of all enacted vetoes. These advance reporting requirements provide Congress or its committees with a window of opportunity to take proactive steps to affect a pending action. While not explicitly stated, report and wait provisions may implicitly require legislative approval (Fisher 1985). At the very least, legislators are afforded with advance notice that allows for further scrutiny of executive action.

Conclusion 277

Current and Future Prospects

The gulf between the branches remains wide, but we may have reached a tenuous equilibrium on this controversial type of oversight. In recent decades, one-House vetoes are essentially nonexistent and dual-House vetoes are most often tied to joint, instead of concurrent, resolutions. These changes bring veto oversight into compliance with the *Chadha* holding that the one-House veto lacked bicameralism and presidential presentment. Dual-House deliberative vetoes remain, as do committee deliberative vetoes, which are the most common variety. In some cases, presidents and cabinet secretaries have expressed resistance to providing Congress with information in advance of certain actions, but, more often than not, legislators receive the information they request. As presidents have expressed in signing statements, some veto requirements governing actions of the president and high-ranking cabinet-level officials are especially troubling. Though it is altogether possible that high-profile conflict over a particular veto statute emerges at some point in the future, a continuation of the status quo where we observe a balance between rhetoric and compliance from the executive branch seems more likely.

The policy applications of legislative veto oversight remain broad with a disproportionate skew toward defense and foreign policy matters. This study demonstrated consistent patterns in terms of how the veto is used to oversee different issue areas. Regardless of the partisanship of the president or the majority party in Congress, vetoes are most frequently applied to the Department of Defense and the State Department. If a noticeable interbranch standoff over the veto emerges in the future it will almost certainly involve one of these two issue areas. From a congressional perspective, Republican and Democratic majorities use the oversight device in a similar fashion. Because the veto's implementation does not appear sensitive to changing partisan majorities it is likely to persist. Other reasons for its expected continuation are many.

Absent an external shock, such as another Supreme Court ruling, the legislative veto will almost certainly remain one of Congress's most important oversight resources. The committee veto in particular has become a popular way to qualify grants of power to the executive by reserving some type of postpassage influence on a law's execution. It is difficult to quantify just how often committees actually direct executive action through these procedures, but the sheer number of committee vetoes passed by recent Congresses provides a strong indicator of the importance legislators place on this type of oversight. Extrapolating into the future based on existing trends suggests that these types of statutes will become more frequent. In the post-*Chadha* period, the number of committee vetoes has increased by an average of 24 percent each term. Though this term-by-term increase has not been linear, it is possible to envision Congresses beyond 2020 enacting in excess of 1,000 committee veto statutes.

As the policy-making power of the bureaucracy continues to grow, the president and lawmakers in Congress employ a variety of institutional resources seeking to influence policy outcomes. Despite the constitutional questions raised by each, the legislative veto and the presidential signing statement will likely continue to exist as major weapons in the respective arsenals of the legislative and executive branches. In *Federalist No. 47*, Madison wrote, "The several departments of power are distributed and blended in such a manner, as at once to destroy all symmetry and beauty of form: and to expose some of the essential parts of the edifice to the danger of being crushed by the disproportionate weight of the other parts" (1788). So while the entrenched controversy surrounding the legislative veto will almost certainly persist, we can view the heightened macropolitical conflict of the twenty-first century as evidence that in many ways the U.S. government still operates as the Framers of the eighteenth century intended.

Appendix I

Laws Containing Legislative Vetoes: 1931–2010

Legislative Appropriations for Fiscal Year 1933—Public Law 72-212
Appropriations for Treasury and Post Office for Fiscal Year 1934—Public Law 72-428
Charges for Irrigation on Indian Reservation Projects, 1936—Public Law 74-742
Reorganization Act of 1939—Public Law 76-19
Neutrality Act of 1939—Public Law 76-54
Alien Registration Act of 1940—Public Law 76-670
Act to Promote Defense of the United States—Public Law 77-11
Emergency Price Control Act—Public Law 77-421
Emergency Price Control Act Amendment—Public Law 77-729
War Labor Disputes Act—Public Law 78-89
Navy Public Works Construction Authorization, 1944—Public Law 78-289
Naval Petroleum Reserve Amendment—Public Law 78-343
Federal-Aid Highway Act of 1944—Public Law 78-521
Reorganization Act of 1945—Public Law 79-263
Federal Airport Act of 1946—Public Law 79-377
Strategic Materials Stockpiling Act Amendments, 1946—Public Law 79-520
Disposal of Surplus Vessels and Other Navy Property, 1946—Public Law 79-649
Assistance to Greece and Turkey, 1947—Public Law 80-75
Displaced Persons Act of 1948—Public Law 80-774

Immigration Act Amendment of 1948—Public Law 80–863
Long-Range Proving Ground for Guided Missiles, 1949—Public Law 81–60
Reorganization Act of 1949—Public Law 81–109
Government Printing and Binding Amendment—Public Law 81–156
Return of Rehabilitation Costs of Reclamation Projects, 1949—Public Law 81–335
Federal Civil Defense Act of 1950—Public Law 81–920
Universal Military Training and Service Act—Public Law 82–51
Military and Naval Construction Authorization, 1951—Public Law 82–155
Immigration and Nationality Act of 1952—Public Law 82–414
Military and Naval Construction Authorization Act, 1952—Public Law 82–534
Supplementary Appropriations Act for Fiscal Year 1953—Public Law 82–547
Reorganization Act Amendment, 1953—Public Law 83–3
Interior Department Appropriations for Fiscal Year 1954—Public Law 83–172
Disposal of Government-Owned Rubber-Producing Facilities, 1953—Public Law 83–205
Public Building Purchase Contract Act of 1954—Public Law 83–519
Watershed Protection and Flood Prevention Act, 1954—Public Law 83–566
Internal Revenue Code of 1954—Public Law 83–591
Atomic Energy Act of 1954—Public Law 83–703
Reorganization Act Amendment, 1955—Public Law 84–16
Department of Defense Appropriation for Fiscal Year 1956—Public Law 84–157
Federal-Aid Highway Act of 1956—Public Law 84–627
Authorization Interchange of Agriculture and Defense Lands, 1956—Public Law 84–804
Small Reclamation Projects Act, 1956—Public Law 84–984
Watershed Protection and Flood Prevention Act Amendment, 1956—Public Law 84–1018
Contracts for Plans Affect Exploration, Development and Use of Naval Petroleum Reserves—Public Law 84–1028
Small Reclamation Projects Act Amendment, 1957—Public Law 85–47
Atomic Energy Act Amendment, 1957—Public Law 85–79
Reorganization Act Amendment, 1957—Public Law 85–286

Immigration and Nationality Act Amendments—Public Law 85-316
Atomic Energy Act Amendment, 1958—Public Law 85-479
National Aeronautics and Space Act of 1958—Public Law 85-568
Defense Reorganization Act of 1958—Public Law 85-599
Atomic Energy Act Amendment, 1958—Public Law 85-681
Trade Agreements Extension Act of 1958—Public Law 85-686
Military Code Amendments, 1958—Public Law 85-861
Public Buildings Act of 1959—Public Law 86-249
Military Construction Authorization Act, 1960—Public Law 86-500
Reorganization Act Amendment, 1961—Public Law 87-18
National Aeronautics and Space Administration Authorization for Fiscal Year 1962—Public Law 87-98
Foreign Assistance Act of 1961—Public Law 87-195
Mutual Education and Cultural Exchange Act of 1961—Public Law 87-256
Government-Owned Utilities Used for Bureau of Indian Affairs, 1961—Public Law 87-279
Restoration to Indian Tribes of Unclaimed Payments, 1961—Public Law 87-283
Arms Control and Disarmament Act, 1961—Public Law 87-297
Department of Interior Appropriations for Fiscal Year 1963—Public Law 87-578
National Aeronautics and Space Administration Authorization for Fiscal Year 1963—Public Law 87-584
Surveys of Watershed Areas for Flood Prevention, 1962—Public Law 87-639
Independent Agencies Appropriations for Fiscal Year 1963—Public Law 87-741
Trade Expansion Act of 1962—Public Law 87-794
Naval Petroleum and Oil Shale Reserves, 1962—Public Law 87-796
Foreign Aid Appropriations for Fiscal Year 1963—Public Law 87-872
National Aeronautics and Space Administration Authorization for Fiscal Year 1964—Public Law 88-113
Independent Agencies Appropriations for Fiscal Year 1964—Public Law 88-215
Reorganization Act Amendment, 1964—Public Law 88-351
Civil Rights Act of 1964—Public Law 88-352
National Aeronautics and Space Administration Authorization for Fiscal Year 1965—Public Law 88-369
Water Resources Research Act of 1964—Public Law 88-379

Atomic Energy Act Amendments, 1964—Public Law 88–489
Independent Agencies Appropriations for Fiscal Year 1965—Public Law 88–507
Agricultural Trade Development and Assistance Act Amendments, 1964—Public Law 88–638
Reorganization Act Amendment, 1965—Public Law 89–43
National Aeronautics and Space Administration Authorization for Fiscal Year 1966—Public Law 89–53
Independent Agencies Appropriations for Fiscal Year 1966—Public Law 89–128
Authorizing Construction, Repair and Preservation of Certain Public Works, 1965—Public Law 89–298
Water Resources Research Act Amendments, 1966—Public Law 89–404
National Aeronautics and Space Administration Authorization for Fiscal Year 1967—Public Law 89–528
Title 5, United States Code, "Government Organization and Employees"—Public Law 89–554
Independent Agencies Appropriations for Fiscal Year 1967—Public Law 89–555
Interior Department Research Contracts, 1966—Public Law 89–672
Postmaster General Extension of Leasing Authority, 1967—Public Law 90–15
National Aeronautics and Space Administration Authorization for Fiscal Year 1968—Public Law 90–67
Independent Agencies Appropriations for Fiscal Year 1968—Public Law 90–121
Postal Revenue and Federal Salary Act of 1967—Public Law 90–206
Treasury and Post Office Appropriations for Fiscal Year 1969—Public Law 90–350
National Aeronautics and Space Administration Authorization for Fiscal Year 1969—Public Law 90–373
The Wild and Scenic Rivers Act, 1968—Public Law 90–542
Independent Agencies Appropriations for Fiscal Year 1968—Public Law 90–550
Reorganization Act Extension Amendment—Public Law 91–5
Treasury and Post Office Appropriations for Fiscal Year 1970—Public Law 91–74
National Aeronautics and Space Administration Authorization for Fiscal Year 1970—Public Law 91–119
Authorization of Appropriations for Armed Forces, 1970—Public Law 91–121

Independent Agencies Appropriations for Fiscal Year 1970—Public Law 91–126
Military Construction Authorization, 1970—Public Law 91–142
Public Health Cigarette Smoking Act, 1970—Public Law 91–222
Elementary and Secondary Education Assistance Program Extension—Public Law 91–230
National Traffic and Motor Vehicle Safety Act Amendments—Public Law 91–265
National Aeronautics and Space Administration Authorization for Fiscal Year 1971—Public Law 91–303
Defense Production Act of 1950 Amendment—Public Law 91–379
Treasury and Post Office Appropriations for Fiscal Year 1971—Public Law 91–422
Armed Forces Authorization, 1971—Public Law 91–441
Military Construction Authorization, 1971—Public Law 91–511
Independent Offices and Department of Housing and Urban Development Appropriations for Fiscal Year 1971—Public Law 91–556
River and Harbor and Flood Control Acts, 1970—Public Law 91–611
Federal Pay Comparability Act of 1970—Public Law 91–656
Treasury, Postal Service, Executive and Independent Office Appropriations for Fiscal Year 1972—Public Law 92–49
National Aeronautics and Space Administration Authorization for Fiscal Year 1972—Public Law 92–68
National Science Foundation Authorization, 1972—Public Law 92–86
Military Construction Authorization, 1972—Public Law 92–145
Armed Forces Authorization, 1972—Public Law 92–156
Executive Reorganization Plans Extension, 1971—Public Law 92–179
Foreign Assistance Act of 1972—Public Law 92–226
National Aeronautics and Space Administration Authorization for Fiscal Year 1973—Public Law 92–304
Second Supplemental Appropriations Act for Fiscal Year 1972—Public Law 92–306
Public Buildings Amendments of 1972—Public Law 92–313
Education Amendments of 1972—Public Law 92–318
Treasury, Postal Service, Executive, and Independent Offices Appropriations for Fiscal Year 1973—Public Law 92–351
National Science Foundation Authorization, 1973—Public Law 92–372
Military Construction Authorization, 1973—Public Law 92–545
Pennsylvania Avenue Development Corporation Act of 1972—Public Law 92–578
Renegotiation Amendments of 1973—Public Law 93–66

National Aeronautics and Space Administration Authorization for Fiscal Year 1974—Public Law 93-74
National Science Foundation Authorization for Fiscal Year 1974—Public Law 93-96
Department of Interior Appropriations for Fiscal Year 1974—Public Law 93-120
Indian Claims Judgments Funds, 1973—Public Law 93-134
Treasury, Postal Service and General Government Appropriations for Fiscal Year 1974—Public Law 93-143
War Powers Resolution—Public Law 93-148
Amendments to the Mineral Leasing Act of 1920—Public Law 93-153
Department of Defense Authorizations, 1974—Public Law 93-155
Emergency Petroleum Allocation Act of 1973—Public Law 93-159
Military Construction Authorization, 1974—Public Law 93-16
Menominee Restoration Act—Public Law 93-197
Regional Rail Reorganization Act of 1973—Public Law 93-236
Foreign Assistance Appropriations for Fiscal Year 1974—Public Law 93-240
Supplemental Appropriations Act, 1974—Public Law 93-245
Public Works, Rivers and Harbors and Flood Control Authorization, 1974—Public Law 93-251
Wild and Scenic Rivers Act Amendments, 1974—Public Law 933-279
National Aeronautics and Space Administration Authorization for Fiscal Year 1975—Public Law 933-316
Congressional Budget and Impoundment Control Act of 1974—Public Law 933-344
Department of Defense Authorizations for 1975—Public Law 933-365
Air Transportation Security Act of 1974—Public Law 933-366
Atomic Energy Act Amendments, 1974—Public Law 933-377
Forest and Rangeland Renewable Resources Planning Act of 1974—Public Law 933-378
Education Amendments of 1974—Public Law 933-380
Department of Interior and Related Agencies Appropriations for Fiscal Year 1975—Public Law 933-404
Employees Retirement Income Security Act of 1974—Public Law 933-406
National Science Foundation Authorization for Fiscal Year 1975—Public Law 933-413
Conveyance of Submerged Lands to Guam, Virgin Islands and American Samoa—Public Law 933-435

Federal Election Campaign Act Amendments of 1974—Public Law 933–443
Atomic Energy Act Amendments, 1974—Public Law 933–485
Motor Vehicle and School Bus Safety Amendments of 1974—Public Law 933–492
Presidential Recordings and Materials Preservation Act, 1974—Public Law 933–526
Hopi and Navajo Tribe Act—Public Law 933–531
Military Construction Authorization, 1975—Public Law 933–552
Foreign Assistance Act of 1974—Public Law 933–559
Federal Nonnuclear Research and Development Act of 1974—Public Law 933–577
Trade Act of 1974—Public Law 933–618
Grand Canyon National Park Enlargement Act—Public Law 933–620
Headstart, Economic Opportunity and Community Partnership Act of 1974—Public Law 933–644
Export-Import Bank Amendments of 1974—Public Law 93–646
Foreign Assistance Appropriations for Fiscal Year 1975—Public Law 94–11
Amtrak Improvement Act of 1975—Public Law 94–25
Trust Territory of the Pacific Islands Amendment Act—Public Law 94–27
National Aeronautics and Space Administration Authorization for Fiscal Year 1976—Public Law 94–39
National Science Foundation Authorization for Fiscal Year 1976—Public Law 94–86
Amendment to Social Security Act Child Support Provisions—Public Law 94–88
Board for International Broadcasting Authorization for Fiscal Year 1976—Public Law 94–104
Department of Defense Authorization for Fiscal Year 1976—Public Law 94–106
Military Construction Authorization for Fiscal Year 1976—Public Law 94–107
Sinai Early Warning System Agreement—Public Law 94–110
Department of Transportation and Related Agencies Appropriation Act, 1976, and the Period Ending September 30, 1976—Public Law 94–134
Older Americans Amendments of 1975—Public Law 94–135
Foreign Relations Authorization for Fiscal Year 1976—Public Law 94–141
Education for All Handicapped Children Act of 1975—Public Law 94–142
International Development and Food Assistance Act of 1975—Public Law 94–161

Energy Policy and Conservation Act—Public Law 94–163
Department of Interior and Related Agencies Appropriations for Fiscal Year 1976—Public Law 94–165
Energy Research and Development Administration Authorization Act—Public Law 94–187
Home Mortgage Disclosure Act of 1975—Public Law 94–200
Department of Defense Appropriation Act, 1976—Public Law 94–212
Amendments to the Civil Government of the Trust Territory of the Pacific Islands—Public Law 94–255
Naval Petroleum Reserves Production Act—Public Law 94–258
Fishery Conservation and Management Act of 1976—Public Law 94–265
Federal Election Campaign Act Amendments of 1976—Public Law 94–283
Consumer Product Safety Commission Improvements Act of 1976—Public Law 94–284
National Aeronautics and Space Administration Authorization Act, 1977—Public Law 94–307
International Security Assistance and Arms Export Control Act of 1976—Public Law 94–329
Foreign Assistance and Related Programs Appropriations for 1976—Public Law 94–330
Department of Defense Appropriation Authorization Act, 1977—Public Law 94–361
Department of the Interior and Related Agencies Appropriations Act, 1977—Public Law 94–373
Energy Conservation and Production Act—Public Law 94–385
National Emergencies Act—Public Law 94–412
Electric and Hybrid Vehicle Research, Development, and Demonstration Act of 1976—Public Law 94–413
Military Construction Authorization Act, 1977—Public Law 94–431
Foreign Assistance and Related Programs Appropriations Act, 1977—Public Law 94–441
National Science Foundation Authorization Act, 1977—Public Law 94–471
Environmental Research, Development, and Demonstration Authorization Act of 1976—Public Law 94–475
Veterans' Education and Employment Assistance Act of 1976—Public Law 94–502
National Park System Authorization Act—Public Law 94–578
Federal Land Policy and Management Act of 1976—Public Law 94–579

Alaska Natural Gas Transportation Act of 1976—Public Law 94–586
Fishery Conservation Zone Transition Act—Public Law 95–6
Reorganization Act of 1977—Public Law 95–17
Emergency Unemployment Compensation Extension Act of 1977—Public Law 95–19
Authorizations, Appropriations–Energy Research and Development Administration—Public Law 95–39
Land and Water Conservation Fund Act of 1965 Amendments—Public Law 95–42
Authorizations, Appropriations–San Luis Unit, Central Valley Project—Public Law 95–46
Export Administration Amendments of 1977—Public Law 95–52
Appropriations–Agriculture and Interior Departments—Public Law 95–74
International Navigational Rules Act of 1977—Public Law 95–75
National Aeronautics and Space Administration Authorization Act, 1978—Public Law 95–76
Department of Defense Appropriation Authorization Act, 1978—Public Law 95–79
Military Construction Authorization Act, 1978—Public Law 95–82
Water Resources Research and Saline Conversion Program—Public Law 95–84
Department of Transportation and Related Appropriations Act, 1978—Public Law 95–85
International Security Assistance Act of 1977—Public Law 95–92
Public Works and Energy Research Appropriation Act, 1978—Public Law 95–96
National Science Foundation Authorization Act, Fiscal Year 1978—Public Law 95–99
Department of Defense Appropriation Act, 1978—Public Law 95–111
Export-Import Bank Act of 1945 Amendments—Public Law 95–143
Foreign Assistance and Related Programs Appropriations Act, 1978 Foreign Assistance Act—Public Law 95–148
Environmental Research, Development, and Demonstration Authorization Act of 1978—Public Law 95–155
Energy Research and Development Administration Authorization Act of 1977 and 1978–Military Applications—Public Law 95–183
Social Security Amendments of 1977—Public Law 95–216
Wartime or National Emergency Presidential Powers—Public Law 95–223

Department of Energy Act of 1978—Public Law 95-238
Nuclear Non-Proliferation Act of 1978—Public Law 95-242
Petroleum Marketing Practices Act—Public Law 95-297
Emergency Interim Consumer Product Safety Standard Act of 1978—Public Law 95-319
Department of Transportation and Related Appropriations Act for 1979—Public Law 95-335
New York City Loan Guarantee Act of 1978—Public Law 95-339
Military Construction Authorization Act—Public Law 95-356
Outer Continental Shelf Lands Act Amendments of 1978—Public Law 95-372
International Security Assistance Act of 1978—Public Law 95-384
National Aeronautics and Space Administration Authorization Act—Public Law 95-401
Futures Trading Act of 1978—Public Law 95-405
Amtrak Improvement Act of 1978—Public Law 95-421
International Development and Food Assistance Act of 1978—Public Law 95-424
National Science Foundation Authorization Act—Public Law 95-434
Civil Service Reform Act of 1978—Public Law 95-454
A bill making appropriations for the Department of the Interior and related agencies for the fiscal ending September 30, 1979—Public Law 95-465
Water Research and Development Act—Public Law 95-467
Environmental Research, Development, and Demonstration Authorization Act—Public Law 95-477
Foreign Assistance and Related Programs Appropriations Act—Public Law 95-481
Department of Defense Appropriation Authorization Act—Public Law 95-485
Agricultural Trade Act—Public Law 95-501
Amendment to the Internal Revenue Code of 1954—Public Law 95-502
Airline Deregulation Act of 1978—Public Law 95-504
Department of Energy National Security and Military Applications of Nuclear Energy Authorization Act—Public Law 95-509
Foreign Intelligence Surveillance Act—Public Law 95-511
Housing and Community Development Amendments of 1978—Public Law 95-557
Education Amendments of 1978—Public Law 95-561
Public Utility Regulatory Policies Act of 1978—Public Law 95-617
Natural Gas Policy Act of 1978—Public Law 95-621

National Parks and Recreation Act of 1978—Public Law 95-625
Veterans' Health Care Amendments of 1979—Public Law 96-22
Supplemental Appropriations Act, 1979—Public Law 96-38
Trade Agreements Act of 1979—Public Law 96-39
National Science Foundation Authorization for Fiscal Year 1980—Public Law 96-44
Authorization, Appropriations–National Aeronautics and Space Administration Act, 1980—Public Law 96-48
Authorization, Appropriations–Food Stamp Act, 1977—Public Law 96-58
Department of State Authorizing Act, Fiscal Years 1980 and 1981—Public Law 96-60
Energy and Water Development Appropriations for Fiscal Year 1980—Public Law 96-69
Export Administration Act of 1979—Public Law 96-72
Treasury, Postal Service and General Government Appropriations Act, 1980—Public Law 96-74
Department of Education Organization Act—Public Law 96-88
Emergency Energy Conservation Act of 1979—Public Law 96-102
Department of Housing and Urban Development–Independent Agencies Appropriations Act, 1980—Public Law 96-103
Military Construction Authorization Act, 1980—Public Law 96-125
Department of Interior and Related Agencies Appropriations for Fiscal Year 1980—Public Law 96-126
Department of Justice Authorization Act, Fiscal Year 1980—Public Law 96-132
Department of Energy National Security and Military Applications of Nuclear Energy Authorization Act of 1980—Public Law 96-164
Federal Election Campaign Act Amendments of 1979—Public Law 96-187
United States Insular Areas Appropriation Authorization—Public Law 96-205
Crude Oil Windfall Profit Tax Act of 1980—Public Law 96-223
Environmental Research, Development, and Demonstration Authorization Act of 1980—Public Law 96-229
Extension of the Reorganization Authority of the President—Public Law 96-230
Civil Rights of Institutionalized Persons Act—Public Law 96-247
Federal Trade Commission Improvements Act of 1980—Public Law 96-252
Energy Security Act—Public Law 96-294

Authorization, Appropriations–Nuclear Regulatory Commission—Public Law 96–295
Supplemental Appropriations and Rescission Act of 1980—Public Law 96–304
National Aeronautics and Space Administration Authorization Act, 1981—Public Law 96–316
Marine Protection Research and Sanctuaries Authorization Act—Public Law 96–332
Department of Defense Authorization Act, 1981—Public Law 96–342
Multiemployer Pension Plan Amendments Act of 1980—Public Law 96–364
Energy and Water Development Appropriations Act, 1981—Public Law 96–367
Education Amendments of 1980—Public Law 96–374
Military Construction Authorization Act, 1981—Public Law 96–418
Intelligence Authorization Act for Fiscal Year 1981—Public Law 96–450
Coastal Zone Management Improvement Act of 1980—Public Law 96–464
Solid Waste Disposal Act Amendments of 1980—Public Law 96–482
Alaska National Interest Lands Conservation Act—Public Law 96–487
Comprehensive Environmental Response, Compensation, and Liability Act of 1980—Public Law 96–510
Department of Interior and Related Agencies Appropriations, 1981—Public Law 96–514
National Historic Preservation Act Amendments of 1980—Public Law 96–515
Housing and Urban Development Appropriations, 1981—Public Law 96–526
International Security and Development Cooperation Act—Public Law 96–533
Federal Insecticide, Fungicide and Rodenticide Act—Public Law 96–539
Department of Energy, National Security, and Military Applications Nuclear Energy Authorization Act of 1981—Public Law 96–540
Farm Credit Act Amendments of 1980—Public Law 96–592
Supplemental Appropriations and Recession Act, 1981—Public Law 97–12
Authorizations, Appropriations–Earthquake Hazards Reduction and Fire Prevention and Control Program—Public Law 97–80
Department of Defense Authorization Act, 1982—Public Law 97–86
Energy and Water Development Appropriation Act, 1982—Public Law 97–88

Department of Energy National Security and Military Applications of Nuclear Energy Authorization Act of 1982—Public Law 97-90
A joint resolution making further continuing appropriations for the fiscal year 1982—Public Law 97-92
National Aeronautics and Space Administration Authorization Act, 1982—Public Law 97-96
Military Construction Authorization Act, 1982—Public Law 97-99
Appropriations–Department of the Interior–Fiscal Year 1982—Public Law 97-100
Department of Housing and Urban Development–Independent Agencies Appropriation Act, 1982—Public Law 97-101
Department of Transportation and Related Agencies Appropriations Act, 1982—Public Law 97-102
Agriculture, Rural Development, and Related Agencies Appropriations Act, 1982—Public Law 97-103
International Security and Development Cooperation Act of 1981—Public Law 97-113
Department of Defense Appropriation Act, 1982—Public Law 97-114
Foreign Assistance and Related Program Appropriations Act, 1982—Public Law 97-121
Authorization, Appropriations–Coast Guard for Fiscal Year 1982—Public Law 97-136
Urgent Supplemental Appropriations Act, 1982—Public Law 97-216
Department of State Authorization Act, Fiscal Years 1982 and 1983—Public Law 97-241
Department of Defense Authorization Act, 1983—Public Law 97-252
Supplemental Appropriations Act, 1982—Public Law 97-257
Department of Housing and Urban Development–Independent Agencies Appropriations Act, 1983—Public Law 97-272
Continuing Appropriations, Fiscal Year 1983—Public Law 97-276
Student Financial Assistance Technical Amendments Act of 1982—Public Law 97-301
Military Construction Authorization Act, 1983—Public Law 97-321
National Aeronautics and Space Administration Authorization Act, 1983—Public Law 97-324
Department of Transportation and Related Agencies Appropriations Act, 1983—Public Law 97-369
Further Continuing Appropriations, 1983—Public Law 97-377
Department of the Interior and Related Agencies Appropriation Act, 1983—Public Law 97-394

NRC Authorization—Public Law 97–415
Surface Transportation Assistance Act of 1982—Public Law 97–424
Student Financial Assistance Technical Amendments Act of 1982—Public Law 97–458
Department of Housing and Urban Development–Independent Agencies Appropriation Act, 1984—Public Law 98–45
National Aeronautics and Space Administration Authorization Act, 1984—Public Law 98–52
Supplemental Appropriations Act, 1983—Public Law 98–63
Department of Transportation and Related Agencies Appropriations Act, 1984—Public Law 98–78
Department of Defense Authorization Act, 1984—Public Law 98–94
Continuing Appropriations, 1984—Public Law 98–107
Military Construction Authorization Act, 1984—Public Law 98–115
National Park System and Public Lands—Public Law 98–141
Department of the Interior and Related Agencies Appropriations Act, 1984—Public Law 98–146
Continuing Resolution, 1984—Public Law 98–151
Department of State Authorization Act Fiscal Years 1984 and 1985—Public Law 98–164
Departments of Commerce, Justice, and State, the Judiciary, and Related Agencies Appropriations Act, 1984—Public Law 98–166
Supplemental Appropriations Act, 1984; Domestic Housing and International Recovery and Financial Stability Act—Public Law 98–181
Department of Defense Appropriations Act, 1984—Public Law 98–212
Intelligence Authorization Act for Fiscal Year 1984—Public Law 98–215
Rehabilitation Amendments of 1984—Public Law 98–221
Urgent Supplemental Appropriation Act for the Fiscal Year Ending September 30, 1984, for the Department of Agriculture—Public Law 98–332
Energy and Water Development Appropriation Act, 1985—Public Law 98–360
National Aeronautics and Space Administration Authorization Act of 1984—Public Law 98–361
Land Remote-Sensing Commercialization Act of 1984—Public Law 98–365
Department of Housing and Urban Development–Independent Agencies Appropriation Act, 1985—Public Law 98–371
Departments of Commerce, Justice, and State, the Judiciary, and Related Agencies Appropriation Act, 1985—Public Law 98–411

Continuing Appropriations, 1985–Comprehensive Crime Control Act of 1984—Public Law 98–473
Department of Defense Authorization Act, 1985—Public Law 98–525
Nuclear Regulatory Commission, Authorizations—Public Law 98–553
Coast Guard Authorization Act of 1984—Public Law 98–557
Trade and Tariff Act of 1984—Public Law 98–573
Reorganization Act Amendments of 1984—Public Law 98–614
Urgent Supplemental Appropriations, 1985–African Famine Relief—Public Law 99–10
Export Administration Amendments Act of 1985—Public Law 99–64
International Security and Development Cooperation Act of 1985—Public Law 99–83
Supplemental Appropriations, Fiscal Year 1985—Public Law 99–88
Energy and Water Development Appropriation Act, 1985—Public Law 99–141
Department of Defense Authorization Act, 1986—Public Law 99–145
Military Construction Authorization Act, 1986—Public Law 99–167
National Aeronautics and Space Administration Act of 1986—Public Law 99–170
Military Construction Appropriation Act, 1986—Public Law 99–173
Departments of Commerce, Justice, and State, the Judiciary and Related Agencies Appropriation Act, 1986—Public Law 99–180
Agreement for Nuclear Cooperation Between the United States and China—Public Law 99–183
Further Continuing Appropriations, 1985—Public Law 99–190
Urgent Supplemental Appropriations Act, 1986—Public Law 99–349
Comprehensive Anti-Apartheid Act of 1986—Public Law 99–440
Continuing Appropriations, Fiscal Year 1987—Public Law 99–591
Patent and Trademark Office Authorization Act—Public Law 99–607
Coast Guard Authorization Act of 1986—Public Law 99–640
National Defense Authorization Act for Fiscal Year 1987—Public Law 99–661
Supplemental Appropriations Act, 1987—Public Law 100–71
National Defense Authorization Act for Fiscal Years 1988 and 1989—Public Law 100–180
Continuing Appropriations, Fiscal Year 1988—Public Law 100–202
Foreign Relations Authorization Act, Fiscal Years 1988 and 1989—Public Law 100–204
Energy and Water Appropriations Act, 1989—Public Law 100–371
Omnibus Trade and Competitiveness Act of 1988—Public Law 100–418

Treasury, Postal Service and General Government Appropriations Act, 1989—Public Law 100–440

Department of the Interior and Related Agencies Appropriations Act, 1989—Public Law 100–446

Military Construction Appropriations Act, 1989—Public Law 100–447

Coast Guard Authorization Act of 1988—Public Law 100–448

National Defense Authorization Act, Fiscal Year 1989—Public Law 100–456

Department of Transportation and Related Agencies Appropriations Act, 1989—Public Law 100–457

Departments of Commerce, Justice, and State, the Judiciary and Related Agencies Appropriations Act, 1989—Public Law 100–459

Foreign Operations, Export Financing, and Related Programs Appropriations Act, 1989—Public Law 100–461

Department of Defense Appropriations Act, 1989—Public Law 100–463

Defense Authorization Amendments and Base Closure and Realignment Act—Public Law 100–526

To Implement the Bipartisan Accord on Central America of March 24, 1989—Public Law 101–14

Dire Emergency Supplemental Appropriations and Transfers, Urgent Supplementals, and Correcting Enrollment Errors Act of 1989—Public Law 101–45

Making appropriations for the Department of the Interior and related agencies for the fiscal year ending September 30, 1990—Public Law 101–121

Treasury, Postal Service and General Government Appropriations Act, 1990—Public Law 101–136

Making appropriations for military construction for the Department of Defense for the fiscal year ending September 30, 1990—Public Law 101–148

Departments of Commerce, Justice, and State, the Judiciary, and Related Agencies Appropriations Act, 1990—Public Law 101–162

Department of Transportation and Related Agencies Appropriations Act, 1990—Public Law 101–164

Department of Defense Appropriations Act, 1990—Public Law 101–165

Foreign Operations, Export Financing, and Related Programs Appropriations Act, 1990—Public Law 101–167

National Defense Authorization Act for Fiscal Years 1990 and 1991—Public Law 101–189

International Narcotics Control Act of 1989—Public Law 101–231

Foreign Relations Authorization Act, Fiscal Years 1990 and 1991—Public Law 101–246

Dire Emergency Supplemental Appropriations for Disaster Assistance, Food Stamps, Unemployment Compensation Administration, and Other Urgent Needs, and Transfers, and Reducing Funds Budgeted for Military Spending Act of 1990—Public Law 101–302

Departments of Veterans Affairs and Housing and Urban Development, and Independent Agencies Appropriations Act, 1991—Public Law 101–507

Treasury, Postal Service and General Government Appropriations Act, 1991—Public Law 101–509

National Defense Authorization Act for Fiscal Year 1991—Public Law 101–510

Department of Defense Appropriations Act, 1991—Public Law 101–511

Department of the Interior and Related Agencies Appropriations Act, 1991—Public Law 101–512

Iraq Sanctions Act of 1990—Public Law 101–513

Departments of Commerce, Justice, and State, the Judiciary, and Related Agencies Appropriations Act, 1991—Public Law 101–515

Department of Transportation and Related Agencies Appropriations Act, 1991—Public Law 101–516

Military Construction Appropriations Act, 1991—Public Law 101–519

National and Community Service Act of 1990—Public Law 101–610

Persian Gulf Conflict Supplemental Authorization and Personnel Benefits Act of 1991—Public Law 102–25

Dire Emergency Supplemental Appropriations for Consequences of Operation Desert Shield/Desert Storm, Food Stamps, Unemployment Compensation Administration, Veterans Compensation—Public Law 102–27

Operation Desert Shield/Desert Storm Supplemental Appropriations Act, 1991—Public Law 102–28

Department of Veterans Affairs Health-Care Personnel Act of 1991—Public Law 102–40

Dire Emergency Supplemental Appropriations from Contributions of Foreign Governments and/or Interest for Humanitarian Assistance to Refugees and Displaced Persons in and around Iraq—Public Law 102–55

Department of Veterans Affairs Codification Act—Public Law 102–83

Saguaro National Monument Expansion Act of 1991—Public Law 102–88

Military Construction Appropriations Act, 1992—Public Law 102–136

Foreign Relations Authorization Act, Fiscal Years 1992 and 1993—Public Law 102-138

Departments of Veterans Affairs and Housing and Urban Development, and Independent Agencies Appropriations Act, 1992—Public Law 102-139

Departments of Commerce, Justice, and State, the Judiciary, and Related Agencies Appropriations Act, 1992—Public Law 102-140

Treasury, Postal Service and General Government Appropriations Act, 1992—Public Law 102-141

Department of Transportation and Related Agencies Appropriations Act, 1992—Public Law 102-143

Department of the Interior and Related Agencies Appropriations Act, 1992—Public Law 102-154

Department of Defense Appropriations Act, 1992—Public Law 102-172

To provide for the termination of the application of Title IV of the Trade Act of 1974—Public Law 102-182

Intelligence Authorization Act, Fiscal Year 1992—Public Law 102-183

National Defense Authorization Act for Fiscal Years 1992 and 1993—Public Law 102-190

National Aeronautics and Space Administration Authorization Act, Fiscal Year 1992—Public Law 102-195

Conventional Forces in Europe Treaty Implementation Act of 1991—Public Law 102-228

Operation Desert Shield/Desert Storm Act of 1992—Public Law 102-229

Intermodal Surface Transportation Efficiency Act of 1991—Public Law 102-240

Coast Guard Authorization Act of 1991—Public Law 102-241

American Technology Preeminence Act of 1991—Public Law 102-245

Making further continuing appropriations for the fiscal year 1992—Public Law 102-266

Dire Emergency Supplemental Appropriations Act, 1992, for Disaster Assistance to Meet Urgent Needs Because of Calamities Such as Those Which Occurred in Los Angeles and Chicago—Public Law 102-302

Higher Education Amendments of 1992—Public Law 102-325

Energy and Water Development Appropriations Act, 1993—Public Law 102-377

Military Construction Appropriations Act, 1993—Public Law 102-380

Department of the Interior and Related Agencies Appropriations Act, 1993—Public Law 102-381

Department of Transportation and Related Agencies Appropriations Act, 1993—Public Law 102-388

Departments of Veterans Affairs and Housing and Urban Development, and Independent Agencies Appropriations Act, 1993—Public Law 102-389
Foreign Operations, Export Financing, and Related Programs Appropriations Act, 1993—Public Law 102-391
Treasury, Postal Service, and General Government Appropriations Act, 1993—Public Law 102-393
Departments of Commerce, Justice, and State, the Judiciary, and Related Agencies Appropriations Act, 1993—Public Law 102-395
Department of Defense Appropriations Act, 1993—Public Law 102-396
National Defense Authorization Act for Fiscal Year 1993—Public Law 102-484
Intelligence Authorization Act for Fiscal Year 1993—Public Law 102-496
FREEDOM Support Act—Public Law 102-511
International Dolphin Conservation Act of 1992—Public Law 102-523
Enterprise for the Americas Initiative Act of 1992—Public Law 102-532
Telecommunications Authorization Act of 1992—Public Law 102-538
Futures Trading Practices Act of 1992—Public Law 102-546
Defense Production Act Amendments of 1992—Public Law 102-558
National Oceanic and Atmospheric Administration Authorization Act of 1992—Public Law 102-567
Reclamation Projects Authorization and Adjustment Act of 1992—Public Law 102-575
International Narcotics Control Act of 1992—Public Law 102-583
Oceans Act of 1992—Public Law 102-587
National Aeronautics and Space Administration Authorization Act, Fiscal Year 1993—Public Law 102-588
Supplemental Appropriations Act of 1993—Public Law 103-50
Foreign Operations, Export Financing, and Related Programs Appropriations Act, 1994—Public Law 103-87
Departments of Commerce, Justice, and State, the Judiciary, and Related Agencies Appropriations Act, 1994—Public Law 103-121
Treasury, Postal Service, and General Government Appropriations Act, 1994—Public Law 103-123
Department of the Interior and Related Agencies Appropriations Act, 1994—Public Law 103-138
Department of Defense Appropriations Act, 1994—Public Law 103-139
National Defense Authorization Act for Fiscal Year 1994—Public Law 103-160
Foreign Relations Authorization Act, Fiscal Years 1994 and 1995—Public Law 103-236

To revise, codify, and enact without substantive change certain general and permanent laws, related to transportation, as subtitles II, III, and V–X of Title 49, United States Code, "Transportation," and to make other technical improvements in the Code—Public Law 103–272

Making appropriations for foreign operations, export financing, and related programs for the fiscal year ending September 30, 1995—Public Law 103–306

Departments of Commerce, Justice, and State, the Judiciary, and Related Agencies Appropriations Act, 1995—Public Law 103–317

Treasury, Postal Service and General Government Appropriations Act, 1995—Public Law 103–329

Department of the Interior and Related Agencies Appropriations Act, 1995—Public Law 103–332

Departments of Labor, Health and Human Services, and Education, and Related Agencies Appropriations Act, 1995—Public Law 103–333

Department of Defense Appropriations Act, 1995—Public Law 103–335

National Defense Authorization Act for Fiscal Year 1995—Public Law 103–337

Intelligence Authorization Act for Fiscal Year 1995—Public Law 103–359

California Desert Protection Act of 1994—Public Law 103–443

International Narcotics Control Corrections Act of 1994—Public Law 103–447

Emergency Supplemental Appropriations and Rescissions for the Department of Defense to Preserve and Enhance Military Readiness Act of 1995—Public Law 104–6

Emergency Supplemental Appropriations for Additional Disaster Assistance, for Anti-terrorism Initiatives, for Assistance in the Recovery from the Tragedy That Occurred at Oklahoma City—Public Law 104–19

To amend the Colorado River Basin Salinity Control Act to authorize additional measures to carry out the control of salinity upstream of Imperial Dam in a cost-effective manner—Public Law 104–20

Military Construction Appropriations Act, 1996—Public Law 104–32

Agriculture, Rural Development, Food and Drug Administration, and Related Agencies Appropriations Act, 1996—Public Law 104–37

To amend the Alaska Native Claims Settlement Act—Public Law 104–42

Department of Transportation and Related Agencies Appropriations Act, 1996—Public Law 104–50

Treasury, Postal Service, and General Government Appropriations Act, 1996—Public Law 104–52

Department of Defense Appropriations Act, 1996—Public Law 104–61

National Defense Authorization Act for Fiscal Year 1996—Public Law 104–106
Foreign Operations, Export Financing, and Related Programs Appropriations Act, 1996—Public Law 104–107
Cuban Liberty and Democratic Solidarity (LIBERTAD) Act of 1996—Public Law 104–114
Contract with America Advancement Act of 1996—Public Law 104–121
Greens Creek Land Exchange Act of 1995—Public Law 104–123
Antiterrorism and Effective Death Penalty Act of 1996—Public Law 104–132
Omnibus Consolidated Rescissions and Appropriations Act of 1996—Public Law 104–134
To amend the Foreign Assistance Act of 1961 and the Arms Export Control Act—Public Law 104–164
Iran and Libya Sanctions Act of 1996—Public Law 104–172
Military Construction Appropriations Act, 1997—Public Law 104–196
National Defense Authorization Act for Fiscal Year 1997—Public Law 104–201
Departments of Veterans Affairs and Housing and Urban Development, and Independent Agencies Appropriations Act, 1997—Public Law 104–204
Omnibus Parks and Public Lands Management Act of 1996—Public Law 104–333
1997 Emergency Supplemental Appropriations Act for Recovery from Natural Disasters, and for Overseas Peacekeeping Efforts, Including Those in Bosnia—Public Law 105–18
Department of Defense Appropriations Act, 1998—Public Law 105–56
Treasury and General Government Appropriations Act, 1998—Public Law 105–61
Energy and Water Development Appropriations Act, 1998—Public Law 105–62
Departments of Veterans Affairs and Housing and Urban Development, and Independent Agencies Appropriations Act, 1998—Public Law 105–65
Department of Transportation and Related Agencies Appropriations Act, 1998—Public Law 105–66
Departments of Labor, Health and Human Services, and Education, and Related Agencies Appropriations Act, 1998—Public Law 105–78
Department of the Interior and Related Agencies Appropriations Act, 1998—Public Law 105–83

National Defense Authorization Act for Fiscal Year 1998—Public Law 105–85

Agriculture, Rural Development, Food and Drug Administration, and Related Agencies Appropriations Act, 1998—Public Law 105–86

Intelligence Authorization Act for Fiscal Year 1998—Public Law 105–107

United States Fire Administration Authorization Act for Fiscal Years 1998 and 1999—Public Law 105–108

Veterans' Benefits Act of 1997—Public Law 105–114

Foreign Operations, Export Financing, and Related Programs Appropriations Act, 1998—Public Law 105–118

Departments of Commerce, Justice, and State, the Judiciary, and Related Agencies Appropriations Act, 1998—Public Law 105–119

Small Business Reauthorization Act of 1997—Public Law 105–135

FAA Research, Engineering, and Development Authorization Act of 1998—Public Law 105–155

National Sea Grant College Program Reauthorization Act of 1998—Public Law 105–160

1998 Supplemental Appropriations and Rescissions Act—Public Law 105–174

Telemarketing Fraud Prevention Act of 1998—Public Law 105–184

Internal Revenue Service Restructuring and Reform Act of 1998—Public Law 105–206

National Science Foundation Authorization Act of 1998—Public Law 105–207

To amend the Foreign Assistance Act of 1961—Public Law 105–214

Department of Transportation and Related Agencies Appropriations Act, 1999—Public Law 105–227

Military Construction Appropriations Act, 1999—Public Law 105–237

Higher Education Amendments of 1998—Public Law 105–244

Energy and Water Development Appropriations Act, 1999—Public Law 105–245

Strom Thurmond National Defense Authorization Act for Fiscal Year 1999—Public Law 105–261

Department of Defense Appropriations Act, 1999—Public Law 105–262

Travel and Transportation Reform Act of 1998—Public Law 105–264

Departments of Veterans Affairs and Housing and Urban Development, and Independent Agencies Appropriations Act, 1999—Public Law 105–276

Granite Watershed Enhancement and Protection Act of 1998—Public Law 105–281

Technology Administration Act of 1998—Public Law 105-309
Iraq Liberation Act of 1998—Public Law 105-338
National Parks Omnibus Management Act of 1998—Public Law 105-391
1999 Emergency Supplemental Appropriations Act—Public Law 106-31
Military Construction Appropriations Act, 2000—Public Law 106-52
Water Resources Development Act of 1999—Public Law 106-53
Treasury and General Government Appropriations Act, 2000—Public Law 106-58
National Defense Authorization Act for Fiscal Year 2000—Public Law 106-65
Department of Transportation and Related Agencies Appropriations Act, 2000—Public Law 106-69
Departments of Veterans Affairs and Housing and Urban Development, and Independent Agencies Appropriations Act, 2000—Public Law 106-74
Agriculture, Rural Development, Food and Drug Administration, and Related Agencies Appropriations Act, 2000—Public Law 106-78
Department of Defense Appropriations Act, 2000—Public Law 106-79
Intelligence Authorization Act for Fiscal Year 2000—Public Law 106-120
To improve protection and management of the Chattahoochee River National Recreation Area in the State of Georgia—Public Law 106-154
Iran Nonproliferation Act of 2000—Public Law 106-178
Making appropriations for military construction, family housing, and base realignment and closure for the Department of Defense for the fiscal year ending September 30, 2001—Public Law 106-246
Department of Defense Appropriations Act—Public Law 106-259
Security Assistance Act of 2000—Public Law 106-280
Department of the Interior and Related Agencies Appropriations Act, 2001—Public Law 106-291
Microenterprise for Self-Reliance and International Anti-Corruption Act of 2000—Public Law 106-309
Department of Transportation and Related Agencies Appropriations Act, 2001—Public Law 106-346
Victims of Trafficking and Violence Protection Act of 2000—Public Law 106-386
Agriculture, Rural Development, Food and Drug Administration, and Related Agencies Appropriations Act, 2001—Public Law 106-387
National Aeronautics and Space Administration Authorization Act of 2000—Public Law 106-391

Fish and Wildlife Programs Improvement and National Wildlife Refuge System Centennial Act of 2000—Public Law 106–408

Water Resources Development Act of 2000—Public Law 106–541

Intelligence Authorization Act for Fiscal Year 2001—Public Law 106–567

2001 Emergency Supplemental Appropriations Act for Recovery from and Response to Terrorist Attacks on the United States—Public Law 107–38

Uniting and Strengthening America by Providing Appropriate Tools Required to Intercept and Obstruct Terrorism (USA PATRIOT ACT) Act of 2001—Public Law 107–56

To authorize the President to exercise waivers of foreign assistance restrictions with respect to Pakistan through September 30, 2003—Public Law 107–57

Department of the Interior and Related Agencies Appropriations Act, 2002—Public Law 107–63

Military Construction Appropriations Act, 2002—Public Law 107–64

Energy and Water Development Appropriations Act, 2002—Public Law 107–66

Treasury and General Government Appropriations Act, 2002—Public Law 107–67

Departments of Veterans Affairs and Housing and Urban Development, and Independent Agencies Appropriations Act, 2002—Public Law 107–73

Agriculture, Rural Development, Food and Drug Administration, and Related Agencies Appropriations Act, 2002—Public Law 107–76

Departments of Commerce, Justice, and State, the Judiciary, and Related Agencies Appropriations Act, 2002—Public Law 107–77

Department of Transportation and Related Agencies Appropriations Act, 2002—Public Law 107–87

National Defense Authorization Act for Fiscal Year 2002—Public Law 107–107

Kenneth M. Ludden Foreign Operations, Export Financing, and Related Programs Appropriations Act, Fiscal Year 2002—Public Law 107–115

Departments of Labor, Health and Human Services, and Education, and Related Agencies Appropriations Act, 2002—Public Law 107–116

Making appropriations for the Department of Defense for the fiscal year ending September 30, 2002—Public Law 107–117

2002 Supplemental Appropriations Act for Further Recovery from and Response to Terrorist Attacks on the United States—Public Law 107–206

Trade Act of 2002—Public Law 107–210
To revise, codify, and enact without substantive change certain general and permanent laws, related to public buildings, property, and works, as Title 40, United States Code—Public Law 107–217
Foreign Relations Authorization Act, Fiscal Year 2003—Public Law 107–228
Department of Defense Appropriations Act, 2003—Public Law 107–248
Military Construction Appropriation Act, 2003—Public Law 107–249
Making further continuing appropriations for the fiscal year 2003—Public Law 107–294
Homeland Security Act of 2002—Public Law 107–296
Bob Stump National Defense Authorization Act for Fiscal Year 2003—Public Law 107–314
Afghanistan Freedom Support Act of 2002—Public Law 107–327
E-Government Act of 2002—Public Law 107–347
Russian River Land Act—Public Law 107–362
National Science Foundation Authorization Act of 2002—Public Law 107–368
Consolidated Appropriations Resolution, 2003—Public Law 108–7
Emergency Wartime Supplemental Appropriations Act, 2003—Public Law 108–11
Burmese Freedom and Democracy Act of 2003—Public Law 108–61
United States–Chile Free Trade Agreement Implementation Act—Public Law 108–77
United States–Singapore Free Trade Agreement Implementation Act—Public Law 108–78
Department of Defense Appropriations Act, 2004—Public Law 108–87
Department of Homeland Security Appropriations Act, 2004—Public Law 108–90
Emergency Supplemental Appropriations Act for Defense and for the Reconstruction of Iraq and Afghanistan, 2004—Public Law 108–106
Department of the Interior and Related Agencies Appropriations Act, 2004—Public Law 108–108
Military Construction Appropriations Act, 2004—Public Law 108–132
National Defense Authorization Act for Fiscal Year 2004—Public Law 108–136
Energy and Water Development Appropriations Act, 2004—Public Law 108–137
Vision 100—Century of Aviation Reauthorization Act—Public Law 108–176

Intelligence Authorization Act for Fiscal Year 2004—Public Law 108–177
To approve the Compact of Free Association, as amended, between the Government of the United States of America and the Government of the Federated States of Micronesia, and the Compact—Public Law 108–188
Consolidated Appropriations Act, 2004—Public Law 108–199
NASA Flexibility Act of 2004—Public Law 108–201
United States–Australia Free Trade Agreement Implementation Act—Public Law 108–286
Department of Defense Appropriations Act, 2005—Public Law 108–287
United States–Morocco Free Trade Agreement Implementation Act—Public Law 108–302
Making continuing appropriations for the fiscal year 2005—Public Law 108–309
Military Construction Appropriations and Emergency Hurricane Supplemental Appropriations Act, 2005—Public Law 108–324
Department of Homeland Security Appropriations Act, 2005—Public Law 108–334
Ronald W. Reagan National Defense Authorization Act for Fiscal Year 2005—Public Law 108–375
Consolidated Appropriations Act, 2005—Public Law 108–447
Intelligence Reform and Terrorism Prevention Act of 2004—Public Law 108–458
To amend the National Telecommunications and Information Administration Organization Act to facilitate the reallocation of spectrum from governmental to commercial users—Public Law 108–494
Emergency Supplemental Appropriations Act for Defense, the Global War on Terror, and Tsunami Relief, 2005—Public Law 109–13
Dominican Republic–Central America–United States Free Trade Agreement Implementation Act—Public Law 109–53
Department of the Interior, Environment, and Related Agencies Appropriations Act, 2006—Public Law 109–54
Department of Homeland Security Appropriations Act, 2006—Public Law 109–90
Agriculture, Rural Development, Food and Drug Administration, and Related Agencies Appropriations Act, 2006—Public Law 109–97
Foreign Operations, Export Financing, and Related Programs Appropriations Act, 2006—Public Law 109–102
Energy and Water Development Appropriations Act, 2006—Public Law 109–103

Science, State, Justice, Commerce, and Related Agencies Appropriations Act, 2006—Public Law 109–108
Military Quality of Life and Veterans Affairs Appropriations Act, 2006—Public Law 109–114
Transportation, Treasury, Housing and Urban Development, the Judiciary, the District of Columbia, and Independent Agencies Appropriations Act, 2006—Public Law 109–115
Department of Defense Appropriations Act, 2006—Public Law 109–148
Departments of Labor, Health and Human Services, and Education, and Related Agencies Appropriations Act, 2006—Public Law 109–149
National Aeronautics and Space Administration Authorization Act of 2005—Public Law 109–155
National Defense Authorization Act for Fiscal Year 2006—Public Law 109–163
Trafficking Victims Protection Reauthorization Act of 2005—Public Law 109–164
United States–Bahrain Free Trade Agreement Implementation Act—Public Law 109–169
Emergency Supplemental Appropriations Act for Defense, the Global War on Terror, and Hurricane Recovery, 2006—Public Law 109–234
United States–Oman Free Trade Agreement Implementation Act—Public Law 109–283
Department of Defense Appropriations Act, 2007—Public Law 109–289
Military Personnel Financial Services Protection Act—Public Law 109–290
Iran Freedom Support Act—Public Law 109–293
Department of Homeland Security Appropriations Act, 2007—Public Law 109–295
Darfur Peace and Accountability Act of 2006—Public Law 109–344
SAFE Port Act—Public Law 109–347
John Warner National Defense Authorization Act for Fiscal Year 2007—Public Law 109–364
To exempt from certain requirements of the Atomic Energy Act of 1954 a proposed nuclear agreement for cooperation with India—Public Law 109–401
Palestinian Anti-Terrorism Act of 2006—Public Law 109–446
Marine Debris Research, Prevention, and Reduction Act—Public Law 109–469
Revised Continuing Appropriations Resolution, 2007—Public Law 110–5
U.S. Troop Readiness, Veterans' Care, Katrina Recovery, and Iraq Accountability Appropriations Act, 2007—Public Law 110–28

Implementing Recommendations of the 9/11 Commission Act of 2007—Public Law 110-53

Water Resources Development Act of 2007—Public Law 110-114

Making appropriations for the Department of Defense for the fiscal year ending September 30, 2008, and for other purposes—Public Law 110-116

Energy Independence and Security Act of 2007—Public Law 110-140

Consolidated Appropriations Act, 2008—Public Law 110-161

National Defense Authorization Act for Fiscal Year 2008—Public Law 110-181

Consolidated Natural Resources Act of 2008—Public Law 110-229

Strategic Petroleum Reserve Fill Suspension and Consumer Protection Act of 2008—Public Law 110-232

SAFETEA-LU Technical Corrections Act of 2008—Public Law 110-244

Supplemental Appropriations Act, 2008—Public Law 110-252

Housing and Economic Recovery Act of 2008—Public Law 110-289

Tom Lantos and Henry J. Hyde United States Global Leadership Against HIV/AIDS, Tuberculosis, and Malaria Reauthorization Act of 2008—Public Law 110-293

Consolidated Security, Disaster Assistance, and Continuing Appropriations Act, 2009—Public Law 110-329

To provide authority for the Federal Government to purchase and insure certain types of troubled assets for the purposes of providing stability to and preventing disruption in the economy—Public Law 110-343

United States–India Nuclear Cooperation Approval and Nonproliferation Enhancement Act—Public Law 110-369

Inspector General Reform Act of 2008—Public Law 110-409

Duncan Hunter National Defense Authorization Act for Fiscal Year 2009—Public Law 110-417

To amend Title 49, United States Code, to prevent railroad fatalities, injuries, and hazardous materials releases, to authorize the Federal Railroad Safety Administration, and for other purposes—Public Law 110-432

American Recovery and Reinvestment Act of 2009—Public Law 111-5

Omnibus Appropriations Act, 2009—Public Law 111-8

Omnibus Public Land Management Act of 2009—Public Law 111-11

Supplemental Appropriations Act, 2009—Public Law 111-32

Enhanced Partnership with Pakistan Act of 2009—Public Law 111-73

To authorize the Administrator of General Services to convey a parcel of real property in Galveston, Texas, to the Galveston Historical Foundation—Public Law 111-76

Agriculture, Rural Development, Food and Drug Administration, and Related Agencies Appropriations Act, 2010—Public Law 111–80
Department of Homeland Security Appropriations Act, 2010—Public Law 111–83
National Defense Authorization Act for Fiscal Year 2010—Public Law 111–84
Energy and Water Development and Related Agencies Appropriations Act, 2010—Public Law 111–85
Department of the Interior, Environment, and Related Agencies Appropriations Act, 2010— Public Law 111–88
Consolidated Appropriations Act, 2010—Public Law 111–117
Department of Defense Appropriations Act, 2010—Public Law 111–118
Patient Protection and Affordable Care Act —Public Law 111–148
Caregivers and Veterans Omnibus Health Services Act of 2010—Public Law 111–163
Comprehensive Iran Sanctions, Accountability, and Divestment Act of 2010—Public Law 111–195
Dodd-Frank Wall Street Reform and Consumer Protection Act—Public Law 111–203
Supplemental Appropriations Act, 2010—Public Law 111–212
Intelligence Authorization Act for Fiscal Year 2010—Public Law 111–258
To authorize the Secretary of the Interior to lease certain lands in Virgin Islands National Park, and for other purposes—Public Law 111–261
Security Cooperation Act of 2010—Public Law 111–266
Telework Enhancement Act of 2010—Public Law 111–292
To enact certain laws relating to national and commercial space programs as Title 51, United States Code, "National and Commercial Space Programs"—Public Law 111–314
Continuing Appropriations and Surface Transportation Extensions Act, 2011—Public Law 111–322
America COMPETES Reauthorization Act of 2010—Public Law 111–358
Ike Skelton National Defense Authorization Act for Fiscal Year 2011—Public Law 111–383

Appendix 2

Legislative Veto Court Cases

Federal

Sibbach v. Wilson, 312 U.S. 1 (1941)
Buckley v. Valeo, 424 U.S. 1 (1976)
Clark v. Valeo, 182 U.S. App. D.C. 21 (1977)
McCorkle v. United States, 559 F.2d 1258 (1977)
Atkins v. United States, 556 F.2d 1028, Ct.Cl. (1977)
Pacific Legal Foundation v. Watt, 539 F. Supp. 1194 (1982)
Consumer Energy Council of America v. Federal Energy Regulatory Commission, 673 F.2d 425 D.C. Cir. (1982)
Consumers Union of the United States v. Federal Trade Commission, 691 F.2d 575 (1982)
Immigration and Naturalization Service v. Chadha, 462 U.S. 919 (1983)
Allen v. Carmen, 578 F. Supp. 951 (1983)
EEOC v. All State Insurance Company, 570 F. Supp. 1224 (1983)
EEOC v. Hernando Bank Inc., 724 F.2d 1188 (1984)
EEOC v. CBS, Inc., 743 F.2d 969, 2d Cir. (1984)
City of Alexandria v. United States, 737 F.2d 1022 (1984)
Gulf Oil Corp. v. Dyke, 734 F.2d 797 (1984)
Cranston v. Reagan, 611 F. Supp. 247 (1985)
Bowsher v. Synar, 478 U.S. 714 (1986)
Beacon Products v. Reagan, 633 F. Supp. 1191 U.S. Dist. (1986)
Alaska Airlines, Inc. v. Brock, 480 U.S. 678 (1987)
City of New Haven v. United States, 258 U.S. App. D.C. 59 (1987)

State

Alaska	*State of Alaska v. A.L.I.V.E. Voluntary, Inc.*, 606 p.2d 769 (1980)
Colorado	*Watrous v. Golden Chamber of Commerce*, 121 Colo. 521, 218 P. 2d 498 (1950)
Connecticut	*Maloney v. Pac*, 183 Conn. 313, 439 A.2d 349 (1981)
Idaho	*Idaho Power Co. v. State*, 104 Idaho 570, 661 P.2d 736 (1983)
	Mead v. Arnell, 117 Idaho 660, 791 P.2d 410 (1990)
Kansas	*State ex rel. Stephen v. House of Representatives*, 236 Kan. 45, 687 P.2d 622 (1984)
	State ex rel. Tomasic v. Unified Government of Wyandotte County/Kansas City, 264 Kan. 293, 955 P.2d 1136 (1998)
Kentucky	*Legislative Research Commission ex rel. v. Brown*, 664 S.W.2d 907 (Ky. 1984)
Michigan	*Blank v. Department of Corrections*, 462 Mich. 103, 611 N.W.2d 538 (2000)
Missouri	*Missouri Coalition for the Environment v. Joint Committee on Administrative Rules*, 948 S.W.2d 125 (Mo. 1997)
Montana	*Montana Taxpayers' Association v. Department of Revenue*, No. 47126, Mont. Lewis and Clark Co. (1982)
New Hampshire	*Opinion of the Justices*, 96 N.H. 517, 83 A.2d 738 (1950)
	Opinion of the Justices, 110 N.H. 359, 266 A.2d 823 (1970)
	Opinion of the Justices, 121 N.H. 552, 431 A.2d 783 (1981)
New Jersey	*Enourato v. New Jersey Building Authority*, 90 N.J. 396, 448 A.2d 449 (1982)
	General Assembly of New Jersey v. Byrne, 90 N.J. 376, 448 A.2d 438 (1982)
Oregon	*Gilliam County v. Department of Environmental Quality of Oregon*, 316 Or. 99, 849 P.2d 500 (1993)
Pennsylvania	*Commonwealth v. Sessoms*, 516 Pa. 365, 532 A.2d 775 (1987)
South Carolina	*Reith v. South Carolina State Housing Authority*, 267 S.C. 1; 225 S.E.2d 847 (1976)
West Virginia	*State ex rel. Barker v. Manchin*, 167 W. Va. 155, 279 S.E.2d 622 (1981)
	State ex rel. Meadows v. Hechler, 195 W. Va. 11, 462 S.E.2d 586 (1995)
Wisconsin	*Martinez v. Department of Industry, Labor & Human Relations*, 165 Wis. 2d 687, 478 N.W.2d 582 (1992)

Notes

INTRODUCTION

1. The Congressional Research Service defines legislative vetoes as statutes that provide for "congressional review, deferral, approval or disapproval of proposed executive actions" (Norton 1976, 1).

2. http://www.gpo.gov/fdsys/browse/collection.action?collectionCode=FR.

3. There is some difficulty in compiling a definitive catalogue of presidential signing statements. The U.S. Government Accountability Office notes that the signing statement has "no established definition" (2007a, 2). The presidential signing statement database made available by the American Presidency Project is used as the data source for figure 0.2 (www.presidency.ucsb.edu/signingstatements.php).

CHAPTER ONE

1. At the Constitutional Convention, Madison also unsuccessfully lobbied to grant Congress the power to veto state laws (Steinfeld 2011).

2. A provision included in a 1952 supplemental appropriations bill required the Bureau of the Budget director to receive the approval of the chairperson of the House Appropriations Committee before amending specific budget circulars (66 Stat. 758, Public Law 82–547). This is the only legislative veto enacted in American history that provides veto power to a single individual. On the other end of the spectrum, a trade act passed in 1958 required a two-thirds majority vote in both chambers to sanction directives made by the United States Tariff Commission (72 Stat. 685, Public Law 85–686).

3. Under the Articles of Confederation, Congress created departments of Foreign Affairs, War, Marine, and Treasury in 1781, but these departments were attached to the legislature and led by congressional appointees (Pika and Maltese 2013).

4. The first ratification vote, which occurred on November 19, 1919, resulted in 38 yeas and 53 nays. The second vote occurred on March 19, 1920, and resulted in 49 yeas and 35 nays, seven votes short of ratification (www.senate.gov/artandhistory/history/common/briefing/Treaties.htm).

5. A similar law enacted in 1918 during World War I empowered President Wilson to redistribute agencies whose functions pertained to the American war effort (Millett and Rogers 1941). The law required presidential notification of Congress, but did not permit a congressional veto.

6. http://artandhistory.house.gov/house_history/index.aspx?cong=72.

7. The Hughes Court used a similar rationale in *United States v. Rock Royal Co-Operative* (307 U.S. 533 (1939)).

8. The Federal Energy Administration was created by an executive order issued by President Nixon in 1974. It was merged into the Department of Energy in 1977.

9. The Trade Act of 1974 (88 Stat. 1978, Public Law 93–618) contained 10 legislative vetoes concerning foreign trade agreements. This enactment is discussed further in chapter 5.

10. Hearings before the Subcommittee on Rules of the House of the Committee on Rules, House of Representatives, 97th Congress, 1st Session on Various Legislative Veto Bills Introduced in the 97th Congress. October 7, 28, and November 19, 1981, 200.

11. http://bioguide.congress.gov/scripts/biodisplay.pl?index=L000265.

12. Interview with author. March 13, 2012.

13. Discharge petition number 17, June 22, 1982.

14. Interview with author, March 13, 2012.

15. Massachusetts representative John Moakley sponsored an alternative proposal in the 97th House. With 34 cosponsors, the Regulation Reform Act of 1981 (H.R. 1, 97th Congress) proposed creating a Committee on Regulatory Affairs as a permanent select committee charged with monitoring federal agency rulemaking. Under the proposal, new rules could be vetoed by joint resolution, meaning that the president's signature would be required to block the rule. At least six additional bills providing for a one-House congressional veto of agency regulations were introduced in the House but failed to be reported out of committee (H.R. 97, H.R. 314, H.R. 383, H.R. 458, H.R. 945, and H.R. 1128).

16. On three occasions before the *Chadha* ruling, the House or Senate exercised its veto authority to block FEC rules. In 1975, the Senate vetoed a proposal subjecting congressional office accounts to FEC oversight, and the House vetoed an FEC rule regarding fund-raising-disclosure-report submissions. Shortly before the 1980 election, the Senate vetoed a rule proposal on presidential debates. There have been other occasions when the FEC withdrew rules following a veto threat from the Senate (Alexander 1983).

CHAPTER TWO

1. The only vetoes condoned by the administration were those over presidential reorganization efforts (Fisher 2005b).

2. This policy disproportionately affected persons who had immigrated to Kenya from Asian countries. According to one estimate, there were only 270,000

non-African inhabitants out of Kenya's population of 8.6 million in 1963, most of which were from India and Pakistan (Craig 1988).

3. Representative Eilberg lost his bid for a sixth term in 1978 after being indicted on conflict of interest charge alleging that he received funds to secure a federal grant for a Philadelphia hospital. He pled guilty to the charge in 1979 (Associated Press 1979).

4. Justices Warren Burger, William Brennan, Thurgood Marshall, Harry Blackmun, Lewis Powell, John Paul Stevens, and Sandra Day O'Connor voted with the majority, while Justices White and William Rehnquist dissented. Justice Burger wrote the majority opinion, and Justice Powell wrote a special concurrence opinion. Justices Byron White and Rehnquist each wrote dissenting opinions.

5. The General Accounting Office was renamed the Government Accountability Office in 2004.

6. See *Chevron Oil Co. v. Huson*, 404 U.S. 97 (1971) regarding the Supreme Court's standards in applying its decisions retroactively (Wisner 1985).

7. For example, the reauthorization of presidential reorganization authority replaced the one-House negative veto with a dual-House joint resolution of approval (5 U.S.C. § 901–911). In 1986, lawmakers similarly modified seven legislative vetoes in the Arms Control Export Act concerning military aid and arms sales to foreign countries. Two statutes allowing Congress to veto arms transfers by concurrent resolution were replaced by statutes requiring Congress to enact a law prohibiting a specific transfer (22 U.S.C. § 2753). Another five legislative vetoes allowing for a veto of arms sales by concurrent resolution were modified to joint resolutions (22 U.S.C. § 2776, 2796(b)).

8. One important exception to this came from the ruling in *City of New Haven v. United States*, 258 U.S. App. D.C. 59; 809 F.2d 900 (1987), where appellants argued that as a result of the *Chadha* ruling an entire section of the Budget Impoundment Control Act of 1974 (2 U.S.C. § 684) should be overruled. The ruling by the Second Circuit Court of Appeals asserted that Congress would not have granted presidential recession authority absent the opportunity for a congressional veto. This holding compelled the court to find the legislative veto inseverable from its enabling law.

9. A direct appeal to the Supreme Court was permitted in this instance pursuant to the Judicial Code and Judiciary Act of 1948 (62 Stat. 928, Public Law 80–733).

10. Chief Justice John Roberts likewise used this principle in the monumental 2012 Supreme Court ruling on the Patient Protection and Affordable Care Act by citing rulings in *Hooper v. California*, 155 U. S. 648 (1895), and *United States v. Harris*, 106 U. S. 629 (1883) as the basis for the Court's "general reticence to invalidate the acts of the Nation's elected leaders" (*National Federation of Independent Business v. Sebelius*, 567 U.S. 2012, 6).

11. S.J. Res. 135, 98th Congress, 1st Session, 129 Congressional Record S11, 15–17.

12. Hearing before the Subcommittee on the Constitution of the Committee on the Judiciary on S.J. Res 135. 98th Congress, Second Session, Senate Hearing 98–1162, March 2, 1984.

13. It is possible, of course, that a constitutional amendment such as this may accrue support in the future. In *The Liberty Amendments*, best-selling author Mark

Levin (2013) makes the case for the ratification of an amendment requiring any executive regulation with an estimated economic impact of more than $100 million to receive approval from a joint committee of Congress before going into effect.

14. Supreme Court precedent has upheld report and wait provisions as a legitimate condition on delegated powers by stating that "the rules were submitted to the Congress so that that body might examine them and veto their going into effect if contrary to the policy of the legislature" (*Sibbach v. Wilson*, 312 U.S. 1 (1941)). Also see *City of Alexandria v. United States*, 737 F.2d 1022 (1984), where an appellate court similarly upheld the constitutionality of a report and wait provision included in the Tucker Act (28 U.S.C. § 1491) concerning government land sales, calling them "perfectly constitutional."

15. Vetoes of a similar nature were affirmed by a federal court of claims in *Atkins v. United States*, 556 F.2d 1028, Ct.Cl. (1977), which permitted a congressional veto that, when executed, simply maintained the status quo. It is unclear whether the TPA veto would be upheld in a similar fashion since the *Atkins* ruling was issued prior to *Chadha*.

16. TPA expired again in 2007 and President Obama did not lobby Congress to reenact it during his first term. In 2013, the president expressed hope that Congress could pass a bipartisan bill reauthorizing TPA. It remains to be seen whether such a bill would impose the same extension procedure, design a new one, or preclude the possibility of an extension altogether.

17. The science and financial services committees are next on this list, but each comprise just over 1 percent of the committee veto total.

18. Interview with the author, August 16, 2007, Washington DC.

19. The review timeline varies depending on whether the rule is designated as a "major rule," which is defined as those expected to have an estimated economic impact of $100,000,000 or more (110 Stat. 873, Public Law 104–121).

20. S.J.Res. 6, 107th Congress—Ergonomics; S.J.Res. 17, 108th Congress—Broadcast media ownership; and S.J.Res. 4, 109th Congress—Establishment of minimal risk zones for introduction of mad cow disease.

21. The proposal defines a major rule as those with "(A) an annual effect on the economy of $100,000,000 or more; (B) a major increase in costs or prices for consumers, individual industries, Federal, State, or local government agencies, or geographic regions; or (C) significant adverse effects on competition, employment, investment, productivity, innovation, or on the ability of United States based enterprises to compete with foreign-based enterprises in domestic and export markets" (H.R. 10, S. 299, 112th Congress, Sec. 804).

22. Interview with the author, November 16, 2012.

CHAPTER THREE

1. Notable court cases challenging delegation include *Cargo of the Brig Aurora v. United States*, 11 U.S. 382 (1813), *Wayman v. Southard*, 23 U.S. (10 Wheat.) 1 (1825), *J. W. Hampton, Jr. & Co. v. United States*, 276 U.S. 394 (1928), *A.L.A. Schechter Poultry Corp. v. United States*, 295 U.S. 495 (1935), and *Panama Refining Co. v. Ryan*, 293 U.S. 388 (1935).

2. I am grateful to former representative and current Senator Mark Udall (D–CO) for providing several of these reports.
3. Funding from the Dirksen Congressional Research Center (2007 Congressional Research Award) and the National Science Foundation (NSF award number SES–0720308) provided support that enabled the hiring of several research assistants to collect veto data in this manner.
4. http://constitution.org/uslaw/sal/sal.htm.
5. http://thomas.loc.gov.
6. The search was limited to enrolled bills, which are bills that have received a majority vote in both chambers of Congress and are sent to the president for approval. Focusing on enrolled bills made the data collection more manageable and also concentrated the analysis on legislation reported out of committee.
7. http://thomas.loc.gov.
8. http://voteview.com/dwnomin_joint_house_and_senate.htm.
9. A Poisson model was not employed since the dependent variable's variance is greater than its mean. A Vuong test comparing the estimates of a negative binomial regression model with those of a zero-inflated negative binomial regression model indicated that the zero-inflated model is most appropriate. This is to be expected given that about 94 percent of the laws included in the data set do not contain a legislative veto.
10. Interviews were conducted by the author in Washington, DC, in August 2007 and April 2008.

CHAPTER FOUR

1. Interview Elliott Levitas. March 13, 2012.
2. Hearings before the Subcommittee on Agency Administration of the Senate Judiciary Committee, 97th Congress, 1st Session on Various Legislative Veto Proposals. April 23, 1981.
3. In one recent Congress, compulsory legislation corresponded to a mere 3 percent of bills introduced and 25 percent of enacted laws, while trivial legislation accounted for 9 percent of all introduced bills and 20 percent of enacted laws. In total, non-discretionary legislation corresponded to 12 percent of introduced bills and nearly half of the laws passed by Congress (Adler and Wilkerson 2005).
4. During the 104th Congress, President Clinton vetoed an Emergency Supplemental Appropriations bill (H.R. 1158), the National Defense Authorization Act (H.R. 1530), the Foreign Relations Authorization Act (H.R. 1561), the Department of the Interior and Related Agencies Appropriations Act (H.R. 1977), the Departments of Commerce, Justice, and State, the Judiciary, and Related Agencies Appropriations Act (H.R. 2076), the Departments of Veterans Affairs and Housing and the Urban Development, and Independent Agencies Appropriations Act (H.R. 2099), each of which contained multiple legislative veto provisions.
5. The empirics presented in table 4.2 were also estimated using a dependent variable that excluded pocket vetoes as instances of presidential vetoes. With the exception of the dummy variables for the Clinton and George W. Bush administrations, the sign and significance of the remaining independent variables were identi-

cal to the models estimated that included pocket vetoes as vetoes. Because of this, the models including all instances of presidential vetoes are reported.

6. The 107th Congress, which witnessed a within majority party term change is coded as unified government for each of the bills that were introduced prior to June 6, 2001, when Senator Jim Jeffords officially switched his party affiliation from Republican to independent. All bills introduced after this date are coded as belonging to a period of divided government.

7. Public approval variables were compiled by the author using data from the Gallup Organization and the *Washington Post*. Presidential public approval data are monthly averages of all Gallup polls taken in a given month. Congressional public approval data from 1993 to 2010 are monthly averages of all Gallup polls taken in a given month. Congressional public approval data from 1989 to 1993 use quarterly polls conducted by the *Washington Post*.

8. Rare events logit (King and Zeng 1999) models with identical specifications were also ran, which produced nearly identical results in terms of the sign and significance of the coefficients for all of the variables.

9. On rare occasions, presidents have attached two signing statements to a single bill. This has occurred approximately 12 times: see, for example, H.R. 2346 (111th Congress) or H.R. 4200 (108th Congress).

10. Following in this tradition, Attorney General Eric Holder announced in February 2014 that state attorneys general should not enforce existing bans on gay marriage if they were believed to be unconstitutional (Apuzzo 2014).

11. A bill seeking to further clarify acceptable interrogation techniques was vetoed by President Bush on March 8, 2008 (110th Congress, H.R. 2082).

CHAPTER FIVE

1. According to the *New York Times*, an additional 26 detainees have been transferred out of the Guantanamo Bay facility since the prisoner exchange for Bergdahl (http://projects.nytimes.com/guantanamo/timeline). The press relations office of the House Armed Services Committee claimed that the committee received 30 days advance notice in each of these instances.

2. Five hundred veto provisions were randomly selected for a second round of coding to test the reliability of these policy codes. Intercoder reliability for these codes in these cases was 96.9 percent.

3. The *Policy Agendas Project* and *Congressional Bills Project* are available at www.policyagendas.org and www.congressionalbillsproject.org.

4. The House and Senate Armed Services committees assumed these veto powers following the passage of the Legislative Reorganization Act of 1946 (60 Stat. 812, Public Law 79–601).

5. Congress has also implemented committee deliberative vetoes on other arms sales, which require the president to submit notice to the House Committee on International Relations and the Senate Committee on Foreign Relations 30 days in advance of such transactions (39 U.S.C. § 2778).

6. Some have argued that this 60-day window had the unintended consequence of actually strengthening presidential warmaking power by providing the

president with a two-month period to deploy troops absent any congressional authorization.

7. After the *Chadha* ruling, Congress considered amending the War Powers Resolution to replace the concurrent resolution with a joint resolution. The Senate passed a bill on October 23, 1983, to this effect (Grimmett 2010b). Rather than amend the WPR, lawmakers passed a free-standing measure providing for expedited consideration of any joint resolution calling for a redeployment of U.S. forces (97 Stat. 1062, Public Law 98–164).

8. Since the enactment of the War Powers Resolution, lawmakers in Congress have filed lawsuits against alleged presidential violations of the act on eight different occasions spanning four administrations. Federal courts have yet to make a ruling on the merits of such a case (Garcia 2012).

9. This is in addition to powers claimed pursuant to the authorizations for the use of military force of 2001 (115 Stat. 224, Public Law 107–40) and 2002 (116 Stat. 1498, Public Law 107–243).

10. The Base Realignment and Closure Commission made closure and realignment recommendations to Congress in 1988, 1991, 1993, 1995, and 2005. It is scheduled to issue another round of recommendations in 2015.

11. Legislators also tried, unsuccessfully, to impose a legislative veto over loan repayment terms.

12. U.S. aid to Pakistan was severed in 1979 with the invocation of the Symington Amendment to the Foreign Assistance Act of 1961 (82 Stat. 1322, Public Law 90–629), which banned military aid to countries determined to be trafficking or developing nuclear technology or materials outside of International Atomic Energy Agency monitoring. This, however, was not a legislative veto pursuant to the Foreign Assistance Act.

13. These measures have been inserted into comprehensive foreign trade reforms bills such as the Omnibus Trade and Competitiveness Act of 1988 (102 Stat. 1107, Public Law 100–418) and Bipartisan Trade Promotion Authority Act of 2002 (116 Stat. 1008, Public Law 107–210), as well as individualized trade agreements with nations including Chile, Singapore, Australia, Morocco, Bahrain, Oman, and the Dominican Republic.

14. For each model, a Hausman test, which tests for a statistically significant difference between the estimates provided by fixed and random effects models, showed no statistical difference between the two sets of coefficients.

15. Replicating the models from table 5.2 without the dichotomous 108th Congress variable, the only substantive changes to the results are that the divided government variable coefficients are each insignificant, and the coefficients for the post-*Chadha* variable each become significant. This demonstrates the weight of this congressional term's veto activity.

16. The figures report greater numbers of vetoes relative to table 5.1 since some veto statutes apply to multiple departments.

17. Hausman test results for these models showed a statistical difference between the coefficient estimates of random and fixed effects models. Given this discrepancy, the consistent but less efficient estimates of the fixed effects models are presented.

18. Department of War and Navy vetoes passed before the passage of the National Security Act of 1947 (61 Stat. 495, Public Law 80–253), which reorganized these departments into the Department of Defense, are coded as Defense Department veto statutes.

CHAPTER SIX

1. Some state constitutions permit a legislative veto over gubernatorial reorganization plans including Alaska (Article III, Section 23), Illinois (Article V, Section 11), Kansas (Article I, Section 6), Maryland (Article II, Section 24), Massachusetts (Article LXXXVII, Section 1), Michigan (Article V, Section 2), North Carolina (Article III, Section 5), and South Dakota (Article IV, Section 8). In at least eight other states, legislatures hold independent veto power over executive reorganization by virtue of statutory authorization (Benjamin and Keck 2010/2011).

2. A constitutional amendment approved by Arkansas voters in 2014 permits the legislature to design a system requiring committee approval of new rules.

3. For the first time in 2010, revisions to the MSAPA included a section providing for a legislative veto of rules deemed objectionable by a rules review committee. Regarding the veto mechanism, the act suggested that "states should use the alternative that complies with their state constitution."

4. The incorporation of the legislative veto into the Michigan constitution occurred when voters ratified an entirely new constitution in 1963.

5. At the federal level, concurrent resolutions require agreement in the House and Senate, but do not require a presidential signature. The nomenclature at the state level varies, but in this instance the governor's signature was not necessary for the Kansas legislature to veto agency rules.

6. The exact distribution of rules vetoed by concurrent resolution and by statute is indeterminate because the report only identifies the total number of vetoed rules for certain years.

7. On what amounted to a technicality, while the court found the dual-House veto constitutional, it overturned the specific veto challenged in this case on the grounds that the language used in the concurrent resolution did not specifically state that the rules adopted by the board violated the legislature's intent when delegating this power.

8. Previously, however, the Idaho Supreme Court did strike down a statute passed in 1977 that provided for a veto by concurrent resolution of water management plans proposed by the state Water Resources Board (*Idaho Power Co. v. State*, 104 Idaho 570, 661 P.2d 736, 1983). The difference between this ruling and the one upholding the generic concurrent resolution veto procedure in 1990 was the fact that the water board's authority to adopt water plans was derived directly from the constitution (Heffron 1994).

9. Despite being struck down in 1980, the legislative veto statute was not repealed until 2004 (SLA 2004, chap. 164, § 7).

10. By a simple majority vote the committee can adopt a formal objection to a rule that will be printed alongside the rule in the Iowa Administrative Bulletin and the Iowa Administrative Code. However, this action has no direct effect on the rule itself.

11. Annual state spending data from Klarner (2012) are used to create a change in total state spending variable. To standardize spending data over time, I used the Bureau of Economic Analysis's national GDP implicit price deflator to convert all figures into 2009 dollars. The variable used in the analysis indicates the percentage change in total spending from the prior year in constant 2009 dollars.

12. The remaining case of suspension system adoption in Nebraska (1978) is omitted from this analysis on account of its nonpartisan legislature. Nebraska's adoption of a nullification system (1953) is also omitted from this table.

13. Iowa first adopted a nullification system in 1984 with the ratification of a constitutional amendment.

14. This sums to 10 because the 1981 veto issued by New Jersey governor Brendan Byrne was over legislation permitting the legislature to suspend or nullify rules.

15. The second model in the table omits both legislative partisanship variables since there are no cases of nullification system adoption under divided legislative control.

16. Given his advocacy for the oversight device, it is conceivable that Congressman Levitas was strategically seeking to downplay the use of the veto at the state level in order to make the case that members of Congress would likewise be conservative in blocking executive actions if a generic legislative veto was permitted at the federal level.

Bibliography

Aberbach, Joel D. 1990. *Keeping a Watchful Eye: The Politics of Congressional Oversight.* Washington, DC: Brookings Institution.

Achen, Christopher H. 2000. "Why Lagged Dependent Variables Can Suppress the Explanatory Power of Other Independent Variables." Paper presented at the 2000 political methodology section of the American Political Science Association annual meeting, Los Angeles, July 20–22.

Adler, David Gray. 1996. "Court, Constitution, and Foreign Affairs." In *The Constitution and the Conduct of American Foreign Policy*, edited by David Gray Adler and Larry N. George. Lawrence: University Press of Kansas.

Adler, E. Scott, and John S. Lapinski. 2006. *The Macropolitics of Congress.* Princeton: Princeton University Press.

Adler, E. Scott, and John Wilkerson. 2005. "The Scope and Urgency of Legislation: Reconsidering Bill Success in the House of Representatives." Paper presented at the 2005 annual meetings of the American Political Science Association, Washington, DC, September 1–4.

Adler, E. Scott, and John Wilkerson. 2011. *Congressional Bills Project.* NSF 00880066 and 00880061.

Adler, E. Scott, and John D. Wilkerson. 2012. *Congress and the Politics of Problem Solving.* Cambridge: Cambridge University Press.

Ainsworth, Scott, Brian Harward, Ken Moffett, and Laurie Rice. 2014. "Congressional Response to Statements of Administration Policy and Presidential Signing Statements." *Congress & the Presidency* 41 (3): 312–34.

Alexander, Herbert E. 1983. "FECA and the Legislative Veto Decision." *Campaigns & Elections* (Fall): 40–42.

Anderson, Jerry L., and Christopher Poynor. 2012. "A Constitutional and Empirical Analysis of Iowa's Administrative Rules Review Committee Procedure." *Drake Law Review* 61: 1–84.

Apuzzo, Matt. 2014. "Holder Sees Way to Curb Bans on Gay Marriage." *New York Times*, February 24.

Arnold, R. Douglas. 1979. *Congress and the Bureaucracy*. New Haven: Yale University Press.
Associated Press. 1979. "Former U.S. Rep. Eilberg Pleads Guilty to Conflict." February 25.
Ball, Carlos A. 2011. "When May a President Refuse to Defend a Statute? The Obama Administration and DOMA." *Northwestern University Law Review Colloquy* 106: 77–95.
Balla, Steven J. 2000. "Legislative Organizations and Congressional Review of Agency Regulations." *Journal of Law, Economics, and Organization* 16:424–48.
Banks, Jeffery S., and Barry R. Weingast. 1992. "The Political Control of Bureaucracies under Asymmetric Information." *American Journal of Political Science* 36 (2): 509–24.
Baranowski, Michael. 2001. "Legislative Professionalism and Influence on State Agencies." *Politics & Policy* 29 (1): 147–61.
Barron, David. 2000. "Constitutionalism in the Shadow of Doctrine: The President's Non-Enforcement Power." *Law and Contemporary Problems* 63 (1): 61–106.
Barron-Lopez, Laura. 2014. "McConnell to Force Vote on EPA Carbon Regs." *The Hill*, January 16.
Baumgartner, Frank, and Bryan Jones. 1993. *Agendas and Instability in American Politics*. Chicago: University of Chicago Press.
Bawn, Kathleen. 1995. "Political Control vs. Expertise: Congressional Choice about Administrative Procedures." *American Political Science Review* 92: 663–73.
Bawn, Kathleen. 1997. "Choosing Strategies to Control the Bureaucracy: Statutory Constraints, Oversight, and the Committee System." *Journal of Law, Economics, and Organization* 13 (1): 101–26.
Beck, Nathaniel, and Jonathan N. Katz. 1995. "What to Do (and Not to Do) with Time-Series Cross-Section Data." *American Political Science Review* 89 (3): 634–47.
Bendor, Jonathan. 1988. "Formal Models of Bureaucracy." *British Journal of Political Science* 18 (3): 353–95.
Benjamin, Gerald, and Zachary Keck. 2010/2011. "Executive Orders and Gubernatorial Authority to Reorganize State Government." *Albany Law Review* 74 (4): 1613–35.
Berry, Michael J. 2009. "Controversially Executing the Law: George W. Bush and the Constitutional Signing Statement." *Congress & the Presidency* 36 (3): 244–71.
Bertelli, Anthony M., and Christian R. Grose. 2011. "The Lengthened Shadow of Another Institution? Ideal Point Estimates for the Executive Branch and Congress." *American Journal of Political Science* 55 (4): 766–80.
Beth, Richard S. 2001. "Disapproval of Regulations by Congress: Procedure under the Congressional Review Act." RL31160. Washington, DC: Congressional Research Service.
Binder, Sarah A. 2001. "Congress, the Executive, and the Production of Public Policy." In *Congress Reconsidered*, 7th ed., edited by Lawrence C. Dodd and Bruce I. Oppenheimer. Washington, DC: CQ Press.
Binder, Sarah A. 2003. *Stalemate: Causes and Consequences of Legislative Gridlock*. Washington, DC: Brookings Institution.

Binder, Sarah A., and Forrest Maltzman. 2009. "The Politics of Advice and Consent: Putting Judges on the Federal Bench." In *Congress Reconsidered*, 9th ed., edited by Lawrence C. Dodd and Bruce I. Oppenheimer. Washington, DC: CQ Press.

Bloomenthal, Harold S. 1963. "The Revised Model State Administrative Procedure Act—Reform or Retrogression?" *Duke Law Journal* 12 (4): 593–628.

Boerner, Robert D. 2005. "Legislative Oversight in the States." *NCSL LegisBrief* 13 (45).

Bolton, John R. 1977. *The Legislative Veto: Unseparating the Powers*. Washington, DC: American Enterprise Institute for Public Policy Research.

Bonfield, Arthur Earl. 1986. *State Administrative Rulemaking*. Boston: Little, Brown and Company.

Bonfield, Arthur Earl. 1993. *State Administrative Rulemaking: 1993 Supplement Current to June 15, 1993*. Boston: Little, Brown and Company.

Bowers, James R. 1990. Regulating the Regulators: An Introduction to Legislative Oversight and Administrative Rulemaking. New York: Praeger.

Box-Steffensmeier, Janet M., and Christopher J.W. Zorn. 2002. "Duration Models for Repeated Events." *The Journal of Politics* 64(4): 1069–94.

Boyd, F. Scott. 1993. "Legislative Checks on Rulemaking Under Florida's New APA." *Florida State University Law Review* 24: 309–51.

Bradbury, Steven G. 2005. "Application of United States Obligations under Article 16 of the Convention Against Torture to Certain Techniques That May Be Used in the Interrogation of High Value al Qaeda Detainees." U.S. Department of Justice, Office of Legal Counsel Memo. May 30.

Bradley, Curtis A., and Eric A. Posner. 2006. "Presidential Signing Statements and Executive Power." *Constitutional Commentary* 23 (3): 307–64.

Broder, David, and Cass Peterson. 1983. "Supreme Court Strikes Down 'Legislative Veto.'" *Washington Post*, June 24, A1.

Bruff, Harold H., and Ernest Gellhorn. 1977. "Congressional Control of Administrative Regulation: A Study of Legislative Vetoes." *Harvard Law Review* 90 (7): 1369–1440.

Bush, George W. 2001a. "Statement on Signing the Agriculture, Rural Development, Food and Drug Administration, and Related Agencies Appropriations Act, 2002." *Public Papers of the President*, November 28. Book 2: 1457–58.

Bush, George W. 2001b. "Statement of Administration Policy: H.R. 2330—Department of Agriculture, Rural Development, Food and Drug Administration, and Related Agencies Appropriations Bill, FY 2002." June 27.

Bush, George W. 2002. "Statement of Administration Policy: H.R. 3009—Andean Trade Preference Expansion Act." May 8.

Bush, George W. 2004. "Statement on Signing the Consolidated Appropriations Act, 2005." *Public Papers of the President*, December 8. Book 3: 3058–61.

Bush, George W. 2005. "Statement on Signing the Department of Defense, Emergency Supplemental Appropriations to Address Hurricanes in the Gulf of Mexico, and Pandemic Influenza Act, 2006." *Weekly Compilation of Presidential Documents* 41: 1918. December 30..

Bush, George W. 2008. "Statement on Signing the Duncan Hunter National Defense Authorization Act for Fiscal Year 2009." *Weekly Compilation of Presidential Documents* 44: 1346. October 14.

Calvert, Randall L., Mathew D. McCubbins, and Barry R. Weingast. 1989. "A Theory of Political Control and Agency Discretion." *American Journal of Political Science* 33 (3): 588–611.
Cameron, Charles M. 2000. *Veto Bargaining: Presidents and the Politics of Negative Power.* Cambridge: Cambridge University Press.
Carter, James. 1978. "Legislative Vetoes—Message to Congress." *Public Papers of the President,* June 21. Book 1: 1146–49.
Carter, James. 1979. "Standby Gasoline Rationing Plan: Message to Congress Transmitting Contingency Plan No. 5." *Public Papers of the President,* May 7, 1979. Book 1: 813–15.
Carter, James. 1981. "*Chadha v. Immigration and Naturalization Service*: White House Statement on Justice Department Appeal of the Decision to the Supreme Court." *Public Papers of the President,* January 13. Book 3: 2882–83.
Cavanagh, M. Suzanne, Rogelio Garcia, and Clark F. Norton. 1982. "Congressional Veto Legislation: 97th Congress." Washington, DC: Congressional Research Service.
Chubb, John E. 1983. *Interest Groups and the Bureaucracy: The Politics of Energy.* Stanford: Stanford University Press.
Chubb, John E., and Paul E. Peterson. 1989. *Can the Government Govern?* Washington, DC: Brookings Institution.
Clark, Donald E. 1986–1987. "Nuclear Nonproliferation Legislation after *Chadha*: Nonjusticiable Political Questions and the Loss of the Legislative Veto." *Syracuse Law Review* 37: 899–922.
Clingermayer, James C. 1991. "Administrative Innovations as Instruments of State Legislative Control." *Western Political Quarterly* 44 (2): 389–403.
Clingermayer, James C., and William F. West. 1992. "Imposing Procedural Constraints on State Administrative Agencies: An Empirical Investigation of Competing Explanations." *Policy Studies Review* 11 (2): 37–56.
Clinton, Joshua D., and David E. Lewis. 2008. "Expert Opinion, Agency Characteristics, and Agency Preferences." *Political Analysis* 16 (1): 3–20.
Clinton, William J. 1994. "Statement on Signing Transportation Legislation." *Public Papers of the President.* July 5. Book 1: 1198–99.
Clinton, William J. 1995. "Message to the House of Representatives Returning Without Approval the National Defense Authorization Act for Fiscal Year 1996." December 28. Book 2: 1929–30.
Coase, Ronald H. 1937. "The Nature of the Firm." *Economica* 4 (16): 386–405.
Cooper, Frank E. 1965. *State Administrative Law.* Indianapolis: Bobbs-Merrill Company.
Cooper, Joseph. 1970. *The Origins of the Standing Committees and the Development of the Modern House.* Houston: William Marsh Rice University.
Cooper, Joseph. 1985. "The Legislative Veto in the 1980s." In *Congress Reconsidered,* 3rd ed., edited by Lawrence C. Dodd and Bruce I. Oppenheimer. Washington, DC: CQ Press.
Cooper, Joseph, and Patricia Hurley. 1983. "The Legislative Veto: A Policy Analysis." *Congress & the Presidency* 10 (1): 1–24.
Cooper, Joseph, and Cheryl Young. 1989. "Bill Introduction in the Nineteenth Century: A Study of Institutional Change." *Legislative Studies Quarterly* 14: 67–106.

Cooper, Phillip J. 2002. *By Order of the President: The Use and Abuse of Executive Direct Action*. Lawrence: University Press of Kansas.

Cooper, Phillip J. 2005. "George W. Bush, Edgar Allan Poe, and the Use and Abuse of Presidential Signing Statements." *Presidential Studies Quarterly* 35 (3): 515–32.

Copeland, Gary W. 1983. "When Congress and the President Collide: Why Presidents Veto Legislation." *Journal of Politics* 45 (3): 696–710.

Corwin, Edward S. 1940. *The President: Office and Powers*. New York: New York University Press.

Council of State Governments. 2012. *The Book of the States*. Lexington: Council of State Governments.

Cox, Gary W., and Matthew D. McCubbins. 1991. "Control of Fiscal Policy." In *The Politics of Divided Government*, edited by Gary W. Cox and Samuel Kernell. Boulder, CO: Westview Press.

Cox, James H. 2004. *Reviewing Delegation: An Analysis of the Congressional Reauthorization Process*. Westport, CT: Praeger.

Crabb, Cecil V., and Pat M. Holt. 1989. *Invitation to Struggle: Congress, the President, and Foreign Policy*. Washington, DC: Congressional Quarterly Press.

Craig, Barbara Hinkson. 1983. *The Legislative Veto: Congressional Control of Regulation*. Boulder, CO: Westview.

Craig, Barbara Hinkson. 1988. Chadha: *The Story of an Epic Constitutional Struggle*. Berkeley: University of California Press.

Crews, Wayne. 2014. "CEI's 2014 Unconstitutionality Index: 56 Regulations for Every Law." Competitive Enterprise Institute. January 7. http://www.openmarket.org/2014/01/07/ceis-2014-unconstitutionality-index-56-regulations-for-every-law/.

Crouch, Jeffrey, Mark J. Rozell, and Mitchel A. Sollenberger. 2013. "President Obama's Signing Statements and the Expansion of Executive Power." *Presidential Studies Quarterly* 43 (4): 883–99.

Daley, Dorothy M., Donald P. Haider-Markel, and Andrew B. Whitford. 2007. "Checks, Balances, and the Cost of Regulation: Evidence from the American States." *Political Research Quarterly* 60 (4): 696–706.

Davidson, Roger H. 1988. "'Invitation to Struggle': An Overview of Legislative-Executive Relations." *Annals of the American Academy of Political and Social Science* 499: 9–21.

Davidson, Roger H., Walter J. Oleszek, and Frances E. Lee. 2012. *Congress and Its Members*. 13th ed. Washington, DC: CQ Press.

Davis, Christopher M. 2005. "'Fast Track' Congressional Consideration of Recommendations of the Base Realignment and Closure (BRAC) Commission." RS22144. Washington, DC: Congressional Research Service.

Dean, Kenneth D. 1992. "Legislative Veto of Administrative Rules in Missouri: A Constitutional Virus." *Missouri Law Review* 57:1157–1231.

DeConcini, Dennis. 1983. "Should Congress Act Now to Preserve the Legislative Veto?" *Congressional Digest* 62(12): 296–302.

DeConcini, Dennis, and Robert Faucher. 1984. "The Legislative Veto: A Constitutional Amendment." *Harvard Journal on Legislation* 21 (1): 29–60.

DeFigueiredo, Rui J. P., and Richard G. Vanden Bergh. 2004. "The Political Econ-

omy of State-Level Administrative Procedure Acts." *Journal of Law and Economics* 47 (2): 569–88.
Dellinger, Walter. 1993. "The Legal Significance of Presidential Signing Statements: Memorandum for Bernard N. Nussbaum, Counsel to the President." November 3.
Dellinger, Walter. 1995. "Legal Opinion from the Office of Legal Counsel to the Honorable Abner J. Mikva." *Arkansas Law Review* 48: 313–32.
Denzau, Arthur T., and Robert J. Mackay. 1983. "Gatekeeping and Monopoly Power of Committees: An Analysis of Sincere and Sophisticated Behavior." *American Journal of Political Science* 27 (4): 740–61.
Destler, I. M. 2005. *American Trade Politics*. 4th ed. Washington, DC: Institute for International Economics.
Devaney, Tim. 2015. "GOP Finds Its Secret Weapon." *The Hill*, January 19. http://thehill.com/regulation/legislation/229936-gop-finds-its-secret-weapon.
Dodd, Lawrence, and Richard Schott. 1979. *Congress and the Administrative State*. New York: John Wiley & Sons.
Eisenhower, Dwight D. 1955. "Special Message to the Congress upon Signing the Department of Defense Appropriations Act." *Public Papers of the President*, July 13, 688–90.
Eisenhower, Dwight D. 1956. "Veto of Bill Authorizing Certain Construction at Military Installations." *Public Papers of the President*, July 16, 596–98.
Ellis, Joseph J. 2007. *American Creation: Triumphs and Tragedies at the Founding of the Republic*. New York: Knopf.
England, Catherine. 1981. "Legislative Veto: A Review of Current Proposals." Heritage Foundation Issue Bulletin 75, December 8.
Epstein, David, and Sharyn O'Halloran. 1996. "Divided Government and the Design of Administrative Procedures: A Formal Model and Empirical Test." *Journal of Politics* 58 (2): 373–79.
Epstein, David, and Sharyn O'Halloran. 1999. *Delegating Powers: A Transaction Cost Politics Approach to Policy Making under Separate Powers*. Cambridge: Harvard University Press.
Ethridge, Marcus E. 1981. "Legislative-Administrative Interaction as 'Intrusive Access': An Empirical Analysis." *Journal of Politics* 43 (2): 473–92.
Ethridge, Marcus E. 1984a. "Consequences of Legislative Review of Agency Regulations in Three U.S. States." *Legislative Studies Quarterly* 9 (1): 161–78.
Ethridge, Marcus E. 1984b. "A Political-Institutional Interpretation of Legislative Oversight Mechanisms and Behavior." *Polity* 17 (2): 340–59.
Feinstein, Dianne. 2014. "Statement on Intel Committee's CIA Detention, Interrogation Report." March 11. http://www.feinstein.senate.gov/public/index.cfm/press-releases?ID=db84e844-01bb-4eb6-b318-31486374a895.
Fiorina, Morris P. 2003. *Divided Government*. 2nd ed. New York: Longman.
Fisher, Louis. 1985. "Judicial Misgivings about the Lawmaking Process: The Legislative Veto Case." *Public Administration Review* 45: 705–11.
Fisher, Louis. 1993. "The Legislative Veto: Invalidated, It Survives." *Law and Contemporary Problems* 56: 273–92.
Fisher, Louis. 1998. *The Politics of Shared Power: Congress and the Executive*. College Station: Texas A&M University Press.

Fisher, Louis. 2004. *Presidential War Power.* 2nd ed. Lawrence: University Press of Kansas.

Fisher, Louis. 2005a. "Legislative Vetoes after *Chadha.*" Washington, DC: Report RS22132. Congressional Research Service.

Fisher, Louis. 2005b. "Committee Controls of Agency Decisions." Report RL33151. Washington, DC: Congressional Research Service.

Fisher, Louis. 2007. *Constitutional Conflicts between Congress and the President.* 5th ed., rev. Lawrence: University Press of Kansas.

Flanigan, Timothy E. 1992. "Issues Raised by Provisions Directing Issuance of Official or Diplomatic Passports." Office of Legal Counsel, January 17.

Ford, Gerald. 1976. "Statement on Signing the Federal Election Campaign Act Amendments of 1976." *Public Papers of the President,* May 11, 1976. Book 2:. 1529–31.

Franck, Thomas M., and Clifford A. Bob. 1985. "The Return of Humpty-Dumpty: Foreign Relations Law after the *Chadha* Case." *American Journal of International Law* 79 (4): 912–60.

Friel, Brian. 2006. "Caught in the Middle." *National Journal.* June 19.

Gailmard, Sean. 2002. "Expertise, Subversion, and Bureaucratic Discretion." *Journal of Law, Economics, and Organization* 18 (2): 536–55.

Gailmard, Sean. 2009. "Discretion Rather Than Rules: Choice of Instruments to Control Bureaucratic Policy Making." *Political Analysis* 17: 25–44.

Gailmard, Sean. 2009. "Multiple Principals and Oversight of Bureaucratic Policy-Making." *Journal of Theoretical Politics* 21 (2): 161–86.

Gailmard, Sean, and John W. Patty. 2007. "Slackers and Zealots: Civil Service, Policy Discretion, and Bureaucratic Expertise." *American Journal of Political Science* 51 (4): 873–89.

Galemore, Gary L. 2001. "The Presidential Veto and Congressional Procedure." Report 98–156. Washington, DC: Congressional Research Service.

Gamm, Gerald, and Kenneth Shepsle. 1989. "Emergence of Legislative Institutions: Standing Committees in the House and Senate, 1810–1825." *Legislative Studies Quarterly* 14 (1): 39–66.

Garcia, Michael John. 2007. "Interrogation of Detainees: Overview of the McCain Amendment." RL33655. Washington, DC: Congressional Research Service.

Garcia, Michael John. 2012. "War Powers Litigation Initiated by Members of Congress since the Enactment of the War Powers Resolution." RL30352. Washington, DC: Congressional Research Service.

Gazell, James A., and Darrell L. Pugh. 1987. "The Legislative Veto and the Administrative State: Implications for the Federal Government." *American Review of Public Administration* 17 (4): 17–37.

Gerber, Brian J., Cherie Maestas, and Nelson C. Dometrius. 2005. "State Legislative Influence over Agency Rulemaking: The Utility of Ex Ante Review." *State Politics and Policy Quarterly* 5 (1): 24–46.

Gerber, Brian J., and Paul Teske. 2000. "Regulatory Policymaking in the American States: A Review of Theories and Evidence." *Political Research Quarterly* 53 (4): 849–86.

Gibson, Martha Liebler. 1992. *Weapons of Influence: The Legislative Veto, American Foreign Policy, and the Irony of Reform.* Boulder, CO: Westview Press.

Gibson, Martha Liebler. 1994. "Managing Conflict: The Role of the Legislative Veto in American Foreign Policy." *Polity* 26 (3): 441–72.
Gilligan, Thomas W., and Keith Krehbiel. 1987. "Collective Decision-Making and Standing Committees: An Informational Rationale for Restrictive Amendment Procedures." *Journal of Law, Economics, and Organization* 3: 287–335.
Gilmour, John B. 2002. "Institutional and Individual Influences on the President's Veto." *Journal of Politics* 61 (1): 198–218.
Gilmour, Robert S. 1982. "The Congressional Veto: Shifting the Balance of Administrative Control." *Journal of Policy Analysis and Management* 2 (1): 13–25.
Gilmour, Robert S., and Barbara H. Craig. 1984. "After the Congressional Veto: Assessing the Alternatives." *Journal of Policy Analysis and Management* 3 (3): 373–92.
Ginnane, Robert W. 1953. "The Control of Federal Administration by Congressional Resolutions and Committees." *Harvard Law Review* 66 (4): 569–611.
Goldberg, David Howard. 1990. *Foreign Policy and Ethnic Interest Groups: American and Canadian Jews Lobby for Israel*. Westport, CT: Greenwood Press.
Grady, Dennis O., and Kathleen M. Simon. 2002. "Political Restraints and Bureaucratic Discretion: The Case of State Government Rule Making." *Politics & Policy* 30 (4): 646–79.
Greiner, John. 1988. "Two State Issues on Ballot Legislative Veto, Hospital Levy Proposed." *The Oklahoman*. March 6.
Grimmett, Richard F. 1979. "The Legislative Veto and U.S. Arms Sales." Washington, DC: Congressional Research Service.
Grimmett, Richard F. 2010a. "Instances of Use of United States Armed Forces Abroad, 1798–2009." Washington, DC: Congressional Research Service.
Grimmett, Richard F. 2010b. "The War Powers Resolution: After Thirty-Six Years." Washington, DC: Congressional Research Service.
Grimmett, Richard F. 2012. "Arms Sales: Congressional Review Process." Washington, DC: Congressional Research Service.
Habig, Douglas B. 1981. "The Constitutionality of the Legislative Veto." *William and Mary Law Review* 23 (1): 123–38.
Hagel, Chuck. 2014. "Statement on the Transfer of Detainees before the House Armed Services Committee." June 11. http://www.defense.gov/Speeches/Speech.aspx?SpeechID=1860.
Hahn, Robert. 2000a. *Reviving Regulatory Reform*. Washington, DC: AEI-Brookings Joint Center for Regulatory Studies.
Hahn, Robert W. 2000b. "State and Federal Regulatory Reform: A Comparative Analysis." *Journal of Legal Studies* 29 (S2): 873–912
Hall, Thad. 2004. *Authorizing Policy*. Columbus, OH: The Ohio State University Press.
Hall, Thad. 2008. "Steering Agencies with Short-Term Authorizations." *Public Administration Review* 68 (2): 366–79.
Hallett, Brien. 2012. "The 112th Congress, the War Powers Resolution, and the 2011 Libya Operation: A Normative Analysis of Functional and Organizational Incapacity." Paper presented at the 2012 annual meetings of the Western Political Science Association, Portland, OR, March 22–24.
Hamm, Keith E., and Roby D. Robertson. 1981. "Factors Influencing the Adoption of New Methods of Legislative Oversight in the U. S. States." *Legislative Studies Quarterly* 6 (1): 133–50.

Hammond, Thomas H., and Jack H. Knott. 1996. "Who Controls the Bureaucracy? Presidential Power, Congressional Dominance, Legal Constraints, and Bureaucratic Autonomy in a Model of Multi-Institutional Policy-Making." *Journal of Law, Economics, & Organization* 12 (1): 119–66.

Harris, Joseph P. 1964. *Congressional Control of Administration*. Washington, DC: Brookings Institution.

Harris, Milton, and Artur Raviv. 1979. "Optimal Incentive Contracts with Imperfect Information." *Journal of Economic Theory* 20: 231–59.

Harvard Law Review. 2007. "Oversight and Insight: Legislative Review of Agencies and Lessons from the States." *Harvard Law Review* 121: 613–35.

Hebers, John. 1983. "Government Power Poised for a Grand Realignment." *New York Times*, June 26, section 4, 1.

Heffron, Florence A. 1994. "Legislative Review of Administrative Rules under the Idaho Administrative Procedure Act." *Idaho Law Review* 30: 369–79.

Helco, Hugh. 1994. "What Has Happened to the Separation of Powers?" In *Separation of Powers and Good Government*, edited by Bradford P. Wilson and Peter W. Schramm. London: Rowman & Littlefield.

Herz, Michael. 1997. "The Legislative Veto in Times of Political Reversal: *Chadha* and the 104th Congress." *Constitutional Commentary* 14 (2): 319–36.

Hoover, Herbert. 1933. "Veto of a Bill to Supply Deficiency and Supplemental Appropriations." Public Papers of the President January 24. Book 1: 968–77.

Hoover, Herbert. 1951. *The Memoirs of Herbert Hoover: The Cabinet and the Presidency*. New York: Macmillan.

Horr, Samuel. 1991. "Saying No: Presidential Support and Veto Use, 1889–1989." *American Politics Quarterly* 19 (3): 310–23.

Howe, David L. 1955–56. *Current Trends in State Legislation*. Ann Arbor: Legislative Research Center.

Howell, William G. 2003. *Power without Persuasion: The Politics of Direct Presidential Action*. Princeton: Princeton University of Press.

Howell, William, Scott Adler, Charles Cameron, and Charles Riemann. 2000. "Divided Government and the Legislative Productivity of Congress, 1945–94." *Legislative Studies Quarterly* 25 (2): 285–312.

Huber, John D., and Charles R. Shipan. 2000. "The Costs of Control: Legislators, Agencies, and Transaction Costs." *Legislative Studies Quarterly* 25 (1): 25–52.

Huber, John D., and Charles R. Shipan. 2002. *Deliberate Discretion? The Institutional Foundations of Bureaucratic Autonomy*. Cambridge: Cambridge University Press.

Huber, John D., Charles R. Shipan, and Madelaine Pfahler. 2001. "Legislatures and Statutory Control of Bureaucracy." *American Journal of Political Science* 45 (2): 330–45.

Jackson, Robert H. 1953. "A Presidential Legal Opinion." *Harvard Law Review* 66 (8): 1353–61.

Jacobson, Gary C. 1990. *The Electoral Origins of Divided Government*. Boulder, CO: Westview Press.

Jensen, Christian B., and Robert J. McGrath. 2011. "Making Rules about Rulemaking: A Comparison of Presidential and Parliamentary Systems." *Political Research Quarterly* 64 (3): 656–67.

Johnsen, Dawn E. 2000. "Presidential Non-Enforcement of Constitutionally Objectionable Statutes." *Law and Contemporary Problems* 63 (1): 7–60.

Johnsen, Dawn E. 2008. "What's a President to Do? Interpreting the Constitution in the Wake of Bush Administration Abuses." *Boston University Law Review* 88: 395–419.

Jones, Bradford S., and Regina P. Branton. 2005. "Beyond Logit and Probit: Cox Duration Models of Single, Repeating, and Competing Events for State Policy Adoption." *State Politics & Policy Quarterly* 5 (4): 420–44.

Jones, Charles O. 2005. *The Presidency in a Separated System.* Washington, DC: Brookings Institution.

Kaiser, Frederick M., Walter J. Oleszek, T. J. Halstead, Morton Rosenberg, and Todd B. Tatelman. 2007. "Congressional Oversight Manual." In *Congress of the United States: Oversight, Processes, and Procedures*, edited by Carol S. Plesser. New York: Nova.

Kansas Legislative Research Department. 2006. "Legislative Procedure in Kansas." http://www.kslegislature.org/li/m/pdf/kansas_legislative_procedure.pdf.

Kansas Legislative Research Department. 2010. "Report on the Oversight Activities of the Joint Committee on Administrative Rules and Regulations." http://skyways.lib.ks.us/ksleg/KLRD/2010CommRepts/jcarr-cr.pdf.

Karl, Barry Dean. 1963. *Executive Reorganization and Reform in the New Deal: The Genesis of Administrative Management, 1900–1939.* Cambridge: Harvard University Press.

Kasperowicz, Pete. 2011. "House Dems Mock GOP's Disapproval Resolution on Debt-Ceiling Vote." *The Hill*, September 14.

Keefe, William J., and Morris S. Ogul. 1981. *The American Legislative Process: Congress and the States.* Englewood Cliffs, NJ: Prentice-Hall.

Kelley, Christopher S. 2006. "The Significance of the Presidential Signing Statement." In *Executing the Constitution: Putting the President Back into the Constitution*, edited by Christopher S. Kelley. Albany: State University of New York Press.

Kelley, Christopher S. 2007a. "A Matter of Direction: The Reagan Administration, the Signing Statement, and the 1986 Westlaw Decision." *William and Mary Bill of Rights Journal* 16 (1): 283–306.

Kelley, Christopher S. 2007b. "The Law: Contextualizing the Signing Statement." *Presidential Studies Quarterly* 37 (4): 737–48.

Kelley, Christopher S., and Bryan W. Marshall. 2008. "The Last Word: Presidential Power and the Role of Signing Statements." *Presidential Studies Quarterly* 38 (2): 248–67.

Kelley, Christopher S., and Bryan W. Marshall. 2009. "Assessing Presidential Power: Signing Statements and Veto Threats as Coordinated Strategies." *American Politics Research* 37 (3): 508–33.

Kernell, Samuel. 1997. *Going Public: New Strategies of Presidential Leadership.* Washington, DC: CQ Press.

Kiewiet, Roderick D., and Mathew McCubbins. 1991. *The Logic of Delegation: Congressional Parties and the Appropriations Process.* Chicago: University of Chicago Press.

King, Gary, Michael Tomz, and Jason Wittenberg. 2000. "Making the Most of Statistical Analyses: Improving Interpretation and Presentation." *American Journal of Political Science* 44 (2): 341–55.

King, Gary, and Langche Zeng. 1999. "Logistic Regression in Rare Events Data." *Political Analysis* 9 (2): 137–63.

Klarner, Carl. 2012. "State Economic Data." http://www.indstate.edu/polisci/klarnerpolitics.htm.

Korn, Jessica. 1996. *The Power of Separation: American Constitutionalism and the Myth of the Legislative Veto*. Princeton: Princeton University Press.

Korte, Gregory. 2014. "Special Report: America's Perpetual State of Emergency." *USA Today*, October 23.

Krause, George. 1999. *A Two-Way Street: The Institutional Dynamics of the Modern Administrative State*. Pittsburgh: University of Pittsburgh Press.

Krehbiel, Keith. 1991. *Information and Legislative Organization*. Ann Arbor: University of Michigan Press.

Krutz, Glen S. 2001. *Omnibus Legislating in the U.S. Congress*. Columbus: Ohio State University Press.

Lambert, R. Bradley. 1982. "The Legislative Veto: A Survey, Constitutional Analysis, and Empirical Study of Its Effect in Michigan." *Wayne Law Review* 29:91–148.

Lardner, George, Jr. 1983. "Safety Commission Could Lose Powers." *Washington Post*, June 29.

Lee, Jong R. 1975. "Presidential Vetoes from Washington to Nixon." *Journal of Politics* 37 (2): 522–46.

Levin, Mark R. 2013. *The Liberty Amendments: Restoring the American Republic*. New York: Threshold Editions.

Levinson, L. Harold. 1982. "Legislative and Executive Veto of Rules of Administrative Agencies: Models and Alternatives." *William and Mary Law Review* 24 (1): 79–119.

Levinson, L. Harold. 1987. "The Decline of the Legislative Veto: Federal/State Comparisons and Interactions." *Publius* 17 (1): 115–32.

Levitas, Elliott H. 1981. "Prepared Statement of Congressman Elliott H. Levitas." Hearings before the Subcommittee on Agency Administration of the Senate Judiciary Committee, 97th Congress, 1st Session on Various Legislative Veto Proposals, April 23.

Levitas, Elliott H., and Stanley M. Brand. 1984. "The Post Legislative Veto Response: A Call to Congressional Arms." *Hofstra Law Review* 12: 593–616.

Lewis, David E. 2003. *Presidents and the Politics of Agency Design*. Redwood City, CA: Stanford University Press.

Lowi, Theodore J. 1969. *The End of Liberalism: Ideology, Policy, and the Crisis of Public Authority*. New York: Norton.

Lowi, Theodore J. 1991. "Toward a Legislature of the First Kind." In *Knowledge, Power, and the Congress*, edited by William H. Robinson and Clay H. Wellborn. Washington, DC: Congressional Quarterly Press.

MacDonald, Jason A. 2010. "Limitation Riders and Congressional Influence over Bureaucratic Policy Decisions." *American Political Science Review* 104 (4): 766–82.

Madison, James, Alexander Hamilton, and John Jay. 1788 [2003]. *The Federalist Papers*. New York: Signet Classic.

Maltzman, Forrest, and Charles R. Shipan. 2008. "Change, Continuity, and the Evolution of the Law." *American Journal of Political Science* 52 (2): 252–67.

Maltzman, Forrest, and Steven S. Smith. 1994. "Principals, Goals, Dimensionality, and Congressional Committees." *Legislative Studies Quarterly* 19 (4): 457–76.

Martin, Elizabeth M. 1997. "An Informational Theory of the Legislative Veto." *Journal of Law, Economics, and Organization* 13 (2): 319–43.

May, Christopher N. 1998. *Presidential Defiance of "Unconstitutional" Laws*. Westport, CT: Greenwood Press.

Mayer, Kenneth R. 2001. *With the Stroke of a Pen*. Princeton: Princeton University Press.

Mayhew, David. 1991. *Divided We Govern: Party Control, Lawmaking, and Investigations, 1946–1990*. New Haven: Yale University Press.

Mayhew, David. 2005. *Divided We Govern: Party Control, Lawmaking, and Investigations, 1946–2002*. 2nd ed. New Haven: Yale University Press.

McCarty, Nolan M., and Keith T. Poole. 1995. "Veto Power and Legislation: An Empirical Analysis of Executive and Legislative Bargaining from 1961 to 1986." *Journal of Law, Economics, and Organization* 11: 282–312.

McCarty, Nolan, Keith T. Poole, and Howard Rosenthal. 2006. *Polarized America: The Dance of Ideology and Unequal Riches*. Cambridge: MIT Press.

McClure, Barbara. 1979. "Legislative Veto Provisions under the Immigration Laws." Washington, DC: Congressional Research Service.

McCubbins, Mathew D. 1985. "The Legislative Design of Regulatory Structure." *American Journal of Political Science* 29 (4): 721–48.

McCubbins, Mathew D., Roger G. Noll, and Barry R. Weingast. 1987. "Administrative Procedures as Instruments of Political Control." *Journal of Law, Economics, & Organization* 3 (2): 243–77.

McCubbins, Mathew D., Roger G. Noll, and Barry R. Weingast. 1989. "Structure and Process, Politics, and Policy: Administrative Arrangements and the Political Control of Agencies." *Virginia Law Review* 75: 431–82.

McCubbins, Mathew D., and Thomas Schwartz. 1984. "Congressional Oversight Overlooked: Police Patrols versus Fire Alarms." *American Journal of Political Science* 28 (1): 165–79.

Mezey, Michael L. 1989. *Congress, the President, and Public Policy*. Boulder, CO: Westview Press.

Miller, Gary J. 2005. "The Political Evolution of Principal–Agent Models." *Annual Review of Political Science* 8: 203–25.

Miller, Gary, and Terry Moe. 1983. "Bureaucrats, Legislators, and the Size of Government." *American Political Science Review* 77: 297–322.

Millett, John D., and Lindsay Rogers. 1941. "The Legislative Veto and the Reorganization Act of 1939." *Public Administration Review* 1 (2): 176–89.

Mitchell, William D. 1933. United States Attorney General Opinion. 37: 56.

Moe, Terry M. 1985. "Control and Feedback in Economic Regulation." *American Political Science Review* 79: 1094–1116.

National Association of Secretaries of State. 2012. *2012–2013 State & Federal Survey*. Eagan, MN: Thomson Reuters.

National Conference of State Legislatures, Legislative Improvement and Modernization Committee. 1979. *Restoring the Balance: Legislative Review of Administrative Regulations*. Washington, DC: National Conference of State Legislatures.

Niskanen, William. 1971. *Bureaucracy and Representative Government*. Chicago: Aldine Publishing.
Nixon, Richard M. 1973. "Veto of the War Powers Resolution." *Public Papers of the President*, October 24. Book 1: 893–95.
North, Douglas. 1991. "A Transaction Cost Theory of Politics." *Journal of Theoretical Politics* 2 (4): 355–67.
Norton, Clark F. 1976. "Congressional Review, Deferral, and Disapproval of Executive Actions: A Summary and an Inventory of Statutory Authority." Washington, DC: Congressional Research Service.
Norton, Clark F. 1978. "1976–1977 Congressional Acts Authorizing Prior Review, Approval, or Disapproval of Proposed Executive Actions." Washington, DC: Congressional Research Service.
Norton, Clark F. 1981a. "Statistical Summary of Congressional Approval and Disapproval Legislation, 1932–1980." Washington, DC: Congressional Research Service.
Norton, Clark F. 1981b. "Congressional Veto of Executive and Regulations: Introduction and Disposition of Approval and Disapproval Resolution under Authorizing Statutes." Washington, DC: Congressional Research Service.
Obama, Barack. 2009. "Statement on Signing the Omnibus Appropriations Act, 2009." *Public Papers of the President*, Book 1: 216–17.
Obama, Barack. 2011. "Statement on Signing the Ike Skelton National Defense Authorization Act for Fiscal Year 2011." *Daily Compilation of Presidential Documents*, January 7. DCPD201100010.
Obama, Barack. 2013. "Statement on Signing the National Defense Authorization Act for Fiscal Year 2013." *Daily Compilation of Presidential Documents*, January 2. DCPD-201300004.
Obama, Barack. 2014. "Message to the Congress on Continuation of the National Emergency with Respect to Certain Terrorist Attacks." *Daily Compilation of Presidential Documents*, September 4. DCPD-201400644.
Office of Management and Budget. 2012. "The President's Budget for Fiscal Year 2013: Historical Tables." http://www.whitehouse.gov/omb/budget/Historicals.
Ogul, Morris S. 1976. *Congress Oversees the Bureaucracy: Studies in Legislative Supervision*. Pittsburgh: University of Pittsburgh Press.
Oleszek, Walter. 2010. "Congressional Oversight: An Overview." Washington, DC: Congressional Research Service. Report R41079.
Oleszek, Walter. 2013. *Congressional Procedures and the Policy Process*. 9th ed. Washington, DC: CQ Press.
Olson, Theodore B. 1981. "Congressional Disapproval of AWACS Arms Sale: Memorandum Opinion for the Attorney General." Office of Legal Counsel. October 28.
Ostrander, Ian, and Joel Sievert. 2014. "Presidential Signing Statements and the Durability of the Law." *Congress & the Presidency* 41 (3): 362–83.
Petrocik, John R., William L. Benoit, and Glenn J. Hansen. 2003. "Issue Ownership and Presidential Campaigning, 1952–2000." *Political Science Quarterly* 118 (4): 599–626.
Philpott, A. L., J. Harry Michael, John A. Banks, Frederick T. Gray, John Wingo

Knowles, Andrew P. Miller, and Theodore V. Morrison. 1975. "Report of the Virginia Code Commission to the Governor and General Assembly of Virginia." House Document No. 26.

Pika, Joseph, and John Anthony Maltese. 2013. *The Politics of the Presidency*. Washington, DC: CQ Press.

Polenberg, Richard. 1966. *Reorganizing Roosevelt's Government: The Controversy over Executive Reorganization—1936–1939*. Cambridge: Harvard University Press.

Poole, Keith T. 1998. "Recovering a Basic Space from a Set of Issue Scales." *American Journal of Political Science* 42:954–93.

Poole, Keith T., and Howard Rosenthal. 2000. *Congress: A Political-Economic History of Roll Call Voting*. Oxford: Oxford University Press.

Potoski, Matthew. 1999. "Managing Uncertainty through Bureaucratic Design: Administrative Procedures and State Air Pollution Control Agencies." *Journal of Public Administration Research and Theory* 9 (4): 623–39.

Pregelj, Vladimir N. 2005. "The Jackson-Vanik Amendment: A Survey." Washington, DC: Congressional Research Service.

Rakove, Jack N. 1996. *Original Meanings*. New York: Vintage.

Reagan, Ronald. 1984. "Statement on Signing the Department of Housing and Urban Development—Independent Agencies Appropriation Act, 1985." *Public Papers of the President*, July 18. Book 2: 1056–57.

Reagan, Ronald. 1988. "Statement on Signing the Department of the Interior and Related Agencies Appropriations Act, Fiscal Year 1989." *Public Papers of the President*, September 27. Book 2: 1228.

Relyea, Harold C. 1996. "Executive Branch Reorganization." Washington, DC: Congressional Research Service.

Relyea, Harold. C. 2005. "Martial Law and National Emergency." Washington, DC: Congressional Research Service.

Relyea, Harold C. 2007. "National Emergency Powers." Washington, DC: Congressional Research Service.

Renfrow, Patty D., and David J. Houston. 1987. "A Comparative Analysis of Rulemaking Provisions in State Administrative Procedure Acts." *Policy Studies Review* 6 (4): 657–65.

Renfrow, Patty D., William F. West, and David J. Houston. 1986. "Rulemaking Provisions in State Administrative Procedure Acts." *Public Administration Quarterly* 9: 357–81.

Republican Party Platforms. 1980. "Republican Party Platform of 1980." July 15, 1980. American Presidency Project. http://www.presidency.ucsb.edu/ws/?pid=25844.

Rhyme, Nancy. 1990. "Legislative Review of Administrative Rules and Regulations." Denver: National Conference of State Legislatures.

Ringquist, Evan J., Jeff Worsham, and Marc Allen Eisner. 2003. "Salience, Complexity, and the Legislative Direction of Regulatory Bureaucracies." *Journal of Public Administration Research and Theory* 13 (2): 141–64.

Rohde, David, and Dennis M. Simon. 1985. "Presidential Vetoes and Congressional Response: A Study of Institutional Conflict." *American Journal of Political Science* 29 (3): 397–427.

Roosevelt, Franklin D. 1941. "Memorandum for the Attorney General." April 7.

Roosevelt, Franklin D. 1942. "Executive Order 9250 Establishing the Office of Economic Stabilization." *Public Papers of the President*, October 3. Book 1: 396–406.
Rosenberg, Martin. 2008. "Congressional Review of Agency Rulemaking: An Update and Assessment of the Congressional Review Act after a Decade." Washington, DC: Congressional Research Service.
Rudalevige, Andrew. 2005. *The New Imperial Presidency: Renewing Presidential Power after Watergate*. Ann Arbor: University of Michigan Press.
Sanger, David E. 2006. "Under Pressure, Dubai Company Drops Port Deal." *New York Times*, March 10.
Savage, Charlie. 2007. "Barack Obama's Q&A." *Boston Globe*, December 20.
Savage, Charlie. 2009. "Obama Looks to Limit Impact of Tactic Bush Used to Sidestep New Laws." *New York Times*, March 9.
Scholtz, John. 1981. "State Regulatory Reform and Federal Regulation." *Policy Studies Review* 1: 347–59.
Schwartz, Jason A. 2010. "52 Experiments with Regulatory Review: The Political and Economic Inputs into State Rulemakings." Report No. 6. New York: Institute for Polity Integrity, New York University School of Law.
Schweid, Barry. 1986. "Reagan Withdraws Bid to Sell Arms to Jordan." Associated Press, February 4.
Sek, Lenore. 2003. "Trade Promotion Authority (Fast-Track Authority for Trade Agreements): Background and Developments in the 107th Congress." Washington, DC: Congressional Research Service.
Sek, Lenore. 2005. "Trade Promotion Authority: Possible Vote on Two-Year Extension." Washington, DC: Congressional Research Service.
"Severability of Legislative Veto Provisions: A Policy Analysis." *Harvard Law Review* 97 (5): 1182–97.
Shields, Todd G., and Chi Huang. 1995. "Presidential Vetoes: An Event Count Model." *Political Research Quarterly* 48 (3): 559–72.
Shields, Todd G., and Chi Huang. 1997. "Executive Vetoes: Testing Presidency-versus President-Centered Perspectives of Presidential Behavior." *American Politics Quarterly* 48 (3): 431–57.
Shipan, Charles R. 2004. "Regulatory Regimes, Agency Actions, and the Conditional Nature of Congressional Influence." *American Political Science Review* 98 (3): 467–80.
Shull, Steven A. 2006. *Policy by Other Means: Alternative Adoption by Presidents*. College Station: Texas A&M University Press.
Silverstein, Gordon. 1997. *Imbalance of Powers: Constitutional Interpretation and the Making of American Foreign Policy*. New York: Oxford University Press.
Sinclair, Barbara. 2006. *Party Wars: Polarization and the Politics of National Policy Making*. Norman: Oklahoma University Press.
Slater, Richard Lee. 1987. "Oklahoma's Legislative Veto: Combat Casualty in Separation of Powers War?" *Oklahoma City University Law Review* 12 (1): 129–61.
Smith, J. Malcolm, and Cornelius P. Cotter. 1957. "Administrative Accountability: Reporting to Congress." *Western Political Quarterly* 10 (2): 405–15.
Smith, Keith W. 2010. "Congressional Use of Authorization and Oversight." *Congress & the Presidency* 37:45–63.

Sollenberger, Mitchel A., and Mark J. Rozell. 2012. *The President's Czars: Undermining Congress and the Constitution.* Lawrence: University Press of Kansas.
Sonmez, Felicia. 2012. "House Approves Symbolic Resolution Disapproving of Debt-Ceiling Raise." *Washington Post*, January 18.
Spitzer, Robert J. 1988. *The Presidential Veto: Touchstone of the American Presidency.* Albany: State University of New York Press.
Steinfeld, Robert J. 2010. "The Early Anti-Majoritarian Rationale for Judicial Review." In *Transformations in American Legal History, II*, edited by Daniel W. Hamilton and Alfred L. Brophy. Cambridge: Harvard University Press.
Steinhauer, Jennifer. 2015. "District of Columbia Sees Loophole in Congress's Move to Halt Marijuana Law." *New York Times*, February 7.
Stengle, Dan R., and James Parker Rhea. 1993. "Putting The Genie Back In The Bottle: The Legislative Struggle To Contain Rulemaking By Executive Agencies." *Florida State University Law Review* 21: 415–81.
Stewart, David O. 2009. *Impeached: The Trial of President Andrew Johnson and the Fight for Lincoln's Legacy.* New York: Simon & Schuster.
Strauss, Peter L. 2000. "The President and Choices Not to Enforce." *Law and Contemporary Problems* 63 (1): 107–24.
Strum, Albert L., and Kaye M. Wright. 1978. "State Constitutional Developments during 1977." *National Civic Review* 61(1): 31–36.
Summers, Paul G. 2001. "Authority of Legislative Committee to Review Agency Rules." Attorney General Opinion No. 01–086. May 23.
Tharp, Stacey M. 2001. "Legislative Powers of Rules Review in the States and Congressional Powers of Rules Review." Virginia Administrative Law Advisory Committee, Report of the Subcommittee to Study Petitions for Rulemaking.
Theriault, Sean M. 2008. *Party Polarization in Congress.* New York: Cambridge University Press.
Tichenor, Daniel J. 2005. "The Presidency and Interest Groups: Allies, Adversaries, and Policy Leadership." In *The Presidency and the Political System*, edited by Michael Nelson. Washington, DC: CQ Press.
Time Magazine. 1983. "A Foreigner Who Upset U.S. History." July 4.
Tolchin, Martin. 1989. "Washington Talk: The Legislative Veto, An Accommodation That Goes On and On." *New York Times*, March 31.
Toobin, Jeffrey. 2007. *The Nine: Inside the Secret World of the Supreme Court.* New York: Doubleday.
Tribe, Laurence H. 1985. *Constitutional Choices.* Cambridge: Harvard University Press.
Truman, Harry S. 1951. "Veto of Bill Relating to Land Acquisition and Disposal Actions by the Army, Navy, Air Force, and Federal Civil Defense Administration." *Public Papers of the President*, May 15. Book 1: 280–82.
Tucker, Todd, and Lori Wallach. 2009. *The Rise and Fall of Fast Track Trade Authority.* Washington, DC: Public Citizen's Global Trade Watch.
Udall, Mark. 2011. "Udall Continues Fight for Bark-Beetle Mitigation Funding." *Berthoud Recorder*, Berthoud, CO. April 8.
United Nations General Assembly. 1984. "Convention Against Torture and Other Cruel, Inhuman or Degrading Treatment or Punishment." Resolution 39/46. December 10.

U.S. Congress. House of Representatives. Armed Services Committee. 2014. "The May 31, 2014 Transfer of Five Senior Taliban Detainees." 113th Cong., 2nd Session. June 11.

U.S. General Accounting Office (GAO). 1985. "Potential for Excess Funds in DOD." Publication No. GAO/NSIAD-85-145.

U.S. General Accounting Office. 1986. "Budget Reprogramming: Department of Defense Process for Reprogramming Funds." Publication No. GAO/NSIAD-86-164BR.

U.S. General Accounting Office. 1989. "Economic Assistance: Ways to Reduce the Reprogramming Notification Burden and Improve Congressional Oversight." Publication No. GAO/NSIAD-89-202.

U.S. General Accounting Office. 2001. "Embassy Construction: Better Long-Term Planning Will Enhance Program Decision-Making." Publication No. GAO-01-11.

U.S. Government Accountability Office (GAO). 2004a. "Principles of Federal Appropriations Law." 3rd ed. Publication No. GAO-04-261SP.

U.S. Government Accountability Office. 2004b. "Budget Issues: Reprogramming of Federal Air Marshal Service Funds in Fiscal Year 2003." Publication No. GAO-04-577R.

U.S. Government Accountability Office. 2007a. "Presidential Signing Statements Accompanying the Fiscal Year 2006 Appropriations Acts." GAO B-308603. June 18.

U.S. Government Accountability Office. 2007b. "Presidential Signing Statements—Agency Implementation of Ten Provisions of Law." GAO B-309928. December 20.

U.S. Government Accountability Office. 2011. "Office of Science and Technology Policy—Bilateral Activities with China." Publication No. GAO-B-321982.

U.S. Government Accountability Office. 2014. "Department of Defense—Compliance with Statutory Notification Requirement." Publication No. GAO-B-326013.

U.S. Trade Representative. 2005. "Administration Requests Extension of Trade Promotion Authority." Press release, March 30. http://www.ustraderep.gov/Document_Library/Press_Releases/2005/March/Administration_Requests_Extension_of_Trade_Promotion_Authority.html.

Vibert, Frank. 2007. *The Rise of the Unelected: Democracy and the New Separation of Powers*. Cambridge: Cambridge University Press.

Walsh, Lawrence E. 1993. "Final Report of the Independent Counsel for Iran/Contra Matters."

Warren, Kenneth F. 2004. *Administrative Law in the Political System*. Boulder, CO: Westview.

Watson, H. Lee. 1975. "Congress Steps Out: A Look at Congressional Control of the Executive." *California Law Review* 63 (4): 983–1094.

Watson, Richard A. 1993. *Presidential Vetoes and Public Policy*. Lawrence: University Press of Kansas.

Waxman, Henry. 2010. *The Waxman Report: How Congress Really Works*. New York: Twelve.

Weingast, Barry R. 1984. "The Congressional-Bureaucratic System: A Principal-Agent Perspective." *Public Choice* 44:147–91.

Weingast, Barry R., and William J. Marshall. 1988. "The Industrial Organization of Congress; or, Why Legislatures, Like Firms, Are Not Organized as Markets." *Journal of Political Economy* 96 (1): 132–62.

Weingast, Barry R., and M. J. Moran. 1983. "Bureaucratic Discretion or Congressional Control? Regulatory Policymaking by the Federal Trade Commission." *Journal of Political Economy* 91:765–800.

West, William F., and Joseph Cooper. 1989–90. "Legislative Influence v. Presidential Dominance: Competing Models of Bureaucratic Control." *Political Science Quarterly* 104 (4): 581–606.

Wheeler, Darren A. 2008. "Actor Preference and the Implementation of *INS v. Chadha*." *BYU Journal of Public Law* 23 (1): 83–117.

White House Press Briefing. 2011. "Press Briefing by Press Secretary Jay Carney, 4/18/2011." April 18.

Whitford, Andrew B. 2005. "The Pursuit of Political Control by Multiple Principals." *Journal of Politics* 67 (1): 29–49.

Will, George F. 2012. "Applying REINS to a Runaway Executive." *Washington Post*, June 12.

Wilson, James Q. 1989. *Bureaucracy: What Government Agencies Do and Why They Do It*. New York: Basic Books.

Wisner, Kent F. 1985. "The Aftermath of *Chadha*: The Impact of the Severability Doctrine on the Management of Intragovernmental Relations." *Virginia Law Review* 71 (7): 1211–38.

Wood, B. Dan. 1988. "Principals, Bureaucrats, and Responsiveness in Clean Air Enforcements." *American Political Science Review* 82 (1): 213–34.

Wood, B. Dan, and John Bohte. 2004. "Political Transaction Costs and the Politics of Administrative Design." *Journal of Politics* 66 (1): 176–202.

Wood, B. Dan, and Richard W. Waterman. 1991. "The Dynamics of Political Control of the Bureaucracy." *American Political Science Review* 85 (3): 801–28.

Wood, B. Dan, and Richard W. Waterman. 1993. "The Dynamics of Political-Bureaucratic Adaptation." *American Journal of Political Science* 37 (2): 497–528.

Woods, Neal. 2004. "Political Influence on Agency Rule Making: Examining the Effects of Legislative and Gubernatorial Rule Review Powers." *State & Local Government Review* 36 (3): 174–85.

Woods, Neal D., and Michael Baranowski. 2006. "Legislative Professionalism and Influence on State Agencies: The Effects of Resources and Careerism." *Legislative Studies Quarterly* 31 (4): 585–609.

Woolley, John T. 1991. "Institutions, the Election Cycle, and the Presidential Veto." *American Journal of Political Science* 35:279–304.

Woolley, John T., and Gerhard Peters. The American Presidency Project [online]. University of California, Santa Barbara. http://www.presidency.ucsb.edu/

Yaskin, Judith A. 1981. "Formal Opinion No. 3—1981." New Jersey Attorney General's Office.

Yoo, John C. 2003. "Memorandum for William J. Haynes II, General Counsel of the Department of Defense, Re: Military Interrogation of Alien Unlawful Combatants Held Outside the United States." Office of Legal Counsel. March 14.

Index

Administrative Procedure Act: federal, 37–38, 42–44; state, 212–14, 226–27, 230, 232–36, 235, 243, 245, 247–50, 254, 264, 267
airline industry, 80–82
A.L.A. Schechter Poultry Corp. v. United States, 113
Alaska Airlines, Inc. v. Brock, 81
appropriations, 1–2, 84–89, 123–25, 131–35, 143; reprogramming of, 28–30, 82, 85–87, 121–22, 159
appropriations committees, 2, 25, 28, 85–87, 96–99, 109, 123–25, 133–35, 159–60, 180, 182, 276
Armed Services Committees, 96, 135, 165–67, 170–73, 194, 276
arms sales, 170–73
Articles of Confederation, 19
attorney general. *See* Department of Justice

Baker v. Carr, 57
Balanced Budget and Emergency Deficit Control Act, 73–74
Base Realignment and Closure Commission, 7, 181–82
Bergdahl, Bowe prisoner exchange, 165–67
Bowsher v. Synar, 73–74

Brownlow Committee Report on Administrative Management, 32
Buckley v. Valeo, 52, 54
Bush, George H. W., 94, 139, 144–45, 149
Bush, George W., 11–12, 95–96, 101, 142–46, 152–53, 156–57, 179–80, 189
Burger, Warren, 69, 73–74, 77

campaign finance reform, 52–54
Carter, Jimmy, 11, 60, 77, 139, 141, 144, 189, 269–70
Cabinet, 5, 21, 97–98, 125–26, 202–7, 277
Central Intelligence Agency, 157–58, 174, 202
Chadha, Jagdish Rai, 61–65
Champlin Refining Co. v. Corporation Commission, 75
Civil Rights Act, 6, 28–29
Clinton, Bill, 13–14, 93–95, 125, 142–46, 177–79
Clinton v. City of New York, 161
Congressional Bills Project, 168, 192, 208
Congressional Budget and Impoundment Control Act, 6, 105, 271–72
congressional polarization, 126, 132, 146–48, 273
Congressional Review Act, 100–104
Currin v. Wallace, 33–34

339

delegation, 5–6, 70–72, 84–87, 111–14
Department of Homeland Security, 5, 25, 30, 159, 179–81, 193, 195, 209
Department of Defense, 12, 30, 82, 156, 158–60, 165–67, 170–73, 181–82, 194–95, 198, 202, 205
Department of Justice, 23, 31, 47, 61, 64, 138, 155, 172, 186
Department of Treasury, 21, 31, 160
Department of State, 85–86, 160, 172, 185, 188, 195, 202, 277
Detainee Treatment Act, 156–58
divided government, 126, 130–36, 146–49, 193–207, 249–51, 255–59
Dubai ports controversy, 179–81

Eisenhower, Dwight, 12, 36–37
Eilberg, Joshua, 64–65
enrolled bills, 127, 145–46, 149
Environmental Protection Agency, 101, 123, 196
Equal Employment Opportunity Commission, 76–78
Executive Office of the President, 34, 111, 207
Export-Import Bank, 185

Fast-track authority. *See* Trade Promotion Authority
Federal Election Campaign Act and Amendments, 6, 52–53
Federal Emergency Management Agency, 159, 180
Federal Register, 5, 42
Field v. Clark, 113
Food and Drug Administration, 2–3, 123, 142, 189
Ford, Gerald, 53, 148, 155, 171, 178
foreign aid, 185–88
Foreign Relations Committee (Senate), 96, 172, 190, 276
foreign trade, 94–96, 107, 183–85

General Accounting Office, 73, 82–83, 159–60, 165, 167
General Services Administration, 28, 76, 78–79, 207

Goldwater v. Carter, 46
Guantanamo Bay Naval Base, 164–67

Hamilton, Alexander, 21, 71
Hoover, Herbert, 22–24, 31–32, 58
Hughes, Charles Evans, 33
hybrid legislative veto systems, 244–49

Immigration and Naturalization Service v. Chadha, 8, 61–73, 108–9, 141–42; applying precedent, 76–82; consequences of, 82–96, 129–34, 169–70, 181–82, 189–90, 275–76
impeachment, 50, 111, 154, 176
International Relations Committee (House), 96, 190, 276
Iran-Contra scandal, 173–74

Johnson, Andrew, 154
joint rule review committees, 216–17, 223–24, 230–32, 235–38, 240–47, 255, 265–66
J. W. Hampton, Jr. & Co. v. United States, 113

Kilbourn v. Thompson, 51

League of Nations, 21–22
legislative professionalization, 251–52, 264
legislative veto: by resolution, 104–7; by joint resolution, 26–27, 33, 44, 92, 100–107, 174, 179–84, 187–90, 224, 229–30, 269; committee, 30–31, 35–37, 85–87, 99–99, 123–24, 275–75; committee deliberative, 27–30, 91, 182, 276–77; committee negative, 28, 87; constitutional amendments, 83–84, 217–18; data collection, 105–6, 127–29, 253–55; defense policy, 170–83, 272; dual-House deliberative, 32, 91–92, 276–77; federal courts, 51–57, foreign policy, 183–90; generic, 41–45; immigration law, 7, 61–65; origins, 6–8, 20–24; one-House, 24, 26–28, 32–34, 38–39, 54–56, 65–69, 75–81, 90–96, 228–30; Republican Party platform, 138; severability of, 54, 69, 74–81; typology, 24–30

Lend Lease foreign aid, 3, 6, 188–90
Levitas, Elliott, 41–44, 78, 139, 264
limitation riders, 24–25, 101, 116–17, 121, 174
Lujan v. Defenders of Wildlife, 46

macropolitical conflict, 1–6, 11–14, 125–27, 162–63, 270–72
Madison, James, 19
McCain Amendment. *See* Detainee Treatment Act
McCulloch v. Maryland, 55
Metropolitan Washington Airports Authority v. Citizens for the Abatement of Aircraft Noise, 81–82

National Aeronautics and Space Administration, 85, 207–9
National Emergencies Act, 80, 178–79
National Security Council, 79, 167, 174
Nixon, Richard, 54, 79, 149, 152, 175–76, 272
Nonenforcement, 154–60
nuclear nonproliferation, 181, 188–89
nullification legislative veto systems, 18, 218–34, 255–64

Obama, Barack, 1–2, 102–3, 139–42, 152–54, 164–67, 179
Occupational Health and Safety Administration, 100–101, 107
O'Connor, Sandra Day, 77
Office of Legal Counsel, 156–57, 172
Office of Management and Budget, 86, 103, 126, 204
Office of National Drug Control Policy, 160–61
omnibus bills, 1–2, 87–89, 199–200, 274
O'Neill, Tip, 43, 45

Panama Refining Co. v. Ryan, 34
partisan policy subsystems, 196–202
Patient Protection and Affordable Care Act, 3, 7
Policy Agendas Project, 130, 168
Powell, Lewis, 71
presdiential oath of office, 154–55
presidential reorganization, 7, 22–24, 28–35, 77–78

presidential veto, 123, 139–43, 145–48, 274

Reagan, Ronald, 12–13, 43, 80, 84–85, 138–39, 144, 173–74, 188–89
Regulations from the Executive in Need of Scrutiny Act, 102–4
Rehnquist, William, 68–69, 75, 82
report and wait provisions. *See* legislative veto: committee deliberative
Roberts, John, 84, 155
Roosevelt, Franklin, 3, 5, 32–37, 140, 186–87
Roosevelt, Theodore, 22

Scalia, Antonin, 41
signing statements, 1, 11–14, 53, 85, 93, 139–40, 143–45, 149–58, 165–67, 274–75
Springer v. Philippine Islands, 51
state constitutions, 211–13
state legislative veto powers: Alaska, 216–17, 238–40; Georgia, 244, 248–49, 254; Idaho, 226–28; Illinois, 216, 222–23, 244–46; Iowa, 244, 247–48, 254; Kansas, 211, 223–26; Michigan, 211–12, 222, 234–37, 244, 265; Missouri, 214, 218, 242–44; Nevada, 211–12, 216, 222–23, 246–47, 254; New Jersey, 211, 232–34, 258–59, 267; Ohio, 216–17, 244–45, 266; Oklahoma, 223, 229–30; Virginia, 212, 216, 222–23, 240–42; West Virginia, 212, 230–32, 247, 259; Wisconsin, 216–17, 237–38, 265
statutory debt limit, 3–4
statutory oversight, 9–11, 114–17
suspension legislative veto systems, 18, 216–22, 234–44, 255–64

transaction costs, 9–11, 117–27, 132, 136–138, 197, 204–7, 250
Trade Promotion Authority, 94–96
Treaty of Versailles, 21–22
Truman, Harry, 34–36

unified government, 141–42, 191–93, 255–59

United States Agency for International Development, 183, 190, 207
United States v. Curtiss–Wright Export Corp., 183

War Powers Resolution, 6, 28, 174–78, 272

Washington, DC City Council, 105, 129
Wayman v. Southard, 112
White, Byron, 14, 53, 69–74, 82, 163
White House Special Files, 79
Woodrow Wilson, 21–22